Mistër E's
Eclectic COMPENDIUM
of
WONDROUS HITS

I0112400

Mistër E's

Eclectic COMPENDIUM

of

WONDROUS HITS

THE MUSICAL UNIVERSE OF ONE BOY—HIS 101 FAVORITE SONGS, EVERY YEAR, SINCE 1976

Elias Mondegreen

BEAVER'S POND
PRESS

Mistër E's Eclectic Compendium of Wondrous Hits © 2025 by Elias Mondegreen LLC.
All rights reserved. No part of this book may be reproduced, stored in a retrieval system, in
any form whatsoever, by photography or xerography or by any other means, by broadcast
or transmission, by translation into any kind of language, nor by recording electronically or
otherwise, without permission in writing from the author, except by a reviewer, who may
quote brief passages in critical articles or reviews.

Edited by Kerry Stapley

ISBN 13: 978-1-64343-571-8
Library of Congress Catalog Number: 2025908138
Printed in the United States of America
First Printing: 2025
29 28 27 26 25   5 4 3 2 1

Book design and typesetting by Mayfly book design.

BEAVER'S POND
PRESS

526 Seventh Street West
Saint Paul, MN 55102
(952) 829-8818
www.BeaversPondPress.com

Contact Elias Mondegreen at www.eliasmondegreen.com for speaking engagements,
book club discussions, and interviews.

*A long-distance dedication to Casey Kasem who inspired
a young man to create his annual lists of songs.
(Thanks for Shaggy too!)*

*In memory of Joel Whitburn for his invaluable Record Research guides.
His books continue to provide answers faster than the Internet and were
crucial to validating the dates of my music memories. He legitimized
my love of music charts. Much respect and thanks.*

To Vangelis and Ryuichi Sakamoto.

*While creating this book, two musical heroes left to
perform forever in the heavens.*

To all those lost as I wrote this book. They are missed.

To Kate Bush. No words required.

Then There Is Music
(REM to RPM)

Life is both requisite and required.
Breathing is our performance.
Home, our haven between wanderings.
Love, those places peculiar we roam.
Work, a mere distraction from pleasure.
Fun is the reason we work.

Friends bring our balance.
Dreams connect our dots.

And then there is music . . .
    seeping into crannies
    occupying the time that remains.

Come on, music! Bring it on.

Contents

A perfect song envelops you whole
—it separates you from reality—
may you never reappear.

Introductory Musings

A smile is the universal language,
but music is a close second.

Q: What do Tracy Chapman, The Pretenders, Jon & Vangelis, Supertramp, Timbaland, Seal, Phil Collins, Portishead, Tracey Thorn, Broken Bells, and Kelly Osbourne have *In Common* (#8, 2016)? (See song position #8 in the 2016 year-end list. Follow this rule for other such references. Legacy songs and "songs that got away" are listed only in the Artist Cross-Reference, alphabetized by artist name.)

A: Each artist had the #1 song of the year for me.

This book of lists is simple: a compilation of my favorite songs, ranked 1 to 101, for every year of my life since 1976. There are a few extras (OK, I lie, hundreds more …) along with my musical musings and list explanations. I wrote down and ranked my favorite songs year after year— every song I liked and wanted to remember—no matter the number of songs.

There's an artist within these pages who has three year-end #1s.

I'm certain there are others who have compiled their favorite songs each year, but I may be the only one to share my favorites for world consumption. Who else has done such a thing?

Think of this book as an obscure, alternative song repository merged with a historical snapshot of one person's lifelong musical journey—an introduction to my musical passions and my often-insular musical experience.

Though there are many popular artists in my lists, be forewarned. If you're looking for a book jam-packed with mainstream hits and megastars, this book

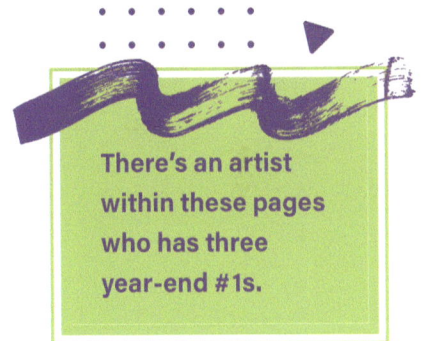

Disclaimer:
_____

I don't declare these songs are the best in the world for any given year; they are simply my favorites.

may not be it. Instead, I suggest purchasing Joel Whitburn's fantastic reference books of *Billboard* hits.

This book often spotlights lesser-known artists and deeper cuts. It's a sort of rebellious, anti-popular anthology comprising the songs I loved; albeit a rather quiet (but fabulous) rebellion, since punk, metal, and death rock . . . oh wait, I'll talk about my musical tastes later.

These are *my* songs. My ode to contemporary music. To be cliché, these songs spoke to me. The songs I vibed, danced, chilled, partied, cried, daydreamed, and sang along to—while the rest of my life carried on over forty-nine years. This is the music that illuminated my life: one boy's attempt to capture his cherished songs forever in a book. A compendium of memories in the shape of music. Seriously, my songs are my book!

I can survive on food, water, and music.

Before I continue:

If You Like . . .

Carly Simon

Bryan Ferry

America

a-ha

Sarah McLachlan

Kool & the Gang

Seal

Morcheeba

Joni Mitchell

Everything But The Girl

Orchestral Manoeuvres In The Dark

Bel Canto

Bee Gees

Bananarama

The Spinners

Talk Talk

Tears For Fears

U2

Hall & Oates

Enigma

Genesis

The Weeknd

Cocteau Twins

Mike Oldfield

Kate Bush

Dido

Eurythmics

Fleetwood Mac

Peter Gabriel

Hooverphonic

XTC

Prince

Depeche Mode

The Alan Parsons Project

ABBA

Journey

Heart

Tori Amos

Olivia Newton-John

The Smiths

Schiller

Lady Gaga

Sarah Brightman

Pet Shop Boys

Madonna

Clannad

R.E.M.

Sade

Jon & Vangelis

Alison Moyet

The Police

Grace Jones

Kylie Minogue

Ultravox

Electric Light Orchestra

Elton John

David Bowie

Split Enz

Simple Minds

Barbra Streisand

The B-52s

Maggie Reilly

Gary Numan

Donna Summer

Röyksopp

Queen

Then you will love . . .

Zazie

Kaskade

Chris Isaak

Snow Patrol

Morgan Page

Stone Age

Little Boots

Chris Rea

Iris

Toni Childs

Nadia Ali

Delerium

Thomas Dolby

The Babys

Kim Carnes

Duffy

Dua Lipa

Ellie Goulding

Prefab Sprout

Poliça

Tiësto

Tangerine Dream

Paula Cole

ATB

Kate Ryan

Texas

David Guetta

Hard-Fi

The Human League

Ryuichi Sakamoto

Erasure

London Grammar

Icehouse

Bright Light Bright Light

Empire Of The Sun

Jake Bugg

The Adventures

October Project

Tiromancino

The Dream Academy

Cause & Effect

Sam Phillips

Suzanne Vega

Sandra

Tanya Chua

Uh Huh Her

Kosheen

Ladyhawke

Jimmy Somerville

Patrick O'Hearn

Keane

Happy Rhodes

China Crisis

**These artists, plus hundreds more,
are featured within!**

Welcome To MY World!

(#14, 2023; legacy song, 1964, Jim Reeves)

O'ahu, 1966

My first song memories are from 1966 when my family resided briefly in Hawai'i. I was in kindergarten then. Early one day, I left my open-air classroom and walked through downtown Honolulu to the motel where we temporarily stayed. We'd only been there for a few weeks. (I was always a junior geographer.) My kindergarten classmates were not particularly nice to me, though I will never forget a Chinese American girl who befriended me; we collected and shared seashells found in the playground sand. I wish I knew her name.

I remember when my family watched Don Ho perform his famous *Tiny Bubbles* at the Polynesian Cultural Center. This may have been my first concert. I also recall Tommy James & The Shondells playing on the radio with their song *Hanky Panky* as we drove past a Dole processing plant. That's it, a brief musical image I retain after fifty-eight years, along with a fleeting radio memory of The Beatles's *Michelle* as we drove near Ewa Beach.

My family watched the films *Bambi* and *Born Free* at a drive-in theater during Dad's short military stint on O'ahu. *Bambi* frightened me, but I loved the theme song from *Born Free*.

These are my earliest music-related memories.

Fast-forward to 1971. During fifth-grade music class, auditions were held for a class representative to be in the school talent show. I hadn't planned to enter the competition, but at the last minute I stood up to perform. Spontaneously, I sang *Born Free*, a cappella. Somehow, I was voted the winner. My parents drove me to a nearby mall to purchase sheet music so my music teacher could accompany me on piano at the show. When it was my turn to perform, the teacher began to play as I meekly sang the first words. Then I remember only mouthing the rest of the song. I'm not sure if, or when, I walked off the stage. I learned about stage fright and public embarrassment that day. But I am still alive and still born free.

Note: This is the first of many song memories scattered throughout this book. See the Music Memories chapter for thoughts on the memories we all have in relation to songs in our lives.

A Seed Germinates

I need music like I need humor—for survival.

Imagine (legacy song, 1971, John Lennon) a *Lonely Boy* (#63, 1977) who, in 1976, began to compile and rank his favorite songs of the year. He was *Only Sixteen* (#59, 1976). He continued this project every year since then, and he will do so going forward.

He didn't realize back then that forty-nine years later, he would still search, compile, track, and rank his favorite songs as he heard them. *Sometimes* (#71, 1987) he would miss a song, but more about this grievous error later. (He really didn't know what he was in for.) He tracked and compiled through the end of his high school years, through the excitement and new experiences of college and early adulthood, and through numerous moves, jobs, friendships, loves, and vacations. Through years of maturation, detachment, sadness, work entanglements, life distractions, and amid glorious years of happiness, he tracked. Music became his unpaid, part-time job, even in retirement. Music was a time suck, but such a lovely waste of his time.

Music was there when he needed it and brought light to his darkness.

Music heals the ugly we each face in our lives.

That boy is me. And within these pages are my songs.

The next chapter contains the documented results. All 4,900+ songs as I ranked them annually from number 1 to 101.

The Year-End Lists

If you play it, others will hear!

Here are my unadulterated, annual lists of 101 favorite songs each year from 1976 to 2024. These lists are the reason for this book, so I present them now before musing further. You may read more about me and other matters related to my songs and lists later.

The song titles and artist names are chronicled as found on their original release, or as printed on my album or CD.

I cannot promise that all commas or "ands, ampersands, and plus-symbols" are 100 percent accurate within song titles or group names (e.g., Diana Ross And The Supremes; Mel & Kim; Florence + The Machine). Dear readers, forgive me if minor mistakes exist in these lists. Please ignore many of the perceived spelling or punctuation errors, though such trivial variations occur between websites and reissues. Still my goal is correctness.

For consistency, all song titles and artist names are capitalized unless specifically denoted by the artist.

Extra, ranked songs are included each year beyond the top 101. For explanation, see the Year-End List Controversies subsection—Songs That Got Away (Part I) later in this book.

As you will learn in an upcoming chapter, Year-End List Controversies (subsection—Double Hits), I have many double hits on my lists for various reasons. Double hit listings contain a forward slash (/) inserted between the songs in my year-end lists *and* the artist cross-reference.

The following types of double-hit titles are documented with *no* spaces surrounding the forward slash:

1. songs that segue seamlessly into each other as one blended song
2. songs with an intro, outro, or reprise
3. songs with a legitimate B-side
4. songs released as double-sided hits.

These types of double hits are documented as shown in these respective examples:

1. *Discoteca/Single* by Pet Shop Boys (#41, 1996)
2. *Chromatica I/Alice* by Lady Gaga (#8, 2020)
3. *Good Times Roll/All Mixed Up* by The Cars (#18, 1979)
4. *This Beat Goes On/Switchin' To Glide* by The Kings (#39, 1980)

To visibly differentiate two distinct songs that I ranked as one combined chart hit (a "smashed" double hit), the forward slash will be surrounded by spaces as shown in these double-hit examples:

- *Take The Long Way Home / Breakfast In America* by Supertramp (#8, 1979)
- *Topaz / Follow Your Bliss* by The B-52s (#35, 1989)

For consistency and to save space, artists who are featured on a recording will be preceded by "f/." If an artist is listed as being "with" another artist, then their name will be preceded by "w/" in the song listing. Some favorite artists who were not officially listed on a song but who had a prominent role in the song may be listed in parentheses and also found in the Artist Cross-Reference.

For non-English songs, I present and spell the song title in the language format of the original song. I had assistance from international friends and the Internet for title and artist spellings and translations.

For non-English song titles that use the Roman alphabet, I leave the translation legwork to my readers.

If an artist used a different name in the US market due to copyright or other issues, the US name will be listed in parentheses.

I've said enough, for now.

It's been a joy to relive my past life through these songs and memories as I typed each list—a COVID-masked man in the library. I'm surprised by how much more I've learned about the artists, and about music in general, by writing this book. There were so many songs and artists I hadn't thought of in

(Option) If you haven't already done so, peruse the alphabetical Artist Cross-Reference (page 157 – indicated by colored index pages) to search for your favorite artists. Then, return to the year-end lists and read the rest of my humble musings, though, as I will remind you, this book is about the music and not about me.

years, and so many songs I felt relieved to see in my year-end lists. There are songs I had to revisit just to remember the melody. When you have over two thousand albums and CDs in your collection, it is impossible to remember them all! (I haven't counted the actual number for decades.) My collection is a significant portion of my so-called living room décor.

I Hope (#99, 2020) you find a forgotten gem from your past within my lists, and that numerous songs *Flood* (#34, 1996) your soul with *Memories* (#77, 2001) and *Happiness* (#94, 1979; #19, 2014). In retrospect, these lists are a beautiful snapshot of one person's musical life and ear, a solo study of one music lover's mind. I feel as if I am baring my soul as I share these songs.

That being said, *Let's Go* (#11, 1979; #92, 2014)! I present to you, Mistër E's wondrous year-end top 101 hits. The year-end position, title, and artist are recorded for each song.

Once I had a voice,
Once I found my voice,
I could sing!

The Lists

1976

#	Song Title	Artist
1	Devil Woman	Cliff Richard
2	(Don't Fear) The Reaper	Blue Öyster Cult
3	Rock'n Me	Steve Miller Band
4	Crazy On You	Heart
5	Love Is Alive	Gary Wright
6	Golden Years	David Bowie
7	Boogie Fever	The Sylvers
8	Love Machine (Part 1)	The Miracles
9	You Should Be Dancing	Bee Gees
10	More Than A Feeling	Boston
11	Rhiannon (Will You Ever Win)	Fleetwood Mac
12	More, More, More	Andrea True Connection
13	Play That Funky Music	Wild Cherry
14	(Shake, Shake, Shake) Shake Your Booty	KC And The Sunshine Band
15	Dream Weaver	Gary Wright
16	A Fifth Of Beethoven	Walter Murphy & The Big Apple Band
17	Mamma Mia	ABBA
18	You Sexy Thing	Hot Chocolate
19	Don't Go Breaking My Heart	Elton John and Kiki Dee
20	Do You Feel Like We Do	Peter Frampton
21	Funeral For A Friend/Love Lies Bleeding	Elton John
22	Evil Woman	Electric Light Orchestra
23	Shannon	Henry Gross
24	Magic Man	Heart
25	Get The Funk Out Ma Face	The Brothers Johnson
26	Fly, Robin, Fly	Silver Convention
27	December, 1963 (Oh, What A Night)	Frankie Valli And The Four Seasons
28	Fanny (Be Tender With My Love)	Bee Gees
29	Right Back Where We Started From	Maxine Nightingale
30	You're My Best Friend	Queen
31	Dream On	Aerosmith
32	Love To Love You Baby	Donna Summer
33	Takin' It To The Streets	The Doobie Brothers
34	Say You Love Me	Fleetwood Mac
35	I Only Want To Be With You	Bay City Rollers
36	Love Hangover	Diana Ross
37	That's The Way (I Like It)	KC And The Sunshine Band
38	Love Rollercoaster	Ohio Players
39	Moonlight Feels Right	Starbuck
40	If You Leave Me Now	Chicago
41	Still The One	Orleans
42	I'd Really Love To See You Tonight	England Dan & John Ford Coley
43	Sky High	Jigsaw
44	I'll Be Good To You	The Brothers Johnson
45	Movin'	Brass Construction
46	Wham Bam (Shang-A-Lang)	Silver
47	Nice 'N' Naasty	The Salsoul Orchestra
48	Love Hurts	Nazareth
49	Jeans On	David Dundas
50	Nights Are Forever Without You	England Dan & John Ford Coley
51	Turn The Beat Around	Vicki Sue Robinson
52	With Your Love	Jefferson Starship
53	Get Up And Boogie (That's Right)	Silver Convention
54	Over My Head	Fleetwood Mac
55	The Boys Are Back In Town	Thin Lizzy
56	Shop Around	Captain & Tennille
57	She's Gone	Daryl Hall & John Oates
58	Bohemian Rhapsody	Queen
59	Only Sixteen	Dr. Hook
60	Let 'Em In	Wings
61	Theme From S.W.A.T.	Rhythm Heritage
62	Take It To The Limit	Eagles
63	Show Me The Way	Peter Frampton
64	Let's Do It Again	The Staple Singers
65	Fox On The Run	Sweet
66	Get Closer	Seals & Crofts
67	Love So Right	Bee Gees
68	Afternoon Delight	Starland Vocal Band
69	Ave Satani	Jerry Goldsmith
70	Fool For The City	Foghat

1976

#	Song Title	Artist
71	Beth	KISS
72	You Are The Woman	Firefall
73	Strange Magic	Electric Light Orchestra
74	Convoy	C. W. McCall
75	Livin' Ain't Livin'	Firefall
76	Sweet Love	Commodores
77	The Rubberband Man	The Spinners
78	Take The Money And Run	Steve Miller Band
79	Tonight's The Night (Gonna Be Alright)	Rod Stewart
80	Fernando	ABBA
81	It's A Long Way There	Little River Band
82	Baretta's Theme ("Keep Your Eye On The Sparrow")	Rhythm Heritage
83	Lonely Nights (Angel Face)	Captain & Tennille
84	Welcome Back	John Sebastian
85	All By Myself	Eric Carmen
86	Island Girl	Elton John
87	You Are My Starship	Norman Connors
88	Good Vibrations	Todd Rundgren
89	Theme From Mahogany (Do You Know Where You're Going To)	Diana Ross
90	Silly Love Songs	Wings

#	Song Title	Artist
91	Rock And Roll All Nite	KISS
92	Let Her In	John Travolta
93	Disco Lady	Johnnie Taylor
94	Rock And Roll Love Letter	Bay City Rollers
95	Sara Smile	Daryl Hall & John Oates
96	Squeeze Box	The Who
97	Best Disco In Town	The Ritchie Family
98	Fooled Around And Fell In Love	Elvin Bishop
99	Disco Duck	Rick Dees & His Cast Of Idiots
100	It's Over	Boz Scaggs
101	Highfly	John Miles

1976 EXTRAS

#	Song Title	Artist
113	TVC 15	David Bowie
117	Tell Me Something Good	Rufus f/ Chaka Khan
119	Free Bird	Lynyrd Skynyrd
120	I Love Music	The O'Jays
121	How Long	Ace
125	Don't Touch Me There	The Tubes
127	The Wreck Of The Edmund Fitzgerald	Gordon Lightfoot
128	Enjoy Yourself	The Jacksons
148	Breakaway	Art Garfunkel

1977

#	Song Title	Artist
1	I Just Want To Be Your Everything	Andy Gibb
2	Dreams	Fleetwood Mac
3	Give A Little Bit	Supertramp
4	Strawberry Letter 23	The Brothers Johnson
5	Boogie Nights	Heatwave
6	I Feel Love	Donna Summer
7	Couldn't Get It Right	Climax Blues Band
8	Keep It Comin' Love	KC And The Sunshine Band
9	Isn't It Time	The Babys
10	Star Wars Theme/ Cantina Band	Meco
11	Indian Summer	Poco
12	You Make Loving Fun	Fleetwood Mac
13	Help Is On Its Way	Little River Band
14	Boogie Child	Bee Gees
15	Undercover Angel	Alan O'Day
16	N.Y., You Got Me Dancing	Andrea True Connection
17	Blinded By The Light	Manfred Mann's Earth Band
18	Cold As Ice	Foreigner
19	Got To Give It Up (Pt. 1)	Marvin Gaye
20	Life In The Fast Lane	Eagles
21	I Wouldn't Want To Be Like You	The Alan Parsons Project
22	Barracuda	Heart
23	Stone Cold Sober	Crawler
24	The Things We Do For Love	10cc
25	It's Ecstasy When You Lay Down Next To Me	Barry White
26	Do Ya	Electric Light Orchestra
27	Ariel	Dean Friedman
28	I'm Your Boogie Man	KC And The Sunshine Band
29	Rich Girl	Daryl Hall & John Oates
30	Dusic	Brick
31	I Go Crazy	Paul Davis
32	Sentimental Lady	Bob Welch

#	Song Title	Artist
33	It's So Easy	Linda Ronstadt
34	Go Your Own Way	Fleetwood Mac
35	You Make Me Feel Like Dancing	Leo Sayer
36	Knowing Me, Knowing You	ABBA
37	How Much Love	Leo Sayer
38	So In To You (So Into You)	Atlanta Rhythm Section
39	Hotel California	Eagles
40	Telephone Line	Electric Light Orchestra
41	Brick House	Commodores
42	Space Intro/Fly Like An Eagle	Steve Miller Band
43	Do Ya Wanna Get Funky With Me?	Peter Brown
44	Sad Eyes	Brooklyn Dreams
45	Cherry Baby	Starz
46	High School Dance	The Sylvers
47	Feels Like The First Time	Foreigner
48	Dancin' Man	Q
49	I'm In You	Peter Frampton
50	Livin' Thing	Electric Light Orchestra
51	Back Together Again	Daryl Hall & John Oates
52	The Killing Of Georgie (Part I And II)	Rod Stewart
53	Baby, What A Big Surprise	Chicago
54	Dazz	Brick
55	Calling Dr. Love	KISS
56	How Deep Is Your Love	Bee Gees
57	Can't It All Be Love	Randy Edelman
58	Old Fashioned Boy (You're The One)	Stallion
59	Your Smiling Face	James Taylor
60	Walk This Way	Aerosmith
61	The First Cut Is The Deepest	Rod Stewart
62	Year Of The Cat	Al Stewart
63	Lonely Boy	Andrew Gold

1977

#	Song Title	Artist
64	Why Do Lovers (Break Each Other's Heart?)	Daryl Hall & John Oates
65	Foreplay/Long Time	Boston
66	Gonna Fly Now (Theme From "Rocky")	Bill Conti
67	Gonna Fly Now (Theme From "Rocky")	Maynard Ferguson
68	She's Not There	Santana
69	Money, Money, Money	ABBA
70	When I Need You	Leo Sayer
71	Telephone Man	Meri Wilson
72	(Remember The Days Of The) Old Schoolyard	Cat Stevens
73	Bite Your Lip (Get up and dance!)	Elton John
74	Don't Stop	Fleetwood Mac
75	We Just Disagree	Dave Mason
76	Dancing Queen	ABBA
77	Carry On Wayward Son	Kansas
78	You Made Me Believe In Magic	Bay City Rollers
79	Hot Line	The Sylvers
80	Best Of My Love	The Emotions
81	Swingtown	Steve Miller Band
82	It Keeps You Runnin'	The Doobie Brothers
83	Time Bomb	Lake
84	Just Remember I Love You	Firefall
85	Lido Shuffle	Boz Scaggs
86	Come Sail Away	Styx
87	Jet Airliner	Steve Miller Band

#	Song Title	Artist
88	A Place In The Sun	Pablo Cruise
89	The Whistler	Jethro Tull
90	Chicago	Kiki Dee
91	Smoke From A Distant Fire	The Sanford/Townsend Band
92	Sir Duke	Stevie Wonder
93	Signed, Sealed, Delivered (I'm Yours)	Peter Frampton
94	(Your Love Has Lifted Me) Higher And Higher	Rita Coolidge
95	Crackerbox Palace	George Harrison
96	Don't Leave Me This Way	Thelma Houston
97	Black Betty	Ram Jam
98	Easy	Commodores
99	Someone To Lay Down Beside Me	Linda Ronstadt
100	She Did It	Eric Carmen
101	Somebody To Love	Queen
1977 EXTRAS		
102	Spirit In The Night	Manfred Mann's Earth Band
105	My Heart Belongs To Me	Barbra Streisand
106	Whatcha Gonna Do?	Pablo Cruise
108	Whodunit	Tavares
113	Stand Tall	Burton Cummings
115	Nobody Does It Better	Carly Simon
124	So You Win Again	Hot Chocolate
131	Spring Rain (Lluvia De Primavera)	Silvetti
136	Just A Song Before I Go	Crosby, Stills & Nash
137	On The Border	Al Stewart

1978

#	Song Title	Artist
1	The Groove Line	Heatwave
2	Let's All Chant	Michael Zager Band
3	Shadow Dancing	Andy Gibb
4	Flash Light	Parliament
5	Don't Let Me Be Misunderstood	Santa Esmeralda f/ Leroy Gomez
6	Night Fever	Bee Gees
7	Follow You, Follow Me	Genesis
8	Dreadlock Holiday	10cc
9	Boogie Oogie Oogie	A Taste Of Honey
10	Before My Heart Finds Out	Gene Cotton
11	Hot Summer Nights	Walter Egan
12	Can We Still Be Friends	Todd Rundgren
13	Stayin' Alive	Bee Gees
14	The Name Of The Game	ABBA
15	I Can't Stand The Rain	Eruption (f/ Precious Wilson)
16	Theme From "Close Encounters Of The Third Kind"	John Williams
17	Theme From Close Encounters	Meco
18	Like A Sunday In Salem (The Amos & Andy Song)	Gene Cotton
19	Got To Have Loving	Don Ray
20	(Love Is) Thicker Than Water	Andy Gibb
21	Forever Autumn	Justin Hayward
22	Grease	Frankie Valli
23	Werewolves Of London	Warren Zevon
24	Le Freak	Chic
25	Miss You	The Rolling Stones
26	Because The Night	Patti Smith Group
27	I Love The Night Life (Disco 'Round)	Alicia Bridges
28	Breakdown	Tom Petty And The Heartbreakers
29	Almost Like Being In Love	Michael Johnson

#	Song Title	Artist
30	Summer Nights	Olivia Newton-John, John Travolta & Cast
31	Time Passages	Al Stewart
32	Baby Come Back	Player
33	You're A Part Of Me	Gene Cotton w/ Kim Carnes
34	Right Down The Line	Gerry Rafferty
35	FM (No Static At All)	Steely Dan
36	Get Off	Foxy
37	I Will Still Love You	Stonebolt
38	Lovely Day	Bill Withers
39	An Everlasting Love	Andy Gibb
40	Voyager/What Goes Up...	The Alan Parsons Project
41	Always And Forever	Heatwave
42	Two Tickets To Paradise	Eddie Money
43	Wrap Your Arms Around Me	KC And The Sunshine Band
44	Who Are You	The Who
45	Life's Been Good	Joe Walsh
46	You Never Done It Like That	Captain & Tennille
47	She's Always A Woman	Billy Joel
48	Sweet Talkin' Woman	Electric Light Orchestra
49	Native New Yorker	Odyssey
50	Sharing The Night Together	Dr. Hook
51	Mr. Blue Sky	Electric Light Orchestra
52	Dance, Dance, Dance (Yowsah, Yowsah, Yowsah)	Chic
53	Dance With Me	Peter Brown f/ Betty Wright
54	Jack And Jill	Raydio
55	(Our Love) Don't Throw It All Away	Andy Gibb
56	5-7-0-5 (5.7.0.5)	City Boy
57	You Belong To Me	Carly Simon
58	Here Comes The Night	Nick Gilder
59	Magnet And Steel	Walter Egan
60	Straight On	Heart

1978

#	Song Title	Artist
61	What's Your Name, What's Your Number	Andrea True Connection
62	Strange Way	Firefall
63	Wuthering Heights	Kate Bush
64	The Power Of Gold	Dan Fogelberg/ Tim Weisberg
65	Turn To Stone	Electric Light Orchestra
66	London Town	Wings
67	Imaginary Lover	Atlanta Rhythm Section
68	Love Theme From "Eyes Of Laura Mars" (Prisoner)	Barbra Streisand
69	Shame	Evelyn "Champagne" King
70	Falling	LeBlanc & Carr
71	So Long	Firefall
72	Don't Want To Live Without It	Pablo Cruise
73	Kiss You All Over	Exile
74	Warm Ride	Rare Earth
75	There's A Place In The World For A Gambler	Dan Fogelberg
76	Paradise By The Dashboard Light: I. Paradise II. Let Me Sleep On It III. Praying For The End Of Time	Meat Loaf
77	You And I	Rick James (& The Stone City Band)
78	Baby Hold On	Eddie Money
79	Double Vision	Foreigner
80	Thank You For Being A Friend	Andrew Gold
81	Silver Dreams	The Babys
82	Thank God It's Friday	Love And Kisses
83	How Much I Feel	Ambrosia
84	Fool (If You Think It's Over)	Chris Rea
85	Movin' Out (Anthony's Song)	Billy Joel

#	Song Title	Artist
86	Only The Good Die Young	Billy Joel
87	Emotion	Samantha Sang
88	Dust In The Wind	Kansas
89	Take A Chance On Me	ABBA
90	Baker Street	Gerry Rafferty
91	We Will Rock You/We Are The Champions	Queen
92	Love Is Like Oxygen	Sweet
93	Hot Child In The City	Nick Gilder
94	Bicycle Race/Fat Bottomed Girls	Queen
95	Hot Love, Cold World	Bob Welch
96	Boogie Shoes	KC And The Sunshine Band
97	Just What I Needed	The Cars
98	You Keep Me Dancing	Samantha Sang
99	You	Rita Coolidge
100	Rocket Ride	KISS
101	Prisoner Of Your Love	Player
1978 EXTRAS		
104	Peg	Steely Dan
106	Serpentine Fire	Earth, Wind & Fire
108	Whenever I Call You "Friend"	Kenny Loggins w/ Stevie Nicks
111	With A Little Luck	Wings
115	If I Can't Have You	Yvonne Elliman
126	Stuff Like That	Quincy Jones
129	Ready For The Times To Get Better	Crystal Gayle
137	Copacabana (At The Copa)	Barry Manilow
139	I'm Gonna Take Care Of Everything	Rubicon
170	Dance (Disco Heat)	Sylvester
211	Second Avenue	Tim Moore

#	Song Title	Artist
1	The Logical Song	Supertramp
2	Are 'Friends' Electric?	Gary Numan + Tubeway Army
3	Love Don't Live Here Anymore	Rose Royce
4	Hold On	Iam Gomm
5	Driver's Seat	Sniff 'n' The Tears
6	Chase	Giorgio Moroder
7	We Are Family	Sister Sledge
8	Take The Long Way Home / Breakfast In America	Supertramp
9	Love Is The Answer	England Dan & John Ford Coley
10	Frederick	Patti Smith Group
11	Let's Go	The Cars
12	My Sharona	The Knack
13	Please Don't Go	KC And The Sunshine Band
14	Cruel To Be Kind	Nick Lowe
15	Cool Breeze	The Jeremy Spencer Band
16	I Will Survive	Gloria Gaynor
17	Gold	John Stewart
18	Good Times Roll/All Mixed Up	The Cars
19	Tragedy	Bee Gees
20	Such A Woman/How Long (Can We Go On)	Tycoon
21	Message In A Bottle	The Police
22	Babe	Styx
23	Up On The Roof	James Taylor
24	Heart Of Glass	Blondie
25	The Day The Earth Caught Fire	City Boy
26	Roxanne	The Police
27	Dancing In The City	Marshall Hain
28	Every 1's A Winner	Hot Chocolate
29	Midnight Wind	John Stewart
30	Is She Really Going Out With Him?	Joe Jackson

#	Song Title	Artist
31	Home And Dry	Gerry Rafferty
32	Damned If I Do	The Alan Parsons Project
33	Every Time I Think Of You/Head First	The Babys
34	Don't Ever Wanna Lose Ya	New England
35	Got To Be Real	Cheryl Lynn
36	Shattered	The Rolling Stones
37	Tusk	Fleetwood Mac
38	Hold On	Triumph
39	Georgy Porgy	Toto
40	Take Me To The River	Talking Heads
41	New York Groove	Ace Frehley
42	Sweet Lui-Louise	Ironhorse
43	I Was Made For Lovin' You	KISS
44	Bad Girls	Donna Summer
45	Saturdaynight	Herman Brood & His Wild Romance
46	Rock 'N' Roll Fantasy	Bad Company
47	Get It Right Next Time	Gerry Rafferty
48	Get A Move On	Eddie Money
49	Head Games	Foreigner
50	Lotta Love	Nicolette Larson
51	Goodnight Tonight	Wings
52	Crazy Love	Poco
53	I Need A Lover	John Cougar (Mellencamp)
54	You're Gonna Get What's Coming	Bonnie Raitt
55	Rolene	Moon Martin
56	Hot Stuff	Donna Summer
57	Shakedown Cruise	Jay Ferguson
58	Dog & Butterfly	Heart
59	I Want Your Love	Chic
60	Children Of The Sun	Billy Thorpe
61	Dream Police	Cheap Trick
62	Love You (Inside Out)	Bee Gees
63	Knock On Wood	Amii Stewart

#	Song Title	Artist
64	One Way Or Another	Blondie
65	Girls Talk	Dave Edmunds
66	No More Tears (Enough Is Enough)	Barbra Streisand/Donna Summer
67	Song On The Radio	Al Stewart
68	Pop Muzik	M
69	Sail On	Commodores
70	Sailing Without A Sail/ When You Come Home	Michael Johnson
71	Lonesome Loser/Shut Down Turn Off	Little River Band
72	Don't You Write Her Off	McGuinn, Clark & Hillman
73	(If Loving You Is Wrong) I Don't Want To Be Right	Barbara Mandrell
74	Lovin', Touchin', Squeezin'	Journey
75	Rise	Herb Alpert
76	Goodbye, I Love You	Firefall
77	Get Used To It	Roger Voudouris
78	Do Ya Think I'm Sexy?	Rod Stewart
79	Goodbye Stranger/ Even In The Quietest Moments	Supertramp
80	Don't Bring Me Down	Electric Light Orchestra
81	Deeper Than The Night	Olivia Newton-John
82	Heartache Tonight	Eagles
83	The Main Event/Fight	Barbra Streisand
84	I Can't Stand It No More	Peter Frampton
85	You Can't Change That	Raydio
86	Hold The Line	Toto
87	Jane	Jefferson Starship
88	Does Your Mother Know	ABBA

#	Song Title	Artist
89	Magazine	Heart
90	Girl Of My Dreams	Bram Tchaikovsky
91	What You Won't Do For Love	Bobby Caldwell
92	September	Earth, Wind & Fire
93	New Lines On Love	Sniff 'n' The Tears
94	Happiness	Pointer Sisters
95	Heart Of The Night	Poco
96	Music Box Dancer	Frank Mills
97	Long Live Rock	The Who
98	Just When I Needed You Most	Randy VanWarmer
99	Don't Hold Back	Chanson
100	Arrow Through Me	Wings
101	You Take My Breath Away	Rex Smith

#	1979 EXTRAS	
103	Come To Me	France Joli
104	I Never Said I Love You	Orsa Lia
109	I Want You To Want Me	Cheap Trick
110	Shake Your Groove Thing	Peaches & Herb
115	A Little More Love	Olivia Newton-John
116	Boogie Wonderland	Earth, Wind & Fire w/ The Emotions
122	Life During Wartime (This Ain't No Party . . . This Ain't No Disco . . . This Ain't No Foolin' Around)	Talking Heads
137	Suspicions	Eddie Rabbitt
167	Bright Eyes	Art Garfunkel
201	Ring My Bell	Anita Ward

#	Song Title	Artist
1	It's Different For Girls	Joe Jackson
2	Games Without Frontiers	Peter Gabriel (w/ Kate Bush)
3	Carrie	Cliff Richard
4	Let My Love Open The Door	Pete Townshend
5	Everybody's Got To Learn Sometime	The Korgis
6	Sara	Fleetwood Mac
7	With You I'm Born Again	Billy Preston & Syreeta
8	Into The Night	Benny Mardones
9	Sailing	Christopher Cross
10	Another Brick In The Wall Part II	Pink Floyd
11	99	Toto
12	Boyss	Strix Q
13	I Can't Tell You Why	Eagles
14	The Seduction (Love Theme)	James Last Band
15	Brass In Pocket (I'm Special)	The Pretenders
16	A Little Is Enough	Pete Townshend
17	Woman In Love	Barbra Streisand
18	Sisters Of The Moon	Fleetwood Mac
19	Another One Bites The Dust	Queen
20	Cars	Gary Numan
21	Stay In Time	Off Broadway usa
22	Why Not Me	Fred Knoblock
23	Video Killed The Radio Star	The Buggles
24	Magic	Olivia Newton-John
25	I'm Alright (Theme From "Caddyshack")	Kenny Loggins
26	Complex	Gary Numan
27	We Live For Love	Pat Benatar
28	Lady	Kenny Rogers
29	Clones (We're All)	Alice Cooper
30	Coming Up (Live At Glasgow)/Coming Up	Paul McCartney & Wings

#	Song Title	Artist
31	That Girl Could Sing	Jackson Browne
32	Turn It On Again	Genesis
33	Wow / Hammer Horror	Kate Bush
34	Whip It	Devo
35	Desire	Andy Gibb
36	Chiquitita	ABBA
37	The Rose	Bette Midler
38	New Romance (It's A Mystery)	Spider
39	This Beat Goes On/ Switchin' To Glide	The Kings
40	Back On My Feet Again	The Babys
41	Lost Her In The Sun	John Stewart
42	Walking On The Moon	The Police
43	Ten Feet Tall	XTC
44	How Does It Feel To Be Back	Daryl Hall & John Oates
45	We Don't Talk Anymore	Cliff Richard
46	Emotional Rescue	The Rolling Stones
47	You're The Only Woman (You & I)	Ambrosia
48	Deadline	Blue Öyster Cult
49	All Out Of Love	Air Supply
50	Touch And Go	The Cars
51	You've Lost That Lovin' Feeling	Daryl Hall & John Oates
52	Do Right	Paul Davis
53	I Could Be Good For You	707
54	Heartbreaker	Pat Benatar
55	Wait For Me	Daryl Hall & John Oates
56	Train In Vain (Stand By Me)	The Clash
57	Headed For A Fall	Firefall
58	On The Radio/There Will Always Be A You	Donna Summer
59	Money (That's What I Want)	The Flying Lizards
60	You Better Run	Pat Benatar
61	Dreamin'	Cliff Richard
62	Sometimes A Fantasy	Billy Joel

#	Song Title	Artist
63	Run Like Hell/Don't Leave Me Now	Pink Floyd
64	Lost In Love	Air Supply
65	Ride Like The Wind	Christopher Cross
66	Walks Like A Lady	Journey
67	Voices	Cheap Trick
68	Hurt So Bad	Linda Ronstadt
69	I Don't Like Mondays	The Boomtown Rats
70	How Do I Survive	Amy Holland
71	Good Morning Girl/ Stay Awhile	Journey
72	Atomic	Blondie
73	All Over The World	Electric Light Orchestra
74	Souvenirs	Jesse Brady Band
75	Him	Rupert Holmes
76	Heart Hotels	Dan Fogelberg
77	The Spirit Of Radio	Rush
78	Midnight Rocks	Al Stewart & Shot In The Dark
79	Last Chance	Shooting Star
80	Without Your Love	Roger Daltrey
81	Refugee	Tom Petty And The Heartbreakers
82	Call Me	Blondie
83	Gimme! Gimme! Gimme! (A Man After Midnight)	ABBA
84	More Love	Kim Carnes
85	Coming Down From Love	Bobby Caldwell
86	Free Me	Roger Daltrey
87	Look What You've Done To Me	Boz Scaggs
88	Sequel	Harry Chapin
89	Why Me	Styx

#	Song Title	Artist
90	Don't Do Me Like That	Tom Petty And The Heartbreakers
91	Set Me Free	Utopia
92	Everything Works If You Let It	Cheap Trick
93	Double Life	The Cars
94	It's Still Rock And Roll To Me	Billy Joel
95	Suddenly	Olivia Newton-John & Cliff Richard
96	You'll Accomp'ny Me	Bob Seger & The Silver Bullet Band
97	Hit Me With Your Best Shot	Pat Benatar
98	Boulevard	Jackson Browne
99	Every Woman In The World	Air Supply
100	Lovin' You With My Eyes	Starland Vocal Band
101	She's So Cold	The Rolling Stones
1980 EXTRAS		
104	Misunderstanding	Genesis
105	He's So Shy	Pointer Sisters
111	Crazy Little Thing Called Love	Queen
114	Guilty	Barbra Streisand & Barry Gibb
118	Fame	Irene Cara
124	Easy To Be Hard	Cheryl Barnes
129	I Remember Romance	Flamin' Oh's
130	Stomp!	The Brothers Johnson
136	Upside Down	Diana Ross
141	Xanadu	Electric Light Orchestra & Olivia Newton-John
161	Turning Japanese	The Vapors

1981

#	Song Title	Artist
1	In The Air Tonight	Phil Collins
2	Same Old Lang Syne	Dan Fogelberg
3	Babooshka	Kate Bush
4	The Friends Of Mr. Cairo	Jon & Vangelis
5	The Wedding List	Kate Bush
6	For Your Eyes Only	Sheena Easton
7	Every Little Thing She Does Is Magic	The Police
8	Heaven	Carl Wilson
9	Fanfare/Chloe	Elton John
10	Waiting For A Girl Like You	Foreigner
11	What Kind Of Fool	Barbra Streisand & Barry Gibb
12	Don't Stop Believin'	Journey
13	One Step Ahead	Split Enz
14	Don't Stand So Close To Me	The Police
15	Who's Crying Now	Journey
16	Time	The Alan Parsons Project
17	De Do Do Do, De Da Da Da	The Police
18	Hard Act To Follow	Split Enz
19	Rapture	Blondie
20	I Will Follow	U2
21	The Party's Over (Hopelessly In Love)	Journey
22	My Mother's Eyes	Bette Midler
23	Don't Want To Wait Anymore	The Tubes
24	Fashion	David Bowie
25	Tomorrow/October	U2
26	The Breakup Song (They Don't Write 'Em)	Greg Kihn Band
27	The Tide Is High	Blondie
28	Tempted	Squeeze
29	Bette Davis Eyes	Kim Carnes
30	Alien	Atlanta Rhythm Section
31	Another Ticket	Eric Clapton
32	The Voice	The Moody Blues
33	Games People Play	The Alan Parsons Project
34	I Got You	Split Enz
35	Generals And Majors	XTC
36	Stop Draggin' My Heart Around/Kind Of Woman	Stevie Nicks w/ Tom Petty And The Heartbreakers
37	History Never Repeats	Split Enz
38	Time Is Time	Andy Gibb
39	Limelight	Rush
40	I Die: You Die	Gary Numan
41	A Woman In Love (It's Not Me)	Tom Petty And The Heartbreakers
42	My Girl (Gone, Gone, Gone)	Chilliwack
43	Ah! Leah!	Donnie Iris
44	While You See A Chance	Steve Winwood
45	The Winner Takes It All	ABBA
46	Promises	Barbra Streisand
47	Stranger	Jefferson Starship
48	Find Your Way Back	Jefferson Starship
49	Skateaway	Dire Straits
50	Endless Love	Diana Ross & Lionel Richie
51	Really Wanna Know You	Gary Wright
52	Sukiyaki	A Taste Of Honey
53	Nobody Wins	Elton John
54	Arc Of A Diver	Steve Winwood
55	Jesse's Girl	Rick Springfield
56	A Heart In New York	Art Garfunkel
57	9 To 5	Dolly Parton
58	Me (Without You)	Andy Gibb
59	Fireflies	Fleetwood Mac
60	Hard To Say	Dan Fogelberg
61	Draw Of The Cards	Kim Carnes
62	The Best Of Times	Styx
63	Her Town Too	James Taylor And J.D. Souther
64	Mirror In The Bathroom	The Beat (The English Beat)
65	Flesh And Blood	Shooting Star

1981

#	Song Title	Artist		#	Song Title	Artist
66	Burnin' For You	Blue Öyster Cult		88	America	Neil Diamond
67	Gotta Have More Love	Climax Blues Band		89	Too Much Time On My Hands	Styx
68	Winning	Santana		90	Boy From New York City	The Manhattan Transfer
69	Stop This Game	Cheap Trick		91	I Loved 'Em Every One	T.G. Sheppard
70	Working In The Coal Mine	Devo		92	Sausalito Summernight	Diesel
71	Hearts	Marty Balin		93	I Missed Again	Phil Collins
72	If It's The Last Night	Toto		94	Talk Of The Town	The Pretenders
73	Tom Sawyer	Rush		95	Just Between You And Me	April Wine
74	Living In A Fantasy	Leo Sayer		96	Promises In The Dark	Pat Benatar
75	Mistaken Identity	Kim Carnes		97	Heavy Metal (Takin' A Ride)	Don Felder
76	I Don't Remember	Peter Gabriel		98	No Reply At All	Genesis
77	Ain't Even Done With The Night	John Cougar (Mellencamp)		99	Urgent	Foreigner
78	The Night Owls	Little River Band		100	A Little In Love	Cliff Richard
79	Rock And Roll Dreams Come Through	Jim Steinman		101	Lady (You Bring Me Up)	Commodores
80	Super Trouper	ABBA			**1981 EXTRAS**	
81	Turn And Walk Away	The Babys		102	Sweetheart	Franke & The Knockouts
82	You Better You Bet	The Who		103	Passion	Rod Stewart
83	We Can Get Together	Icehouse		106	The Theme From Hill Street Blues	Mike Post f/ Larry Carlton
84	Don't Let Go The Coat	The Who		107	New Toy	Lene Lovich
85	Arthur's Theme (Best That You Can Do)	Christopher Cross		113	Somebody's Knockin'	Terri Gibbs
86	Physical	Olivia Newton-John		116	Seven Year Ache	Rosanne Cash
87	You Make My Dreams	Daryl Hall & John Oates		124	No Turning Back	Sherbs

#	Song Title	Artist
1	I'll Find My Way Home	Jon & Vangelis
2	Family Man	Mike Oldfield
3	Almost	Orchestral Manoeuvres In The Dark
4	Why	Carly Simon
5	You Could Have Been With Me	Sheena Easton
6	Making Love / I'm The One	Roberta Flack
7	The Visitors	ABBA
8	Runaways	XTC
9	Chariots Of Fire – Titles	Vangelis
10	Gloria	U2
11	Five Miles Out	Mike Oldfield
12	Tainted Love/Where Did Our Love Go	Soft Cell
13	Icehouse	Icehouse
14	Hard To Say I'm Sorry/ Get Away	Chicago
15	Mesopotamia	The B-52's
16	Down Under	Men At Work
17	I Ran (So Far Away)	A Flock Of Seagulls
18	Sirius/Eye In The Sky	The Alan Parsons Project
19	Fly On The Wall	XTC
20	Genius Of Love	Tom Tom Club
21	Our Lips Are Sealed	Go-Go's
22	Pioneer/Six Months In A Leaky Boat	Split Enz
23	Don't You Want Me	The Human League
24	Souvenir	Orchestral Manoeuvres In The Dark
25	Nice Girls	Eye To Eye
26	Sat In Your Lap	Kate Bush
27	Under Pressure	Queen & David Bowie
28	Man On The Corner	Genesis
29	Enola Gay / Stanlow	Orchestral Manoeuvres In The Dark
30	Target For Life	Our Daughter's Wedding
31	Harden My Heart	Quarterflash
32	Memory	Barbra Streisand

#	Song Title	Artist
33	Your Imagination	Daryl Hall & John Oates
34	Dirty Creature	Split Enz
35	Big Science	Laurie Anderson
36	The Voice	Ultravox
37	Still They Ride	Journey
38	Secret Journey / Invisible Sun	The Police
39	Destination Unknown	Missing Persons
40	Deep Sleep	The B-52's
41	Joan Of Arc (Maid Of Orleans)	Orchestral Manoeuvres In The Dark
42	Steppin' Out	Joe Jackson
43	O Superman (For Massenet)	Laurie Anderson
44	Spirits In The Material World	The Police
45	Talk Talk	Talk Talk
46	Giant Heartbeat	Split Enz
47	Trouble	Lindsey Buckingham
48	Wordy Rappinghood	Tom Tom Club
49	Senses Working Overtime	XTC
50	Gypsy	Fleetwood Mac
51	Blue Eyes	Elton John
52	Gloria	Laura Branigan
53	Space Age Love Song	A Flock Of Seagulls
54	Shock The Monkey	Peter Gabriel
55	Words	Missing Persons
56	Who Can It Be Now?	Men At Work
57	Muscles	Diana Ross
58	We Belong Together	Rickie Lee Jones
59	Maneater	Daryl Hall & John Oates
60	Empty Garden (Hey Hey Johnny)	Elton John
61	Pirates (So Long Lonely Avenue)	Rickie Lee Jones
62	Classic	Adrian Gurvitz
63	Rock The Casbah	The Clash
64	Walking In The Rain	Grace Jones
65	The Look Of Love	ABC

1982

#	Song Title	Artist	#	Song Title	Artist
66	I Can't Go For That (No Can Do)	Daryl Hall & John Oates	89	Let Me Tickle Your Fancy	Jermaine Jackson (w/ Devo)
67	Never Never Land	Lene Lovich	90	Cat People (Putting Out Fire)	David Bowie
68	Paperlate/You Might Recall	Genesis	91	Don't Talk To Strangers	Rick Springfield
69	Hollywood	Shooting Star	92	Edge Of Seventeen (Just Like The White Winged Dove)	Stevie Nicks
70	Nobody Said It Was Easy (Lookin' For The Lights)	LeRoux	93	State Of Independence	Donna Summer
71	I Keep Forgettin' (Every Time You're Near)	Michael McDonald	94	Only The Lonely	The Motels
72	Comin' In And Out Of Your Life	Barbra Streisand	95	Rosanna	Toto
73	Atmospherics (Listen To The Radio)	Tom Robinson	96	Please Be The One	Karla Bonoff
74	When It's Over	Loverboy	97	Pocket Calculator	Kraftwerk
75	A World Without Heroes	KISS	98	Just Can't Win 'Em All	Stevie Woods
76	New World Man	Rush	99	When He Shines	Sheena Easton
77	867-5309/Jenny	Tommy Tutone	100	Only Time Will Tell	Asia
78	I Know What Boys Like	The Waitresses	101	Open Arms	Journey
79	Love Action (I Believe In Love)	The Human League	**1982 EXTRAS**		
80	When All Is Said And Done	ABBA	103	Johnny, Are You Queer?	Josie Cotton
81	I.G.Y. (What A Beautiful World)	Donald Fagen	105	Mickey	Toni Basil
82	Love Plus One	Haircut One Hundred	107	Kids In America	Kim Wilde
83	Vacation	Go-Go's	108	Hot In The City	Billy Idol
84	Since You're Gone	The Cars	111	Love Is In Control (Finger On The Trigger)	Donna Summer
85	Goin' Down	Greg Guidry	114	We Got The Beat	Go-Go's
86	More Than Just The Two Of Us	Sneaker	118	You Should Hear How She Talks About You	Melissa Manchester
87	Night Talk	Gary Numan	126	You Can Do Magic	America
88	abacab	Genesis	128	Man Out Of Time	Elvis Costello & The Attractions
			131	Never Say Never	Romeo Void
			186	Abracadabra	Steve Miller Band

Minnesota to Maine & Back Again, 1982

There were thirty magical days in August and September of 1982 that started with the adventure of my young-man dreams and ended in numbing tragedy. This was a landmark moment in my life.

In mid-August, I began my first solo road trip through the Northeast US. Three weeks, fourteen states, one province. College had ended earlier that summer, though I still had an independent study to complete for my degree. Upon my return from this journey, I'd have only a few weeks left at my summer jobs in my college town.

I made one crucial hotel reservation in Manhattan (near Lincoln Center) using a travel book from the college library. To save money—I didn't have many savings back then—I planned to camp; stay with a few friends along the way; find cheap motels; or sleep in my car, pulling up late at night on side streets and setting my bicentennial alarm clock for 6:00 a.m. to keep the locals none the wiser. It worked, except on the morning when I was in a town near the Amityville horror house and a dog owner greeted me as I crawled out of my hatchback.

I took off with a road atlas, traveler's checks, Bob Damron's gay guide, my cooler, and homemade shrimp pasta salad to eat for a day or two to save money and time. I had promised Mom and Dad that I would call collect every other day (often from phone booths), but I failed once and made sure I did not worry them again. You see, I was still mostly naïve to the world and its ways, so they did worry. It was, after all, my first time to New York City, let alone Cleveland, Philly, and Boston. I drove past Chicago thinking I would see it one day. Sure, the cities along the way seemed scary to me as such a young driver; hence, I drove across the Verrazzano-Narrows Bridge at midnight to bypass the Big Apple and tour Long Island first. Luckily, I am great at reading and memorizing maps.

Being a geographer, I wanted to see everything along

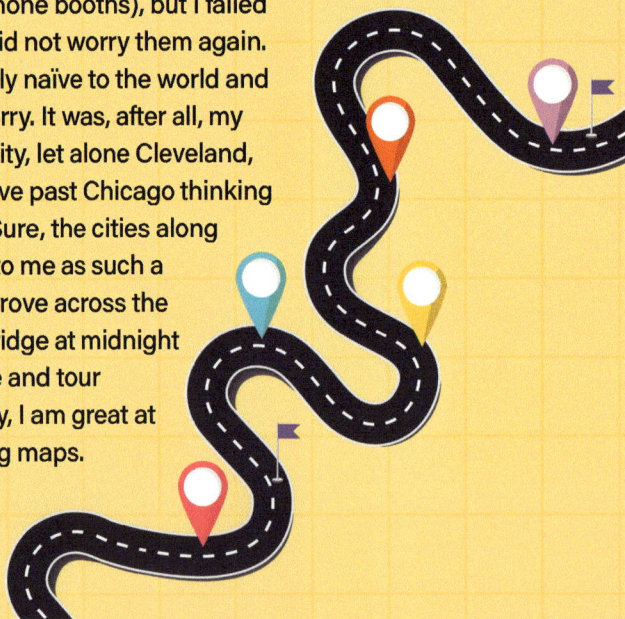

the way: Indiana Dunes, The Hershey Story Museum, Valley Forge, Cape Cod, Acadia, the White and Green Mountains, Finger Lakes, Niagara Falls, Three Mile Island, and Love Canal. Then there was Fire Island, where I was miserably out of my gay comfort zone and obviously seen as an unstylish small-town hick. I never reached Martha's Vineyard (still to this day) on account of being ill for three days in a Woods Hole, Massachusetts, motel. I eventually found some energy and drove to a clinic in Provincetown.

I learned that every adventure can have a change in plans, so I adjusted. How could I complain when I experienced a Yankees game, viewed New York City from the outside rooftop of the World Trade Center South Tower, slept across from Paul Revere's house, tasted my first street-vendor knish with mustard, went to my first nude beach, ate my first lobster roll, toured Edgar Allan Poe's home, and reached the easternmost point of the United States. I saw the Old Man of the Mountain before his face fell off and learned about green-eyed robber flies. The worst moment happened when I woke up as my car traveled 80-some kilometers per hour in the median of a Canadian interstate. Yet, I survived. This trip was a dream despite minor incidents.

Why am I telling you all of this? Because the summer of 1982 was the most magical musical moment in my life. The musical transition from disco to new wave, constrasting with the changes in my life (finishing college, moving back home, facing my future, finding my first full-time job, and moving to the city), created the perfect summer of music.

I fondly recall the exciting songs that summer. My top 101 list for 1982 is dappled with songs from that incredible road trip, especially songs ranked at 1, 4, 12, 14, 16, 17, 18, 23, 25, 31, 39, 42, 48, 51, 52, 82, 83, 89, 93, 94, 105 and 126. And *The Visitors* (#7, 1982), my all-time favorite ABBA song.

But all my road-trip memories and my expectations for the future quickly faded when my dad unexpectedly died in mid-September. Shortly after being with him and hearing his last breath, I heard Michael McDonald's *I Keep Forgettin' (Every Time You're Near)* on my car radio. Dad is near, and reappears in my mind, every time I hear that song.

I was happy and blessed to spend a few months with Mom before I went out on my own. I know she was glad I was there for her. I purchased Peter Gabriel's **Security**, Kate Bush's **The Dreaming**, and Ultravox's **Monument** albums during those months. Final memories of a formative year and a magical summer that remain vivid because of the music.

1983

#	Song Title	Artist		#	Song Title	Artist
1	The Dreaming	Kate Bush		32	Someone Somewhere In Summertime	Simple Minds
2	Pale Shelter (You Don't Give Me Love)	Tears For Fears		33	When I'm With You	Sheriff
3	Genetic Engineering	Orchestral Manoeuvres In The Dark		34	Europa And The Pirate Twins	Thomas Dolby
4	Mad World	Tears For Fears		35	Eyes Of A Stranger	Payola$
5	Today	Talk Talk		36	One Thing Leads To Another	The Fixx
6	Love Is A Battlefield	Pat Benatar		37	Love In Store	Fleetwood Mac
7	Send Her My Love	Journey		38	Blue Monday	New Order
8	Sweet Dreams (Are Made Of This)	Eurythmics		39	The Safety Dance	Men Without Hats
9	The Metro	Berlin		40	Promises, Promises	Naked Eyes
10	She Blinded Me With Science/One Of Our Submarines	Thomas Dolby		41	Auto Music	Our Daughter's Wedding
11	More Than This	Roxy Music		42	Don't Go	Yazoo (Yaz)
12	Wishing (If I Had A Photograph Of You)	A Flock Of Seagulls		43	You're Driving Me Out Of My Mind	Little River Band
13	Hey' Little Girl	Icehouse		44	Major Tom (Coming Home)	Peter Schilling
14	Change	Tears For Fears		45	Great Southern Land / Street Café	Icehouse
15	True	Spandau Ballet		46	Stand Back	Stevie Nicks
16	Mirror Man	The Human League		47	The Rhythm Of The Heat	Peter Gabriel
17	Every Breath You Take	The Police		48	Let's Dance	David Bowie
18	New Year's Day	U2		49	The Day Before You Came	ABBA
19	Nobody's Diary/ State Farm	Yazoo (Yaz)		50	Breaking Us In Two	Joe Jackson
20	Promised You A Miracle	Simple Minds		51	Mama	Genesis
21	There Goes A Tenner	Kate Bush		52	Do You Really Want To Hurt Me	Culture Club
22	Saved By Zero	The Fixx		53	My Jamaican Guy	Grace Jones
23	Africa	Toto		54	Two Hearts Beat As One	U2
24	Let Me Go	Heaven 17		55	Glittering Prize	Simple Minds
25	(Keep Feeling) Fascination	The Human League		56	I Couldn't Say No	Robert Ellis Orrall w/ Charlene Carter
26	King Of Pain	The Police		57	Heart Of The Night	Juice Newton
27	New Gold Dream (81-82-83-84)	Simple Minds		58	Nightmares	A Flock Of Seagulls
28	Candy	Talk Talk		59	The Border	America
29	Lies	Thompson Twins		60	Sunday Bloody Sunday	U2
30	Suspended In Gaffa/ Ne T'en Fui Pas	Kate Bush		61	Old And Wise	The Alan Parsons Project
31	Reap The Wild Wind	Ultravox		62	Only You	Yazoo (Yaz)
				63	Twist Of Fate	Olivia Newton-John
				64	I Know Something's Going On	Frida

1983

#	Song Title	Artist
65	Too Shy	Kajagoogoo
66	Overkill	Men At Work
67	I Have The Touch	Peter Gabriel
68	The Man With The 4-Way Hips	Tom Tom Club
69	Allentown	Billy Joel
70	Love On Your Side	Thompson Twins
71	I Melt With You	Modern English
72	Talking In Your Sleep	The Romantics
73	One On One	Daryl Hall & John Oates
74	Sexual Healing	Marvin Gaye
75	Holiday/Everybody	Madonna
76	You Are A Danger	Gary Low
77	Flashdance...What A Feeling	Irene Cara
78	Hymn	Ultravox
79	Adventures In Success	Will Powers
80	Love Is A Stranger	Eurythmics
81	Can't Shake Loose	Agnetha Fältskog
82	Where Everybody Knows Your Name ("Theme From Cheers")	Gary Portnoy
83	He Is Sailing	Jon & Vangelis
84	Where Is My Man?	Eartha Kitt
85	It's Raining Again	Supertramp
86	Jeopardy	Greg Kihn Band
87	Take Me To Heart	Quarterflash
88	Everyday I Write The Book	Elvis Costello
89	If Anyone Falls	Stevie Nicks
90	Little Red Corvette	Prince
91	Psychobabble	The Alan Parsons Project
92	After The Fall	Journey
93	Be Good Johnny	Men At Work
94	Love Come Down	Evelyn King
95	Burning Down The House	Talking Heads
96	Synchronicity II	The Police
97	China	Red Rockers

#	Song Title	Artist
98	Great Fire	XTC
99	Nipple To The Bottle	Grace Jones
100	Family Man	Daryl Hall & John Oates
101	Back On The Chain Gang/My City Was Gone	The Pretenders
1983 EXTRAS		
103	Total Eclipse Of The Heart	Bonnie Tyler
105	Sex (I'm A...)	Berlin
106	Does It Make You Remember	Kim Carnes
110	Working Girl	Cheri
114	Der Kommissar (two versions)	After The Fire / Falco
115	Poison Arrow	ABC
118	Making Love Out Of Nothing At All	Air Supply
123	White Wedding	Billy Idol
125	Billie Jean	Michael Jackson
126	She's A Beauty	The Tubes
127	Potential New Boyfriend	Dolly Parton
129	Separate Ways (Worlds Apart)	Journey
130	Suddenly Last Summer	The Motels
132	Eminence Front	The Who
133	She Works Hard For The Money	Donna Summer
136	I Eat Cannibals	Toto Coelo (Total Coelo)
151	You And I	Eddie Rabbitt and Crystal Gayle
163	Just Be Good To Me	The S.O.S. Band
165	Mexican Radio	Wall Of Voodoo
179	Beat It	Michael Jackson
182	Living On Video	Trans X
183	Electric Avenue	Eddy Grant
188	Freeez	I.O.U.
192	Dancing In Heaven (Orbital Be-Bop)	Q-Feel
219	Milk From The Coconut (Part 1)	Toto Coelo (Total Coelo)

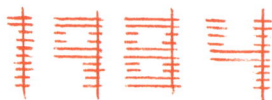

1984

#	Song Title	Artist
1	Wishful Thinking	China Crisis
2	Screen Kiss	Thomas Dolby
3	Talk About Your Life	Mike Oldfield
4	Smalltown Boy	Bronski Beat
5	Such A Shame	Talk Talk
6	Here Comes The Rain Again	Eurythmics
7	Wouldn't It Be Good	Nik Kershaw
8	A Girl In Trouble (Is A Temporary Thing)	Romeo Void
9	Hold Me Now	Thompson Twins
10	Dum Dum Girl	Talk Talk
11	Foreign Affair	Mike Oldfield
12	When The Lights Go Out	Naked Eyes
13	Time After Time	Cyndi Lauper
14	It's My Life	Talk Talk
15	Gold	Spandau Ballet
16	Cruel Summer	Bananarama
17	Pride (In The Name Of Love)	U2
18	Who's That Girl?	Eurythmics
19	Over My Head	Toni Basil
20	Lament	Ultravox
21	When Doves Cry	Prince And The Revolution
22	I Can Hear Your Heartbeat	Chris Rea
23	Love In Motion	Icehouse
24	In High Places	Mike Oldfield (w/ Jon Anderson)
25	Working With Fire And Steel / Hanna Hanna	China Crisis
26	New Song	Howard Jones
27	Dancing With Tears In My Eyes	Ultravox
28	Coming Out Of Hiding	Pamala Stanley
29	Wrapped Around Your Finger	The Police
30	They Don't Know	Tracey Ullman
31	Hard Habit To Break	Chicago

#	Song Title	Artist
32	Owner Of A Lonely Heart	Yes
33	We Belong	Pat Benatar
34	Tonight	Kool & The Gang
35	The More You Live, The More You Love	A Flock Of Seagulls
36	Message To My Girl	Split Enz
37	To France	Mike Oldfield
38	Come Back And Stay	Paul Young
39	Eyes Without A Face	Billy Idol
40	Drive	The Cars
41	Talking Loud And Clear	Orchestral Manoeuvres In The Dark
42	Doctor! Doctor!	Thompson Twins
43	Self Control	Laura Branigan
44	It Ain't Enough	Corey Hart
45	Only When You Leave	Spandau Ballet
46	Locomotion	Orchestral Manoeuvres In The Dark
47	Life On Your Own	The Human League
48	Boys Do Fall In Love	Robin Gibb
49	I'll Fly For You	Spandau Ballet
50	She Bop	Cyndi Lauper
51	Love Of The Common People	Paul Young
52	Inside Of My Head	Annabel Lamb
53	Sister Of Mercy / The Gap	Thompson Twins
54	Hello	Lionel Richie
55	Sunglasses At Night	Corey Hart
56	You Don't Believe	The Alan Parsons Project
57	Wherever I Lay My Hat (That's My Home)	Paul Young
58	Go Insane	Lindsey Buckingham
59	Excellent Birds / This Is The Picture (Excellent Birds)	Laurie Anderson / Peter Gabriel
60	Swept Away	Diana Ross
61	Doot-Doot	Freur
62	Shooting Shark	Blue Öyster Cult

1984

#	Song Title	Artist
63	Louise	The Human League
64	No Way Out	Jefferson Starship
65	My Ever Changing Moods	The Style Council
66	Dream Boy	Annabel Lamb
67	Missing You	John Waite
68	The Lebanon	The Human League
69	The Politics Of Dancing	Re-Flex
70	Suffer The Children	Tears For Fears
71	Nightbird	Stevie Nicks
72	Sound Of My Heart	Sleeping Lions
73	In A Minor Key	Tim Finn
74	Let The Music Play	Shannon
75	Remember The Nights	The Motels
76	Send Me An Angel / Send Me An Angel '89	Real Life
77	Baby I Lied	Deborah Allen
78	Out Of Touch	Daryl Hall & John Oates
79	Runner	Manfred Mann's Earth Band
80	New York / NY	Nina Hagen
81	Independence Day	The Comsat Angels (The C.S. Angels)
82	Prime Time	The Alan Parsons Project
83	Red Red Wine	UB40
84	New Moon On Monday	Duran Duran
85	All Through The Night	Cyndi Lauper
86	This Charming Man	The Smiths
87	Union Of The Snake	Duran Duran
88	Think Of Laura	Christopher Cross
89	The Record Keeps Spinning	Indeep
90	What Difference Does It Make?	The Smiths
91	Tragedy And Mystery	China Crisis
92	Theme From "Terms Of Endearment"	Michael Gore
93	The Ghost In You/ Heartbeat	Psychedelic Furs
94	Leave It	Yes

#	Song Title	Artist
95	Jump (For My Love) / Automatic / I Need You	Pointer Sisters
96	Borderline	Madonna
97	Reel Around The Fountain	The Smiths
98	Theme From "The Natural"	Randy Newman
99	What You Really Want	Melanie Rosales
100	Heaven	Psychedelic Furs
101	Island Heart	The Comsat Angels (The C.S. Angels)
1984 EXTRAS		
102	The Art Of Love	Peter Godwin
105	I Sweat (Going Through The Motions)	Nona Hendryx
113	What's Love Got To Do With It	Tina Turner
116	Show Me	The Pretenders
118	Dance Hall Days	Wang Chung
119	Revenge	Ministry
120	Somebody's Eyes	Karla Bonoff
121	The Blue Hour	Raise The Dragon
123	West End Girls	Pet Shop Boys
132	The Lucky One	Laura Branigan
141	I Would Die 4 U	Prince And The Revolution
142	White Horse	Laid Back
147	Stop Me If You Think You've Heard This One Before	The Smiths
148	Still Loving You	Scorpions
160	Wake Me Up Before You Go-Go	Wham!
163	Blue World	The Moody Blues
197	Heaven	Bryan Adams
207	Birds Fly (Whisper To A Scream)	Icicle Works
224	Ain't Nobody	Rufus f/ Chaka Khan
231	No Parking (On The Dance Floor) / Freak-A-Zoid	Midnight Star

1985

#	Song Title	Artist
1	Running Up That Hill (A Deal With God)	Kate Bush
2	How Soon Is Now?	The Smiths
3	Everybody Wants To Rule The World	Tears For Fears
4	Julia	Eurythmics
5	This Is Not America	David Bowie/Pat Metheny Group
6	Head Over Heels	Tears For Fears
7	Careless Whisper	Wham! f/ George Michael
8	This World Over	XTC
9	Hunting High And Low	a-ha
10	Bangkok/One Night In Bangkok	Murray Head
11	Say I'm Your No. 1	Princess
12	We Don't Need Another Hero (Thunderdome)	Tina Turner
13	Save A Prayer	Duran Duran
14	Pie Jesu	Sarah Brightman & Paul Miles-Kingston
15	Never Could Have Been Worse	Everything But The Girl
16	Into The Groove	Madonna
17	Healing Broken Hearts	Boys Voice
18	The Boys Of Summer	Don Henley
19	Do They Know It's Christmas?	Band Aid
20	Shout	Tears For Fears
21	History	Mai Tai
22	Rough Justice / The Wild Life	Bananarama
23	Cry	Godley & Creme
24	(I'll Never Be) Maria Magdalena	Sandra
25	Moments In Love	The Art Of Noise
26	Hang On To Your Love	Sade
27	All Summer Long	Chris Rea
28	Love Like Blood	Killing Joke
29	Change Your Mind	Sharpe + Numan (Bill Sharpe/Gary Numan)
30	Smooth Operator	Sade

#	Song Title	Artist
31	The Power Of Love/bang...	Frankie Goes To Hollywood
32	Days Are Numbers (The Traveller)	The Alan Parsons Project
33	Frost And Fire	Everything But The Girl
34	Everything She Wants	Wham!
35	Would I Lie To You?	Eurythmics
36	Ivo / Pandora (for Cindy)	Cocteau Twins
37	A View To Kill	Duran Duran
38	Duel	Propaganda
39	Ain't Necessarily So	Bronski Beat
40	I Know Him So Well	Elaine Page And Barbara Dickson
41	Secret	Orchestral Manoeuvres In The Dark
42	Don't Stop The Dance	Bryan Ferry
43	The Story Of A Young Heart	A Flock Of Seagulls
44	Kayleigh	Marillion
45	Life In A Northern Town	The Dream Academy
46	Quisquose	Cocteau Twins
47	Slave To Love	Bryan Ferry
48	Don't Believe Anymore	Icehouse
49	Private Dancer	Tina Turner
50	Desire	Yello
51	Why?	Bronski Beat
52	Take On Me	a-ha
53	So In Love	Orchestral Manoeuvres In The Dark
54	Shame	The Motels
55	Voices Carry	'Til Tuesday
56	Crazy For You	Madonna
57	There Must Be An Angel (Playing With My Heart)	Eurythmics
58	Don't You (Forget About Me)	Simple Minds
59	Our Day	Split Enz
60	Mistake No. 3	Culture Club
61	It Must Be Love	Rickie Lee Jones

1985

#	Song Title	Artist
62	Don't Come Around Here No More	Tom Petty And The Heartbreakers
63	Angel	Madonna
64	Broken Wings	Mr. Mister
65	Why Can't I Have You	The Cars
66	(Everyday Is) Halloween/ All Day	Ministry
67	What About Love	Heart
68	Lie To Me	Depeche Mode
69	Be Near Me	ABC
70	Vicious Games	Yello
71	Alive And Kicking	Simple Minds
72	In My House	Mary Jane Girls
73	Friends	Amii Stewart
74	Take Me With U	Prince (w/ Apollonia)
75	You Belong To The City	Glenn Frey
76	Kiss Me	Stephen 'Tin Tin' Duffy
77	Solid	Ashford & Simpson
78	I Want To Know What Love Is	Foreigner
79	Never Turn Away	Orchestral Manoeuvres In The Dark
80	Ave Maria (Om Ganesha)	West India Company
81	Foolish Heart	Steve Perry
82	Madam Butterfly (Un Bel di Vedremo)	Malcolm McLaren
83	Fortress Around Your Heart	Sting
84	Black Man Ray	China Crisis
85	Never Surrender	Corey Hart
86	I'm On Fire	Bruce Springsteen
87	And She Was	Talking Heads
88	Never Ending Story	Limahl
89	Pop Life	Prince And The Revolution

#	Song Title	Artist
90	I Will	The Fixx
91	Night Shift	Commodores
92	Painted Desert	Pat Benatar
93	Kindred Spirits	Shadowfax
94	Burning Flame	Vitamin Z
95	Too Late For Goodbyes	Julian Lennon
96	Party All The Time	Eddie Murphy
97	Missing You	Diana Ross
98	King In A Catholic Style	China Crisis
99	I'm Falling	The Comsat Angels (The C.S. Angels)
100	Lay Your Hands On Me	Thompson Twins
101	New Attitude / Axel F (two songs by respective artists)	Patti LaBelle / Harold Faltermeyer

	1985 EXTRAS	
102	Raspberry Beret/She's Always In My Hair	Prince And The Revolution
104	Everytime You Go Away	Paul Young
105	The Men All Pause	Klymaxx
106	Hurts To Be In Love	Gino Vannelli
107	People Are People	Depeche Mode
110	Cherish	Kool & The Gang
116	Sight And Touch	Chris DeBurgh
118	Things Can Only Get Better	Howard Jones
119	Who's Zoomin' Who	Aretha Franklin
121	Love & Pride	King
127	One Lonely Night	REO Speedwagon
150	Love Theme From St. Elmo's Fire	David Foster
169	The Only Flame In Town	Elvis Costello & The Attractions
176	19	Paul Hardcastle

#	Song Title	Artist
1	I Don't Believe In You	Talk Talk
2	Experiment IV	Kate Bush
3	Life's What You Make It	Talk Talk
4	No Promises	Icehouse
5	Cloudbusting	Kate Bush
6	Help Me	Bryan Ferry
7	Paradise	Icehouse
8	Love Comes Quickly	Pet Shop Boys
9	Magic Smile	Rosie Vela
10	Left Of Center	Suzanne Vega f/ Joe Jackson
11	Holding Back The Years	Simply Red
12	Mother Stands For Comfort / The Big Sky	Kate Bush
13	Live To Tell	Madonna
14	Give It Up	Talk Talk
15	The Sweetest Taboo	Sade
16	Is Your Love Strong Enough?/Windswept	Bryan Ferry
17	The Wild Cry	Clannad
18	Women III	Orchestral Manoeuvres In The Dark
19	(Forever) Live And Die	Orchestral Manoeuvres In The Dark
20	If I Was	Midge Ure
21	Watching You Without Me	Kate Bush
22	In The Middle Of The Night	Feelabeelia
23	Only A Visitor	Wax (Wax UK)
24	We Work The Black Seam	Sting
25	Adrian	Eurythmics w/ Elvis Costello
26	The Captain Of Her Heart	Double
27	I Believe	Tears For Fears
28	Don't Give Up	Peter Gabriel/Kate Bush
29	Don't Wanna Be Normal	Randy Crawford
30	Johnny Come Home	Fine Young Cannibals
31	Feel The Raindrops	The Adventures

#	Song Title	Artist
32	In A Lifetime	Clannad (w/ Bono)
33	I've Been Losing You	a-ha
34	Bonny / Goodbye Lucille #1	Prefab Sprout
35	The Love Parade	The Dream Academy
36	What About Love	'Til Tuesday
37	How To Bring A Blush To The Snow	Cocteau Twins
38	Sledgehammer	Peter Gabriel
39	Oxygen	Feelabeelia
40	Summer Of Love	The B-52's
41	The Sun Always Shines On T.V./Driftwood	a-ha
42	Human	The Human League
43	Eurasian Eyes	Corey Hart
44	Angela	Vitamin Z
45	Some Girls Are Bigger Than Others	The Smiths
46	I'm Not The One	The Cars
47	It's Alright (Baby's Coming Back)	Eurythmics
48	Opportunities (Let's Make Lots Of Money)	Pet Shop Boys
49	Something About You	Level 42
50	Closer To Your Heart	Clannad
51	Gift Of Freedom	China Crisis
52	Sweet Love	Anita Baker
53	Ain't Nothin' Goin' On But The Rent	Gwen Guthrie
54	In Your Eyes	Peter Gabriel
55	Russians / I Burn For You	Sting
56	Good Friends	Joni Mitchell (w/ Michael McDonald)
57	Saturday Love	Cherrelle w/ Alexander O'Neal
58	Walking On Ice	Keats
59	World Where You Live	Crowded House
60	These Dreams	Heart
61	Silhouette	Randy Goodrum
62	I Like You	Phyllis Nelson

#	Song Title	Artist
63	Oh, People	Patti LaBelle
64	Impossible Dreamer	Joni Mitchell
65	Let's Go All The Way	Sly Fox
66	Mask: Movement 2	Vangelis
67	Seven Steps To The Wall	Jane Siberry
68	Send My Heart	The Adventures
69	Word Up	Cameo
70	Blasphemous Rumours / It's Called A Heart	Depeche Mode
71	Your Fascination	Gary Numan
72	Light Of The World	The Alan Parsons Project
73	Slave To The Rhythm	Grace Jones
74	I Didn't Mean To Turn You On	Robert Palmer
75	Nothing In Common	Thompson Twins
76	Losing Yourself / Everybody's Young	Sandra Bernhard
77	Lives In The Balance	Jackson Browne
78	Nobody Home	Heart
79	Never As Good As The First Time	Sade
80	Papa Don't Preach	Madonna
81	Girl Can't Help It	Journey
82	Cities In Dust	Siouxsie And The Banshees
83	I Wanna Be A Cowboy	Boys Don't Cry
84	Take Me On The Subway	Linda Thompson
85	Pink Orange Red	Cocteau Twins
86	La Femme Accident	Orchestral Manoeuvres In The Dark
87	Letter To Brezhnev Theme	Alan Gill
88	Stick Around	Julian Lennon
89	All The Things She Said	Simple Minds

#	Song Title	Artist
90	Two Of Hearts	Stacey Q
91	Mountains	Prince And The Revolution
92	She Cried	Midge Ure
93	When Love Breaks Down	Prefab Sprout
94	ρ – Machinery (p:Machinery)	Propaganda
95	Artificial Heart	Cherrelle
96	I Can't Wait	Nu Shooz
97	One More Colour	Jane Siberry
98	A Question Of Time / A Question Of Lust	Depeche Mode
99	Mothers Talk/Sea Song	Tears For Fears
100	Addicted To Love	Robert Palmer
101	Physical Presence	Level 42
1986 EXTRAS		
105	Hé! Stranger	Anne Pigalle
106	Rumors	Timex Social Club
108	Tarzan Boy	Baltimora
109	Kyrie	Mr. Mister
111	Walk Like An Egyptian	Bangles
112	The Way It Is	Bruce Hornsby And The Range
116	Silent Running (On Dangerous Ground)	Mike + The Mechanics
117	Nasty	Janet Jackson
122	Here Comes A Regular	The Replacements
123	True Colors	Cyndi Lauper
128	The Rain	Oran "Juice" Jones
131	All Cried Out	Lisa Lisa And Cult Jam w/ Full Force
135	Easier Said Than Done	Jon Anderson
136	Rock Me Amadeus	Falco
163	100% Chance Of Rain	Gary Morris

1987

#	Song Title	Artist
1	The Kingdom	Icehouse
2	Oscillate Wildly	The Smiths
3	The Cutting Edge	The Comsat Angels (The C.S. Angels)
4	Angel Street	Icehouse
5	Strange Charm	Gary Numan
6	Waiting	The Style Council
7	Ain't It A Shame	The B-52's
8	Blow Wind Blow	Alison Moyet
9	Little Lies	Fleetwood Mac
10	What Have I Done To Deserve This?	Pet Shop Boys & Dusty Springfield
11	Disenchanted	The Communards
12	Dear God	XTC
13	Sign '☮' The Times	Prince
14	Another Satellite	XTC
15	Never Let Me Down Again/Pleasure, Little Treasure	Depeche Mode
16	Lie To Me	Chris Isaak
17	Hole In The River	Crowded House
18	Interlude	Rosie Vela
19	Leaving Me Now	Level 42
20	The Right Stuff	Bryan Ferry
21	Reach Out	Joan Armatrading
22	True Faith (The Morning Sun)	New Order
23	My Breathing	Gary Numan
24	The Living Daylights	a-ha
25	The Right Thing	Simply Red
26	Why You Treat Me So Bad	Club Nouveau
27	Love You Down	Ready For The World
28	Heroine (Theme From "Captive")	The Edge w/ Sinéad O'Connor
29	Ever Fallen In Love	Fine Young Cannibals
30	Sunday	Rosie Vela
31	Fool's Paradise	Rosie Vela
32	A Trick Of The Night	Bananarama
33	Solitude Standing	Suzanne Vega

#	Song Title	Artist
34	Happiness Is Easy	Talk Talk
35	She's Like The Wind	Patrick Swayze f/ Wendy Fraser
36	First We Take Manhattan	Jennifer Warnes
37	Fascinated	Company B
38	(I Know) I'm Losing You	Dave Stewart/ Barbara Gaskin
39	Living In Another World	Talk Talk
40	Stay The Night	Benjamin Orr
41	Love In Chains	The Adventures
42	I Still Haven't Found What I'm Looking For	U2
43	Land Of Confusion	Genesis
44	I Want To Make The World Turn Around	Steve Miller Band
45	Big Time	Peter Gabriel
46	Girl From Ipanema Goes To Greenland	The B-52's
47	Suffer	Simply Red
48	Hampton Beach	China Crisis
49	Stripped	Depeche Mode
50	With Or Without You	U2
51	It's Over	Level 42
52	The One I Love	R.E.M.
53	We'll Be Together	Sting
54	So Cold The Night	The Communards
55	It's A Sin	Pet Shop Boys
56	Citizen Jane	Bernie Taupin
57	Luka	Suzanne Vega
58	Plain Brown Wrapper	Gary Morris
59	Criticize	Alexander O'Neal
60	In Dreams	Pete Bardens
61	Pleasure And Pain	Steve Jones
62	Heart And Soul	T'Pau
63	Oh L'Amour	Erasure
64	Alone/Mama K(2)	This Mortal Coil
65	Lessons In Love	Level 42
66	Cross The Border	Icehouse
67	New Thing From London Town	Sharpe + Numan (Bill Sharpe/Gary Numan)

1987

#	Song Title	Artist
68	Arizona Sky	China Crisis
69	I'm Not Perfect (But I'm Perfect For You)	Grace Jones
70	Respectable	Mēl & Kim
71	Sometimes	Erasure
72	This Independence	Marc Jordan
73	Indian Summer	The Dream Academy
74	You'll Never Know	The Comsat Angels (The C.S. Angels)
75	Standing On Higher Ground / Inside Looking Out	The Alan Parsons Project
76	Cry Like This	Blue Room
77	Holiday	The Other Ones
78	Are You Ever Coming Back?	The Human League
79	Don't Dream It's Over	Crowded House
80	More Than Physical	Bananarama
81	Big Love	Fleetwood Mac
82	Cry Wolf	a-ha
83	Same Old Story	Ultravox
84	Silent Morning	Noel
85	U Got The Look	Prince & Sheena Easton
86	Maybe Someday...	Simply Red
87	Misfit	Curiosity Killed The Cat
88	Coming Up Close	'Til Tuesday
89	Don't Turn Away	Thomas Dolby f/ Cherry Bomb
90	Grass	XTC
91	One Chance	Stan Meissner
92	Bigmouth Strikes Again	The Smiths

#	Song Title	Artist
93	I'll Still Be Loving You	Restless Heart
94	House Of Love	Blue Yonder
95	Waterfall	Wendy And Lisa
96	Strangelove	Depeche Mode
97	Need A Minit	Pete Shelley
98	Skin Trade	Duran Duran
99	Seven Wonders	Fleetwood Mac
100	Jane's Getting Serious	Jon Astley
101	L Is For Lover	Al Jarreau
1987 EXTRAS		
103	Looking Glass	Yanni
104	Sweet Sixteen	Billy Idol
105	High Priority	Cherrelle
106	La Sagrada Familia	The Alan Parsons Project
108	Boom! There She Was	Scritti Politti w/ Roger
112	Islands	Mike Oldfield (w/ Bonnie Tyler)
113	Love Power	Dionne Warwick & Jeffrey Osborne
114	Wild Horses	Gino Vannelli
122	Hymn To Her	The Pretenders
124	Still A Thrill	Jody Watley
132	Need You Tonight	INXS
136	Sky Juice	Patrick O'Hearn
158	Mind Over Matter	E.G. Daily
164	Gettin' Away With Murder	Randy Crawford
165	Songbird	Kenny G
275	Is This Love	Whitesnake

1980s

#	Song Title	Artist		#	Song Title	Artist
1	North Point	Mike Oldfield		34	Nothing Can Come Between Us	Sade
2	Be Kind To My Mistakes	Kate Bush		35	Be Still My Beating Heart	Sting
3	King's Cross	Pet Shop Boys		36	Hand To Mouth / Monkey	George Michael
4	I'm Gonna Lose You	Simply Red		37	Broken Land	The Adventures
5	The Itchy Glowbo Blow	Cocteau Twins		38	Tubular Bells/Pretty Boys And Pretty Girls	Book Of Love
6	This Woman's Work	Kate Bush		39	The Longest Night	Bee Gees
7	Suedehead	Morrissey		40	The Look Of Love	Madonna
8	Rent	Pet Shop Boys		41	The Things You Said	Depeche Mode
9	Surrender	Swing Out Sister		42	Im Nin'Alu	Ofra Haza
10	Something To Believe In	Clannad (w/ Bruce Hornsby)		43	Carolyn's Fingers	Cocteau Twins
11	Without Someone	Electric Light Orchestra		44	My Brain Is Like A Sieve	Thomas Dolby
12	E·S·P/E·S·P (Vocal Reprise)	Bee Gees		45	Carve You In Marble	Tim Finn
13	Man Of Colours	Icehouse		46	Power To Believe	The Dream Academy
14	Beethoven (I Love To Listen To)	Eurythmics		47	Heart	Pet Shop Boys
15	Fast Car	Tracy Chapman		48	Time And Tide	Basia
16	Dreamer	Toni Childs		49	One Earth	The Art Of Noise
17	Did I Make You Up	Joan Armatrading		50	On Tuesday	Men Without Hats
18	For A Friend	The Communards		51	Circle In The Sand	Belinda Carlisle
19	No Thunder, No Fire, No Rain	Tim Finn		52	Talkin' Bout A Revolution	Tracy Chapman
20	Reunion	Patrick O'Hearn		53	Ship Of Fools	Erasure
21	Cry Freedom	George Fenton / Jonas Gwangwa		54	Under The Milky Way	The Church
22	Sirius	Clannad		55	The Time Has Come	Mike Oldfield
23	Father Figure	George Michael		56	Hold On Tight	The Communards
24	Chains Of Love	Erasure		57	Lover's Night	Jane Wiedlin
25	Tomorrow	The Communards		58	In The Hands Of Love	The Dream Academy
26	Inheritance	Talk Talk		59	Limbo	Bryan Ferry
27	Bad Reputation	Al Stewart		60	Nite And Day/Nuit Et Jour	Al B. Sure!
28	Rush Hour	Jane Wiedlin		61	Full Of Love (1986 version – "Perfume From Spain")	Dr. Calculus
29	Kiss And Tell	Bryan Ferry		62	In Love With Love	Debbie Harry
30	Desert Love	Roger Hodgson		63	What I Am	Edie Brickell & New Bohemians
31	Inside A Dream	Jane Wiedlin		64	Giving Up The Ghost	Bee Gees
32	Last Night I Dreamt That Somebody Loved Me	The Smiths		65	Mercedes Boy	Pebbles
33	Sorrow About To Fall	Electric Light Orchestra		66	Apron Strings	Everything But The Girl

#	Song Title	Artist
67	Suspicion Of Love	Chris Isaak
68	Soldier Of Fortune	Marc Jordan
69	Everyday Is Like Sunday	Morrissey
70	Liar, Liar	Debbie Harry
71	There's The Girl	Heart
72	Shattered Dreams	Johnny Hates Jazz
73	Turning Tide	Clannad
74	You Have Placed A Chill In My Heart	Eurythmics
75	A Word In Spanish	Elton John
76	Foolish Beat	Debbie Gibson
77	You Don't Have To Cry Anymore	The Adventures
78	Indigo Eyes	Peter Murphy
79	Orpheus	David Sylvian
80	You Came	Kim Wilde
81	Sleep Like Breathing	Alison Moyet
82	I Feel Possessed	Crowded House
83	Top Of The World (The Glass Bead Game)	Jon Anderson
84	Seasons Change	Exposé
85	Tango In The Night	Fleetwood Mac
86	Fragil / Fragile	Sting
87	Stay On These Roads	a-ha
88	(The World Don't Need) Another Lover	Giant Steps
89	Gypsy/Wooden Horse (Caspar Hauser's Song)	Suzanne Vega
90	Powaqqatsi	Philip Glass

#	Song Title	Artist
91	You Owe Me Some Kind Of Love	Chris Isaak
92	Many Roads	Clannad
93	Gold	Pete Bardens
94	If There Was A Man	The Pretenders
95	Cat Scan	Tangerine Dream
96	Everywhere	Fleetwood Mac
97	Victim Of Love	Erasure
98	The White Tent The Raft	Jane Siberry
99	Calling You	Jevetta Steele
100	I Ching	Marc Jordan
101	Paradise	Sade
1988 EXTRAS		
102	I Don't Want To Go On With You Like That	Elton John
104	Primitive Painters	Felt f/ Elizabeth Fraser
105	Soviet Snow	Shona Laing
107	Price Of The Fire	John Stewart (w/ Rosanne Cash)
112	Never Gonna Give You Up	Rick Astley
113	Sign Your Name	Terence Trent D'Arby
114	Girlfriend	Pebbles
123	Don't You Want Me	Jody Watley
125	Behind The Wheel/ Route 66	Depeche Mode
142	Dinner With Gershwin	Donna Summer
156	Piano In The Dark	Brenda Russell
224	Waiting For A Star To Fall	Boy Meets Girl

1980s

#	Song Title	Artist
1	Blue Bell Knoll	Cocteau Twins
2	Orinoco Flow (Sail Away)	Enya
3	The Sensual World	Kate Bush
4	Sowing The Seeds Of Love	Tears For Fears
5	Nothing Has Been Proved	Dusty Springfield
6	Wicked Game	Chris Isaak
7	Twist In My Sobriety	Tanita Tikaram
8	I'm Not Scared	Pet Shop Boys
9	Oh Father	Madonna
10	St. Saviour Square	China Crisis
11	Vox	Sarah McLachlan
12	Compulsion	Martin L. Gore
13	The Will Of The Wind	Vangelis
14	Hell To Heaven	Midge Ure
15	Cursum Perficio	Enya
16	กรุงเทพมหานคร (Bangkok/Krung Thep Mahanakhon)	อัสนี-วสันต์ โชติกุล (Asanee-Wasan)
17	Secret Land	Sandra
18	Channel Z	The B-52's
19	Another Day In Paradise	Phil Collins
20	Galbi	Ofra Haza
21	Diary Of A Hollow Horse	China Crisis
22	Voix	Gary Numan
23	Strange Kind Of Love	Love And Money
24	Out Of The Shadows	Sarah McLachlan
25	She Drives Me Crazy	Fine Young Cannibals
26	Chalkhills And Children	XTC
27	Into Temptation	Crowded House
28	Tell Me Why	Nick Heyward
29	Don't Drop Bombs	Liza Minnelli
30	Teardrops	Womack & Womack
31	Eden	Talk Talk
32	I'm Not Scared/ J'ai Pas Peur	Eighth Wonder
33	Orange Crush	R.E.M.
34	Do We See The Light Of Day	Dave Stewart/ Barbara Gaskin
35	Topaz / Follow Your Bliss	The B-52's
36	Respect	Gary Numan
37	Love Song	The Cure
38	Everything Is Coming Up Roses	Black
39	We'll Be Together	Sandra
40	I Believe In You	Talk Talk
41	On The Beach	Chris Rea
42	It's Only Love	Simply Red
43	Crossroads	Tracy Chapman
44	Personal Jesus	Depeche Mode
45	World Leader Pretend	R.E.M.
46	This Is Your Land	Simple Minds
47	Suboceana	Tom Tom Club
48	Air Of December	Edie Brickell & New Bohemians
49	A Little Respect	Erasure
50	Good Life	Inner City
51	No Condom, No Sex	Cruise Control
52	I'll Be There (Voodoo)	BoDeans
53	Good Thing	Fine Young Cannibals
54	For My Lover	Tracy Chapman
55	Mothers Of Rain	Tangerine Dream
56	Shaday	Ofra Haza
57	Wonderful Life	Black
58	She Took My Soul In Istanbul	Marc Almond
59	You Are My Heroin	Boy George
60	Where Do You Live?	The Big Dish
61	Rockland	The Lilac Time
62	Cold Hearted	Paula Abdul
63	Knock On Wood	Prefab Sprout
64	The Feeling Begins	Peter Gabriel
65	Walk The Last Mile	Love And Money
66	Mother Tongue	Dead Can Dance
67	Stop!	Sam Brown
68	All Night Long	Peter Murphy

#	Song Title	Artist
69	Don't Ask Me Why	Eurythmics
70	We Didn't Start The Fire	Billy Joel
71	ยินดีไม่มีปัญหา (Happy, No Problem)	อัสนี-วสันต์ โชติกุล (Asanee-Wasan)
72	Never Turn Your Back On Mother Earth	Martin L. Gore
73	Song Of The Factory	Jane Wiedlin
74	Toy Soldiers	Martika
75	The Stroll	Patrick O'Hearn
76	Something To Believe In	Bangles
77	Straight Up	Paula Abdul
78	Just For You	Midge Ure
79	Shaking The Tree	Youssou N'Dour w/ Peter Gabriel
80	Hey, I Was Right You Were Wrong!	Black
81	I Drove All Night	Cyndi Lauper
82	Sweetest Smile	Black
83	Voices Of Babylon	The Outfield
84	It's My Neighborhood	Bee Gees
85	Fascination Street	The Cure
86	Dear God	Midge Ure
87	For All These Years	Tanita Tikaram
88	Prayers For Rain	The Cure
89	Fuck You	Dean And The Weenies

#	Song Title	Artist
90	Anna Stesia	Prince
91	Early In The Morning	Robert Palmer
92	Don't Make Me Dream About You	Chris Isaak
93	Bound By The Beauty	Jane Siberry
94	Salaam Bombay!	L. Subramaniam
95	Back To Life	Soul II Soul f/ Caron Wheeler
96	Don't Let It End This Way	Johnny Hates Jazz
97	It's Alright	Pet Shop Boys
98	Discipline	Joe Jackson
99	Storms In Africa	Enya
100	Closer To Fine	Indigo Girls
101	Downtown	One 2 Many

1989 EXTRAS		
103	Sweet Jane	Cowboy Junkies
115	Happy Ever After	Julia Fordham
121	All She Wants Is	Duran Duran
125	My Prerogative	Bobby Brown
127	Like A Prayer	Madonna
128	She's A Mystery To Me	Roy Orbison
144	Friends	Jody Watley w/ Eric B. & Rakim
160	Love Shack	The B-52's
161	The Look	Roxette

1980s

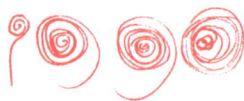

#	Song Title	Artist
1	Between A Man And A Woman	Kate Bush
2	Black Sheep Wall	The Innocence Mission
3	Never Be Mine	Kate Bush
4	Don't Know What To Do (Without You)	Jimmy Somerville
5	Machine Gun Ibiza	Prefab Sprout
6	Watchlar	Cocteau Twins
7	November Spawned A Monster	Morrissey
8	Intravenous	Bel Canto
9	Earth Moving	Mike Oldfield
10	Clear To You	The Innocence Mission
11	Your Wildlife	Propaganda
12	Chattahoochee Field Day	Patrick O'Hearn
13	Holding On To The Earth	Sam Phillips
14	Here's Where The Story Ends	The Sundays
15	Wonder Of Birds	The Innocence Mission
16	Rusted Pipe / Rusted Pipe (Tom's Mix) (two versions)	Suzanne Vega / DNA f/ Suzanne Vega
17	Heaven Here On Earth (With Your Love)	Jimmy Somerville
18	A Shoulder To The Wheel	Bel Canto
19	A Strange Kind Of Love	Peter Murphy
20	Feel So Different	Sinéad O'Connor
21	Cruising For Bruising	Basia
22	Rescue Mission	Luka Bloom
23	Imagining America	Everything But The Girl
24	Enjoy The Silence	Depeche Mode
25	Cut Flowers	The Smithereens
26	Behind The Mask	Fleetwood Mac
27	Woman In Chains	Tears For Fears (w/ Oleta Adams)
28	A Lover Spurned	Marc Almond
29	The Hunter	Clannad
30	This Time	Tracy Chapman
31	Steaming	Sarah McLachlan

#	Song Title	Artist
32	Up In Flames	Koko Taylor
33	In A Manner Of Speaking	Martin L. Gore
34	Levi Stubbs' Tears	Dave Stewart/ Barbara Gaskin
35	Cuts You Up	Peter Murphy
36	If There Was Love	Liza Minnelli
37	Justify My Love	Madonna
38	Heads We're Dancing	Kate Bush
39	Everybody Knows	Concrete Blonde
40	Scarlet	The Adventures
41	The Only One I Know	The Charlatans (UK)
42	You Surround Me	Erasure
43	Born To Fight	Tracy Chapman
44	In The Back Of My Mind	Fleetwood Mac
45	Close To You	Maxi Priest
46	Name	Peter Himmelman
47	Butterfly On A Wheel	The Mission (UK)
48	Hold On To Love	Lene Lovich
49	Nothing Compares 2 U	Sinéad O'Connor
50	Where Do We Go From Heaven	The Mighty Lemon Drops
51	The Lost Girl In The Midnight Sun	The Lilac Time
52	Dreaming Girl	Bel Canto
53	Shape Of Things To Come	Love And Money
54	Driving	Everything But The Girl
55	Dry County	The B-52's
56	Marilyn Monroe	Phoebe Legere
57	World Of Difference	Clannad
58	Waltz Darling	Malcolm McLaren And The Bootzilla Orchestra
59	Awara Hoon	3 Mustaphas 3
60	Don't Wait For Me	Vitamin Z
61	Vicious Circle	Propaganda
62	Steady On	Shawn Colvin
63	Machine Gun (Welcome, Machine Gun)	Hubert Kah
64	Innocent	Mike Oldfield

1990s

42

#	Song Title	Artist
65	Blue Spanish Sky	Chris Isaak
66	Rotation's Logic	Vangelis
67	Getting Away With It	Electronic (w/ Neil Tennant)
68	Dirty Cash (Money Talks)	The Adventures Of Stevie V
69	New York Minute	Don Henley
70	Rhythm Of Life	Oleta Adams
71	Pure	The Lightning Seeds
72	The Last Time	Agnetha Fältskog
73	You Hurt Me (And I Hate You)	Eurythmics
74	Empty Beach	Tricia Leigh Fisher
75	Hippychick	Soho
76	I Found Out	The Christians
77	It's Me, Cathy (Follow My Heart)	Hubert Kah
78	Sacrifice	Elton John
79	Washington Deceased	The Adventures
80	Sister And Brother	Midge Ure (w/ Kate Bush)
81	In My Heart	One 2 Many
82	Dreamtime	The Heart Throbs
83	Roam	The B-52's
84	Wish You Were Here	Bee Gees
85	Cairo By Night	Dissidenten
86	Policy Of Truth	Depeche Mode
87	Whisper	Schnell Fenster
88	Into The Night	Julee Cruise

#	Song Title	Artist
89	The Hurt Stays Home	H Factor
90	Hold On	En Vogue
91	I Want You Now	Liza Minnelli
92	Commercial Rain	Inspiral Carpets
93	He Is So	Deborah Harry
94	A Face In The Crowd	Tom Petty
95	Dear Jessie / Till Death Do Us Part	Madonna
96	Perfect Day	Jimmy Somerville
97	Ever On	Dan Fogelberg
98	I've Got U Under My Skin	Neneh Cherry
99	Just The Way It Is, Baby	The Rembrandts
100	Black Velvet	Alannah Myles
101	Vogue	Madonna
1990 EXTRAS		
106	Downtown	Lloyd Cole
112	A Girl Like You	The Smithereens
113	Love Is A Shield	Camouflage
114	You're The Voice	John Farnham
116	Prelude To The Garden/ The Secret Garden (Sweet Seduction Suite)	Quincy Jones f/ Al B Sure!, James Ingram, El DeBarge & Barry White
118	Thieves In The Temple	Prince
129	The Ways Of Love	Neil Young & Linda Ronstadt
131	I Still Believe	The Call
146	It Must Have Been Love	Roxette

1990s

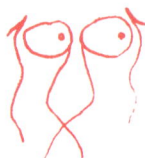

#	Song Title	Artist	#	Song Title	Artist
1	Born For A Purpose	The Pretenders	32	House Of Hope	Toni Childs
2	Road, River And Rail	Cocteau Twins	33	Frou-Frou Foxes In Midsummer Fires	Cocteau Twins
3	Safe From Harm	Massive Attack	34	The Sea Still Sings	Marc Almond
4	Then	The Charlatans (UK)	35	Subterranean Homesick Blues	Dave Stewart & Barbara Gaskin
5	Woman In The Garden	The Judybats	36	Mr Reed	Dave Stewart And The Spiritual Cowboys
6	The Windfall (Everything For Nothing)	Joni Mitchell	37	Tomorrow, Wendy	Concrete Blonde
7	Tripping Over Gravity	Sam Phillips	38	The Shadow	Mary Black
8	Columbus	Mary Black	39	Ascension Day	Talk Talk
9	Mea Culpa	Enigma	40	Rebound	The Human League
10	This Must Be The Place I Waited Years To Leave	Pet Shop Boys	41	Spirit	Dead Can Dance
11	Dead Of The Night	Shawn Colvin	42	Get The Message	Electronic
12	Intro/Banging On The Door	Simple Minds	43	Redhills Road	Candyflip
13	Apollo XI	Orchestral Manoeuvres In The Dark	44	The Boy Who's Never Found	Katydids
14	Sadeness Part I	Enigma	45	And Hiding Away	The Innocence Mission
15	The Stars Are Going Out	The Human League	46	Crazy	Seal
16	Texarkana	R.E.M.	47	Devils Lake	Patrick O'Hearn
17	The Shore Down Under	Xymox	48	See The Lights	Simple Minds
18	The Means Becomes The End	9 Ways To Sunday	49	I'll Give You My Skin	Indigo Girls & Michael Stipe
19	Good To See You	Vangelis	50	Across The Way	Aleka's Attic
20	Heaven On Earth	Laurie Freelove	51	Within The Lost World	Jonathan Elias f/ Jon Anderson
21	A Dream In The Night	Clannad	52	Losing My Religion	R.E.M.
22	Doo-Wop In Harlem	Prefab Sprout	53	Bedspring Kiss	Jellyfish
23	Antelope	Hex	54	Birds Of Passage	Bel Canto
24	Pitch The Baby	Cocteau Twins	55	Scarlet Nights	Prefab Sprout
25	Being Boring	Pet Shop Boys	56	The Fog	Kate Bush
26	Shotgun Down The Avalanche	Shawn Colvin	57	Real Life	Simple Minds
27	May This Be Your Last Sorrow	Banderas	58	It Won't Be Long	Alison Moyet
28	The Living And Their Stillborn	Danielle Dax	59	Side Streets	Vangelis
29	Follow In My Footsteps	Jonathan Elias f/ Simon Le Bon w/ Susanna Hoffs	60	Idiot Country	Electronic
30	The Sheffield Song	Soul Family Sensation	61	My Book	The Beautiful South
31	There's A World	Psychedelic Furs	62	It's Lonely Out Here	Susanna Hoffs
			63	Smells Like Truth	Laurie Freelove
			64	Don't Be A Girl	Psychedelic Furs

#	Song Title	Artist
65	So Like Candy	Elvis Costello
66	Pilgrimage	Suzanne Vega
67	Love	The Dream Academy
68	Hollywood In Winter	Hex
69	The Chant Movement	Jonathan Elias f/ Grace Jones & Jim Morrison
70	I Want A Cure	Rosanne Cash
71	Gypsy Woman (She's Homeless) (La Da Dee La Da Da)	Crystal Waters
72	Too Darn Hot	Erasure
73	You're Not Very Well	The Charlatans (UK)
74	There She Goes	The La's
75	Sweetness And Light	Lush
76	Love To Hate You	Erasure
77	Lily Was Here	David A. Stewart introducing Candy Dulfer
78	Satisfied	Squeeze
79	Paint The Ending	Grace Pool
80	The King Is Half-Undressed	Jellyfish
81	Every Beat Of The Heart	The Railway Children
82	More	The Sisters Of Mercy
83	It'll Never Happen Again	The Dream Academy
84	Love... Thy Will Be Done	Martika
85	Smells Like Teen Spirit	Nirvana
86	How Can You Expect To Be Taken Seriously?	Pet Shop Boys
87	Big Space/Predictions	Suzanne Vega
88	Deaths Diary	Marc Almond
89	You Can't Fool That Girl	Merchants Of Venus
90	Now I Can't Find The Door	Sam Phillips

#	Song Title	Artist
91	Drive That Fast	Kitchens Of Distinction
92	Obscurity Knocks	The Trash Can Sinatras
93	Crush Story	Too Much Joy
94	I Get A Kick	The Jungle Brothers
95	She Lives (In A Time Of Her Own)	The Judybats
96	The Comfort Of Faith	Banderas
97	She's In A Trance	The Heart Throbs
98	Monsters And Angels	Voice Of The Beehive
99	Early Morning	a-ha
100	Why Should I Cry For You?	Sting
101	Chocolate Cake	Crowded House
1991 EXTRAS		
102	Diabaram	Ryuichi Sakamoto (w/ Youssou N'Dour)
107	Miss America	The Big Dish
109	Ooops	808 State f/ Björk
111	Unbelievable	EMF
112	Feeding Off The Love Of The Land	Stevie Wonder
121	Radio Song	R.E.M.
124	3 A.M. Eternal	The KLF
125	Strange Minaret	Sheila Chandra
131	Right Here Right Now	Jesus Jones
132	Luck Of The Draw	Bonnie Raitt
140	X Y & Zee	Pop Will Eat Itself
164	Change Myself	Todd Rundgren
173	I've Been Thinking About You	Londonbeat
171	Looking For The Summer	Chris Rea
210	Addams Groove	MC Hammer

#	Song Title	Artist
1	Summer	Bel Canto
2	War Dance	XTC
3	If This Is Love	Pamela Golden
4	Shimmering, Warm And Bright	Bel Canto
5	Caribbean Blue	Enya
6	Step Up	This Picture
7	Words Weren't Made For Cowards	Happy Rhodes
8	Untogether	Lush
9	Keep Me From Harm	Peter Murphy
10	The Old Ways	Loreena McKennitt
11	Ignoreland	R.E.M.
12	The Days Of Pearly Spencer	Marc Almond
13	Feed The Fire	Happy Rhodes
14	Spiderdust	Bel Canto
15	All Souls Night	Loreena McKennitt
16	Into The Fire	Sarah McLachlan
17	Lisa Of The Wind	Pamela Golden
18	Raised On Promises	Sam Phillips
19	Cé Leis	Maíre Brennan
20	瀟洒走一回 (Walk Gracefully/Cool Walk)	葉蒨文 (Sally Yeh/Sally Yip/Yip-Sin-Man)
21	This Used To Be My Playground	Madonna
22	Tomorrow	Morrissey
23	Only Today	Two Nice Girls
24	Visions Of You	Jah Wobble's Invaders Of The Heart f/ Sinéad O'Connor
25	Constant Craving	k.d. lang
26	Precious Things	Tori Amos
27	Sweetness Follows	R.E.M.
28	99.9F°	Suzanne Vega
29	The Poison Glen	Clannad
30	For Love	Lush
31	Laid So Low (Tears Roll Down) / Tears Roll Down	Tears For Fears
32	Why Worry?	Clannad

#	Song Title	Artist
33	Phobos	Happy Rhodes
34	So Sad	Grashüpfer (Grasshopper / 草蜢) & Shirley Kwan
35	Crucify	Tori Amos
36	Wisdom Chain	Jon & Vangelis
37	Beginning The World	The Innocence Mission
38	Ripple	The Church
39	Cradle	Heidi Berry
40	Never Too Late	Alison Moyet
41	Fifty-Fifty Clown	Cocteau Twins
42	Soledad	Jah Wobble's Invaders Of The Heart
43	Common Threads / Sweet In The Mornin'	Bobby McFerrin / f/ Voicestra
44	Blood Makes Noise	Suzanne Vega
45	Coast Is Clear	Curve
46	It Takes Time	Patti Smith & Fred Smith
47	In Liverpool	Suzanne Vega
48	Money	Jon & Vangelis
49	Afer Ventus	Enya
50	Ladykiller	Nicky Holland
51	Revolution Earth	The B-52's
52	Winter Came Too Soon	The Heart Throbs
53	Steam	Peter Gabriel
54	No Easy Way	Maíre Brennan
55	Hooligan	The Heart Throbs
56	No More	Youssou N'Dour
57	Four Seasons In One Day	Crowded House
58	Stay By Me	Annie Lennox
59	Be A Good Friend Of Mine	Jon & Vangelis
60	Zoo Station	U2
61	O My Heart	Laurie Freelove
62	War Of Man	Neil Young (w/ Linda Ronstadt)
63	Standing Still	Sam Phillips
64	I Want To Touch You	Catherine Wheel
65	焚心以火 (Throw Heart To Fire)	葉蒨文 (Sally Yeh/Sally Yip/Yip-Sin-Man)

#	Song Title	Artist
66	Money Can't Buy It	Annie Lennox
67	Heartbeat (Tainai Kaiki II) - returning to the womb	Ryuichi Sakamoto w/ David Sylvian/Ingrid Chavez
68	When The Rain Doesn't Come	Sandra
69	Strange Jane	Thompson Twins
70	Street Of Dreams	Lindsey Buckingham
71	Whispers And Moans / Fall At Your Feet	Crowded House
72	You're So Close	Peter Murphy
73	Bird	Dead Can Dance
74	Digging In The Dirt	Peter Gabriel
75	The Invisible Man/ The Saint	Thompson Twins
76	Crashing Back To You	Wire Train
77	The Sweetest Drop	Peter Murphy
78	Book Of Days	Enya
79	Book Of Roses	Andreas Vollenweider
80	Black Metallic	Catherine Wheel
81	Faît Accompli	Curve
82	Anywhere You Are	The Smithereens
83	Until The End Of The World	U2
84	I Need Love	Luka Bloom
85	Breaking The Girl	Red Hot Chili Peppers
86	Daw Da Hiya	Ofra Haza (w/ Iggy Pop)
87	It's A Fine Day	Opus III
88	Success Has Made A Failure Of Our Home	Sinéad O'Connor
89	Princess Of Power	Two Nice Girls

#	Song Title	Artist
90	Black	Sarah McLachlan
91	Something Good	Utah Saints (w/ Kate Bush)
92	Hero In Me	Jeffrey Gaines
93	Dealing With The Night	John Stewart
94	Why	Annie Lennox
95	Silent All These Years	Tori Amos
96	Rí Na Cruinne	Clannad
97	(No One) Not Even The Rain	The Charlatans (UK)
98	Tiny Feet	The Heart Throbs
99	Believe Me Sometimes	Xymox
100	Pain Lies On The Riverside	Līve
101	Against The Wind	Maíre Brennan
1992 EXTRAS		
106	Calling All Angels	Jane Siberry & k.d. lang
111	Hazard	Richard Marx
112	Born Of Frustration	James
121	The Trouble With Andre	Shakespears Sister
130	太胡鬧 (Too Mischievous)	Dominic Chow 周啓生
134	Come As You Are	Nirvana
141	Everybody's Free (To Feel Good)	Rozalla
147	Just Another Day	Jon Secada
179	Finally	CeCe Peniston
181	Lithium	Nirvana
242	Disappointed	Electronic
243	Killer	Seal / Adamski (two versions)

1993

#	Song Title	Artist
1	Easy Way Out	Praise
2	Illusory Me	Love Spirals Downwards
3	Big Stripey Lie	Kate Bush
4	Jacksie	Over The Rhine
5	Know Who You Are At Every Age	Cocteau Twins
6	Sleeping Satellite	Tasmin Archer
7	My Dead Friend	The Judybats
8	Bad Girl	Madonna
9	Dance Without Sleeping	Melissa Etheridge
10	Chinatown	Praise
11	Come Undone	Duran Duran
12	Somebody's Daughter	Tasmin Archer
13	Pretty	The Cranberries
14	Theft, And Wandering Around Lost	Cocteau Twins
15	Pearls	Sade
16	Elemental	Tears For Fears
17	Constellation Of The Heart	Kate Bush
18	I Still Do	The Cranberries
19	Coming	Jimmy Somerville
20	And So Is Love	Kate Bush
21	Age Of Loneliness (Carly's Song)	Enigma
22	Make Me A Mask	Fleetwood Mac
23	Waltzing Back	The Cranberries
24	Waking Will	Bel Canto
25	Out Like A Lamb	Happy Rhodes
26	World On A Wing	The Telling
27	Can You Forgive Her?	Pet Shop Boys
28	I've Been Slipping	Over The Rhine
29	I Cannot Go On	Happy Rhodes
30	Ground Level	Stereo MC's
31	Not Sorry	The Cranberries
32	Fish Out Of Water	Tears For Fears
33	By Now	Sarah Brightman
34	Lily	Kate Bush
35	Closer	Happy Rhodes

#	Song Title	Artist
36	Guardian Angel	The Telling
37	Ordinary World	Duran Duran
38	And The Wood Comes Into Leaf	Love Spirals Downwards
39	In Your Care	Tasmin Archer
40	Locust	a-ha
41	Further Than We Know	Pete Bardens
42	Shiva Descending	The Comsat Angels (The C.S. Angels)
43	Rubberband Girl	Kate Bush
44	In This Life / Why's It So Hard	Madonna
45	Walking In My Shoes	Depeche Mode
46	Follow	Heidi Berry
47	Always Near	The Comsat Angels (The C.S. Angels)
48	Neon Sisters	Thomas Dolby
49	Deep Forest	Deep Forest
50	Goodnight Song	Tears For Fears
51	I Will Find You (Theme From 'The Last Of The Mohicans')	Clannad
52	Dreaming Of The Queen	Pet Shop Boys
53	If You Could See Me Now	Devonsquare
54	Shape Of My Heart	Sting
55	Venus As A Boy	Björk
56	Numb	U2
57	The Happy Worker / Workers	Tori Amos / The Cast Of Toys
58	What Can You Do For Me	Utah Saints (w/ Gwen Guthrie, Annie Lennox)
59	Can't Do A Thing (To Stop Me)	Chris Isaak
60	Banba Óir	Clannad
61	Incredible Bittersweet	The Judybats
62	Rhapsodie	Over The Rhine
63	Avenue	Saint Etienne
64	Runners	Happy Rhodes
65	I Should've Known	Aimee Mann
66	The Second Element/The Second Element II	Sarah Brightman

1990s

1993

#	Song Title	Artist
67	World Keeps Turning	Starclub
68	I Put A Spell On You	Bryan Ferry
69	Brand New Day	Praise
70	Temple	Jane Siberry
71	Feel No Pain	Sade
72	Linger	The Cranberries
73	89 Lines	Terri Nunn
74	I Want To Live	Gavin Friday
75	Jacob Marley's Chain	Aimee Mann
76	What About Your Friends	TLC
77	What's Up	4 Non Blondes
78	Love Song For A Vampire / Little Bird	Annie Lennox
79	Cold As Stone	a-ha
80	Altered State/Maya Gold	Mike Oldfield
81	So Cold	Praise
82	Bohemia	Mae Moore
83	Where In The World?	Gavin Friday
84	Sail Across The Water	Jane Siberry
85	Last Chance	John Mellencamp
86	Miranda	The Moon Seven Times
87	Property	TR-i (Todd Rundgren)
88	I Feel You	Depeche Mode

#	Song Title	Artist
89	Being Simple	The Judybats
90	Put Me Down	The Cranberries
91	Mr Time	Alan Parsons
92	Halfway To Heaven	Tasmin Archer
93	There For You	Clannad
94	Take To The Sky	Tori Amos
95	Soul To Squeeze	Red Hot Chili Peppers
96	The Answer	Starclub
97	Two Worlds Collide	Inspiral Carpets
98	Say Anything	Aimee Mann
99	Playing With Fire	Stereo MC's
100	Solution	Utah Saints
101	Conehead Love	Beldar & Prymaat w/ Nan Shaefer

1993 EXTRAS		
107	Creep	Stone Temple Pilots
114	Read My Lips	A Thousand Points Of Night (Don Was)
115	All That She Wants	Ace Of Base
118	I'd Die Without You	P.M. Dawn
130	Rhythm Is A Dancer	Snap!
135	I See Your Smile	Gloria Estefan
160	The Crying Game	Boy George

1994

#	Song Title	Artist
1	Kiss From A Rose	Seal
2	Plenty	Sarah McLachlan
3	Possession	Sarah McLachlan
4	Saturn Girl	Paula Cole
5	Sour Times (Nobody Loves Me)	Portishead
6	Living In Danger	Ace Of Base
7	Collective Heart	Happy Rhodes
8	Zombie	The Cranberries
9	Bang And Blame	R.E.M.
10	Chiaroscuro	Paula Cole
11	Germaine/Fire On Babylon	Sinéad O'Connor
12	Something's Always Wrong	Toad The Wet Sprocket
13	Take Me As I Am	October Project
14	Same Changes	Sam Phillips
15	God	Tori Amos
16	Ragga Steady	Midi Maxi & Efti
17	Fear	Sarah McLachlan
18	She Said	Cause & Effect
19	Hold Me	Happy Rhodes
20	You Made Me The Thief Of Your Heart	Sinéad O'Connor
21	Newborn Friend	Seal
22	Selling The Drama	Līve
23	Hold On	Sarah McLachlan
24	Delicate	Terence Trent D'Arby (w/ Des'ree)
25	Within Without	Over The Rhine
26	Urban Clearway	Saint Etienne
27	Superstar	Sonic Youth
28	Cornflake Girl	Tori Amos
29	Girls & Boys / (Pet Shop Boys Remix)	Blur
30	Lay Down Your Pain	Toni Childs
31	Secret	Madonna
32	Same Rain	Sam Phillips
33	Refuse To Dance	Céline Dion

#	Song Title	Artist
34	Private Universe	Crowded House
35	Stay (I Missed You)	Lisa Loeb & Nine Stories
36	Bury My Lovely	October Project
37	Light From A Dead Star	Lush
38	Every Generation Got Its Own Disease	Fury In The Slaughterhouse
39	Never-Never	Lush
40	Prayer For The Dying	Seal
41	Look Up To The Sky	The Indians
42	You Gotta Be	Des'ree
43	I Don't Sleep, I Dream	R.E.M.
44	Wait	Sarah McLachlan
45	Am I Wrong	Love Spit Love
46	Sex Kills	Joni Mitchell
47	Return To Innocence	Enigma
48	Fall Down	Toad The Wet Sprocket
49	No Excuses	Alice In Chains
50	You Won't See Me Cry	B-Tribe
51	Take A Walk	Urge Overkill
52	The Bonny Swans	Loreena McKennitt
53	Getting Into Something	Alison Moyet
54	Be My Hero	October Project
55	Mmm Mmm Mmm Mmm	Crash Test Dummies
56	Elsewhere	Sarah McLachlan
57	Same Dream, Same Destination	Ryuichi Sakamoto
58	Inside Out	Cause & Effect
59	Happy Home	Paula Cole
60	It's Over Now	Cause & Effect
61	Space Dog	Tori Amos
62	Becoming More Like God	Jah Wobble's Invaders Of The Heart (w/ Anneli Drecker)
63	Purple Haze	The Cure
64	Lovetown	Peter Gabriel
65	Take You There	The Glee Club
66	Absolutely Fabulous	Pet Shop Boys
67	Here Comes The Hotstepper	Ini Kamoze

1990s

#	Song Title	Artist
68	Come In Number 21	The Charlatans (UK)
69	I Am So Ordinary	Paula Cole
70	Predator	Toni Childs
71	Amor Real	Jon Anderson
72	What I Can Do For You	Sheryl Crow
73	In The Name Of The Father	Bono & Gavin Friday
74	Wall Of Silence	October Project
75	Ode To My Family	The Cranberries
76	I Wouldn't Wanna Be You	Reba McEntire
77	New Star	Tears For Fears
78	Pieces Of Clay	Mae Moore
79	Doll Parts	Hole
80	Touched By The Sun	Carly Simon
81	Clock	Milla (Jovovich)
82	Lifted By Love	k.d. lang
83	You Kill Me	Babble
84	The More You Ignore Me, The Closer I Get	Morrissey
85	Gemini Moon	Bryan Ferry
86	On The Shore	Saint Etienne
87	Crystal	Curve
88	I Never Want An Easy Life If Me And He Were Ever To Get There	The Charlatans (UK)

#	Song Title	Artist
89	Closer	Nine Inch Nails
90	Following You	LaTour
91	Never Said	Liz Phair
92	Black Hole Sun	Soundgarden
93	When You Made The Mountain	Opus III
94	Philadelphia	Neil Young
95	Don't Want To Know	Bryan Ferry
96	American Dreaming	Dead Can Dance
97	Nadie Entiende	B-Tribe
98	Stone Girl	Cause & Effect
99	Big Empty	Stone Temple Pilots
100	Summerhead	Cocteau Twins
101	Charmed	Fem2Fem

1994 EXTRAS		
104	Cantaloop (Flip Fantasia)	Us3
105	About A Girl	Nirvana
109	I'll Remember (Theme From "With Honors")	Madonna
110	Landslide	Smashing Pumpkins
113	Heartbeats Accelerating	Linda Ronstadt
119	Found Out About You	Gin Blossoms

#	Song Title	Artist
1	Roads	Portishead
2	A Girl Like You	Edwyn Collins
3	Missing / (Todd Terry Mix)	Everything But The Girl
4	Sellet	Stone Age (Stone Edge)
5	Vision (O Euchari In Leta Via)	Vision
6	Kokerikero	Dao Dezi
7	Dawa (the cradlesong)	Sacred Spirits
8	Crazy Baby	Joan Osborne
9	God's Child (Baila Conmigo)	Selena f/ David Byrne
10	Three	Massive Attack
11	Kalon Mari (Marie's Heart)	Stone Age (Stone Edge)
12	St. Teresa	Joan Osborne
13	Sunday Morning Yellow Sky	October Project
14	Raoul And The Kings Of Spain	Tears For Fears
15	Supermodel Sandwich	Terence Trent D'Arby
16	You Learn	Alanis Morissette
17	Always With Me	The Colour Of Memory
18	Human Nature	Madonna
19	Natural One	Folk Implosion
20	You Oughta Know	Alanis Morissette
21	No More "I Love You's"	Annie Lennox
22	Misty Eyed Adventures	Maíre Brennan
23	Praise For The Mother (O Virga Ac Diadema)	Vision
24	Rigmarole	The Colour Of Memory
25	Carnival	Natalie Merchant
26	Here And Now	Letters To Cleo
27	Pure	The Golden Palominos (w/ Lori Carson)
28	Que Mala Vida	B-Tribe
29	Hypnotised	Simple Minds
30	Filling Up With Heaven	The Human League
31	Hand In My Pocket	Alanis Morissette
32	Ti Eliz Iza	Dao Dezi

#	Song Title	Artist
33	Heartbeat	Jimmy Somerville
34	Ridiculous Thoughts	The Cranberries
35	Going South	The Wolfgang Press
36	I Walked	Wanderlust
37	Wonderwall (two versions)	Oasis / The Mike Flowers Pops
38	By Your Side	Jimmy Somerville
39	The World I Know	Collective Soul
40	Ladder	Joan Osborne
41	Quantum Mechanic	Thomas Dolby
42	Dreaming Of Now	Opus III
43	Bouncing Around The Room	Phish
44	A Dream Gone Wrong	Jimmy Somerville
45	Write In Water	Love Spirals Downwards
46	Something More Than This	October Project
47	Down By The Water	PJ Harvey
48	Boheme	Deep Forest (w/ Márta Sebestyén)
49	The Icicle Melts	The Cranberries
50	That Was Another Country	The Innocence Mission
51	Protection	Massive Attack (f/ Tracey Thorn)
52	Crush With Eyeliner	R.E.M.
53	Nanita	B-Tribe f/ Deborah Blando
54	You'll See	Madonna
55	Shadows In A Mirror	Chris Isaak
56	That's Just What You Are	Aimee Mann
57	Don't Let It Bring You Down	Annie Lennox
58	Who The Hell Is Sonia Rykiel?	Malcolm McLaren
59	Do You Sleep?	Lisa Loeb & Nine Stories
60	Ghost Dance	Robbie Robertson & The Red Road Ensemble
61	December	Collective Soul
62	Marta's Song	Deep Forest (w/ Márta Sebestyén)

#	Song Title	Artist
63	Haunted House	Bee Gees
64	One Of Us	Joan Osborne
65	What Would You Say	Dave Matthews Band
66	Decadence	Pet Shop Boys
67	Cotton Eye Joe	Rednex
68	Too Much Of A Good Thing	Jimmy Somerville
69	Disappointment	The Cranberries
70	Back For Good	Take That
71	Perfecting The Art Of Common Ground	Ultravox
72	My Friends	Red Hot Chili Peppers
73	Interlude Dirigible/Valley Of The Morning Sun	Kendra Smith
74	Sanctuary	Madonna
75	Love Tried To Welcome Me	Madonna
76	Look No Further	Rozalla
77	Queer	Garbage
78	Animus	Fem2Fem
79	Graduation Day	Chris Isaak
80	Machine Punch Through	Moist
81	Here	Mae Moore
82	One Man In My Heart	The Human League
83	Gangsta's Paradise	Coolio f/ L.V.
84	Where Did Love Go	Fem2Fem
85	Sails Wave Goodbye	Peter Murphy
86	Macarena/ (Bayside Boys Mix)	Los Del Rio

#	Song Title	Artist
87	In The Name Of The Father	Black Grape
88	I Believe	Blessid Union Of Souls
89	Another Night	Real McCoy
90	Tsche Mischod	Yulduz Usmanova
91	Stinging Rain	Capercaillie
92	Whip-Smart	Liz Phair
93	Let's Go (Nothing For Me)	New Order
94	Hold Me, Thrill Me, Kiss Me, Kill Me	U2
95	The Grace	The Colour Of Memory
96	Gun	The Golden Palominos (w/ Lori Carson)
97	The Best Of What's Around	Dave Matthews Band
98	Yeha-Noha (wishes of happiness & prosperity)	Sacred Spirits
99	I Know	Dionne Farris
100	The Labyrinth	Kate Price
101	Genuine	Mae Moore
	1995 EXTRAS	
103	Waterfalls	TLC
107	(When I Kiss You) I Hear Charlie Parker Playing	Sparks
111	Runaway	Janet Jackson
113	The Strangest Party (These Are The Times)	INXS
114	Believe	Elton John
115	Connection	Elastica
117	Take A Bow	Madonna

#	Song Title	Artist
1	Didn't You Know It?	Bel Canto
2	Slapstick Heart	Sam Phillips
3	Where Have All The Cowboys Gone?	Paula Cole
4	Wrong	Everything But The Girl
5	From Your Heart	Clannad
6	Black Fields	Capercaillie
7	Me And My Big Ideas/ Los Reyes Católicos (Reprise)	Tears For Fears (w/ Oleta Adams)
8	Captive Heart	Selena
9	Place With No Name	Yosefa
10	To Step Aside	Pet Shop Boys
11	In The Absence Of Sun	Duncan Sheik
12	Casual Match	Suzanne Vega
13	Live Forever	Midge Ure
14	Rumour	Bel Canto
15	Farewell Love	Clannad
16	Winter, Fire & Snow	ANÚNA
17	Coast Line	Yosefa
18	Help Yourself	Sam Phillips
19	Only Talking Sense	Finn Brothers
20	While The Earth Sleeps	Peter Gabriel & Deep Forest
21	Don't Let Go (Love)	En Vogue
22	Nocturne	Secret Garden
23	Edge Of Heaven	Ace Of Base
24	Liquid	Jars Of Clay
25	Don't Speak	No Doubt
26	Road To Dead	Paula Cole
27	Caught A Lite Sneeze	Tori Amos
28	Single	Everything But The Girl
29	Suffer Never	Finn Brothers
30	Entertainmen	Sam Phillips
31	Ready To Go	Republica
32	Heaven Beside You	Alice In Chains
33	Set It Off	Organized Noize f/ Queen Latifah & Andrea Martin

#	Song Title	Artist
34	Flood	Jars Of Clay
35	Too Close To The Sun	Alan Parsons
36	Before	Pet Shop Boys
37	Moog Island/The Music That We Hear (1998) (two versions)	Morcheeba
38	Zo Laret (It Is Said)	Stone Age (Stone Edge)
39	Children	Robert Miles
40	Angry Johnny	Poe
41	Discoteca/Single	Pet Shop Boys
42	Hi Rim Bo	Capercaillie
43	Seanchas	Clannad
44	Freelunch In The Jungle	Bel Canto
45	Adiemus	Adiemus (w/ Miriam Stockley)
46	As The End Draws Near	Manufacture w/ Sarah McLachlan
47	Let Me Be Around	Chimera
48	You're Makin' Me High/ Let It Flow	Toni Braxton
49	Nobody Lives Without Love	Eddi Reader
50	She Runs Away	Duncan Sheik
51	Humdrum And Humble	Tears For Fears
52	La Jument De Mishao	Dao Dezi
53	Everything Changes	Iona
54	Birth-Day (Love Made Real)	Suzanne Vega
55	Breathe	Midge Ure
56	Athair Ar Neamh	Enya
57	Wisdom	Iona
58	Leviticus: Faggot	Me'Shell NdegéOcello
59	No Talking Just Head	The Heads w/ Debbie Harry
60	Seekers Who Are Lovers	Cocteau Twins
61	Losing Sleep (Still, My Heart)	Vangelis w/ Paul Young
62	Before Today	Everything But The Girl
63	Fable	Robert Miles
64	Trail Of Tears	Midge Ure

#	Song Title	Artist		#	Song Title	Artist
65	Keep On, Keepin' On	MC Lyte f/ Xscape		89	Counting Blue Cars	Dishwalla
66	Inside	Patti Rothberg		90	Falling Down	Tears For Fears
67	Refazenda	Gilberto Gil		91	Nierika	Dead Can Dance
68	Love Has No Name	Babble		92	Barely Breathing	Duncan Sheik
69	Who Will Save Your Soul	Jewel		93	Catch Me	Chimera
70	Erin Shore (Traditional Intro)/Forgiven Not Forgotten	The Corrs		94	I'll Be True	First Kiss
				95	Stranger In A Strange Land	Paul Mounsey
71	Oceania/Only Time Will Tell	Mike Oldfield		96	Without Love	Donna Lewis
72	Sleepwalker	Bel Canto		97	Batucada	Towa Tei w/ Bebel Gilberto
73	Tiago	Chimera		98	In Zenith	Bel Canto
74	I Would Die For You	Jann Arden		99	In The Beginning/Let There Be Light	Mike Oldfield
75	Un-Break My Heart	Toni Braxton				
76	Leave	R.E.M.		100	Fanfare	Eric Matthews
77	Stupid Girl	Garbage		101	A Common Disaster	Cowboy Junkies
78	Bone Of Contention	Spirit Of The West		**1996 EXTRAS**		
79	All Over Now	Aimee Mann		102	Trippin' On A Hole In A Paper Heart	Stone Temple Pilots
80	Secrets	Tears For Fears				
81	The Box	Orbital		104	Trigger Happy Jack (Drive By A Go-Go)	Poe
82	Beyond The Invisible	Enigma				
83	Crystal Clear	Mike Oldfield		106	California Love	2Pac f/ Dr. Dre & Roger Troutman
84	Photograph	The Verve Pipe				
85	Jesus To A Child	George Michael		121	One By One	Cher
86	It's Alright, It's OK	Leah Andreone		128	I Love You Always Forever	Donna Lewis
87	Hollywood	The Cranberries				
88	Cavan Potholes	Sharon Shannon		146	Doin It	LL Cool J

1997

#	Song Title	Artist
1	Nuestra Única Ilusíon	Cielo y Tierra
2	To The Moon And Back	Savage Garden
3	I Loved You	Sarah Brightman
4	Irresistible Force	Bee Gees
5	Sweet Surrender	Sarah McLachlan
6	Child On A Cloud	Brigid Boden
7	6 Underground	Sneaker Pimps
8	Claire In Heaven	Capercaillie
9	Feelin' Love	Paula Cole
10	It's No Good	Depeche Mode
11	In The Heat Of The Night/Elena	Maggie Reilly
12	Havana	Brother Sun Sister Moon
13	Sleeping Beauty	Brigid Boden
14	Falling Into You	Céline Dion
15	Building A Mystery	Sarah McLachlan
16	Only The Lonely	The Heads f/ Gordon Gano
17	Your Woman	White Town
18	Tubthumping	Chumbawamba
19	Don't Call Me (You're Not Mine)	Grace
20	Carry On Dancing	Savage Garden
21	2Wicky	Hooverphonic
22	Stomp	God's Property f/ Kirk Franklin & 'Salt'
23	Los Cuatro Elementos	Cielo y Tierra
24	Absolution	Amanda Ghost
25	Drop Dead Gorgeous	Republica
26	The Fire Of The Spirit (O Ignis Spiritus Paracliti)	Illumination (Richard Souther)
27	Laddie, Lie Near Me	Connie Dover
28	If I Could Fly	Grace
29	Crazy Times	Jars Of Clay
30	Fall Into Your Dreams	Cyndi Lauper
31	Above The Lone	Love Spirals Downwards
32	Out Of My Mind	Duran Duran
33	Teri Akhiyan	Bally Sagoo
34	Freed From Desire	Gala (Rizzatto)
35	Black & White	Sarah McLachlan
36	Extremis	Hal f/ Gillian Anderson
37	Oh How I Cry	Brigid Boden
38	Eye Goes Blind (Aya)	Vision II
39	Walking Wounded	Everything But The Girl
40	Níl Sí I nGrá	Capercaillie
41	World Before Columbus	Suzanne Vega
42	2:1	Elastica
43	Sunny Came Home	Shawn Colvin
44	Wannabe	Spice Girls
45	Bangkok	Brother Sun Sister Moon
46	In My Arms	Erasure
47	Blue Skies	BT f/ Tori Amos
48	From The Lips Of The One I Love	Joy Askew
49	Yéku	Marcomé
50	Not Over Yet	Grace
51	If You Could Only See	Tonic
52	Quit Playing Games (With My Heart)	Backstreet Boys
53	One More Night	Amber
54	Foolish Games	Jewel
55	Torn Between Lovers	Maggie Reilly
56	Duden	Natacha Atlas
57	I Want You/Tears Of Pearls	Savage Garden
58	Ghost In The Machinery	Sarah Brightman
59	Never An Easy Way	Morcheeba
60	Todo Por Ti	Trilogía
61	With My Eyes Closed	Bee Gees
62	Staring At The Sun	U2
63	Barbie Girl	Aqua
64	Since You've Been Gone	Fine Young Cannibals
65	Multi-Family Garage Sale	Land Of The Loops
66	Tree Of Wonders (O Vos Felices Radices)/ [Sanctus]	Illumination (Richard Souther)
67	Sisters Of Avalon	Cyndi Lauper

1997

#	Song Title	Artist	#	Song Title	Artist
68	Female Of The Species	Space	90	Sick & Beautiful	Artificial Joy Club
69	The Voyager	Mike Oldfield	91	Time To Say Goodbye (Con Te Partirò)	Sarah Brightman & Andrea Bocelli
70	Mesa Drive	Jenifer Smith	92	Men In Black	Will Smith
71	Nicosia	Brother Sun Sister Moon	93	Everlong	Foo Fighters
72	Only You	Portishead	94	Madras	Love Spirals Downwards
73	Fool's Game	Richard Marx	95	Tattva	Kula Shaker
74	Walkin' On The Sun	Smash Mouth	96	Sex And Candy	Marcy Playground
75	Don't Go Breaking My Heart	Sonic Dream Collective	97	Together As One (Luminous)	Moodswings
76	Jaan	Talvin Singh f/ Amar	98	Mother Tongue	Leah Andreone
77	So Long So Wrong	Alison Krauss & Union Station	99	Alright	Jamiroquai
78	A World So Rare	Joy Askew	100	Aïcha	Khaled (Cheb Khaled)
79	Nobody's Girl	Nicky Holland	101	I Don't Want To Wait	Paula Cole
80	Home	Depeche Mode		**1997 EXTRAS**	
81	Navigate	Wayquay	102	Legend Of A Cowgirl	Imani Coppola
82	Don't You Ever	Republica	109	This Is Your Night	Amber
83	Always There	UB40	110	Return Of The Mack	Mark Morrison
84	T.N.T. For The Brain	Enigma	114	Mama	Spice Girls
85	Flipside	Everything But The Girl	117	Elegantly Wasted	INXS
86	Crazy (D-Influence Mix)	Mark Morrison	118	Do You Miss Me	Jocelyn Enriquez
87	In Your Wildest Dreams	Tina Turner f/ Barry White	123	Truly Madly Deeply	Savage Garden
88	Spanish Harbour	Vangelis	128	You're Not Alone	Olive
89	Dream	Forest For The Trees	164	Ooh Aah... Just A Little Bit	Gina G

1998

#	Song Title	Artist
1	Silence	Delerium f/ Sarah McLachlan
2	Human Beings	Seal
3	The Mummers' Dance	Loreena McKennitt
4	Unbound	Robbie Robertson
5	Of This Land	Clannad
6	Club Montepulciano	Hooverphonic
7	Black Eyed Boy	Texas
8	What About	Janet Jackson
9	She Smiles/Filmstar	Mulu
10	Campus Stella/ Field Of Stars	Pilgrimage
11	An Gleann	Clannad
12	Walk This Earth Alone	Lauren Christy
13	Sky Fits Heaven	Madonna
14	救你 (Save You)	杜德伟 (Alex To/ Du De Wei)
15	Revolver	Hooverphonic
16	Fear And Love	Morcheeba
17	Shelter	Capercaillie
18	Son Of A Time Machine	Sandra
19	Teardrop	Massive Attack (w/ Elizabeth Fraser)
20	Rose	Dominique Dalcan w/ Zazie
21	Tell Me	Billie Myers
22	Ray Of Light	Madonna
23	Velvet Rope / Rope Burn	Janet Jackson f/ Vanessa-Mae
24	Pilgrimage	Pilgrimage
25	This Love	Craig Armstrong w/ Elizabeth Fraser
26	Inhaler	Hooverphonic
27	The Dreaming/ Fionnghuala	The Spirit Of Eden
28	Frozen	Madonna
29	The Boy Is Mine	Brandy & Monica
30	Child Of Mine (I Have Come)	Jaci Velasquez
31	Fun For Me	Moloko

#	Song Title	Artist
32	煙 (The Smoke)	辛曉琪 (Winnie Hsin/Xin Xiaoqi)
33	Fade To Grey	Jars Of Clay
34	No Good For Me	The Corrs
35	Wishful Thinking	Duncan Sheik
36	Life In Mono	Mono
37	Eden	Hooverphonic
38	Holy Moses	Jann Arden
39	Nothing Really Matters	Madonna
40	If I Had Wings	Simple Minds
41	Perfect Time	Maíre Brennan
42	Crush	Jennifer Paige
43	The Angel Wars/ Absolution	Gary Numan
44	Euphoria (Firefly)	Delerium
45	Uselink/Useless	Depeche Mode
46	Jóga	Björk
47	Love Song (Dr. Lunatic's Keemovision)	Ofra Haza
48	Dominion Day	Gary Numan
49	Believe	Cher
50	The Sea	Morcheeba
51	Dark Skies	Pilgrimage
52	Beyond Reach	Curve
53	Mansun's Only Love Song	Mansun
54	海上花 Flowers Of Shanghai: Theme Song	Yoshihiro Hanno / 莫文蔚 (Karen Mok)
55	Boomerang Bang	Lauren Christy
56	Everyday Life	Robert Miles
57	My Favourite Game	The Cardigans
58	Bittersweet Symphony	The Verve
59	Feel It	The Tamperer f/ Maya
60	Amnesia	Chumbawamba
61	Let Me See	Clannad
62	Dark Sky	Jimmy Somerville
63	Leave Me Alone	Natalie Imbruglia
64	Skin	Madonna
65	On The Run	OMC

#	Song Title	Artist
66	Ray (Back From The Offworld)	Happy Rhodes
67	Let Me See	Morcheeba
68	The Power Of Good-Bye/ To Have And Not To Hold	Madonna
69	Freedom	Robert Miles (w/ Kathy Sledge)
70	Breakable	Fisher
71	Only When I Sleep	The Corrs
72	Without Within	Pete Belasco
73	Never You Mind	Semisonic
74	Something In The Air	Sarah Brightman f/ Tom Jones
75	Sweet Little Truth	Tasmin Archer
76	The Tree	Capercaillie
77	Friction	Morcheeba
78	Dead Heaven	Gary Numan
79	Planet Unknown	Forest For The Trees
80	Viva Forever	Spice Girls
81	Are You Jimmy Ray?	Jimmy Ray
82	Rise	Craig Armstrong
83	Beautiful Wasteland	Capercaillie
84	Man In The Rain	Mike Oldfield
85	Vem Kommer Såra Vem Ikväll	Anni-Frid Lyngstad (Frida)
86	Sleepy Maggie	Ashley MacIsaac w/ Mary Jane Lamond

#	Song Title	Artist
87	Alane	Wes (Madiko)
88	Film Noir	Philippe Saisse
89	La Guapa	B-Tribe
90	My Favorite Mistake	Sheryl Crow
91	Silicone	Mono
92	Sinner	Neil Finn
93	By Your Side	Love Spirals Downwards
94	You're Still The One	Shania Twain
95	You Look So Fine	Garbage
96	Song For The Tribes	Simple Minds
97	Pussycat	Mulu
98	Snow On The Sahara	Anggun
99	The Big Rock	Maíre Brennan
100	Penthouse Girl, Basement Boy	Crush
101	Your Loving Arms	Billie Ray Martin
1998 EXTRAS		
112	Torn	Natalie Imbruglia
113	I Want You Back	*NSYNC
132	Adia	Sarah McLachlan
152	My Heart Will Go On	Céline Dion
153	Everybody (Backstreet's Back)	Backstreet Boys
197	Free	Ultra Naté
233	One Week	Barenaked Ladies

1990s

#	Song Title	Artist
1	All That My Heart Can Hold	Maggie Reilly
2	Les Naufragés	Mitsou
3	Discovering Yourself	Emma Shapplin
4	Ça Fait Mal Et Ça Fait Rien	Zazie
5	Maureen Maguire	Stone Age
6	Detour	Bis
7	Tuva Groove	Ondar
8	Erase/Rewind	The Cardigans
9	Blue	Chantal Kreviazuk
10	Beautiful Stranger	Madonna
11	Hunter	Dido
12	I Believe In Love	Paula Cole Band
13	Tous Des Anges	Zazie
14	Bongo Bong/Je Ne T'Aime Plus	Manu Chao
15	Maribrengaël	Stone Age
16	A Rose In The Wind	Anggun
17	Only An Ocean Away	Sarah Brightman
18	Ameno	Era
19	Don't Think Of Me	Dido
20	Come Around	Kim Richey
21	Deliver Me / Eden	Sarah Brightman
22	Don't Wanna Lose	Maggie Reilly
23	Be Careful (Cuidado Con Mi Corazón)	Ricky Martin & Madonna
24	Happiness Is An Option	Pet Shop Boys
25	The Source Of Secrets	Mike Oldfield
26	If You Want Me	Total f/ Mase
27	State Of Grace	Seal
28	Saltwater	Chicane f/ Maíre Brennan
29	My Sensual Mind	Anggun
30	Muse / Cochise	Mike Oldfield
31	Lost My Faith	Seal
32	Gotta Stay High	New Radicals
33	Consume Me	dc Talk
34	Excerpt From	Seal
35	Hamam/Istanbul Uyurken (Hamam Trance Version)	Trancendental
36	Is This Real?	lisahall
37	Words Needed	Scripture
38	Debout Dans Les Flammes	Judith Bérard
39	The Hush	Texas
40	Tu	Sarah Brightman
41	Amen	Paula Cole Band
42	Here With Me	Dido
43	My Lover's Gone	Dido
44	Five Fathoms	Everything But The Girl
45	Top Of The World	Dudearella
46	No Regrets	Robbie Williams (w/ Neil Tennant)
47	Saint	Texas
48	...Baby One More Time	Britney Spears
49	Not Only Human	Heather Nova
50	History Repeating	Propellerheads w/ Miss Shirley Bassey
51	Sexual (Li Da Di)	Amber
52	Whisper To The Wild Water	Maíre Brennan
53	Sombra De Tí	Shakira
54	Everytime We Touch ('98)	Maggie Reilly
55	Enae Volare (Mezzo)	Era
56	Press Rewind	Alan Parsons
57	Summer Son	Texas
58	Octavo Día	Shakira
59	That Girl	Esthero
60	One	Alanis Morissette
61	In Our Lifetime	Texas
62	Horny	Mousse T. vs. Hot 'n' Juicy
63	Lung	Hooverphonic
64	Stars All Seem To Weep	Beth Orton
65	Show Me The Meaning Of Being Lonely	Backstreet Boys

#	Song Title	Artist
66	Graduale	Gala
67	Taxi Taxi	Cher
68	Californication	Red Hot Chili Peppers
69	A Wing And A Prayer	Laurel MacDonald
70	This Time	The Verve
71	Don't Want You Back	Backstreet Boys
72	Millennium	Robbie Williams
73	Forgive And Forget	Blondie
74	Enchanted	Delerium
75	Sway	Bic Runga
76	The World Is Not Enough	Garbage
77	Please	Chris Isaak
78	Prayer	Secret Garden
79	Sleep With The Ancients	The Spirit Of Eden
80	Secret Smile	Semisonic
81	Culture Clash	Sacred Spirit (Indigo Spirit)
82	Someday Soon	Jimmy Somerville
83	Sing It Back	Moloko
84	Red	Sister Soleil
85	I'm Alive	Heather Nova
86	Eight O'Clock	Amina (Annabi)
87	Electro Shock Faders	Hooverphonic
88	Oh My People	Joi
89	Podour Bihan	Stone Age

#	Song Title	Artist
90	Eurodisco	Bis
91	A Thousand Years	Sting
92	Honey / Natural Blues	Moby
93	Au Nom De La Rose	Moos
94	Stolen Car	Beth Orton
95	What Will I Do?	Clannad
96	Here I Am	Jimmy Somerville
97	Ends	Everlast
98	If You Had My Love	Jennifer Lopez
99	Larger Than LIfe	Backstreet Boys
100	Metaforce	The Art Of Noise
101	Dis-Moi Pourquoi	Amina
1999 EXTRAS		
102	Breathe	Sixpence None The Richer
107	Right Now	Chris Gaines (Garth Brooks)
113	What It's Like	Everlast
114	This Kiss	Faith Hill
119	Smooth	Santana w/ Rob Thomas
120	When You Believe	Whitney Houston & Mariah Carey
123	Talisman	Air
133	Right Here, Right Now	Fatboy Slim
135	Genie In A Bottle	Christina Aguilera

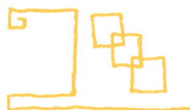

#	Song Title	Artist
1	Wedding Song	Tracy Chapman
2	Shame	BT
3	Minor Earth Major Sky	a-ha
4	Out Of Sight	Hooverphonic
5	Smile	Olive
6	我給的愛 (I Give You Love)	楊乃文 (Faith Yang)
7	Every Word	Sade
8	Images	Bel Canto
9	Conflict Junkie	Layla Kaylif
10	Shallow End	Morcheeba
11	It Feels So Good	Sonique
12	So Long	黃大煒 (David Wong)
13	Tonight And The Rest Of My Life	Nina Gordon
14	Move Your Body	Eiffel 65
15	Into The Dark	Melissa Etheridge
16	Pure Shores	All Saints
17	Unsung Psalm	Tracy Chapman
18	Follow The Word	Maíre Brennan
19	Move Closer	Sonique
20	秋天1944 (The Fall Of 1944)	黃大煒 (David Wong)
21	Made In Love	Zazie
22	To Be Free	Emilíana Torrini
23	Beltain – Beltane	Ceredwen
24	Damaged	Plumb
25	Enigmatism	Mike Oldfield
26	Unforgivable Sinner	Lene Marlin
27	Shakespeare In Love	Layla Kaylif
28	La Lune/Winter In July	Sarah Brightman
29	插曲 (Episode/Chaqu)	鄭秀文 (Sammi Cheng)
30	Mindless Moments	Moodorama
31	The Time Machine (Part 1)/(Part 2)	Alan Parsons
32	Temperamental	Everything But The Girl
33	Object Of Your Desire	Amber
34	The Doge's Palace	Mike Oldfield

#	Song Title	Artist
35	Apples And Diamonds (Lord-Alge Remix)	Bertine
36	Don't Give Up	Chicane f/ Bryan Adams
37	This Life	Mandalay
38	A Song For The Lovers	Richard Ashcroft
39	Mad About You	Hooverphonic
40	It's OK	Tracy Chapman
41	Show Me	Ofra Haza
42	With You	Nomad
43	My Life	Dido
44	Time Stood Still	Madonna
45	Live & Breathe	Tina Cousins
46	Slide	Dido
47	Mastermind	Mike Oldfield
48	Days To Dust	Grey Eye Glances
49	911	Wyclef Jean f/ Mary J. Blige
50	Don't Call Me Baby	Madison Avenue
51	Y Bryn Gwyn – The White Hall	Ceredwen
52	Meltdown	Lisa Gerrard and Pieter Bourke
53	發熱發亮 (Shining Bright/Hot And Bright)	鄭秀文 (Sammi Cheng)
54	Desert Rose	Sting f/ Cheb Mami
55	I Won't Forget Her	a-ha
56	Only Time	Enya
57	Heaven's Earth	Delerium w/ Kristy Thirsk
58	Snow	Grey Eye Glances
59	On A Night Like This	Kylie Minogue
60	Brave New World	Julia Taylor-Stanley/ Miriam Stockley
61	Never The Same	Supreme Beings Of Leisure
62	Vampires	Pet Shop Boys
63	Kotahitanga (Union)	Oceania
64	The Sweetest Find	Layla Kaylif
65	Şimarik	Tarkan
66	Dreaming	BT f/ Kirsty Hawkshaw
67	Blue (Da Ba Dee)	Eiffel 65

#	Song Title	Artist
68	Closer To Heaven	Pet Shop Boys
69	Forever My Heart	Miriam Stockley
70	You Can Still Be Free	Savage Garden
71	Stranded	Plumb
72	Out Of The Blue	Alan Parsons (w/ Tony Hadley)
73	Sitting Down Here	Lene Marlin
74	Pukaea (The Trumpet)	Oceania
75	Push	Olive
76	Rome Wasn't Built In A Day	Morcheeba
77	Wishing On A Star	Miriam Stockley / Anne Dudley
78	Ahava	Ofra Haza
79	Better Off Alone	Alice Deejay
80	Goldie	Sarah Cracknell
81	Bye Bye Bye	*NSYNC
82	When We Are Together	Texas
83	Where I'm Headed	Lene Marlin
84	Bringin' Da Noise	*NSYNC
85	Very Close To Far Away	Orchestral Manoeuvres In The Dark
86	Autumn Tactics	Chicane f/ Justine Suissa
87	Take A Picture	Filter
88	Gotta Tell You	Samantha Mumba
89	Jacky Cane	Hooverphonic

#	Song Title	Artist
90	Bu Gece	Tarkan
91	Rock DJ	Robbie Williams
92	No More	Ruff Endz
93	Dizzy	98°
94	Never Just For A Ring	Toni Braxton
95	I Get My Beat	Richard Ashcroft
96	Goodtime	Beyond (黃家駒)
97	I Put A Spell On You	Sonique
98	Colour Me	Dot Allison
99	Good Bye	Martina McBride
100	Boom Boom Ba	Métisse
101	Mind Of A King	Blaque
2000 EXTRAS		
105	Porcelain	Moby
108	Caligula	Macy Gray
113	Playground Love	Air (sung by Gordon Tracks)
114	Be With You	Enrique Iglesias
117	Oops! . . . I Did It Again	Britney Spears
130	Butterfly	Smile (Smile.dk)
137	Amazed	Lonestar
142	The Bad Touch	The Bloodhound Gang
178	Petals	Mariah Carey
249	Liquid Dreams	O-Town

2000s

#	Song Title	Artist	#	Song Title	Artist
1	Glorious / (NUM Remix)	Andreas Johnson	35	Golden Boys	Res
2	Talking To Myself	Maggie Reilly	36	Fallen Icons	Delerium f/ Jenifer McLaren
3	Straight To...Number One	Touch And Go	37	Design	Merrie Amsterburg
4	Summer Moved On	a-ha	38	Clutch	Shea Seger
5	Drive	Incubus	39	Immigrant	Sade
6	Luna (Only You)	Alessandro Safina	40	Nobody Wants To Be Lonely	Ricky Martin w/ Christina Aguilera
7	B777	Utah Saints	41	The Sun Never Shone That Day	a-ha
8	Give Me Strength	Over The Rhine	42	Whenever, Wherever / Suerte (Whenever, Wherever)	Shakira
9	Wednesday's Child	Emilíana Torrini			
10	Bullets For Brains	Roland Orzabal	43	Erase Her	LFO
11	It's Been Awhile	Staind	44	Crystal	New Order
12	Born To Love Her	Spain	45	Pedestal	Astronaut Wife
13	Veni Redemptor Gentium	State Of Grace (Paul Schwartz f/ Lisbeth Scott)	46	Freelove	Depeche Mode
			47	Cherry Popsicle	Jann Arden
14	Tighinn Air a'Mhuir Am Fear A Phosas Mi	Capercaillie	48	Ticket To The World	Roland Orzabal
			49	Penitent	Suzanne Vega
15	Dela Dela	Sacred Spirit	50	The Summer	ATB
16	Adelena	Maggie Reilly	51	Replay	Maggie Reilly
17	Low Life	Roland Orzabal	52	Amazing	Madonna
18	Light Years	Kylie Minogue	53	The Magnificent Tree	Hooverphonic
19	You're Not There	Jaci Velasquez	54	One More Time	Daft Punk
20	Impressive Instant	Madonna	55	Love Will Find You	ATB and Heather Nova
21	Everytime We Live Together We Die A Bit More	Hooverphonic	56	Daylight	Delerium f/ Matthew Sweet
22	Runaway Crush	Stella Soleil	57	Nobody's Perfect / Gone	Madonna
23	Ghost Of You And Me	BBMak	58	Yellow	Coldplay
24	Wildwood	Eliza Carthy	59	Fallin'	Alicia Keys
25	Nightfall	Solar Twins	60	Family Affair / Family Affair (Dance For Me) (two versions, Guetta remix released in 2022)	Mary J. Blige / David Guetta f/ Mary J. Blige
26	Aht Uh Mi Hed	Shuggie Otis			
27	What You're Afraid Of	Bis			
28	All I Ever Wanted	The Human League			
29	Aaroma Of A Man	Pru	61	Human	Rod Stewart
30	Piece Of It All	Jann Arden	62	'Til I Whisper U Something	Sinéad O'Connor
31	Let Me Be The One	Sasha Alexander			
32	Ondeia (Água)	Dulce Pontes	63	Salva Me	Libera
33	Imperfect	Stella Soleil	64	Man In The Middle	Bee Gees
34	Earthbound	Solar Twins	65	Dream On	Depeche Mode

#	Song Title	Artist	#	Song Title	Artist
66	She's Got My Number	Semisonic	91	Trouble In Shangri-La	Stevie Nicks
67	I Feel Loved	Depeche Mode	92	King Of Sorrow	Sade
68	Angel Face	Stella Soleil	93	Bed	Semisonic
69	The Dinosaur-Slipper-Man	Bel Canto	94	Harder, Better, Faster, Stronger	Daft Punk
70	In The End	Linkin Park	95	Androgyny	Garbage
71	All Around The World (La La La La La)	ATC (A Touch Of Class)	96	Massive / Sun / Punk Club	Utah Saints (w/ Michael Stipe)
72	Truth Calling	Capercaillie	97	Dandelion	LFO f/ Kelis
73	Not Of This Earth	Robbie Williams	98	Clint Eastwood	Gorillaz
74	Butterfly	Kylie Minogue	99	Lebanese Blonde	Thievery Corporation
75	The World Can Wait	Over The Rhine	100	Land Of Promise	Sacred Spirit
76	The Time Is Now	Moloko	101	Innocente	Delerium f/ Leigh Nash
77	Memories	Maggie Reilly			
78	Omen Sore	Era	104	Ms. Jackson	Outkast
79	Breathing	Andreas Johnson	105	I'm Outta Love	Anastacia
80	This Is Where I Came In	Bee Gees	108	Angel Boy	Tim McGraw
81	Alleluias	Solar Twins	110	I'll Fly With You (L'Amour Toujours) (Bla Bla Bla)	Gigi D'Agostino
82	Cowboy's Dream/All The Pretty Horses (Medley)	Marty Stuart/Kristin Wilkinson/Larry Paxton	111	Fill Me In	Craig David
83	Exploration B/Haunted	Poe	122	Hit 'Em Up Style (Oops!)	Blu Cantrell
84	Pushing Me Away	Linkin Park	124	Superman (It's Not Easy)	Five For Fighting
85	Judith	Heather Duby	136	Everything In Its Right Place	Radiohead
86	Butterfly	Crazy Town	141	Don't Come Around Here	Rod Stewart w/ Helicopter Girl
87	Glamour And Pain	Joe Jackson w/ Dale De Vere	146	Desire	Ultra Naté
88	In My Pocket	Mandy Moore			
89	Hindi Sad Diamonds	Nicole Kidman/John Leguizamo/Alka Yagnik			
90	Une Femme	Anggun			

2001 EXTRAS

2000s

2002

#	Song Title	Artist
1	Check The Meaning	Richard Ashcroft
2	Did Anyone Approach You?	a-ha
3	Damascus/Center Of The Sun	Conjure One (w/ Poe)
4	Hungry	Kosheen
5	Sandriam	Perry Blake
6	Moi...Lolita	Alizée
7	Annie, Would I Lie To You	Iris
8	Insensible	Mandalay
9	Lifelines	a-ha
10	Train Song	Eliza Carthy
11	Rock And A Hard Place	Supreme Beings Of Leisure
12	Can't Get You Out Of My Head	Kylie Minogue
13	Rapture (Tastes So Sweet)	iiO
14	Caravan	Shabaz
15	Tsugaru	Uttaru-Kuru
16	Die Another Day	Madonna
17	Love Affair	Kylie Minogue
18	Wild Butterfly	Balligomingo
19	Tuesday Afternoon	Jennifer Brown
20	Catch	Kosheen
21	Hummingbirds	Luminous (Brother Sun Sister Moon) f/ Orbital
22	God Put A Smile Upon Your Face	Coldplay
23	Love To See You Cry	Enrique Iglesias
24	J.B.G.	Alizée
25	Rue De La Paix	Zazie
26	The Shame Of Life	Butthole Surfers
27	Aqualung	Morcheeba
28	Otherwise	Morcheeba
29	Beautiful Girl	Eliza Carthy
30	Making Out	No Doubt
31	Turn Smile Shift Repeat	Phantom Planet
32	Losing You	Eiffel 65
33	Destiny	Zero 7

#	Song Title	Artist
34	Perfect Touch	Sandra
35	Cover	Kosheen
36	Still Lives	Perry Blake
37	I See Right Through To You	DJ Encore f/ Engelina
38	She's So Gone	Cause & Effect
39	On Éteint	Zazie
40	Get Over You	Sophie Ellis-Bextor
41	Here	Pet Shop Boys
42	The Music's No Good Without You	Cher
43	Don't Panic	Coldplay
44	Forgive Me	Sandra
45	Six Feet Under Theme	Thomas Newman
46	So Blu	Blu Cantrell
47	Breathe	Télépopmusik
48	Real?	Cause & Effect
49	River, Sea, Ocean	Badly Drawn Boy
50	Days Go By	Dirty Vegas
51	Forever Not Yours	a-ha
52	Anywhere	Beth Orton
53	Such A Shame	Sandra
54	Walking Away	Craig David
55	It Makes Me Wonder	Suzanne Vega
56	Save Yourself	Sense Field
57	Full Moon	Brandy
58	Sometimes	Hooverphonic
59	I DJ With The Fire	Eiffel 65
60	Abigail	Bertine
61	Endangered Species (Galleon Remix)	Deep Forest
62	Someone Like You	New Order
63	Oranges On Appletrees	a-ha
64	Bother	Stone Sour
65	Voodooman	Todmobile
66	One Day In Your Life	Anastacia
67	Electrical Storm	U2
68	Thoughts	Védís

2000s

2002

#	Song Title	Artist
69	Purify	Balligomingo
70	Snowdrop	Roland Orzabal
71	To Be Free	Mike Oldfield
72	Shine	Bond
73	Cherry Lips (Go Baby Go!)	Garbage
74	Ready For The Good Times	Shakira
75	Something	José Padilla
76	The Hands That Built America (Theme From "Gangs Of New York")	U2
77	Twisted / Twisted (Reprise)	Fused
78	Hypnoculture	Roland Orzabal
79	On The Sly	Thunderball
80	Bamboo Dance	Shao Rong (邵容)
81	Lamb Of God	Rebecca St. James
82	Lost	Balligomingo
83	You Owe Me Nothing In Return	Alanis Morissette
84	Sunlight	Natalie Imbruglia
85	Ehad	Zöhar
86	Orange Meadows	Aria
87	Volveré Junto A Ti	Laura Pausini
88	Good In My Head	Anika Moa

#	Song Title	Artist
89	Cannot Hide	a-ha
90	Freak Like Me	Sugababes
91	Gotta Get Thru This	Daniel Bedingfield
92	A Sorta Fairytale	Tori Amos
93	Hold You	ATB (f/ Roberta Carter Harrison)
94	Break 4 Love	Peter Rauhofer + Pet Shop Boys = The Collaboration
95	Optimistique-Moi	Mylène Farmer
96	Veni Vedi Vici	Alizée
97	A New Day Has Come	Céline Dion
98	Come Into My World	Kylie Minogue
99	A Different Kind Of Love Song	Cher
100	Lost Cause	Beck
101	Ghosts	Dirty Vegas
2002 EXTRAS		
113	May It Be	Enya
118	Aserejé [The Ketchup Song (Hey Hah)]	Las Ketchup
129	Es Por Ti	Juanes
131	Dare You To Move	Switchfoot
132	Without Me	Eminem
139	If I Could Fall In Love	Lenny Kravitz

2000s

#	Song Title	Artist	#	Song Title	Artist
1	Truly	Delerium f/ Nerina Pallot	36	Hayling	FC/Kahuna
2	One Fine Day	Jakatta (f/ Beth Hirsch)	37	Peacekeeper	Fleetwood Mac
3	Move This Mountain	Sophie Ellis-Bextor	38	Make A Wish	Conjure One (f/ Poe)
4	Loneliest Star	Seal	39	All I Know	Anneli Drecker
5	Reveal	Céline Dion	40	Talking To Myself	Cousteau
6	Let Go	Frou Frou	41	Whatever	Iris
7	Out There	DJ Encore f/ Engelina	42	Are You For Real	Astronaut Wife
8	Disappear Club 5	Bel Canto	43	Gloria Deo Patri	Classical Spirit (The Brave)
9	Pick A Card	Jessy Moss	44	Humilitas	Lesiëm (f/ Maggie Reilly)
10	Remind Me	Röyksopp	45	Hollywood	Madonna
11	Psychobabble	Frou Frou	46	Mysterious Days	Sarah Brightman f/ Ofra Haza
12	My Vision	Jakatta f/ Seal	47	Maybe Tomorrow	Stereophonics
13	It's All Here	Anneli Drecker	48	Only You	Jann Arden
14	Close Your Eyes	Grey Eye Glances	49	You Can Be Replaced	Dot Allison
15	Magical Love	Kate Ryan	50	Intro/Are You Happy Now?	Michelle Branch
16	Addictive	Faithless	51	Crazy	Leaves
17	Sand In My Shoes	Dido	52	Tundra (Mánaiga)	Anneli Drecker
18	Dorothy's Victory	Bel Canto	53	Sleep	Conjure One
19	Alone In Kyoto	Air	54	Snow Patrol (Part 1)/ (Part 2)	Alpinestars
20	Manic Star	Conjure One	55	Growing Pains	Mia Doi Todd
21	You Rock My World Tonight	Bel Canto	56	Come Into Our Room	Clinic
22	Into The Light	Cause & Effect	57	A Thousand Beautiful Things	Annie Lennox
23	Home Away From You	Jakatta	58	Guide Me God	Ghostland f/ Sinéad O'Connor + Natacha Atlas
24	After All	Delerium f/ Jaël	59	It's A Beautiful Day / Beautiful	Sarah Brightman
25	You're The Answer	Iris	60	Fides	Lesiëm (f/ Maggie Reilly)
26	Wasting My Time	Kosheen	61	Run For It	Delerium f/ Leigh Nash
27	Waiting For You	Seal	62	Sparkle	Sophie Ellis-Bextor
28	Famous Monsters	Saliva	63	Late Now	Astronaut Wife
29	Tears From The Moon	Conjure One (f/ Sinéad O'Connor)	64	I'll Be There	Weekend Players
30	Quattro (World Drifts In)	Calexico	65	My Culture	1 Giant Leap f/ Robbie Williams and Maxi Jazz
31	A Contre-Courant	Alizée	66	Crawling	Kosheen
32	All The Things She Said	t.A.T.u.			
33	Smile At You	Fleetwood Mac			
34	L'Alizé	Alizée			
35	Must Be Dreaming	Frou Frou			

2000s

#	Song Title	Artist	#	Song Title	Artist
67	It's My Life	No Doubt	87	Give Up	Supreme Beings Of Leisure
68	Sunrise	Cause & Effect	88	We Used To Be Friends	The Dandy Warhols
69	Poor Leno	Röyksopp	89	Sorrow Expert	Iris
70	Inner Smile / Inner Child (two versions)	Texas / Justin Guarini	90	Sleeping Girl	Simple Minds
71	Jacob's Ladder	Chumbawamba	91	Leave The Lights On / Intuition	Jewel
72	Beg	Lisbeth Scott	92	Youpidou	Alizée
73	Digital	Mia Doi Todd	93	Show Me Love	t.A.T.u.
74	Jericho	Weekend Players	94	In The Great Unknown	Mary Fahl
75	Human Interest	Hooverphonic	95	Love Somebody	Robbie Williams
76	Taxi Ride	Tori Amos	96	Night Wants To Forget	Mario Frangoulis
77	Drama	Airlock	97	Fallen	Sarah McLachlan
78	I Don't Wanna Stop	ATB	98	I'm So Stupid	Madonna
79	Righteously	Lucinda Williams	99	Closer To You	The Wallflowers
80	Montana	Venus Hum	100	Look Of Today	Enigma
81	What Your Soul Sings	Massive Attack (f/ Sinéad O'Connor)	101	Return Of The Cranes	Bruno Coulais
82	Night Lady	Bel Canto		**2003 EXTRAS**	
83	Single By Choice / Song For A Good Son	Bangles	103	Toxic	Britney Spears
84	Nothing Fails	Madonna	104	S.O.B.	Lisa Marie Presley
85	Silver Girl	Fleetwood Mac	113	Numb	Linkin Park
86	At The End	iiO	114	Slow	Kylie Minogue
			116	Provider (Zero 7 Mix)	N*E*R*D

#	Song Title	Artist	#	Song Title	Artist
1	Beautiful Things	Andain	34	Sway	Lostprophets
2	Dice	Finley Quaye & William Orbit f/ Beth Orton	35	One Way Or The Other	Chumbawamba
3	24	Jem	36	Home	Zero 7
4	Miracles	Pet Shop Boys	37	When I Close My Eyes	Natacha Atlas & Myra Boyle
5	For Reasons Unexplained	Casey Stratton	38	Baby Be Brave/Silver Strand	The Corrs
6	I Thought You Were My Boyfriend	The Magnetic Fields	39	You Promised Me (Tu Es Foutu)	In-Grid
7	Somewhere A Clock Is Ticking	Snow Patrol	40	Fallen	Delerium f/ Rani
8	Lovers In The Backseat	Scissor Sisters	41	Alive	Sonique
9	Hummingbirds	Venus Hum	42	Attitude	Suede (The London Suede)
10	Tits On The Radio	Scissor Sisters	43	I'd Rather Dance With You	Kings Of Convenience
11	Your Eyes Open	Keane	44	Holding Out For A Hero	Frou Frou
12	Sweet Misery	Tiësto	45	Ecstasy	ATB
13	Cherry Blossom Girl	Air	46	Let It Go	Etro Anime
14	Stoned	Dido	47	We Might As Well Be Strangers	Keane
15	Blood	Casey Stratton	48	Somnambulist (Simply Being Loved)	BT f/ JC Chasez
16	Life Got Cold	Girls Aloud	49	This Is The World We Live In	Alcazar
17	Everything Is Everything	Phoenix	50	The Rain	Kate Ryan
18	Stay	Cause & Effect	51	Low Ambition	Lambchop
19	Across The Universe Of Time	Hayley Westenra	52	Coming Home	Kosheen
20	Crying At The Discoteque	Alcazar	53	Familiar Feeling	Moloko
21	The Dead Sea	Casey Stratton	54	Careful What You Wish For	Texas
22	Touched	Delerium f/ Rachel Fuller	55	Taste The Summer	Duran Duran
23	Steppin' Out	Kaskade	56	Comfortably Numb	Scissor Sisters
24	Show Me (Jakatta Mix)	Moya Brennan	57	(Reach For The) Sunrise	Duran Duran
25	I Go Shopping	Alcazar	58	They	Jem
26	Quiet Ones	Tears For Fears	59	Sunrise	Simply Red
27	Here In My Room	Incubus	60	Hard To Know	Mindy Smith
28	Lonely	Maria (Jensen)	61	Hope On Fire	Vienna Teng
29	We Play The Game	Alan Parsons	62	Come To Me	JC Chasez
30	An Area Big Enough To Do It In	Prophet Omega	63	Hidden Track (the sky above, the earth below me) (bonus song #12)	Jessy Greene
31	Soul Deep	Laura Turner			
32	The World Outside	Paloalto			
33	Untitled 1 / Sunshine	Keane			

2000s

#	Song Title	Artist	#	Song Title	Artist
64	Fly Again	Kristine W	87	Promises	Kylie Minogue
65	Dear To Me	Amel Larrieux	88	Little Boy	Kosheen
66	The Space Between	Zero 7	89	Run	Snow Patrol
67	Flawless (Go To The City)	George Michael	90	Somewhere Only We Know	Keane
68	I Give, You Take	Maria (Jensen)	91	New Favorite Thing	Balligomingo f/ Lucy Woodward
69	Red Blooded Woman	Kylie Minogue	92	Gather The Horses	Charlie Mars
70	Ocean	Casey Stratton	93	The House Of Jupiter	Casey Stratton
71	You Will Be My Ain True Love	Alison Krauss (w/ Sting)	94	Let Your Head Go	Victoria Beckham
72	Wait / She	ZOEgirl	95	Get Me	Twista (w/ The Three Degrees)
73	Automatic Lover	Jay-Jay Johanson	96	About Her	Malcolm McLaren
74	Talk Amongst Yourselves (Sasha Involver Remix)	Grand National (w/ Sasha)	97	Marrakech	ATB
75	Angels	Junkie XL f/ Gary Numan	98	Agnus Dei	Magna Canta
76	Greeting Card Aisle	Sarah Harmer	99	Paris	Delerium
77	Scandalous	Mis-Teeq	100	Want That Life	The Fixx
78	Nowhere Without You	Sophie Ellis-Bextor	101	Somebody Told Me	The Killers
79	Counting Stars / Destination Anywhere	Sugarcult		**2004 EXTRAS**	
80	Ways & Means	Snow Patrol	103	Save A Horse (Ride A Cowboy)	Big & Rich
81	No Phone	Cake	109	The District Sleeps Alone Tonight	The Postal Service
82	Wild West Show	Big & Rich	110	Woman	Maroon 5
83	Blame It On The Moon	Katie Melua	120	Turn Me On	Kevin Lyttle
84	Don't Pass Go	Chumbawamba	138	Boulevard Of Broken Dreams	Green Day
85	Me And The Moon	Something Corporate	139	Do You Realize??	The Flaming Lips
86	Time Of Our Lives	Paul van Dyk f/ Vega 4			

2000s

#	Song Title	Artist
1	One Word (Chris Cox Remix)	Kelly Osbourne
2	White Shadows	Coldplay
3	Bana Sen Lazımsın	Rafet El Roman
4	Due Destini	Tiromancino
5	How To Be Invisible	Kate Bush
6	Cash Machine	Hard-Fi
7	Endless Dream	Conjure One
8	What Else Is There?	Röyksopp
9	I've Seen It All (two versions)	Schiller f/ Sarah Brightman / Maya Saban
10	Have You Got It In You?	Imogen Heap
11	Rodéo	Zazie
12	Heartbeat	Annie
13	Living In My City (Theme From The Turin Winter Olympic Games 2006)	Eiffel 65
14	Fuck Them All	Mylène Farmer
15	I Feel You	Schiller f/ Heppner
16	Peut-Être Toi	Mylène Farmer
17	Nothing Else Matters	Bedroom Rockers
18	La Pluie Et Le Beau Temps	Zazie
19	King Of The Mountain	Kate Bush
20	Broken	Junkie XL f/ Grant Nicholas
21	Son's Gonna Rise	Citizen Cope
22	The Engine Driver	The Decemberists
23	Still Breathing	Duran Duran
24	Yamah Tövbeler	Mustafa Sandal
25	Left Outside Alone	Anastacia
26	Hung Up	Madonna
27	Versace	Bettie Serveert
28	It Generates	Iris
29	Low	Coldplay
30	Where No One Knows Me	Jann Arden
31	Dracula's Castle	New Order
32	Antidote	Morcheeba
33	Clear The Area	Imogen Heap
34	Destroy Everything You Touch	Ladytron
35	Whirlwind	Beauty's Confusion
36	Can't Take It	The All-American Rejects
37	Desire	Schiller f/ Veljanov
38	I've Been Thinking	Handsome Boy Modeling School f/ Cat Power
39	Miles From Monterey	West Indian Girl
40	Benim İçin N'Apadın	Gökhan Özen
41	Into Everything	Télépopmusik f/ Deborah Anderson
42	Porno Graphique	Mylène Farmer
43	The Time We Lost Our Way	Thievery Corporation f/ LouLou
44	Precious	Depeche Mode
45	Lands Of Fire	Iris
46	Walk Into The Sun	Dirty Vegas
47	Don't Stop	Brazilian Girls
48	What Are You Afraid Of	West Indian Girl
49	I Believe	Conjure One
50	Could It Be Love	Jimmy Somerville
51	Soul Meets Body	Death Cab For Cutie
52	Muovo Le Ali Di Nuovo	Tiromancino
53	Dream Of You	Schiller f/ Heppner
54	Struggle	Ringside
55	Hide And Seek	Imogen Heap
56	It's Great To Be Here Again!	The Posies
57	Tired Of Being Sorry (aka Spanishfaster)	Ringside
58	What's Wrong With Being Lonely	Colette
59	Thinking About You	Ivy
60	Sergio's Theme	Deep Dish
61	Finest Hour	Duran Duran
62	Feel Good Inc	Gorillaz
63	C'est Écrit	Anggun
64	Wonders Never Cease	Morcheeba
65	Surfing	Mike Oldfield

#	Song Title	Artist
66	An Honest Mistake	The Bravery
67	Doolididom	Zazie
68	Mindstalking	Lunascape
69	I Still Feel	Martina Topley-Bird
70	A Million Ways	Dirty Vegas
71	(You Can't Blame It On) Anybody/ Congratulations	Phoenix
72	One Word	Conjure One
73	Exodus '04	Utada (Hikaru)
74	Roses	Dirty Vegas
75	Dangerous And Moving (Intro)/All About Us	t.A.T.u.
76	Dragostea Din Tei (Numa Numa/Ma Ya Hi)	O-Zone
77	My Poor Old Heart	Alison Krauss & Union Station
78	Homme	Brazilian Girls
79	This Is How A Heart Breaks	Rob Thomas
80	Sleepsong	Secret Garden
81	LoveLife	Alcazar
82	Do Pal	Lata Mangeshkar, Sonu Nigam
83	Gabriel	Lamb
84	Say Hello	Deep Dish
85	Jerk It Out	Caesars
86	Bir Anda Sevmiştim	Demet Akalın
87	Don't Break My Heart	Nicola
88	Sweet The Sting / Parasol	Tori Amos

#	Song Title	Artist
89	Conversations	The Posies
90	(Can't Believe) This Is Me	Jennifer Lopez
91	Despertar	Federico Aubele
92	Just Let Go	Fischerspooner
93	Tell Me Now (What You See)	Moya Brennan
94	Ecce Gratum (Club Mix)	Qntal
95	De Usuahia Al A Quiaca	Gustavo Santaolalla
96	Free Me / (Dr. Octavo Mix)	Emma (Bunton)
97	Very	Moby
98	Let's Never Stop Falling In Love / Lilly	Pink Martini
99	I Miss You / Mittelerde (Middle Earth)	Schiller f/ Maya Saban
100	Queen Of Night	Damian & London Symphony Orchestra
101	Marching The Hate Machines (Into The Sun)	Thievery Corporation f/ The Flaming Lips
2005 EXTRAS		
106	Summertime Cowboy	Husky Rescue
113	Don't Cha	The Pussycat Dolls
119	Don't Phunk With My Heart	The Black Eyed Peas
125	Fortress	Pinback
128	Born Under A Good Sign	Teenage Fanclub
135	Seasons Of Love (movie version)	Rent Cast

#	Song Title	Artist		#	Song Title	Artist
1	Spiral	William Orbit f/ Kenna & Sugababes		35	You Never Know	The Shapeshifters (Shape:UK)
2	Move On Now	Hard-Fi		36	Opaline	Casey Stratton
3	Shut Your Eyes	Snow Patrol		37	Closing In	Imogen Heap
4	The Other Side	Scissor Sisters		38	π	Kate Bush
5	Is It Love	iiO		39	Set The Fire To The Third Bar	Snow Patrol w/ Martha Wainwright
6	Crazy	Andy Bell		40	Craving (I Only Want What I Can't Have)	t.A.T.u.
7	How High/Isaac	Madonna		41	Wake Up	Hooverphonic
8	You Don't Have To Change	Anneli Drecker		42	Extraordinary Way	Conjure One
9	Be Still	Kaskade		43	Forever Lost	Conjure One
10	Get Down Tonight	Texas		44	Anyone Can Lose	Euphoria w/ Tracy Bonham
11	What About Us	Texas		45	Secret	Sophie Barker
12	Celice	a-ha		46	All Things Are Quite Silent | Forever	Maggie Reilly
13	Maybe For A Minute	Casey Stratton		47	Today	Zero 7
14	Somewhere In Between	Kate Bush		48	Miles And Miles	Schiller f/ Moya Brennan
15	Numb	Pet Shop Boys		49	You Are Water	Hayley Westenra
16	Stay With Me Till Dawn (two versions)	Judie Tzuke / Lucid		50	If You Talk Too Much (My Head Will Explode)	People In Planes
17	Sinners And Saints	Euphoria f/ Tina Dico		51	Love Show	Skye (Edwards)
18	Nothing In My Way	Keane		52	Ride The Lights	Morningwood
19	Morning Yearning	Ben Harper		53	Jump	Madonna
20	Make This Go On Forever	Snow Patrol		54	Just 4 Christmas	Fabrizio Faniello
21	Black Is The Colour	The Corrs		55	Fleeting Instant	Delerium f/ Kirsty Hawkshaw
22	I'm With Stupid	Pet Shop Boys		56	Makin Me Crazy	Tommy Lee w/ Dirty Harry
23	Stop This	Anneli Drecker		57	Twentieth Century	Pet Shop Boys
24	Sick And Tired	Anastacia		58	Follow My Ruin	Röyksopp
25	No Bravery	James Blunt		59	Look On The Floor (Hypnotic Tango)	Bananarama
26	Face To Face	Brídín Brennan		60	Headlock	Imogen Heap
27	Head Shop	Tina Dico		61	Don't Do Me Any Favours	a-ha
28	Nocturn/Aerial	Kate Bush		62	Losing	Tina Dico
29	Is It Any Wonder?	Keane		63	Prayer	Hayley Westenra
30	Kiss You (Bailey Edit)	iiO		64	Wish U Were There/ Wish U Were Here	Bliss
31	Sorry	Madonna				
32	Just Be Me / Just Be (different titles)	Kirsty Hawkshaw / Tiësto				
33	Only This Moment	Röyksopp				
34	Satellite	Guster				

_2006_

#	Song Title	Artist
65	Die Nacht...Du Bist Nicht Allein	Schiller
66	Can't Resist	Texas
67	Integral	Pet Shop Boys
68	Love Oneself	Andy Bell w/ Claudia Brücken
69	Out Of My Mind	James Blunt
70	All Good Things (Come To An End)	Nelly Furtado
71	The Way I Feel	Oakenfold f/ Ryan Tedder
72	Face The Music	Conjure One
73	Keys To The World	Richard Ashcroft
74	謎 (Mystery)	Evonne (Hsu) 許慧欣
75	Bottom Of The Bottle / Song Noir	Jon Auer
76	Stromata	Charlotte Martin
77	Rip It Up	Tina Cousins
78	Will You Be Around	Platinum Weird
79	Faster Kill Pussycat	Oakenfold f/ Brittany Murphy
80	All I'm Made Of	Eliot
81	Move In My Direction	Bananarama
82	Me & U	Cassie
83	You Are The One/ Le Disko	Shiny Toy Guns
84	This Fine Social Scene	Zero 7 f/ Sia
85	Lovelight	Robbie Williams

#	Song Title	Artist
86	Lonely Night In NY	Robin Gibb
87	Different World (Taormina.Me)	Simple Minds
88	La Mirada Interior	Marian van de Wal
89	What Silence Said	Susheela Raman
90	Grace	Lisbeth Scott
91	Within Me	Lacuna Coil
92	Baby, I Know That You Know	SpiceHouse
93	The X	Kaskade
94	Crazy	Gnarls Barkley
95	Feel For You	Bananarama
96	My Mirror / Use Me	Tina Dico
97	本草綱目 (Herbalist Manual)	Jay Chou (周杰倫)
98	Hell's Coming With Me	Iris
99	We All Float	Hooverphonic
100	Rock Steady	All Saints
101	These Things	She Wants Revenge
2006 EXTRAS		
105	Congratulations	Blue October f/ Imogen Heap
112	Warm	The New Cars
114	Feelin' You	Jesse McCartney
117	Cross That Line	Rick Ro$$ f/ Akon
143	Hips Don't Lie	Shakira f/ Wyclef Jean
151	Glamorous	Fergie f/ Ludacris

2000s

#	Song Title	Artist		#	Song Title	Artist
1	The Way I Are	Timbaland f/ Keri Hilson, D.O.E. & Sebastian		34	Golden Skans	Klaxons
2	Falling Off A Log	Tracey Thorn		35	Machine	Josh Groban w/ Herbie Hancock
3	The King	Hard-Fi		36	Time To Let Go	Sally Shapiro
4	Power Of Three	Brídín Brennan		37	Glittering Cloud (Locusts)	Imogen Heap
5	We Need Love	Hard-Fi		38	The Rain/Never Took The Time	Akon
6	A-Z	Tracey Thorn		39	Apologize	Timbaland w/ OneRepublic
7	Now Or Never	Josh Groban		40	Sacrifice	Casey Stratton
8	I Am The Wind	Brigid Boden		41	Get To Know Me	Joe f/ Nas
9	Chances	Kosheen		42	L'Alba Di Domani	Tiromancino
10	Boring	The Pierces		43	Casino Royale/Sleep (two versions)	Sandra
11	Angoli Di Cielo	Tiromancino		44	Je Suis Un Homme	Zazie
12	Soulmate	Natasha Bedingfield		45	Gimme More	Britney Spears
13	You Are Loved (Don't Give Up)	Josh Groban		46	Pray	Brigid Boden
14	Amazing	Seal		47	Coloured Bedspread	Annie Lennox
15	Muddy Ground	The Charlatans (UK)		48	Bouncing Off Clouds	Tori Amos
16	All Black	Good Charlotte		49	Justify	ATB
17	Des Rails	Zazie		50	Not Fair	Kate Havnevik
18	Halcyon Days	Siobhan Donaghy		51	Number One In Heaven	Nemesis Rising
19	We Are One	Kelly Sweet		52	If I Can't Have You	Kubb
20	夜的第七章 (Twilight's Chapter Seven)	Jay Chou (周杰倫)		53	At The End Of Time	G-Spliff
21	Merry-Go-Round	Moya Brennan		54	I Will Be With You (Where The Lost Ones Go) (two versions)	Sarah Brightman f/ Chris Thompson or Paul Stanley
22	Maboroshi (まぼろし) (Phantom)	Garnet Crow		55	What Is It About Me	Sandra
23	Get Around To It	Tracey Thorn		56	What'd I Do Wrong?	G-Spliff
24	Damage	Kosheen		57	Relax, Take It Easy	Mika
25	Stars Align	Kaskade		58	Traffic And Weather	Fountains Of Wayne
26	Love Hurts	Incubus		59	Love Is The Journey	Brigid Boden
27	Everybody's Someone	LeAnn Rimes & Brian McFadden		60	Jimmy	M.I.A.
28	Love Or Lust	Kate Ryan		61	Sewn	The Feeling
29	Beautiful View	Brookville		62	Rehab	Rihanna
30	Mama's Room	Under The Influence Of Giants		63	Mer Du Japon / Redhead Girl	Air
31	Remain	Kubb				
32	Overkill	Kosheen				
33	Find A New Way	Young Love				

2000s

#	Song Title	Artist
64	Luz Sin Gravedad / See A Little Light (two versions)	Belinda (Peregrín)
65	5:55/AF607105	Charlotte Gainsbourg
66	Something Kinda Ooooh	Girls Aloud
67	Hell No	All Saints
68	Walking On Moonlight	Brookville
69	Medevac	Siobhan Donaghy
70	Bo'ee (Come With Me)	The Idan Raichel Project
71	Breakdown	Brídín Brennan
72	Forever	Meeky Rosie
73	Four In The Morning	Gwen Stefani
74	Home (Tonight)	Onetwo
75	It's Better To Have Loved	Temposhark f/ Imogen Heap
76	Déjame Gritar	Kudai
77	Dreamworld	Rilo Kiley
78	Watch Me Fall Apart	Hard-Fi
79	All The World	Fauxliage
80	I'm Impressed	They Might Be Giants
81	A Conversation With God	Darren Hayes
82	Ixtapa/Stairway To Heaven	Rodrigo y Gabriela
83	Yin Yang	Zazie
84	Christe Redemptor	State Of Grace (Paul Schwartz)

#	Song Title	Artist
85	Head Home	Midlake
86	Myriad Harbour	The New Pornographers
87	The Mating Game	Bitter:Sweet
88	Window Song	Finger Eleven
89	Kaleidoscope	Kate Havnevik
90	Like A Book	Kosheen
91	Undercover	Pete Yorn
92	Take Care	Tasmin Archer
93	City Of The Dead	The Charlatans (UK)
94	What Goes Around... Comes Around	Justin Timberlake
95	Better Already / Sucka Mofo	Northern State
96	Circles (Just My Good Time)	Busface f/ Mademoiselle E.B. (Sophie Ellis-Bextor)
97	Let's Be Alone	Charlotte Church
98	Starts With One	Shiny Toy Guns
99	Better Without You	Kelly Rowland
100	My Love	Justin Timberlake f/ T.I.
101	I Wanna Love You (I Wanna Fuck You)	Akon f/ Snoop Dogg
2007 EXTRAS		
103	Mesmerized	LIfehouse
105	Daydreamin'	Lupe Fiasco f/ Jill Scott
111	Sightlines	Rogue Wave
114	My Moon My Man	Feist

2000s

#	Song Title	Artist		#	Song Title	Artist
1	The Longest Road / (deadmau5 Vocal Remix)	Morgan Page f/ Lissie		33	Cobrastyle (Press Trigger) (two versions)	Teddybears f/ Mad Cobra / Robyn
2	Stepping Stone	Duffy		34	Strangers In The Wind	Cut Copy
3	I Remember	deadmau5 & Kaskade f/ Haley		35	Eyes Wide Open	The B-52s
4	Miles Away	Madonna		36	Inner City Pressure	Flight Of The Conchords
5	Sehnsucht	Schiller w/ Xavier Naidoo		37	4 Minutes	Madonna f/ Justin Timberlake & Timbaland
6	Touch Me	Cass Fox (Cassandra)		38	Move For Me	Kaskade f/ Haley Gibby / deadmau5
7	Unexpected Intro/ Hello Heartbreak	Michelle Williams		39	Expedition Impossible	Hooverphonic
8	Juliet Of The Spirits	The B-52s		40	Rivermouth	Helicopter Girl
9	It Doesn't Get Much Better Than This	Helicopter Girl		41	Speakerphone	Kylie (Minogue)
10	Let's Begin	Roan / Kaskade		42	There I'll Be	Valeriya
11	Into The Nightlife	Cyndi Lauper		43	Pocketful Of Sunshine / Angel	Natasha Bedingfield
12	Devil Wouldn't Recognize You	Madonna		44	À L'infini (Remix)	Lisa Reagan
13	Angel City	Helicopter Girl		45	Step Into The Light	Darren Hayes
14	When The Lights Go Out	Foxy Brown		46	Covered	Uh Huh Her
15	Fame (The Game)	Donna Summer		47	Appelle Mon Numéro	Mylène Farmer
16	Above The Northern Lights	Mannheim Steamroller f/ Gene Nery		48	If It's In My Mind, It's On My Face	Seal
17	Enjoy The Ride	Morcheeba (w/ Judie Tzuke)		49	A Baby Changes Everything	Faith Hill
18	The Right Life	Seal		50	Damaged	Danity Kane
19	Rule The World	Take That		51	Fleurs Du Mal	Sarah Brightman
20	Don't Stop Now	Emmy Rossum		52	Kim & Jessie	M83
21	Par Les Paupières	Alizée		53	Ella Elle L'a	Kate Ryan
22	Bare Hands	Delta Goodrem		54	Let Me Love You	Schiller w/ Kim Sanders
23	Gentle Storm	Hooverphonic		55	How Would You Like It	Jem
24	The Moth & The Flame	Les Deux Love Orchestra		56	Burden Of Beauty	Lunascape
25	A Kind Of Love	Sing-Sing		57	Deviant Ingredient	The B-52s
26	Should You Return	Copeland		58	Let It Rock	Kevin Rudolf f/ Lil Wayne
27	Try Not To Remember	Sheryl Crow		59	Don't Give Up	Ferras
28	Overtures To Ecstasy/ Ecstasy	Les Deux Love Orchestra		60	Raging Storm / Lay Me Down	Cyndi Lauper
29	Daddy Dear	Cass Fox		61	Dark Side Of Night	Foxboro Hot Tubs
30	Sensitized	Kylie (Minogue)		62	Giants Building Giants	Helicopter Girl
31	Outside	Lunascape		63	No Air	Jordin Sparks w/ Chris Brown
32	I Feel Safe	X-Perience		64	Personal Heaven	X-Perience f/ Midge Ure

2000s

#	Song Title	Artist		#	Song Title	Artist
65	Don't Believe In Love	Dido		88	Gained The World	Morcheeba
66	6 Of 1 Thing	Craig David		89	A Modern Girl	Sing-Sing
67	Loaded	Seal		90	Bad Girl	Danity Kane f/ Missy Elliott
68	Dance Like There's No Tomorrow	Paula Abdul & Randy Jackson		91	I Stand	Idina Menzel
69	Give It 2 Me	Madonna		92	Slow Me Down	Emmy Rossum
70	Blue Chair	Morcheeba (w/ Judie Tzuke)		93	L.I.L.Y.	Kate Ryan
71	Mercy	Duffy		94	Melody	Sharleen Spiteri
72	Endless Love I / II (神话) (美麗的神話 I / II)	Jackie Chan & Kim Hee-Seon		95	Where Are You?	Valeriya
73	Take Back The City	Snow Patrol		96	The Lightning Strike: (i) What If This Storm Ends?	Snow Patrol
74	Spiralling	Keane		97	Rapture	Toby Emerson
75	FM Air	Zazie		98	Crawl, End Crawl	Four Tet
76	Crimewave	Crystal Castles vs. Health		99	No One / Out Of Control	Valeriya
77	Just Dance	Lady Gaga f/ Colby O'Donis		100	Corporate Cannibal	Grace Jones
78	Underworld	Barry Gibb		101	Love Is Gone	David Guetta f/ Chris Willis
79	Trains And Winter Rains	Enya			**2008 EXTRAS**	
80	She's Too Much	Duran Duran		108	American Boy	Estelle f/ Kanye West
81	None Shall Pass	Aesop Rock		111	What's Your Name	Usher f/ will.i.am
82	No More Rain	Kylie (Minogue)		112	We Walk	The Ting Tings
83	La Passion	Fabien Cahen & Zazie		117	This Is The Life	Amy Macdonald
84	Mademoiselle Juliette	Alizée		119	Jai Ho / Jai Ho! (You Are My Destiny)	A .R. Rahman f/ Sukwinder Singh & Tanvi Shah / The Pussycat Dolls f/ Nicole Scherzinger
85	Worry Free Lifestyle	These Modern Socks		120	Black & Gold	Sam Sparro
86	Hot Stuff (Let's Dance)	Craig David		122	Electric Feel	MGMT
87	Stoned In Love	Chicane f/ Tom Jones				

#	Song Title	Artist	#	Song Title	Artist
1	Goodbye	Balligomingo	35	The Keeper	Yanni f/ Leslie Mills
2	Rain On Your Parade	Duffy	36	Safe	Olivia Broadfield
3	We Are The People	Empire Of The Sun	37	Foot Of The Mountain	a-ha
4	So Happy I Could Die	Lady Gaga	38	Back To The Start	Lily Allen
5	The Bandstand	a-ha	39	My First Love	Craig David
6	Better Alone	Carolina Liar	40	Strip	Brooke Hogan
7	Dusk Till Dawn	Ladyhawke	41	Unusual You	Britney Spears
8	Vision One	Röyksopp (f/ Anneli Drecker)	42	Bodies	Robbie Williams
9	Merry Christmas Mr. Lawrence – FYI	Utada Hikaru	43	Tears Of An Angel	RyanDan
10	Common Reaction	Uh Huh Her	44	Gold Guns Girls	Metric
11	Fire To Your Plain	Tori Amos	45	I Like It Rough	Lady Gaga
12	Cómo Te Extraño	Fonseca	46	R U Feeling Me	Sandra
13	Love Etc.	Pet Shop Boys	47	Here On Earth/ Always Near	Tiësto f/ Cary Brothers
14	Life Like	The Rosebuds	48	Telephone	Lady Gaga f/ Beyoncé
15	Poker Face	Lady Gaga	49	Symphony	Susan Borges & The Broken Singles
16	Sunny Mystery	a-ha	50	Rock That Body	The Black Eyed Peas
17	Return The Favor	Keri Hilson f/ Timbaland	51	Let The Feelings Go	AnnaGrace
18	Tears Of Yesterday	Hoobastank	52	On A Good Day	OceanLab
19	Lifeboats	Snow Patrol	53	Whataya Want From Me	Adam Lambert
20	The Sound Of Missing You	Ameerah	54	Cold Cold Summer	Shontelle
21	Bottles&Cans	Rehab	55	Far From Home	Hinder
22	Crash And Burn	Nadia Ali	56	Everywhere	Common f/ Martina Topley-Bird
23	Doesn't Everybody	LeAnn Rimes	57	Believe Again	Delta Goodrem
24	Susan's Industry	Helicopter Girl	58	More Than A Dream	Pet Shop Boys
25	This Must Be It	Röyksopp	59	History	Kleerup f/ Linda Sundblad
26	Magic	Ladyhawke	60	Alive	The Black Eyed Peas
27	The Tree Knows Everything	Adam F f/ Tracey Thorn	61	Maggie Creek Road	Reba (McEntire)
28	Stuck On Repeat	Little Boots	62	Symmetry	Little Boots
29	Troublemaker	Akon f/ Sweet Rush	63	Miracle	Sally Shapiro
30	With Every Heartbeat	Robyn f/ Kleerup	64	Graffiti Soul	Simple Minds
31	It's The Way You Love Me	David Guetta/Kelly Rowland	65	What If	Sandra
32	Spinning	Balligomingo	66	I Gotta Feeling	The Black Eyed Peas
33	Crashing Down	Olivia Broadfield	67	Like The Sun	RyanDan f/ Bailey & Judie Tzuke
34	Hearts Collide	Little Boots			

#	Song Title	Artist
68	Star Of Wonder / Our New Year	Tori Amos
69	Fifth Moon	Maggie Reilly
70	New In Town	Little Boots
71	Save Your Love	Sally Shapiro
72	First Train Home	Imogen Heap
73	This Boy's In Love	The Presets
74	Moscow Underground	Simple Minds
75	Tête À Tête	Sandra
76	This Is How It Goes (Kaskade's Grand Club Edit)	Kaskade / Haley (Gibby)
77	Walking On A Dream	Empire Of The Sun
78	The Best Revenge	Fischerspooner
79	In For The Kill	La Roux
80	If There's A Rocket Tie Me To It	Snow Patrol
81	We Cry	The Script
82	Eva	Mónica Naranjo
83	Last Days Of Disco	Robbie Williams
84	The Way It Used To Be	Pet Shop Boys
85	The Girl And The Robot	Röyksopp (w/ Robyn)
86	Mad World	Adam Lambert
87	Four Long Years	Wire
88	Forgiveness, The Enviable Trait	PlayRadioPlay! (Analog Rebellion)

#	Song Title	Artist
89	When Love Takes Over	David Guetta & Kelly Rowland
90	Long Gone	Chris Cornell
91	Light Travels	Simple Minds
92	No One Will Ever Love You	Susan Borges & The Broken Singles
93	Magical / Mathematics	Little Boots
94	Motherlover	The Lonely Island f/ Justin Timberlake
95	S.O.S. (Let The Music Play)	Jordin Sparks
96	Looking For My Name	Mylène Farmer + Moby
97	Two Silver Trees	Calexico
98	Love, Where Is Your Fire?	Brooke Fraser
99	Love Don't Live Here	Ladyhawke
100	Williams' Blood	Grace Jones
101	Fine Print	Nadia Ali
2009 EXTRAS		
108	Celebration	Madonna / Oakenfold
119	Cue The Rain	Queen Latifah
121	Evacuate The Dancefloor	Cascada
123	Heartless	Kanye West
125	3	Britney Spears
145	Bad Romance	Lady Gaga

2000s

#	Song Title	Artist
1	Sex And Violence	Scissor Sisters
2	Fight For You	Morgan Page f/ Lissie
3	Traces Remain	Morgan Page f/ Jan Burton
4	OMG	Usher f/ will.i.am
5	Feels So Good	Armin van Buuren f/ Nadia Ali
6	Aphrodite	Kylie (Minogue)
7	History	Groove Armada
8	3 Words	Cheryl Cole f/ will.i.am
9	In The Dark	Morgan Page
10	Can You Feel It	Timbaland f/ Esthero & Sebastian
11	Save Me	Orchestral Manoeuvres In The Dark (w/ Aretha Franklin)
12	Kentish Town	Tracey Thorn
13	Happy?	Cause & Effect
14	All That I Have	Findlay Brown
15	Everything Is Beautiful	Kylie (Minogue)
16	Love With A Stranger	Marié Digby
17	Where You Are	JES
18	Wonderful Life	Hurts
19	Butterfly, Butterfly (The Last Hurrah)	a-ha
20	Photograph	Rihanna f/ will.i.am
21	If I'm Any Closer	Seal
22	Weight Of My Mistakes	Seal
23	Unleash The Beat	JES
24	Burn It Up	Jessie James
25	It's Been So Long	AM
26	Your Love	Keane
27	Monster	Lady Gaga
28	DHDQ	Andy Bell
29	Just For Tonight	Groove Armada
30	Believe / Strange Condition	Morgan Page (f/ Lissie)
31	Can't Hear My Eyes	Ariel Pink's Haunted Graffiti
32	Archer's Arrows	Crowded House

#	Song Title	Artist
33	Happy Hour	Cheryl Cole
34	Even Though	Morcheeba
35	Night Life	Scissor Sisters
36	Howl	Florence + The Machine
37	Love Can Kill You	BT
38	Starstruck	Robbie Williams
39	The Best	Michael Bolton f/ Ne-Yo
40	Clear Skies	Keane
41	Commander	Kelly Rowland
42	DJ Got Us Fallin' In Love	Usher f/ Pitbull
43	This Is Who I Am	Cause & Effect
44	Fly On The Wall	t.A.T.u.
45	Tell Me Why	Morgan Page f/ Angela McCluskey
46	Could You Believe	ATB
47	Try	Schiller w/ Nadia Ali
48	Like Ice	Conjure One
49	Same High	Uh Huh Her
50	Acts Of Man	Midlake
51	Rain On Me	Cheryl Cole
52	Bulletproof Heart	Lostboy! AKA Jim Kerr
53	Soldier Of Love	Sade
54	Will You Be There?	Andy Bell
55	Harder You Get	Scissor Sisters
56	Let It Rise	Schiller w/ Midge Ure
57	Difficult For Weirdos	Robbie Williams
58	Don't Stop	Annie
59	Playing With Madness	Schiller w/ Mia Bergström
60	Dust In Gravity	Delerium f/ Keesha Turner
61	In Sleep	Lissie
62	Teenage Dream	Katy Perry
63	Heart Of Stone	The Raveonettes
64	Human Reactor	Kaskade f/ Polina
65	Higher (two versions)	Taio Cruz f/ Kylie (Minogue) or Travie McCoy
66	Never Stop	Reni Lane

#	Song Title	Artist
67	Tonight	Mary J. Blige & Akon
68	Clap Your Hands	Sia
69	You Can Dance	Bryan Ferry
70	Something Like This	Scissor Sisters
71	Get Outta My Way	Kylie (Minogue)
72	Drive Me Crazy	Gyptian
73	Murder My Heart	Michael Bolton f/ Lady Gaga
74	Waves Of Change	Samantha James
75	Closer To Real	Iris
76	Nothing Wrong	Emma Shapplin
77	Les Collines (Never Leave You)	Alizée
78	Loose Change/On Time	Disco Biscuits / f/ Tu Phace
79	Such A Long Time / Lovesong	JES
80	Fortune	Little Dragon
81	Sea Dreams/Misery Loves Companies	Dreaming In Stereo
82	Why Does The Wind?	Tracey Thorn
83	Get Away With Murder	Jeffree Star
84	Pass Out	Chris Brown f/ Eva Simons
85	Hunt	Goldfrapp
86	My Love Is Better	Annie
87	Give It To Me Right	Melanie Fiona
88	Keep Drivin'	Katharine McPhee

#	Song Title	Artist
89	Need You Now	Lady Antebellum
90	Gotta Boyfriend?	Frankmusik
91	No One's Gonna Love You	Renée Fleming
92	Superbad (11:34)	Travie McCoy
93	On A Hot Summer Night/ Just Another Summer (Hebrew Version)	Yehonathan
94	The Ghost Inside	Broken Bells
95	Take A Moment	Armin van Buuren
96	Spaceship	Benny Benassi f/ Kelis, Jean-Baptiste & apl. de.ap
97	What You Get	Junior Caldera f/ Billy Bryan
98	Bottles / Back In Time	V V Brown
99	Eleven Days	David Byrne & Fatboy Slim f/ Cyndi Lauper
100	I Will Follow You	Schiller f/ Henree
101	Heartbeat	Nneka

#	2010 EXTRAS	
104	Sweet Dreams	Beyoncé
105	Dancing On My Own	Robyn
109	TiK ToK	Ke$ha
112	Only Girl (In The World)	Rihanna
115	Sundown Syndrome	Tame Impala
125	Heartbreak Warfare	John Mayer
165	Panamericana	Gotan Project

#	Song Title	Artist
1	Sunday Version 02	Schiller f/ Despina Vandi
2	White Horse	Jessica 6
3	You Will Be Mine	Lenka
4	Somewhere With You	Kenny Chesney
5	The Hours On The Fields	Emma Shapplin
6	Wine Song	Barry Manilow
7	Starry Eyed	Ellie Goulding
8	Set Fire To The Rain	Adele
9	Crimson Skies	The Cinematic Orchestra f/ Lou Rhodes
10	Rocketeer	Far☆East Movement f/ Ryan Tedder
11	Lights	Ellie Goulding
12	All I Need	iiO
13	You'll Be Mine	The Pierces
14	Happiness Is Alien	Cause & Effect
15	You And I	Washed Out f/ Caroline Polachek
16	Norwegian Skies	Hooverphonic
17	When I'm Alone	Lissie
18	Wild Man	Kate Bush
19	In The Air	Morgan Page, Sultan + Ned Shepard and BT f/ Angela McCluskey
20	Under The Sheets	Ellie Goulding
21	Sunday	Hurts
22	My Boy	Duffy
23	Nightcall	Kavinsky f/ Lovefoxxx
24	Burning The Harbor	Kate Voegele
25	Far Away	Washed Out
26	Circle The Drain	Katy Perry
27	Electric Chapel	Lady Gaga
28	Oui Mais... Non	Mylène Farmer
29	Starlight	Sophie Ellis-Bextor
30	Pulse	Orchestral Manoeuvres In The Dark
31	Number One	Chrisette Michele
32	One Two Three	Hooverphonic
33	Stereo Love	Edward Maya & Vika Jigulina

#	Song Title	Artist
34	Don't Stop (Color On The Walls)	Foster The People
35	I See Stars	The Knux f/ Jack Davey
36	Atlantic	The Midway State
37	It'll Be Like	iiO
38	Nothing New Under The Sun	Thomas Dolby
39	Now That I'm Real (How Does It Feel?)	Chad Valley
40	See The New Hong Kong	Josie Cotton
41	Katy On A Mission	Katy B
42	Llove	Kaskade f/ Haley
43	Never Let Me Go	The Human League
44	Heavy Metal Lover	Lady Gaga
45	Better Than Love	Hurts
46	Mirage	Ladytron
47	Waiting For You	The Rosebuds
48	I Dream In Colour	Conjure One
49	Don't Look Now	Far☆East Movement f/ Keri Hilson
50	Summertrain	Greyson Chance
51	Bright Lights Bigger City	CeeLo Green
52	Slow Motion	Holy Ghost!
53	A Whole Lotta Love Run Riot	Erasure
54	What's Next	Donell Jones f/ Inessa
55	I Wrote The Book	Beth Ditto
56	Animal	Ellie Goulding
57	Beautiful People	Chris Brown & Benny Benassi
58	Prisoner Of Love	Jessica 6 f/ Antony Hegarty (ANOHNI)
59	Barbra Streisand	Duck Sauce
60	Together	Pet Shop Boys
61	Rolling In The Deep	Adele
62	Flower Of The Mountain / Song Of Solomon (2011)	Kate Bush
63	久遠の河 (River Of Eternity) (Red Cliff theme)	alan (Alan Dawa Dolma) (阿兰)

2010s

#	Song Title	Artist
64	Wait & See	Holy Ghost!
65	S&M	Rihanna
66	Night By Night	Chromeo
67	Dystopia (The Earth Is On Fire)	YACHT
68	MoneyGrabber	Fitz And The Tantrums
69	Philosophy	Uh Huh Her
70	Promises	Andain
71	Where You Are	ATB f/ Kate Louise Smith
72	Do It In The AM	Frankmusik f/ Far☆East Movement
73	Leave A Light On	Duran Duran
74	Changes	Dirty Vegas
75	How's Never	Ivy
76	All I Can See Is The Face Of Bruce Lee	Josie Cotton
77	Hanging On / Johnny Belinda	Active Child
78	Determinate / Breakthrough	Lemonade Mouth Cast
79	Life's What You Make It	Duncan Sheik
80	Love Is Found	Sade
81	The Day Is Coming	My Morning Jacket
82	Judas	Lady Gaga
83	Intro/Ghosts	Fefe Dobson
84	Holiday	iiO
85	Love You Like A Love Song	Selena Gomez & The Scene

#	Song Title	Artist
86	Sun Of A Gun	Oh Land
87	Mussels	Modern Archetypes
88	Call My Name	Sultan & Ned Shepard f/ Nadia Ali
89	Revolution	Sophie Ellis-Bextor
90	The Future, The Past, And Forever After	Orchestral Manoeuvres In The Dark
91	Perfect Nightmare	Shontelle
92	August Town	Etana
93	No Church In The Wild	Jay-Z & Kanye West f/ Frank Ocean
94	21st Century	Dirty Vegas
95	Season's Trees	Danger Mouse + Daniele Luppi f/ Norah Jones
96	Shine	Cause & Effect
97	Lightning	The Midway State
98	Baby	Alcazar
99	Zombie	Natalia Kills
100	Pumped Up Kicks	Foster The People
101	Here To Stay	Lenka
2011 EXTRAS		
103	Gone	Nelly f/ Kelly Rowland
107	Last Name London	Theophilus London
114	Busted	Wanda Jackson
126	Wintersun	Brendan Perry
145	On The Floor	Jennifer Lopez f/ Pitbull
170	Moves Like Jagger	Maroon 5 f/ Christina Aguilera

2010S

#	Song Title	Artist	#	Song Title	Artist
1	Yeah Yeah	Cheryl Cole f/ Travie McCoy	33	Timebomb	Kylie Minogue
2	State Of The Art	Gotye	34	Fire In The House	Hard-Fi
3	Karmatron	Elton John Vs PNAU	35	Consciousness Of Love	Delerium f/ Stef Lang
4	Dark Star	Poliça	36	Let You Go	Ferry Corsten f/ Sarah Bettens
5	Casualties Of War	Gossip	37	Wrong Opinion	Chairlift
6	Losing	Joe	38	Troubleman	Electric Guest
7	Hanging On	Ellie Goulding (f/ Tinie Tempah)	39	Love Is Real	Theophilus London
8	Love Is War	Joe McElderry	40	Annie You Save Me	Graffiti6
9	Insecurity	Scars On 45	41	Wrecking Ball	Frankmusik
10	Lessons In Love / Lessons In Love (All Day, All Night) (two versions)	Neon Trees f/ Kaskade / Kaskade & Neon Trees	42	Good Intent	Kimbra
11	Breathing	Jason Derulo	43	Some Girls	Madonna
12	ABCDario	Fonseca	44	A Face Like That	Pet Shop Boys
13	Many Colors	Uh Huh Her	45	Awake	Electric Guest
14	Keep The Sun Away	Morten Harket	46	Featherlight	Skye
15	Video	Morgan Page f/ Tegan and Sara	47	Show Me Love	School Of Seven Bells
16	Chokehold	Adam Lambert	48	Little Dreams	Ellie Goulding
17	Skyfall	Adele	49	Fallen Empires	Snow Patrol
18	Ghost Tonight	Chairlift	50	Straight Back	Washed Out
19	Every Little Lie	Skye	51	Outlaws Of Love	Adam Lambert
20	Candy	Thomas White	52	Inevitable	Scissor Sisters
21	Only If For A Night	Florence + The Machine	53	Observations	The Raveonettes
22	Girl Gone Wild	Madonna	54	I Owe You This	Chad Valley f/ Twin Shadow
23	Just Believe It	Morten Harket	55	Keep It For Your Own	Pop Etc
24	Broken English	Adam Lambert	56	You Ain't Seen Nothin' Yet	Lisa Marie Presley
25	Tightly	Kosheen	57	One More Night	Maroon 5
26	Carry Me	Morgan Page And Nadia Ali	58	Waste	Kosheen
27	Alive	Schiller w/ Adam Young	59	Between Me & The Moon	Sandra
28	Good Morning To The Night	Elton John Vs PNAU	60	Body Work	Morgan Page f/ Tegan And Sara
29	Tomorrow's Started	Jason Lytle	61	Liar	Haley Reinhart
30	Power's Out	Nicole Scherzinger & Sting	62	Marstorm	Uh Huh Her
31	Beautiful Killer	Madonna	63	Make Me Say Yes	Gloria Estefan
32	Form	Poliça	64	Blue Jeans	Lana Del Rey
			65	Leaving	Pet Shop Boys
			66	Turn Up The Sound	Andain
			67	Diamonds	Rihanna

#	Song Title	Artist
68	Amnesia	Dead Can Dance
69	Flutes	Hot Chip
70	Looking 4 Myself	Usher f/ Luke Steele
71	Human	Ellie Goulding
72	Nakshi Mrembo	Alikiba
73	Edge Of Evolution	Alanis Morissette
74	Crystals	Magic Wands
75	The Boys	Keane
76	Stone In My Heart	Graffiti6
77	Fist Teeth Money	Poliça
78	The Weight Of Love	Snow Patrol
79	Room For Happiness	Kaskade f/ Skylar Grey
80	This Head I Hold	Electric Guest
81	Give Me All Your Luvin'	Madonna f/ Nicki Minaj & M.I.A.
82	Rolling The Dice	Sander van Doorn w/ Sidney Samson & Nadia Ali
83	Brilliant	Ultravox
84	Burn Money Burn	Morten Harket
85	One By One	The Ting Tings
86	Involved	Gossip
87	The Actor	Morgan Page f/ Richard Walters

#	Song Title	Artist
88	DJ, Ease My Mind	Niki And The Dove
89	Sweet Nothing	Calvin Harris f/ Florence Welch
90	Ultramarin	Schiller
91	Scream	Usher
92	Paddling Out	Miike Snow
93	Chasing The Sun	The Wanted
94	Live Your Life	Yuna
95	Somebody That I Used To Know	Gotye f/ Kimbra
96	Ruin	Cat Power
97	Don't Let Me Die	Bobby Brown
98	Don't You Worry Child	Swedish House Mafia f/ John Martin
99	Leave Your World Behind	Andy Moor f/ Hysteria!
100	Masterpiece	Madonna
101	Perfect World	Gossip
2012 EXTRAS		
111	On'n'On	Justice
122	Reboot The Mission	The Wallflowers f/ Mick Jones
127	Good Feeling	Flo Rida (w/ Etta James)
140	How Quickly You Forget	Eli Young Band

2013

#	Song Title	Artist		#	Song Title	Artist
1	Horizon Flame	Alison Moyet		35	Elle A Dit	Mylène Farmer
2	Lux/DNA	Empire Of The Sun		36	En Brazos De Ella	Pablo Alborán
3	Remind Yourself	Alison Moyet		37	Within	Daft Punk
4	Madness	Kate Ryan		38	Only You	Ellie Goulding
5	Epic Shores	Schiller w/ Meredith Call		39	End Of Night	Dido
6	I Was A Fool	Tegan And Sara		40	Broken Record	Little Boots
7	Long Gone	The-Dream (Terius Nash)		41	The Game Of Love	Daft Punk
8	Awakening	Empire Of The Sun		42	Stay Awake	Ellie Goulding & Madeon
9	Wicked Games	The Weeknd		43	Atmosphere	Kaskade
10	Sonne	Schiller w/ Unheilig		44	The Conversation	Texas
11	Two Coins	City And Colour		45	Love Dance	Mylène Farmer
12	Applause	Lady Gaga		46	Somebody Loves Somebody	Céline Dion
13	Chain My Name	Poliça		47	All I Know	Washed Out
14	Under Control	Ellie Goulding		48	The Song In Your Heart	Clannad
15	Face Of Danger	Morcheeba f/ Chali 2NA		49	Must Be The Love	BT w/ Arty & Nadia Ali
16	I'll Be Around	Empire Of The Sun		50	四季列車 (Four Seasons Train)	Jay Chou (周杰倫)
17	All For You	Little Boots		51	Heart's A Mess	Gotye
18	High Life	Skye		52	My Blood	Ellie Goulding
19	Go Dreaming	Dido		53	Walking On Air	Katy Perry
20	Brave Enough	Clannad f/ Duke Special		54	Missing You	Kaskade & School Of Seven Bells
21	Cola	Lana Del Rey		55	Monkey Me	Mylène Farmer
22	Ritual	Ellie Goulding		56	Desert Empire	Schiller
23	Magnetized	Johnny Hates Jazz		57	Bonnie & Clyde	Tricky
24	Closer	Sarah Brightman (w/ Mike Oldfield)		58	Dark Again	Gold Fields
25	Celebrate	Empire Of The Sun		59	Island	Whitewaits
26	If It Doesn't Rain	Sally Shapiro		60	Bedi	Deep Forest f/ Olyza
27	Further Away (Romance Police)	Lissie		61	Stars Dance	Selena Gomez
28	Instant Crush	Daft Punk f/ Julian Casablancas		62	Days Are Gone	HAIM
29	Days Turn Into Nights	Delerium f/ Michael Logen		63	Changeling	Alison Moyet
30	Closest I Could Get	Gold Fields		64	Get Lucky	Daft Punk f/ Pharrell Williams
31	Stars At Night	Maggie Reilly		65	All My Life	Sally Shapiro
32	Walk To The Beat	Kate Ryan		66	No Part Of You	98°
33	Make It Wonderful	Erasure		67	Final Song	Orchestral Manoeuvres In The Dark
34	Confusion	Little Boots		68	Forever	HAIM

2010s

2013

#	Song Title	Artist
69	Liar Liar	Avicii (f/ Aloe Blacc & Blondfire)
70	Summertime Sadness (Cedric Gervais Mix)	Lana Del Rey
71	There'll Be No Tomorrow!	Erasure
72	Exile	Hurts
73	It All Feels Right	Washed Out
74	The Man I Knew	Dessa
75	Get A New One	Kosheen
76	Moonshine	Bruno Mars
77	Seré	Pablo Alborán
78	Intro (In The Hearts Tonight)/Return Of A Queen	Dawn Richard
79	Spectrum	Zedd f/ Matthew Koma
80	Tears In The Rain	The Weeknd
81	Leggo	B. Smyth f/ 2 Chainz
82	My Songs Know What You Did In The Dark (Light Em Up)	Fall Out Boy
83	7th Heaven	Sarah Brightman
84	Animal	Berlin
85	Love Into The Light	Ke$ha
86	Hell	Pet Shop Boys
87	You Belong To You	Johnny Hates Jazz
88	Line Of Fire	Junip

#	Song Title	Artist
89	Show Me The Way	Allure f/ JES
90	Scream & Shout	will.i.am f/ Britney Spears
91	So Much To Prove	Fantasia
92	Burn	Ellie Goulding
93	Hurricane	MS MR
94	Gaudete	Erasure
95	Falling	HAIM
96	Introduction/Hail Bop	Django Django
97	Cold Nites	How To Dress Well
98	I Wanna Be Your Hand	Holy Ghost!
99	Safe And Sound	Capital Cities
100	Young Lady	Kid Cudi f/ Father John Misty
101	Blizzard / Grand Canyon	Kavinsky
	2013 EXTRAS	
104	I Love It	Icona Pop f/ Charli XCX
106	Te Perdiste Mi Amor	Thalía f/ Prince Royce
110	Atomium	Karl Bartos
111	I Don't Want To See	STRFKR
112	Snow	Chrisette Michele
120	Scene Of The Crime	Placebo
125	Science/Visions	CHVRCH≡S
127	Who Did That To You?	John Legend
129	Reflektor	Arcade Fire

2014

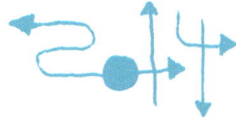

#	Song Title	Artist
1	The Changing Lights	Broken Bells
2	Thinking Of You	The Night VI
3	Grace	The Crystal Method f/ LeAnn Rimes
4	Feeling Is Gone	Active Child
5	Holding On For Life	Broken Bells
6	La La La	Naughty Boy f/ Sam Smith
7	NYC	Dido
8	Going Home	Ásgeir
9	Bloodstream / (Rudimental Remix)	Ed Sheeran / & Rudimental
10	Innocence	Uh Huh Her
11	할말 있어요 (Gotta Talk To U)	Seungri
12	An Open Heart	Bright Light Bright Light
13	Spiritual	Katy Perry
14	Do What U Want	Lady Gaga f/ R. Kelly
15	Win	Jarell Perry
16	Fine	Kylie (Minogue)
17	After The Disco	Broken Bells
18	Hypnotized	Morcheeba f/ Ana Tijoux
19	Happiness	Bright Light Bright Light
20	Subtle	Active Child f/ Mikky Ekko
21	Whatever We Started	Richard Marx
22	Love Me Harder	Ariana Grande & The Weeknd
23	I Heard The Owl Call My Name	Snowbird
24	Dust Clears	Clean Bandit f/ Noonie Bao
25	The Old And The Young	Midlake
26	Liar Liar	Cris Cab
27	Written In Reverse	Tiësto & Hardwell f/ Matthew Koma
28	It's Going Down	Midlake
29	Monument / (T.I.E. Version) (two versions)	Röyksopp & Robyn
30	Can't Take It Back	Lissie
31	Break Of Day	Maggie Reilly
32	Lovers On The Sun	David Guetta f/ Sam Martin
33	Ordinary Love	U2
34	Love Part II	Bright Light Bright Light
35	You Hoooo!!!	Seungri
36	Against The World	Morgan Page & Michael S.
37	Amalfi	Hooverphonic
38	阿貓阿狗 (Cat & Dog)	陳奕迅 (Eason Chan)
39	Nice And Slow	Max Frost
40	넘버나인 (No. 9)	T-ara (티아라)
41	Prayer In C (Robin Schulz Mix)	Lilly Wood & The Prick
42	ARTPOP	Lady Gaga
43	Minds Without Fear	Imogen Heap
44	Do It Again	Röyksopp & Robyn
45	The Habit	Lissie
46	Spilling Lines	Poliça
47	Footprints	Tiësto f/ Cruikshank
48	Sordid Affair	Röyksopp f/ Man Without Country
49	Sit! Stay! Wait! Down! / Love Story	Namie Amuro (安室奈美惠)
50	Million Miles	Kylie (Minogue)
51	Are We Connected	Midge Ure
52	Still Holding On	Conjure One f/ Aruna
53	The Heart Wants What It Wants	Selena Gomez
54	Ventre Della Città	Mario Venuti
55	Your Love's Keepin' Me Tonight	Blake Rayne
56	Provider/Provider Reprise	Midlake
57	Alive	Namie Amuro
58	Driving Me Wild	Bryan Ferry
59	Donatella/Fashion!	Lady Gaga
60	West Coast	Lana Del Rey
61	Monsters	Sarah McLachlan
62	Outside	Calvin Harris f/ Ellie Goulding

2010s

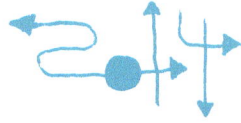

#	Song Title	Artist
63	Mai Saputo Il Tuo Nome	Tiromancino
64	Save Your Tears	Kosheen
65	Hustle Me	Uh Huh Her
66	First Time	Jarell Perry
67	I Want To Drag You Around	Blondie
68	All I Feel Is You	Natalia Safran & Mick Jaroszyk
69	Too Wild	Afrojack f/ Wiz Khalifa + Devin Cruise
70	Feel It	Bright Light Bright Light
71	Netzwerk (Falls Like Rain)	Klangkarussell
72	Hurt You	Toni Braxton & Babyface
73	Dead Of Night	Erasure
74	Fragili	Club Dogo f/ Arisa
75	Lifeline	Imogen Heap
76	How To Make A Heart	Bright Light Bright Light
77	Fireflies	Lange w/ Cate Kanell
78	Polygon Dust	Porter Robinson f/ Lemaitre
79	'Cos You're Beautiful	Dannii Minogue
80	Shiiine	Uh Huh Her
81	Yesterday	David Guetta f/ Bebe Rexha
82	I Had This Thing	Röyksopp f/ Jamie Irrepressible
83	Sissy That Walk	RuPaul
84	Chariots	Mike Oldfield
85	Jealous	Nick Jonas

#	Song Title	Artist
86	Animals	Maroon 5
87	Il Tramonto	Mario Venuti
88	Happy Idiot	TV On The Radio
89	Blonde	Alizée
90	Ice Age (deadmau5 Remix)	How To Destroy Angels / deadmau5
91	Tribute	John Newman
92	Let's Go	Namie Amuro
93	Rimbaud Eyes	Dum Dum Girls
94	One In The Chamber	Salaam Remi f/ Akon
95	Fall In Love	Phantogram
96	Emotions	Jennifer Lopez
97	Extraordinary	Clean Bandit f/ Sharna Bass
98	Intro/Animal Urges	Lo-Fang
99	Renaissance Girls	Oh Land
100	The Walker	Fitz And The Tantrums
101	Blame	Calvin Harris f/ John Newman

#	Song Title	Artist
2014 EXTRAS		
111	A Rose By Any Name	Blondie f/ Beth Ditto
114	Cool Kids	Echosmith
115	Waves	Mr. Probz
116	The Hands Of Love	Sam Roberts Band
117	Under Control	Calvin Harris, Alesso f/ Hurts
119	Hideaway	Kiesza
137	R.I.P. / Roc The Life	Rita Ora
139	Happy	Pharrell Williams

2010s

#	Song Title	Artist
1	Ocean Drive	Duke Dumont
2	My Eyes Are Still Bright	Scars On 45
3	I Do This For You	Giorgio Moroder f/ Marlene
4	Pray To God	Calvin Harris f/ HAIM
5	I Can Change	Brandon Flowers
6	Kaleidoscope	Hurts
7	Rewired	Iris
8	Get Things Done	Little Boots
9	How Deep Is Your Love	Calvin Harris & Disciples
10	Dangerous	David Guetta f/ Sam Martin
11	My Paradise	Julia Thompson w/ Zachary Zamarripa
12	Safe Till Tomorrow	Morgan Page f/ Angelika Vee
13	A Night To Remember	Betty Who
14	Love Story	Indila
15	Where You Belong	The Weeknd
16	Beautiful Goodbye	Richard Marx
17	Tesada'a Bemeen (تصدق بمين) (Who Do You Believe In?)	Elissa (إليسا)
18	Summer Breaking/ Daffodils	Mark Ronson f/ Kevin Parker
19	Can't Deny My Love	Brandon Flowers
20	Another Way	Iris
21	Trigger	Morgan Page f/ Rosette & Dirty Audio
22	Who Can You Trust	Ivy Levan
23	Love Me Like You Do	Ellie Goulding
24	High Society	Betty Who
25	One Last Night	Vaults
26	Black Sun	Death Cab For Cutie
27	Mini World	Indila
28	HeartBreakCity	Madonna
29	Your Secret's Safe	Julie Thompson w/ Super8 & Tab
30	Blue Sky Action	Above & Beyond f/ Alex Vargas
31	Stanley	Jazmine Sullivan

#	Song Title	Artist
32	Cheyenne	Jason Derulo
33	Open Heart	Morgan Page w/ Lissie
34	One Night Stand	Bryan Ferry
35	Things I Didn't Say	Adam Lambert
36	Human	Of Monsters And Men
37	Towards The Sun	Rihanna
38	Save Me	Röyksopp f/ Susanne Sundfør
39	Firestone	Kygo f/ Conrad Sewell
40	Writing's On The Wall	Sam Smith
41	Ray	Delerium f/ Kristy Thirsk
42	We're All We Need	Above & Beyond f/ Zoë Johnston
43	Loop De Li	Bryan Ferry
44	Got To Work It Out	Robyn & La Bagatelle Magique
45	Inside Out	Madonna
46	Adventure Of A Lifetime	Coldplay
47	Skulls	Röyksopp
48	Hearts	Jimmy Somerville
49	Earned It (Fifty Shades Of Grey)	The Weeknd
50	Laws Of Motion	Man Without Country f/ White Sea
51	Entitled	Leighton Meester
52	On My Mind	Ellie Goulding
53	Hello	Adele
54	Body Language	Marlon Roudette
55	All We Do	Oh Wonder
56	Charles Est Stone	Alizée
57	Sun Is Shining	Axwell Λ Ingrosso
58	Right Here, Right Now	Giorgio Moroder f/ Kylie Minogue
59	Generate	Eric Prydz
60	The Hanging Tree (Rebel Remix)	James Newton Howard f/ Jennifer Lawrence
61	Temptation	Active Child
62	When The Beat Drops Out	Marlon Roudette
63	Never Far Away	Active Child

#	Song Title	Artist
64	River From The Sky	The Weepies
65	74 Is The New 24	Giorgio Moroder
66	Ain't Nobody (Loves Me Better)	Felix Jaehn f/ Jasmine Thompson
67	Music To Watch Boys To	Lana Del Rey
68	Life On The Dancefloor	Seal
69	Leave Me Alone	MS MR
70	Thank You	Röyksopp
71	Paradise	Little Boots
72	Something Better	Audien f/ Lady Antebellum
73	What A Feeling	One Direction
74	Sweet Harmony	Man Without Country
75	World Order (Welcome To Tokyo Remix)	World Order
76	Can't Feel My Face	The Weeknd
77	Honest Town	Simple Minds
78	What About Love?	Traci Braxton
79	East Liberty	PARTYNEXTDOOR
80	Forest Fire	a-ha
81	Cold Front	Laura Welsh
82	The Humming	Enya
83	Ghost Town	Adam Lambert
84	Peanut Butter Jelly	Galantis
85	Desire	Years & Years
86	Before I Sleep	Joy Williams

#	Song Title	Artist
87	Are You With Me	Lost Frequencies
88	Sugar	Robin Schulz f/ Francesco Yates
89	Me & The Rhythm	Selena Gomez
90	Wayseer	Iris
91	Talking Body	Tove Lo
92	Cry Baby	The Neighbourhood
93	Does Not Bear Repeating	The Weepies
94	I Can't Think About It Now	Dawes
95	Hot To The Touch	Grace Potter
96	Echoes In Rain	Enya
97	Awake	Snoop Dogg
98	Ghosttown	Madonna
99	Do It Again	The Ting Tings
100	When The Lights Turn Out	Twin Shadow
101	Living For Love	Madonna
2015 EXTRAS		
103	Tutti Frutti	New Order f/ La Roux
111	Paradis Perdus	Christine And The Queens
124	You And The Beach / Night One	Luke Bryan
130	Hotline Bling	Drake
133	What In The World	Cynthia Erivo

#	Song Title	Artist
1	Fly	Andy Bell
2	Daylight Saving	Seal
3	Castle In The Snow	The Avener & Kadebostany
4	Corvette/Shelter	Sasha
5	Somebody	Salt Ashes
6	Kiss For Kiss	Bright Light Bright Light w/ Jake Shears
7	Starboy	The Weeknd f/ Daft Punk
8	In Common / (Kaskade Remix)	Alicia Keys / Alicia Keys x Kaskade
9	I Miss You	Adele
10	Badaboum	Hooverphonic
11	Padded Cell	Seal
12	Strange Species (異類的同類)	Tanya Chua (蔡健雅)
13	Only Love	Schiller w/ Emma Hewitt
14	Aphasia (失語者)	Tanya Chua (蔡健雅)
15	Let Yourself	Seal
16	Banks Of Allatoona	Larkin Poe
17	Hiding In A Song	Hooverphonic
18	Flesh Without Blood	Grimes
19	First	The Ready Set
20	100 Degrees	Kylie w/ Dannii Minogue
21	Faded / (Restrung Remix)	Alan Walker f/ Iselin Solheim
22	Rằng Em Mãi Ở Bên (That You Will Always Be By My Side)	Bích Phương
23	Go!	M83 f/ Mai Lan
24	You're My Favorite	Gwen Stefani
25	DJ (The Magic Key)	Dieselle
26	Broken Record	Krewella
27	New Song	Warpaint
28	Burn For You	Kreo'
29	Don't You Give Up On Me	Lissie
30	Young Rich And Radical	Club Cheval
31	Before The Fire	Santigold
32	Blue Fires	Delerium f/ Mimi Page
33	Brick England	Jean-Michel Jarre f/ Pet Shop Boys
34	Zero	Chris Brown
35	Rise	Katy Perry
36	I Do What I Like	The Corrs
37	Music Takes Me	School Of Seven Bells
38	Somebody Else	The 1975
39	Scars	Tove Lo
40	The Queen (后會無期)	C AllStar f/ GiGi Leung (梁詠琪)
41	Tawny Moon	Kate Bush & Albert McIntosh
42	One Carat (一克拉)	Tanya Chua (蔡健雅)
43	Land Of A Thousand Dreams	Byrne & Kelly
44	How Would U Feel	David Morales f/ Lea-Lorién
45	Tu Sauras	Céline Dion
46	I	Taeyeon (태연) f/ Verbal Jint
47	Without Your Love	Kim Wilde
48	Lime Habit	Poliça
49	Best Way To Die (活著是最好的死亡)	Tanya Chua (蔡健雅)
50	Burn	Pet Shop Boys
51	Keeping Me Alive	Bob Moses
52	Wilderness	Salt Ashes
53	Deep Forest	Hooverphonic
54	Easily	Grimes
55	Soap	Melanie Martinez
56	E.V.A. / The Race For Space	Public Service Broadcasting
57	Give Me Your Love	Sigala f/ John Newman, Nile Rodgers
58	Panama	The Avener
59	Reverie	Chris Isaak
60	On My Heart	School Of Seven Bells
61	Chase You Down	RUNAGROUND
62	Never Ever	Röyksopp f/ Susanne Sundfør

#	Song Title	Artist
63	Once Upon A Time I / Once Upon A Time II	Schiller
64	Here For You	Jean-Michel Jarre f/ Gary Numan
65	Higher	The Naked And Famous
66	Stolen Car	Mylène Farmer & Sting
67	Cut Your Teeth	Kyla La Grange
68	Meteorite	Years & Years
69	Faint Of Heart	Tegan And Sara
70	In The Now	Barry Gibb
71	Light Of Gold	Skye|Ross
72	i hate u, i love u	gnash f/ Olivia O'Brien
73	Buy Car Buy House (上車咒)	C AllStar
74	Sadeness Part II	Enigma f/ Anggun
75	Fantasy	Alina Baraz & Galimatias
76	This Is What You Came For	Calvin Harris f/ Rihanna
77	Can I Help You Sir? (先生有事嗎?)	Tanya Chua (蔡健雅)
78	The Getaway	Red Hot Chili Peppers
79	Walking In A Circle	Santigold
80	Don't Be So Shy	Imany
81	Dancing Around It	Charles Kelley
82	The Ocean	Mike Perry f/ Shy Martin
83	Thick As Thieves	The Temper Trap
84	In Bits	Pet Shop Boys
85	Water Under The Bridge	Adele

#	Song Title	Artist
86	Smoke Filled Room	Mako
87	Gotta Go!	RubberBand (最新派台歌) f/ Jun Kung (恭碩良)
88	Sweet Symphony (My Heart Beats Again)	Schiller w/ Sheppard Solomon
89	Pity Party	Melanie Martinez
90	Whole Lot Of Love	Duffy
91	Cake By The Ocean	DNCE
92	The Fighter	Keith Urban & Carrie Underwood
93	I Wanna Know	Alesso f/ Nico & Vinz
94	Ablaze	School Of Seven Bells
95	Put 'Em High	StoneBridge f/ Therese
96	Eagle Will Fly Again	Howard Jones
97	Ordinary	Two Door Cinema Club
98	I Like The Way I Dance	Hooverphonic
99	Drive It Like You Stole It	Hudson Thames
100	Dancing With Myself	The Knocks
101	Everybody Needs Somebody To Hurt	Richard Ashcroft
2016 EXTRAS		
105	Aberdeen / The Weight	Judy Collins & Ari Hest
108	Rockin'	The Weeknd
109	High And Low	Empire Of The Sun
114	The Right Song	Tiësto + Oliver Heldens f/ Natalie La Rose
118	BOSS	Disclosure

#	Song Title	Artist
1	Indigo Blue	Jake Bugg
2	Burn Down The Summer	Vittoria And The Hyde Park
3	Just A Feeling	Phantoms f/ Vérité
4	Lover, Go	Alison Moyet
5	A.I.	OneRepublic f/ Peter Gabriel
6	Eyes Closed	Halsey
7	Scared To Be Lonely	Martin Garrix/Dua Lipa
8	New York City	The Chainsmokers
9	Unforgettable	French Montana f/ Swae Lee
10	Secrets	The Weeknd
11	The Love We're Hoping For	Jake Bugg
12	Route 66/Faith	ATB & Anova / ATB f/ Tilsen
13	Can't Control	Texas
14	Chained To The Rhythm	Katy Perry f/ Skip Marley
15	Swansea	Dusky f/ Gary Numan
16	Save Me A Place	Mono Mind
17	Bum Bum Bum	Cass McCombs
18	Body 2 Body	Dragonette
19	Lost On You / (Swanky Tunes & Going Deeper Remix)	LP
20	Places	Martin Solveig f/ Ina Wroldsen
21	Sunny Days	Armin van Buuren f/ Josh Cumbree
22	You Don't Know Me	Jax Jones f/ RAYE
23	Falling	Alesso
24	It Was Up To You	Texas
25	Hey Baby	Dimitri Vegas & Like Mike vs Diplo & Kid Ink f/ Deb's Daughter
26	Same Old Lie	Jim James
27	Guys My Age	Hey Violet
28	Lust For Life	Lana Del Rey f/ The Weeknd
29	Love Can't Touch Me Now	Dragonette

#	Song Title	Artist
30	Breathe	Seeb f/ Neev
31	Crying In The Club	Camila Cabello
32	There's No Need	Empire Of The Sun
33	One Mississippi	Zara Larsson
34	Last Night On Mars	Chen Hui-Ting (陳惠婷) (The Huiting)
35	Never Without You	ATB f/ Sean Ryan
36	Darth Vader	Dragonette
37	不畏誰 (Amistad)	許 書豪 (Xu Shu Hao, Haor Xu)
38	Love To Lay	The Weeknd
39	After	MUNA
40	On My Mind	3LAU f/ Yeah Boy
41	Swedish Guns	The Radio Dept.
42	Art Eats Art	Orchestral Manoeuvres In The Dark
43	Fool's Gold	Aaron Carter
44	Piccoli Miracoli	Tiromancino
45	Digital Life	Empire Of The Sun
46	Lose My Number	James Blunt
47	Sexual	Neiked f/ Dyo
48	Other People	LP
49	Déjà Vu	Katy Perry
50	Passionfruit	Drake
51	Attention	Charlie Puth
52	I Need You	Armin van Buuren & Garibay f/ Olaf Blackwood
53	I Love You But I'm Lost	Tears For Fears
54	Alone	Halsey
55	Rollin	Calvin Harris f/ Future & Khalid
56	Fiction	Todd Rundgren
57	Looking For The Rain	UNKLE f/ Mark Lanegan/ ESKA
58	Where Have You Been (All My Night)	Hey Violet
59	New Rules	Dua Lipa
60	When It Ends It Starts Again	ATB & Sean Ryan

#	Song Title	Artist
61	Army	Lady Antebellum
62	Party Monster	The Weeknd
63	Limitless	Sam F f/ Sophie Rose
64	Deeper In The Water	The Lone Bellow
65	Stay	Delerium & JES
66	Be Mine	Ofenbach
67	Another Life	Afrojack & David Guetta f/ Ester Dean
68	Lonely Soul	Blackfield
69	Would I Lie To You	John Gibbons
70	So Special	MUNA
71	High Ticket Attractions	The New Pornographers
72	Ready To Go	Hurts
73	Oxygen	Dirty Heads
74	Alone	Alan Walker
75	Hide In Plain Sight	Jim James
76	The Queen Of Hearts	Offa Rex & Olivia Chaney
77	Bigger Than Me	Katy Perry
78	Instruction	Jax Jones f/ Demi Lovato, Stefflon Don
79	Now Or Never	Halsey
80	Skyscraper (摩天大樓)	Chen Hui-Ting (陳惠婷)
81	I Germinate	Alison Moyet
82	Paris	The Chainsmokers
83	Say It With Your Body	INNA
84	In My World	Lindsey Buckingham, Christine McVie

#	Song Title	Artist
85	Sun-Wave	Anneli Drecker
86	Hard To Say Goodbye	Washed Out
87	Silence	Marshmello f/ Khalid
88	Chameleon Days	Neil Finn
89	Bro Code	Brantley Gilbert
90	Everything Is Never Enough	Goldfrapp
91	Call The Police	G Girls (Alexandra Stan, Lori, Antonia & INNA)
92	The Cure	Lady Gaga
93	Good Day	Yellowclaw f/ DJ Snake & Elliphant
94	On The Loose	Niall Horan
95	Witness	Katy Perry
96	Shape Of You	Ed Sheeran
97	After Hebden	Saint Etienne
98	You + Me Vs The World	Barenaked Ladies
99	Ti Amo	Phoenix
100	Laughable	Ringo Starr
101	Love	Lana Del Rey
2017 EXTRAS		
102	We Are Strong	Pitbull f/ Kiesza
107	Give You More	Ledisi f/ John Legend
111	Cycles	Brett Eldredge
115	Feels	Calvin Harris f/ Pharrell Williams, Katy Perry, Big Sean
121	Green Light	Lorde

2018

#	Song Title	Artist
1	Smoke	Tracey Thorn
2	Non Believer	London Grammar
3	Future Ghost	Dragonette
4	Diamond Dust	Way Out West
5	So Far Away	Martin Garrix & David Guetta f/ Jamie Scott, Romy Dya
6	Side Effects	The Chainsmokers w/ Emily Warren
7	I Found My Soul At Marvingate	Mono Mind
8	Shittosaserubeki Jinsei (嫉妬されるべき人生, A Life to Be Envied)	Utada Hikaru (宇多田 ヒカル)
9	Promises	Calvin Harris f/ Sam Smith
10	A Matter Of Time	Sennek
11	One Kiss	Calvin Harris & Dua Lipa
12	The Right Thing	Lo Moon
13	Indian Summer	My Indigo
14	Why We Call Each Other	Dustin Lynch
15	Nothing In The World	PNAU
16	Tomorrow's Party	Chen Hui-Ting (陳惠婷)
17	High Horse	Kacey Musgraves
18	Find You	Nick Jonas
19	Back On It	Dustin Lynch
20	Change Your Mind	Miike Snow
21	This Town	Kygo f/ Sasha Sloan
22	Machinist	Japanese Breakfast
23	What We Remember	Anggun
24	Tokyo Nights	Digital Farm Animals x Shaun Frank x Dragonette
25	In My Head	PNAU
26	Deadly Valentine	Charlotte Gainsbourg
27	The Only Ones?	Solsun
28	Like Crazy	Basia
29	Drive	Black Coffee & David Guetta f/ Delilah Morgan
30	Leave The War With Me	London Grammar
31	Never Enough	Loren Allred

#	Song Title	Artist
32	Go Bang	PNAU f/ Kira Divine
33	This Is It	Lo Moon
34	Bittersweet & Blue	Above & Beyond
35	Riding Shotgun	Kygo f/ Bonnie McKee
36	Searching For Answers (答案之書)	Joey Yung (容祖兒 / 容祖儿)
37	Black Velvet Sun	My Indigo
38	Agree	Poliça & s t a r g a z e
39	Damn, Dis-Moi (Girlfriend)	Christine And The Queens f/ Dâm-Funk
40	Paris Sur Mer	Morcheeba f/ Benjamin Biolay
41	I Believe	Bob Sinclar & Tonino Speciale
42	Where Is My Love	My Indigo
43	Palo Santo	Years & Years
44	Breathe	Jax Jones f/ Ina Wroldsen
45	Follow Me	Sarah Brightman
46	Ganja Burns	Nicki Minaj
47	On The Line	Julian Peretta
48	Honey	Robyn
49	The Science Of Dust/ Siren Call	Solsun
50	My Indigo	My Indigo
51	Beam Me Up	Django Django
52	Bones	Equinox
53	Solo	Clean Bandit f/ Demi Lovato
54	DaNcing in a RoOm	EZI
55	If Our Love Is Wrong	Calum Scott
56	Finest Hour	Cash Cash f/ Abir
57	Cruising (So They Say)	Claptone f/ Kele Okereke
58	no tears left to cry	Ariana Grande
59	Window (창문)	G-Dragon (지드래곤)
60	First Time	M-22 f/ Medina
61	Why Did You Do That?	Lady Gaga
62	Sister	Tracey Thorn f/ Corinne Bailey Rae
63	Something Exciting	Era
64	Nevermind	Dennis Lloyd

2010s

98

#	Song Title	Artist
65	Don't Go Breaking My Heart	Backstreet Boys
66	Phoenix	Rhye
67	Gentlewomen	Jolin Tsai
68	Out Of Nowhere Girl	Luke Bryan
69	Under The Moon	Claptone f/ Nathan Nicholson
70	She Works Out Too Much	MGMT
71	New Light	John Mayer
72	N'Oublie Pas	Mylène Farmer w/ LP
73	Play A Love Song	Utada Hikaru
74	Cheveux Noirs	Davine
75	Diving Woman / Here Come The Tubular Bells	Japanese Breakfast
76	Done For Me	Charlie Puth f/ Kehlani
77	Right Now	Nick Jonas, Robin Schulz
78	Alone	Claptone f/ Blaenavon
79	Til I'm Done	Paloma Faith
80	Because It's In The Music	Robyn
81	Raining Glitter	Kylie (Minogue)
82	Hair Body Face	Lady Gaga
83	Ignite	K-391 & Alan Walker f/ Julie Bergan/Seungri
84	Ocean	Martin Garrix f/ Khalid
85	Tied To The Weather	Cut Copy
86	Sex, Love & Water	Armin van Buuren f/ Conrad Sewell
87	Joyride	Tinashe
88	A Moment Apart	ODESZA

#	Song Title	Artist
89	Come On Back	Shungudzo
90	17	MK (Mark Kinchen)
91	Running Away	Way Out West f/ Eli & Fur
92	Promise Not To Fall	Human Touch
93	Mystery Of Love	Sufjan Stevens
94	Put It On The Line	The Aces
95	Kill The Fear	Conjure One
96	Fly To Paradise	Sarah Brightman
97	7 Seconds	Era
98	Sylvia Says	Charlotte Gainsbourg
99	Still Rolling Stones	Lauren Daigle
100	It's Summertime	Morcheeba
101	You're The Best Thing About Me	U2 vs Kygo
2018 EXTRAS		
106	Gatekeeper Julie	Capital Cities f/ Jim Svejda
107	Otherside	Post Malone
110	Without Me	Halsey
112	The Only Thing Worth Fighting For	Rosanne Cash
114	Gemini	Keith Urban
115	Rewrite The Stars	Zac Efron & Zendaya
116	Eastside	benny blanco, Halsey & Khalid
119	Pray For Me	The Weeknd/Kendrick Lamar
125	Dusk Till Dawn	ZAYN f/ Sia

2010s

#	Song Title	Artist
1	Never Say Die	Stealth
2	Peace Of Mind	Avicii f/ Vargas & Legola
3	Turn The Light	Danger Mouse & Karen O
4	Càng Níu Giữ Càng Dễ Mất (The More You Hold, The More You Lose)	Mr. Siro
5	Dancing With A Stranger	Sam Smith & Normani
6	Send To Robin Immediately	Robyn
7	Còn Là Gì Của Nhau (What's Left Of Each Other)	Châu Khải Phong
8	Love	Schiller w/ Rebecca Ferguson
9	Easier	5 Seconds Of Summer
10	Hypnotised	Years & Years
11	The Mountain	KT Tunstall
12	Thay Thế (Replace)	Hồ Gia Hùng
13	Take You Home	Dido
14	Only Human	Jonas Brothers
15	Karma	Marina (Diamandis)
16	Romantic	Hooverphonic
17	Without You	Junkilla f/ TonyB
18	RU WO	Sara Liu
19	Người Khác (Others)	Phan Mạnh Quỳnh f/ Drum7
20	Missing U	Robyn
21	Hurricanes	Dido
22	Late Night Prelude/Late Night Feelings	Mark Ronson f/ Lykke Li
23	True	Marina
24	Uptight	Hooverphonic
25	Ta Cứ Đi Cùng Nhau (Let's Go Together)	Đen f/ Linh Cáo
26	Overglow	Adam Lambert
27	Doin' Time	Lana Del Rey
28	One Note Symphony	Alan Parsons
29	Say The Word	Chely Wright f/ Jeremy Lister
30	Heal Me	Lady Gaga
31	Castaway	Yuna f/ Tyler, The Creator
32	Panic Room	Au/Ra & CamelPhat
33	Au Au	Filatov & Karas
34	Windswept	Johnny Jewel
35	Every Single Time	Jonas Brothers
36	Worthy/What If	india.arie
37	Người Lạ Thoáng Qua (Glimpse Of Strangers)	Khởi My
38	365	Zedd, Katy Perry
39	Play	Jax Jones & Years & Years
40	Borrowed Love	Metro Boomin f/ Swae Lee, Wizkid
41	Extraordinary Being	Emeli Sandé
42	Dreamcatcher	Schiller w/ Jhyve
43	Diamond Heart	Alan Walker f/ Sophia Somajo
44	Couldn't Believe My Luck	Mono Mind
45	Don't Lie To Me	Barbra Streisand
46	Circles	Post Malone
47	Catch Me If You Can	The Cranberries
48	Baby Please Don't Stop	Emma Bunton
49	Dance Music	Bananarama
50	Away Away Away/In Control	Mono Mind
51	In Between	Schiller w/ Jan Blomqvist
52	Our Pathetic Age	DJ Shadow f/ Samuel T. Herring
53	Vulture, Vulture	Of Monsters And Men
54	Zij Weet Het	Tino Martin
55	Don't Call Me Angel (Charlie's Angels)	Ariana Grande, Miley Cyrus + Lana Del Rey
56	Gold	Sam Feldt x Kate Ryan
57	Hold My Breath Until I Die	Tegan And Sara
58	Nếu Em Còn Tồn Tại (If I'm Still Alive)	Trịnh Đình Quang
59	This Human Chain	Melissa Etheridge
60	Stranger On A Bus	Mono Mind
61	How Do You Sleep?	Sam Smith

2019

#	Song Title	Artist
62	Summer Days	Martin Garrix f/ Macklemore + Patrick Stump (of Fall Out Boy)
63	Love Is Gone	Vanotek
64	Hope	The Chainsmokers f/ Winona Oak
65	Eyes	Rüfüs Du Sol
66	Hello Happiness	Chaka Khan
67	I'm Not Leaving	Keane
68	House Of Cards	Caitlyn Smith
69	Talk	Two Door Cinema Club
70	Kids In The Dark	Bat For Lashes
71	Fire In My Head	C-BooL f/ Cadence XYZ
72	Makeba	Jain
73	(Hey Why) Miss You Sometimes	P!NK
74	Human	Emeli Sandé
75	Dark Ballet/God Control	Madonna
76	Flying On My Own	Céline Dion
77	Best Way To Travel	Mono Mind
78	Hundred	Khalid
79	Ngắm Hoa Lệ Rơi (Watch The Flowers Fall)	Châu Khải Phong
80	Lost In The Fire	Gesaffelstein & The Weeknd
81	Imagination	City And Colour
82	Miracle	Alan Parsons f/ Jason Mraz
83	Heartless	The Weeknd
84	Superpower	Adam Lambert

#	Song Title	Artist
85	Yêu Khác Thương Hại (Love Others Pity)	Thanh Hưng
86	No Place	Rüfüs Du Sol
87	Got What I Got	Jason Aldean
88	Womxnly	Jolin Tsai
89	Baby	Clean Bandit f/ Marina & Luis Fonsi
90	Survive	Don Diablo f/ Emeli Sandé & Gucci Mane
91	Sometimes Always Never	Edwyn Collins & Sean Read
92	Hongkong1	Nguyễn Trọng Tài x San Ji x Double X
93	Intoxicated	Bananarama
94	Nice To Meet Ya	Niall Horan
95	Before The Bombs	Death Cab For Cutie
96	No More	DJ Snake & ZHU
97	Storm In A Shot Glass	Reba McEntire
98	100 Years Of Downton	John Lunn
99	Reach	BJ The Chicago Kid f/ Afrojack
100	작은 것들을 위한 시 (Boy With Luv)	BTS f/ Halsey
101	Transcendance	Berlin
2019 EXTRAS		
106	Thinkin Bout You	Ciara
113	Don't Call Me Up	Mabel
114	Oblivions	The National
116	Byzantine	Weezer
118	Coffee	Tori Kelly
122	Nothing Breaks Like A Heart	Mark Ronson w/ Miley Cyrus

#	Song Title	Artist
1	Enigma/Replay	Lady Gaga
2	Uneventful Days	Beck
3	Fjernsynet	Gundelach
4	I'm With You Now	Maggie Reilly
5	Johannesburg	Africa Express f/ Sibot, Gruff Rhys, Morena Leraba
6	Lonely For You	Armin van Buuren f/ Bonnie McKee
7	Midnight Sky	Miley Cyrus
8	Chromatica I/Alice	Lady Gaga
9	Hallucinate	Dua Lipa
10	Love On Myself	Felix Jaehn f/ Calum Scott
11	Calling You	angela
12	Blinding Lights	The Weeknd
13	i miss u	Jax Jones & Au/Ra
14	Joy Kill	Iris
15	Chromatica II/911	Lady Gaga
16	Tonight (Bright Light Bright Light Remix)	Bananarama
17	The Fear	Duke Dumont f/ Niia
18	All Is Found (two versions)	Kacey Musgraves / Evan Rachel Wood
19	Emotional Machine	Marina
20	Babylon	Lady Gaga
21	Sour Candy	Lady Gaga, BLACKPINK
22	Chemical	Beck
23	Make It To Heaven (Rework)	David Guetta + MORTEN w/ RAYE
24	Don't Look Back	Maggie Reilly
25	In The Mirror	Demi Lovato
26	Wolf At Your Door	Chloe x Halle
27	Chromatica III/Sine From Above	Lady Gaga & Elton John
28	This Is How (We Want To Get High)	George Michael
29	Drive	lovelytheband
30	Speak Out	Iris
31	Falta Amor	Sebastián Yatra & Ricky Martin
32	Remedium	Saszan
33	Cracked	Echosmith
34	Husavik (My Hometown)	Will Ferrell & Molly Sandén (My Marianne)
35	The World We Knew (Over And Over)	Josh Groban
36	Hello, I'm Right Here	Tegan And Sara
37	Lichtjahre	Schiller & Giorgio Moroder
38	I'm On Fire	Bananarama
39	White Horses	Hurts
40	Friday Night	Burak Yeter
41	Say Something	Kylie (Minogue)
42	4 American Dollars	U.S. Girls
43	Phone Down	Armin van Buuren & Garibay
44	Roses	Adam Lambert f/ Nile Rodgers
45	Cruel	Jax Jones
46	Always	Armin van Buuren w/ BT & Nation Of One
47	Carter & Cash	Tor Miller
48	Hypnotized	Purple Disco Machine & Sophie And The Giants
49	Slave To Your Love	Hurts
50	You Make It So Easy, Don't You	Bright Light Bright Light f/ Sam Sparro
51	Cry For Me	Camila Cabello
52	Galaxy	Chloe x Halle
53	Reckless Desires / Game Of Chance	Washed Out
54	Stupid Love	Lady Gaga
55	Violence	Grimes & i_o
56	Fade Away	Lucky Daye
57	My Life Is Going On	Burak Yeter & Cecelia Krull
58	Black Swan (Japanese Version)	BTS
59	Basic	Electric Guest
60	The Dream Is Over	Maggie Reilly

#	Song Title	Artist
61	The One To Love You (The Lifelike Mix)	Howard Jones & BT
62	Hollow Crown	Ellie Goulding
63	Time Machine	Alicia Keys
64	Kingdom Of One	Maren Morris
65	Voices	Hurts
66	Summer Love	Carly Rae Jepsen
67	It Could Be	Armin van Buuren f/ Inner City
68	Bagsy Not In Net	The 1975
69	Run Away With Me	Sufjan Stevens
70	Try Me	DJ Snake & Plastic Toy
71	Creepin'	Hayley Williams
72	Love Song	Bright Light Bright Light f/ Big Dipper
73	Kill My Mind	Louis Tomlinson
74	Diamonds	Sam Smith
75	Dreamland	Pet Shop Boys f/ Years & Years
76	Touch Me	Antonia (Iacobescu)
77	Numb	Elderbrook
78	Weightless	Active Child
79	Dance Again	Selena Gomez
80	Collide	Shea Couleé & Gess f/ Mykki Blanco
81	Wild Eyes	Kate Ryan
82	Running	Sandro
83	Roses (Imanbek Remix)	SAINt JHN

#	Song Title	Artist
84	Runaway	Armin van Buuren f/ Candace Sosa
85	Levitating	Dua Lipa
86	Stuck	Echosmith
87	Supernova	Kylie (Minogue)
88	Take Yourself Home	Troye Sivan
89	One Last Time	Moby
90	Underdog	Alicia Keys
91	Thin White Lies	5 Seconds Of Summer
92	Double Trouble (Tiësto's Euro 90's Tribute Mix)	Molly Sandén, Will Ferrell & Tiësto
93	Cardigan	Taylor Swift
94	Perfect Girls Of Pop	Elizabeth Cook
95	Third Strike	Iris
96	Tell Your Friends	Liam Payne
97	Flux/Brightest Blue	Ellie Goulding
98	Sunset Lover	Petit Biscuit
99	I Hope	Gabby Barrett f/ Charlie Puth
100	Golden	Harry Styles
101	Hide	Washed Out
2020 EXTRAS		
103	Say So	Doja Cat f/ Nicki Minaj
105	In Your Eyes	The Weeknd
107	March March	The Chicks
108	Domestic Bliss	Glass Animals
110	Runaway Kind	Milo Greene

#	Song Title	Artist		#	Song Title	Artist
1	Drops In The Lake	Lord Huron		32	Répondez-Moi	Gjon's Tears
2	Inner Light	Elderbrook & Bob Moses		33	Breakdown	Tanya Chua (蔡健雅)
3	Call Your Friends	London Grammar		34	Chapter One: The Sleeping Giant/Beautiful Liar	X Ambassadors
4	One More	SG Lewis f/ Nile Rodgers		35	Dancing Away In Tears	Yola
5	Who	Lauv f/ BTS		36	The Kill/Remember Where You Are	Jessie Ware
6	How Does It Feel	London Grammar		37	Prisoner	Miley Cyrus f/ Dua Lipa
7	These Dreams	Bright Light Bright Light f/ The Illustrious Blacks		38	Low Mist Var. 2 (Day One) / (Day Six)	Ludovico Einaudi
8	Ganas De Verte	J Balvin		39	Walk Out!	The Suburbs
9	If I Had To Do It All Again	Yola		40	Enchantment	Maggie Reilly
10	Starlight	Yola		41	The Motto	Tiësto & Ava Max
11	God Only Knows / Timbaland Remix (two versions)	for KING & COUNTRY f/ Dolly Parton or Echosmith		42	Natalie Don't	RAYE
				43	Rabbit Hole	Jake Bugg
12	Just A Ghost	Claptone f/ Seal		44	Belgium In The Rain	Hooverphonic
13	Wish You Well	PVRIS		45	Heights / (Chill Version)	Nick Jonas
14	Lost	Jake Bugg		46	I Am Not A Woman, I'm A God	Halsey
15	Missing	London Grammar		47	Bad Habits	Ed Sheeran
16	Sacrifice	Bebe Rexha		48	Guardian Angel	Schiller x Tricia McTeague
17	Miracle	Schiller x Tricia McTeague		49	The Edge Of The World	Morcheeba f/ Duke Garwood
18	Heartbreak On The Dancefloor	SG Lewis f/ Frances		50	The Tipping Point	Tears For Fears
19	In Your Eyes	Jessie Ware		51	Dry Your Tears/ Keep Moving	Jungle
20	Regardless	RAYE & Rudimental		52	Faraway Look	Yola
21	Bad Girl	Daya		53	Bluebirds	Tanya Chua (蔡健雅)
22	Est./Alibi	Mansionair		54	The Moon Doesn't Mind/ Mine Forever	Lord Huron
23	Convince Me Otherwise	Maroon 5 & H.E.R.		55	The Wrong Place	Hooverphonic
24	Spies	Tori Amos		56	Intro/Californian Soil	London Grammar
25	Lonely Hour	Jake Bugg		57	SHUM	Go_A (Ґоу_Ей)
26	Cold Heart (PNAU Remix) / (Claptone Remix)	Elton John & Dua Lipa		58	My Love	Ladyhawke
27	Keep An Eye On Dan	ABBA		59	Love Me With Your Lie	Kiesza
28	Save A Kiss	Jessie Ware		60	Io Sí (Seen)	Laura Pausini
29	Waves Of Blue	Majid Jordan		61	Speaking With Trees	Tori Amos
30	It's Alright, It's OK	Bright Light Bright Light f/ Caveboy		62	Someone Else	Duncan Laurence
31	날씨를 잃어버렸어 (We Lost The Summer)	TOMORROW X TOGETHER (투모로우바이투게더)				

#	Song Title	Artist
63	Take My Breath	The Weeknd
64	Carrousel	Amir f/ Indila
65	Nightcrawler	Duke Dumont w/ Say Lou Lou
66	This City Will Kill You	Garbage
67	Dark Hearts	Annie
68	Arcade	Duncan Laurence
69	Who Do U Love?	MONSTA X (몬스타엑스) f/ French Montana
70	Dying Is Absolutely Safe	Architects
71	Black Rain	Rhye
72	Blame It On Me	Melanie C
73	On My Knees	Rüfüs Du Sol
74	Justified	Kacey Musgraves
75	Somewhere In Time	Maggie Reilly
76	Yüce Dağ Başında	Altın Gün
77	Give It All Up	Duran Duran f/ Tove Lo
78	Out N Back	The Earth Orchestra
79	Long Lost	Lord Huron
80	Budapest	STRFKR f/ Shy Boys
81	Chasing You	Ben Platt
82	This Is Heaven	Nick Jonas
83	Addition Of Light Divided (+💡÷)	Tori Amos
84	Tonight Tonight	Celeste
85	Pull Me Close Don't Let Go	Lucero
86	Into The Wild	Tanya Chua (蔡健雅) f/ Ayanga (阿云嘎)

#	Song Title	Artist
87	Rosner's Interlude/ Chemicals	SG Lewis
88	Walk Away	Ladyhawke
89	Agreeable	Cautious Clay
90	Planes In The Sky	James Vincent McMorrow
91	No Warning Lights	BT & Emma Hewitt
92	I Don't Wanna Wait	The War On Drugs
93	Falling	Texas
94	A Second To Midnight	Kylie Minogue & Years & Years
95	You	Regard x Troye Sivan x Tate McRae
96	Freedom Feeling	Laura Viers
97	Man On The Moon	Alan Walker & Benjamin Ingrosso
98	Breathing Underwater	Santana w/ Stella Santana, Avi Snow & MVCA
99	Moth To A Flame	Swedish House Mafia + The Weeknd
100	The Love Has Got To Me	Joan As Police Woman, Tony Allen, Dave Okumu
101	Hidden Stories	Hooverphonic
2021 EXTRAS		
106	You Ruined The World For Me Now	The Suburbs
107	Too Good	Arlo Parks
109	V	Balmorhea, Clarice Jensen & Lisa Morgenstern
115	Love Again	Dua Lipa

2012

#	Song Title	Artist
1	Pray For Me	Paul Oakenfold x Velvet Cash
2	19th Floor	Joy Crookes
3	Prada (i like it)	Mura Masa & LEILAH
4	The Next 20th Century	Father John Misty
5	lovely	Billie Eilish & Khalid
6	Alpha Zulu	Phoenix
7	The Ladder	Röyksopp
8	Seen It Coming	Bob Moses
9	In The Dark	Purple Disco Machine, Sophie And The Giants
10	Wounded	Ferry Corsten & Morgan Page f/ Cara Melín
11	Satellite	Claptone f/ Peter Bjorn And John
12	Solo Mission	The Chainsmokers
13	Give That Wolf A Banana	Subwoolfer
14	Hurricane	Cannons
15	Feet Don't Fail Me Now	Joy Crookes
16	Holiday	Fletcher
17	Silver Balloons	Little Boots
18	Come Back Home	070 Shake
19	If This Was A Movie..	Kacey Musgraves
20	Lone Didion	Andrew Bird
21	How Long	Tove Lo
22	My Love	Florence + The Machine
23	Measure Of A Man	FKA twigs f/ Central Cee
24	Love Under Pressure	James Blunt
25	Pieces	Ella Mai
26	Metal Water Wood	Tori Amos
27	One Night	Broken Bells
28	Nothing Ever Changes	Little Boots
29	Miss The Bliss	Hot Chip
30	Forgive Me	SOFI TUKKER w/ Mahmut Orhan
31	Not Alone	Joe Jonas & Khalid
32	Lie Love Lullaby	Girlpool
33	Brand New	Bananarama
34	Strange And Unusual	Years & Years

#	Song Title	Artist
35	Constant Repeat	Charli XCX
36	Hypnotic	Paul Oakenfold x Azaelia Banks x Velvet Cash
37	Mad Girl	Salt Ashes
38	Alive	Poliça
39	Breathe	Röyksopp (w/ Astrid S/ Man Without Country)
40	Believe	Bob Moses
41	Fade Away	Claptone f/ Spelles
42	How Do I Make You Love Me?	The Weeknd
43	Human	John Summit f/ Echoes
44	Let It All Evolve	Tears For Fears
45	Let's Get It Right	Röyksopp
46	Is There Someone Else?	The Weeknd
47	什麼都不必說– (2022 Remix) (Don't Have To Say A Thing)	Billie X NICKTHEREAL (比莉 Billie Wang X 周湯豪)
48	Easy Lover	Ellie Goulding f/ Big Sean
49	Miền Gian Khổ (Endless Hardships) / Nhạt (Light)	Phan Mạnh Quỳnh
50	Distorted Light Beam	Bastille
51	Dark Sun	Schiller
52	Dumb	Envy Of None
53	2 Die 4	Tove Lo
54	Sola Es Mejor	Karol G, Yandar & Yostin
55	Impossible	Röyksopp (w/ Alison Goldfrapp)
56	My Demons	Tears For Fears
57	Less Than Zero	The Weeknd
58	Frozen On Fire / Frozen	Madonna & Sickick / Madonna Vs Sickick f/ 070 Shake
59	Minamata Piano Theme	Ryuichi Sakamoto
60	Siren	Taeyeon (태연)
61	Shame To Humanity	Stone Age
62	Why Did I Say Goodbye	Sally Shapiro f/ Tommy '86
63	Lavender Haze	Taylor Swift
64	Se Mi Ami Davvero	MinaCelentano

2020s

#	Song Title	Artist
65	One More Time	Luka Kloser
66	Prodigal Daughter	Lights
67	Shadows	Bonobo
68	Twennies	Dragonette
69	Call On Me	SG Lewis & Tove Lo
70	Rozenn An Dro	Stone Age
71	Purple Sun	Cannons
72	Love Brand New	Bob Moses
73	Bring Back The Time	New Kids On The Block f/ Salt-N-Pepa, Rick Astley & En Vogue
74	Intro/Carried Away	Lo Moon
75	Need A Little More Time	Bananarama
76	Mirror	Kendrick Lamar
77	Lose	Wonho (원호)
78	The Innocent	AURORA
79	Vengeance	Finneas O'Connell
80	Bluedusk	Sun's Signature
81	Halos	Alan Parsons
82	Intro/Greatest Works Of Art (最偉大的作品)	Jay Chou (周杰倫)
83	Never Say Never	Cole Swindell w/ Lainey Wilson
84	Molly In Mexico	Lauv
85	Beach House	Carly Rae Jepsen
86	Paradigm	The Head And The Heart
87	Mirror Me	Mansionair
88	Oh, Lover	Röyksopp (w/ Susanne Sundfør)
89	Back Seat	Chastity Brown
90	Sweet Dreams & Dynamite	Seeb & Nina Nesbitt
91	Rebirth / Invocation	Clint Mansell

#	Song Title	Artist
92	Anti-Hero	Taylor Swift
93	L'Enfer	Stromae
94	Reclaim The Night	Belle And Sebastian
95	About Damn Time / (Purple Disco Machine Remix)	Lizzo
96	Can't Make You Love Me	Chloe Fredericks
97	Summer Rain	a-ha
98	Virgo's Groove/Summer Renaissance	Beyoncé
99	The Last Goodbye	ODESZA f/ Bettye LaVette
100	Sister Ray	Foxes
101	The White Lotus Theme (Renaissance) (Kabumi Remix / Tiësto Remix) / (Aloha)	Cristobal Tapia de Veer, (Aloha version – Dmitri Vegas & Steve Aoki)
2022 EXTRAS		
102	Different Man	Kane Brown w/ Blake Shelton
103	In Real Life	Mandy Moore
104	Fast Times	Sabrina Carpenter
110	We Don't Talk About Bruno	Carolina Gaitán, Mauro Castillo, Adassa, Rhenzy Feliz, Diane Guerrero, Stephanie Beatriz & Encanto Cast
113	I'm Good (Blue)	David Guetta & Bebe Rexha
115	Devotion	The Staves
117	Tidal Wave	Nickelback
121	Under The Influence	Chris Brown
129	As It Was	Harry Styles
130	Karma	Taylor Swift (f/ Ice Spice)
142	The Evil That Men Do	Hot Chip

#	Song Title	Artist
1	Mayo	Juanes
2	Blue	Kali Uchis
3	Something On My Mind	Purple Disco Machine, Duke Dumont, Nothing But Thieves
4	Anywhere But Here/ Headlights	PVRIS
5	Voices	Jake Shears f/ Kylie Minogue
6	Think Of A Number / (Pet Shop Boys Magic Eye 12" remix)	Noel Gallagher's High Flying Birds
7	Higher Than Heaven	Ellie Goulding
8	Flow	Faith Yang 楊乃文 (Yang Naiwen) f/ Sunset Rollercoaster 落日飛車
9	17th Ward Prelude/ Uneasy	Jon Batiste f/ Lil Wayne
10	Something To Believe In/ Eat The Acid	Kesha
11	Stay Awhile	Röyksopp f/ Susanne Sundfør
12	Holding On	SG Lewis
13	i see america	Joy Oladokun
14	Welcome To MY World	æspa f/ nævis
15	Temptation	Ellie Goulding
16	What Have We Got	Schiller, Ro Nova x Tricia McTeague
17	Genug	Mark Forster
18	Intro/Infatuation	SG Lewis
19	I'd Bet	Tiësto w/ Freya Ridings
20	Intuition	Ellie Goulding
21	So Typically Now	U.S. Girls
22	Begin Again	Jessie Ware
23	Prada	cassö x RAYE x D-Block Europe
24	Forever	Everything But The Girl
25	Samo Mi Se Spava	Luke Black
26	Cure For Love	Ellie Goulding
27	Last Night On Earth	Ava Max
28	Legends Never Die (two versions)	Against The Current, League Of Legends & Mako / Forestella 포레스텔라
29	Jump The Next Train	Young Parisians f/ Ben Lost
30	Another Life	SG Lewis
31	Just Wanted To Know	Röyksopp f/ Astrid S
32	Stars	PNAU w/ Bebe Rexha & Ozuna
33	Heart Wants What It Wants	Bebe Rexha
34	Like A Saviour	Ellie Goulding
35	We're Not In Orbit Yet...	Broken Bells
36	Coast To Coast	Delerium f/ Phildel
37	Run A Red Light	Everything But The Girl
38	People / (sped up+reverb)	Libianca / ft. Ayra Starr & Omah Lay / or Becky G
39	Sorry Isn't Good Enough	Joy Oladokun
40	Midnight Dreams	Ellie Goulding
41	Sunrise	Morgan Wallen
42	City Of Angels	Ladytron
43	I'm Not Scared To Die	Salt Ashes
44	Carretera y Manta	Pablo Alborán
45	Free Yourself	Jessie Ware
46	Learn 2 Love	Tiësto
47	Toy Boy (身體會說話)	HUSH (陳品赫)
48	10 Out Of 10	Kylie (Minogue) w/ Oliver Heldens
49	STAR WALKIN' (League Of Legends Worlds Anthem)	Lil Nas X
50	Tension	Kylie (Minogue)
51	Paradise	Sophie And The Giants x Purple Disco Machine
52	Haute/Ooh La La/ Lipstick Lover	Janelle Monáe f/ Grace Jones
53	Anthropocene	OMD (Orchestral Manoeuvres In The Dark)
54	Loving You	Cannons

#	Song Title	Artist
55	Hurting Interlude/ Lose You	Sam Smith
56	How You Make Me Feel	Smokey Robinson
57	Nobody	Steve Aoki f/ PollyAnna
58	Ein Morgen Im August/ Love And Tears	Schiller w/ Yalda Abbasi
59	Escapism	RAYE f/ 070 Shake
60	Strangers	Kenya Grace
61	Cold Shoulder	James Blunt
62	Claws	Kim Petras
63	Let It Shine (radio edit)	Zazie
64	Moonlight	Kali Uchis
65	Creepin'	Metro Boomin, The Weeknd, 21 Savage
66	Let's Make A Mistake Tonight	Tennis
67	Just Believe	tyDi & JES
68	Padam Padam	Kylie (Minogue)
69	I Inside The Old I Dying	PJ Harvey
70	Silent Running	Gorillaz f/ Adeleye Omotayo
71	Double Fantasy	The Weeknd f/ Future
72	Sweet Relief	Madison Beer
73	Dead Machine	Django Django f/ Stealing Sheep
74	Number One	Shania Twain
75	REACT	Switch Disco f/ Ella Henderson (& Robert Miles)
76	热爱105°C的你 (Love You At 105°C) (two versions)	A Si 阿肆 / Super Idol
77	Who The Hell Is Edgar?	Teya & Salena
78	Funny Kind Of Lonely	Idina Menzel
79	Spotlight	Joy Oladokun
80	Danse Macabre	Duran Duran
81	Ash	SEVENTEEN세븐틴
82	Judadatla Tsisqwa (Spotted Bird)	Kalyn Fay
83	Forbidden Doors	Tennis

#	Song Title	Artist
84	Black Mascara	RAYE
85	Good Life	FAST BOY
86	Miracle Man	Bebe Rexha
87	Let's Party	Kool & The Gang
88	Space	Schiller w/ Tricia McTeague
89	Young Man & Sea	G.E.M.
90	Substitution	Purple Disco Machine x Kungs f/ Julian Perretta
91	Killed The Cowboy	Dustin Lynch
92	Desire	Calvin Harris & Sam Smith
93	Leaving	Hildur Guðnadóttir
94	Beside You	James Blunt
95	Where You Go	Kiana Ledé & Khalid
96	My Sister's Crown	Vesna
97	Is It A Crime?	No Guidnce
98	Saturday/Sunday	Jason Derulo & David Guetta
99	Come Over	Carly Rae Jepsen
100	I Just Want A Lover	Noah Cyrus
101	Synchronize	Milky Chance
2023 EXTRAS		
102	Use Me (Brutal Hearts)	Diplo, Dove Cameron & Johnny Blue Skies (Sturgill Simpson)
103	City Federal Building	St. Paul & The Broken Bones
104	Sirens	Flume f/ Caroline Polachek
108	Full Of Life	Christine And The Queens
111	greedy	Tate McRae
114	Not That Well-Defined	Sparks
119	Dance The Night	Dua Lipa
126	Pumpkin Man南瓜超人	Rhydian Vaughan (鳳小岳)
128	Pa Pa Power	Dead Man's Bones
133	Mind Your Business	will.i.am & Britney Spears

#	Song Title	Artist
1	Car Keys (Ayla)	Alok & Ava Max
2	Towards The Sun	Sia
3	Paladin Strait	Twenty One Pilots
4	Baby Blue Movie	Cigarettes After Sex
5	And Then I Found You	Hooverphonic
6	Connecticut	Lo Moon
7	Last Time I Saw You	Nicki Minaj
8	Somebody	Jungkook
9	In The Mist (雾里)	Yao Liu Yi (姚六一)
10	DIFFICULT	Tierra Whack
11	alife	Slowdive
12	The Door	Teddy Swims
13	If You Love Her	Tokyo Tea Room
14	Low Sun	Hermanos Gutiérrez
15	Butterfly Net (2 versions)	Caroline Polachek / f/ Weyes Blood
16	Two Wrongs Right	Hooverphonic
17	One Lonely Island	Kenny Chesney
18	Changes	Empire Of The Sun
19	Komet	Udo Lindenberg x Apache 207
20	Shades 22	Simply Red
21	House	London Grammar
22	Là Où Je Vais	Zazie
23	Özünlə Apar	Fahree f/ Ilkin Dovlatov
24	I'd Like To Give Up	Faith Yang 楊乃文 (Yang Naiwen) f/ Our Shame
25	Afterlife	Temples
26	We Still Don't Trust You	Future & Metro Boomin w/ The Weeknd
27	Kintsugi	Lindsey Stirling
28	Inhale/Music Is Better	Rüfüs Du Sol
29	Calling All Saviors	Paula Cole
30	Higher	London Grammar, CamelPhat
31	Years That Fall	Snow Patrol
32	What If I'm Not Ready	Dessa
33	Iqual Que Un Ángel	Kali Uchis f/ Peso Pluma
34	Houdini	Dua Lipa
35	Enjoy Youth	Bright Light Bright Light w/ Beth Hirsch

#	Song Title	Artist
36	A Tear In Space (Airlock)	Glass Animals
37	Floating Parade	Michael Kiwanuka
38	Heaven's Gift	Kool & The Gang
39	Body Moving	Calvin Harris, Eliza Rose
40	Put It To Rest	Carly Rae Jepsen
41	Eye Of The Untold Her	Lindsey Stirling
42	Fly To You	Caroline Polachek f/ Grimes & Dido
43	My Oh My	Kylie w/ Bebe Rexha & Tove Lo
44	Lost In Space	Foster The People
45	Come Right Back	Morgan Page
46	How You Leave A Man	Paloma Faith
47	Not Ashamed	Billy Porter w/ MNEK
48	I Adore You	Hugel, Topic, Arash f/ Daecolm
49	Cardinal	Kacey Musgraves
50	Bodyguard	Beyoncé
51	I Like You	Fil Bo Riva
52	Spillhaugen	Beirut
53	Shiver	John Summit w/ Hayla
54	Drown	Justin Timberlake
55	Stuck	Thirty Seconds To Mars
56	Luktelk	Silvester Belt
57	Heaven Can Wait	Christopher von Deylen (Schiller)
58	"Vocal song from the film Ashes (Kül)"	Artist Unknown (Mistër E's first mystery in this book) *
59	17	Madison Beer
60	The Best Day Of Our Life	Hooverphonic
61	Feel	Pet Shop Boys
62	Something Beautiful (2023 version)	Tina Turner
63	Nothing Compares To You	Britti
64	Future Enemies	Yola
65	Turn The Card Slowly	Gossip
66	Unfolding	Lindsey Stirling f/ Rachel Platten
67	Bittersweet	Dolly Parton f/ Michael McDonald

2020s

#	Song Title	Artist
68	Wait On You	Washed Out
69	Hell Is Near	St. Vincent
70	Immortal Queen	Sia f/ Chaka Khan
71	Wild Flame	Moby f/ Danaé Wellington
72	Wave	FAST BOY, Raf
73	Some Horses	Old Dominion
74	Love And Pain	Enrique Iglesias
75	Teresa & Maria	alyona alyona & Jerry Heil
76	Thinkin' Bout	Kenny Chesney
77	Intro To Everything / Expensive Money	Blu DeTiger
78	Tears	John Summit w/ Paige Cavell
79	Salvation Adagio	Robbie Robertson
80	Someone For Me	Kylie
81	Illusion	Dua Lipa
82	Couleur	Zazie
83	Kingdom Come	The Kills
84	The Paradigm	Lil Yachty
85	Neverender	Justice starring Tame Impala
86	Evolution	Sheryl Crow
87	Dancing And Crying	Kiesza
88	Want	Dua Saleh
89	Die With A Smile	Lady Gaga & Bruno Mars
90	Skater	Four Tet
91	Altay	Ummet Ozcan X Otyken
92	Inner Gold	Lindsey Stirling f/ Royal & the Serpent
93	Черные Цветы (Chernye Cvety)	Molchat Doma
94	Love Bites	Nelly Furtado f/ Tove Lo And SG Lewis
95	Olorun	Asake
96	La Fuerte	Shakira x Bizarrap
97	Dark Day	TR/ST

#	Song Title	Artist
98	Columbus & 89th	Sarah Jarosz
99	Television	Empire Of The Sun
100	You Are Here	Real Estate
101	Fool 4 U	Galantis & JVKE f/ Enisa
2024 EXTRAS		
102	HE KNOWS	Camila Cabello f/ Lil Nas X
103	Free	Calvin Harris, Ellie Goulding
104	Don't Go To The Woods	The Decemberists
105	lock / unlock	j-hope f/ benny blanco & Nile Rodgers
106	Don't Go Nowhere	Jason Derulo
107	One Of The Girls	The Weeknd, JENNIE (Kim) & Lily-Rose Depp
108	Disappearing	Blu DeTiger f/ Magdalena Bay
110	Mwaki	Zerb f/ Sofiya Nzau
111	Quiet In A World Full Of Noise	Dawn Richard And Spencer Zahn
112	Birds Of A Feather	Billie Eilish
114	Road To Joy (Bright-Side Mix)	Peter Gabriel
116	interspace 3/Chizzlers	STRFKR
117	we can't be friends (wait for your love)	Ariana Grande
121	2 Year Itch	girli
122	I Don't Know You	Mannequin Pussy
124	The Lighthouse	Stevie Nicks
127	Whispering Love	Beth Gibbons
129	True Blue Interlude/ Image	Magdalena Bay
137	Queen Of Wind	Nymphia Wind
138	Hummingbird	Carly Pearce

*If you discover the artist's name, please tell me!

2020s

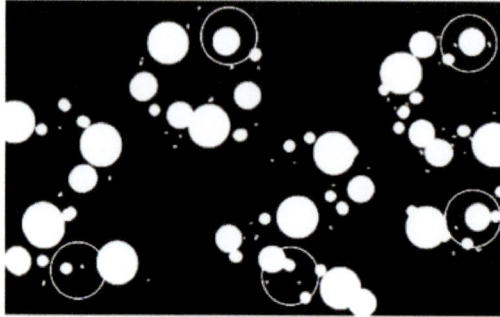

As this book goes to print, I begin to compile my songs for consideration in 2025's list. Stay tuned to your music. And stay tuned for an online location of my future lists.

The music goes on forever.

Further Machinations of a Curious Boy

*Music is there for friends in need,
music is a friend indeed.*

Now that you have seen my year-end lists, what was my purpose for creating them? Good question!

My weekly charts and annual lists began as a whim but became my musical log and subsequently the memory journal of my life—my life attached to music. And now, inadvertently, this book is an observational study of one person's changes in musical tastes and the music he owned. My lists were a way to remember the songs that made me feel something. It became necessary for me to document my favorite songs each year; scouring each new release I purchased looking for my hits.

Throughout life, my music "project" was mostly a secret from those who knew me. I mean, wouldn't others think of me as a bit odd to go to such lengths to track music? They didn't know how I truly needed it, especially during high school when I escaped to music in my solitary, internal life. Music was my friend when I felt there was no one else. I still feel this way on bored or lonely nights. When I was younger, I didn't know I would survive life; music saved me.

Through the years, I would share my favorite songs of the moment with *Friends* (#73, 1985; #144, 1989; legacy song, 1971, Elton John) or in a music-based conversation with a *Beautiful Stranger* (#10, 1999) at a party. Over the years, only my closest music-oriented friends became aware of the extent of, and the time I spent tracking, my *Obsession* (a song-that-got-away, 1985, Animotion). This quiet lifelong project was mine alone. Until now, when I decided to publish my favorite song lists for the world to see.

You may ask why anyone would care about this. Exactly! In the grand scheme of life, how important are my lists to others? Who cares that I spent decades tracking my favorite songs?

At a minimum, fellow music freaks may find my lists interesting.

Maybe I share the same musical tastes as others. I do have friends with whom I share at least a 45-percent Venn-diagram crossover of music and artist favorability. Maybe someone will discover new songs and artists they never heard before. Music *is* an art form that's easily paid forward to the benefit of both artist and listener.

Maybe musicologists, music supervisors, list makers, or music psychologists will find these year-end lists intriguing. *Maybe Someday . . .* (#86, 1987) people will purchase the work of the artists found within.

For instance, look at Kate Bush's surge in popularity by the inclusion of one of her songs in a 2022 TV series. (More about that historical occurrence later!) Perhaps these artists and songs will gain a bigger audience by their presence here. The likelihood seems small, but I have big musical hopes and dreams.

What music flows into your life and accompanies your soul?

Sadly, any song list I create is bound to be flawed on some level. To capture every great song among thousands released around the world each year would be a Herculean feat for anyone, so I know I am forever limited to the music I am exposed to. Imagine any human with the time for, and exposure to, every great song in the world. Or songs from alien worlds if music exists out there. (This is foreshadowing; I believe some haphazard, music-related thoughts necessitate further examination later. So buckle in, and hang with me.)

Pardon me if I bore you with my scatterbrained ramblings; I wish to convey a sense of who I am and what kind of music drives me happily *Crazy* (#46, 1991; #51, 2003; #6, 2006; #94, 2006). If music was personified, *She Drives Me Crazy* (#25, 1989).

Before I go off on other music tangents, my next chapter introduces music-memory tales. Further tales are scattered throughout the remainder of this book.

Music Memories

Some songs are best enjoyed alone (or drunk).

All our senses can bring back memories. We recall textures through touch and teeth. Photos or faces transport us to a distant or recent past. Smells, like those reminiscent of a relative's farm, or the scent of a flower drifting on the wind from the neighbor's yard, fling us back in time. Yet, it is music that brings back the most memorable past moments for me. Without a song connection, some memories, large or miniscule, would have been lost to me.

Some songs became my favorites because of the memories attached to them. We all have such memories. Songs connected to a person or place or event (vivid memories especially come of vacations). Songs linked with the smell of a moment, the restaurant where you dined, the film you had just seen. Then, there are songs that lingered on a particular nothing-sort-of-night, but yet that nothingness became attached, and that song and moment remain forever linked in your brain. Who would necessarily remember, decades later, waiting in line or riding an elevator if it weren't for a great song playing on the sound system?

Many of my memories are attached to the moment I first heard a song, no matter what I was doing at the time. Similar to how I remember the most mundane location and moment I saw an unusual bird species, even when the bird was an LBJ ("little brown job"). Blah bird, great moment; blah moment, great song. Believe me, you would remember where in nature you saw your first cock-of-the-rock, hoopoe, or secretary bird, if you had the opportunity.

Talk about bird and music memories, whenever I hear *Jolene* (Dolly Parton) or *Fancy* (Bobbie Gentry or Reba McEntire) I now think of two rare kiwi birds: the rowi which were given these names at a nature reserve on South Island, New Zealand. My small birding troop quietly tracked Jolene on a highly regulated night search and were successful. Besides being rare, the rowi are skittish; so our troop was diligent in following the strict tracking rules. By the way, Jolene may have been a male.

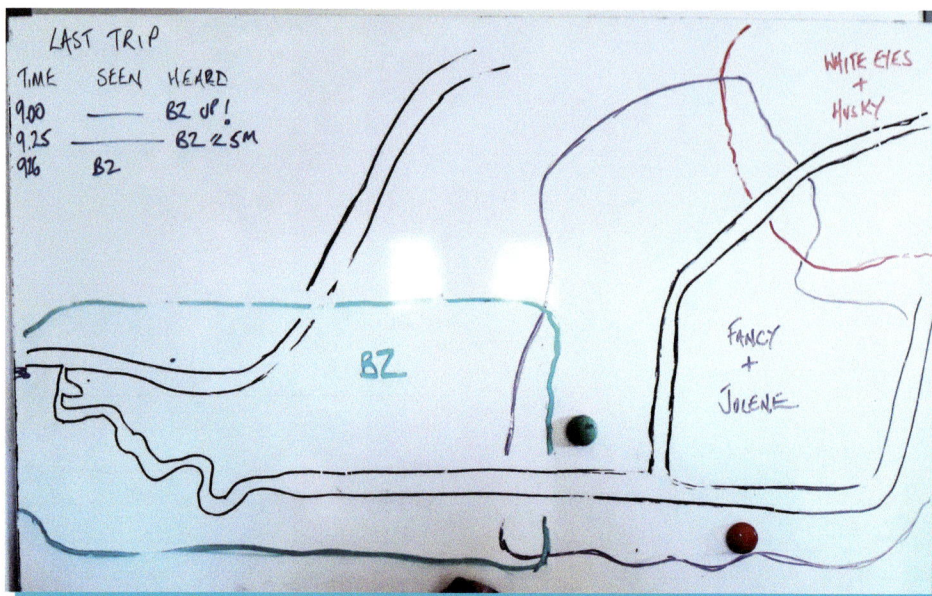

Jethro Tull's *Bungle in the Jungle* and Poco's *Indian Summer* forever remind me of decoration themes I suggested for our high school homecoming dance. The school's homecoming committee advisor immediately stifled the idea of any bungling in the gymnasium, especially after dark.

I always remember when I flipped from albums to compact discs because Kate Bush's *A Sensual World* was my last LP purchase. I bought the CD version within months, in early 1990. I rather doubt I will ever switch to mp3, unless it is the only option available.

I don't want a cloud,
I want music in my hands and home.

Tiësto's *Footprints* will always remind me of my one-time vision to have a Facebook friend from every country in the world before I realized the world was not as kind as it used to be, at least online. I innocently dreamed of leaving my "footprints" around the world by knowing others. I took a chance, and I was glad I did, since I gained and met some wonderful friends. By the end of that innocent online mission, I had a "friend" from 183 of 197 countries. I never did find a friend from Vatican City.

There are songs from my life that I sang to myself every day so I would not forget the melody and whatever I could discern of the lyrics. *Check The Meaning* by Richard Ashcroft comes to mind. It wasn't until I returned home from a trip that I discovered I could find a match merely by adding the word "lyrics" to my online search. I have hummed songs in Hong Kong record stores and clerks have found the Chinese artist for me. Mind you, some of these moments occurred before I ever had a cellphone.

There is my memory of Martika's version of *Love . . . Thy Will Be Done* when I initially heard it "sung" by a drag queen, back when drag wasn't a refined art. The lip syncing was terrible despite this performance illusion being her main job requirement.

I have associative memories of songs I sang at weddings, played in pep band, or sang during my own high school graduation. (About the latter, such ceremonial double-tasking happens when you attend a small-town high school.) There are memories to songs I knew from my stint as a college DJ at a radio station with an orgasmic call sign. City Boy's *The Day The Earth Caught Fire* comes to mind . . .

Since I am anonymous, I use pseudonyms for friends and family mentioned in my stories. Surreptitiously, a version of my immediate family members' first names is found within the song titles or artists. And my friend, and personal editor, has the honor of being the only person whose actual name is the same as an artist in my lists.

I can't hear certain songs without immediately thinking of a particular friend for specific or traceable reasons. Of course, I especially think of friends named in a song: Mary, Carol, Gary, Tami, Johnny, Jack, Jill, Sara, Pamela, Arthur, Laura, Billy, Judy, Vincent, Jennifer, Dan, Peg, Alejandro, Molly, or Lorelei. I could go on . . .

Previously, I presented a few song memories. Some of my memories are vague; others more detailed. I hope you will enjoy these music-related side trips scattered throughout this book.

Who Am I?

I may forget someone's name ten seconds later, but I can hum 1,000 songs.

Since my songs are so personal, this story should be too.

I am Elias Mondegreen, a lover of music. A bit of a fanatic I suppose. A guy who remembers where he purchased half of his music collection (from San Francisco to Sault Ste. Marie and Oslo to Taipei). A man unable to whistle, but who will sing songs out loud with little attention to the true lyrics. (This is your cue to research *mondegreen* if you are not aware of my last name's meaning.)

A favorite mondegreen originated with a friend/former coworker's sister who once sang, "I've been cheated, chop this tree dead . . ." during Linda Ronstadt's version of *When Will I Be Loved*. I cannot listen to *Our Lips Are Sealed*, by the Go-Go's, without hearing a friend's rendition of "grabbing my ass, well, that's no surprise." Then again, on an Aerosmith classic, I used to sing "born to swing" instead of *Walk This Way*. I still think somewhere in *Waterloo,* ABBA sings, ". . . how does it feel to be waterboy." People are crazy weird, aren't they?

I am a left-handed, right-brained, Midwestern, middle-aged, white guy who feels like a child and who happens to be gay. I am an uncomplicated guy with quiet expectations for myself and the world. Someone who has never been popular, but who is certainly affable in most situations. Others may recognize me as being *Too Shy* (#65, 1983). Overall, I'm rather goofy and proudly quirky. I'm a vamp, a scamp, and a bit camp.

When you know me, I blossom like a crescendo.

I use a *nom de plume* for two reasons:

- Primarily for privacy. Mistër E's second mystery for you—a *Sunny Mystery* (#16, 2009). My real name is, surprisingly, the only one of its kind on the planet, so anonymity feels right; besides, I am no authority on music. Does being a high school band and choir nerd grant me expertise? I may not know all the facts, words, or background of my favorite songs and artists, but I know I love the songs within.

- Secondly, I use a pseudonym because this book isn't about me. It's about the songs and artists that influenced my life. I am just a *Vehicle* (legacy song, 1970, The Ides of March), a mere purveyor, a musical pipeline sharing these great songs. The book *is* about the music, no matter what else I tell you. LOL, I may possibly be the Daft Punk, deadmau5, Marshmello, or Claptone of music authors.

  (By the way, I wanted my title to be *Mr. E's Eclectic Compendium* but, to avert online confusion and potential copyright issues, my title name became Mistër E, which I rather enjoy, especially with the unnecessary umlaut. A nod to BÖC and early Jason Derulo.)

Just recently (all right, as I wrote this book) I learned that I am a melomaniac due to my inordinate need for music. That explains everything! I've been passionate about music for as long as I can remember.

As a child, I loved hearing a great song blaring in the car on a surprisingly crisp summer eve, the road sandwiched between cornfields. With the windows down, you could smell the alfalfa as the sounds of gravel and grasshoppers blended with the melody. My mind would *Drift Away* (legacy song, 1973, Dobie Gray). Those were simpler times for me before music became my part-time job. I'm not complaining. I am so very grateful I tracked my songs.

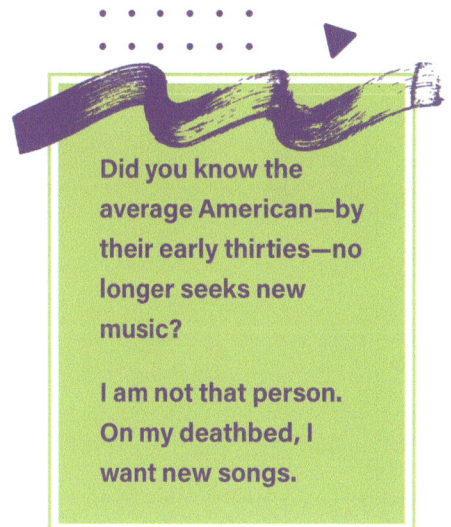

Did you know the average American—by their early thirties—no longer seeks new music?

I am not that person. On my deathbed, I want new songs.

Mankato, 1976

Talk about vague moments attached to a song . . . I can see my family driving down Mankato's Front Street before they tore up downtown to create the Mankato Mall. The car radio began playing Electric Light Orchestra's latest single, *Livin' Thing*, at the exact moment our cream-colored, faux-wood-paneled Pontiac Grand Safari station wagon passed The Lost Chord record store on one side of the street and Marti's Pizza on the other. (I believe this occurred after Marti's overhang sign crashed onto the sidewalk and possibly hurt a pedestrian. If memory serves me well, I think they outlawed overhang signs in town after that incident.) Supposedly, Marti's Pizza was where Billie Joe Armstrong met his wife when Green Day played there in the 1980s.

It's such a nothing memory, but it stays with me each time I hear this song. I am certain it is common for others to recall where they were when they first heard a song they really loved, or the moment they realized the specialness of a song. It is odd, but not surprising, how many of my childhood music memories were spawned by the car radio.

English Class, c. 1977

Though you don't really know me, I am hoping this story does not frighten or concern you in any way. It certainly would play out differently in today's world. My memory is about a short story, titled "More Than a Feeling," which I wrote for English class in my junior year of high school. After all these years, I must thank my remarkable teacher, Mr. Moor, for understanding exactly who I was as a boy, and for never questioning what I was trying to say.

In my short story, a boy was forced by his parents to play the violin even though he did not have any passion for, nor ambition to play, the instrument. When the boy was older, his father was driving him to his next recital. Both parents were in the front as the boy fumed in the back seat. He dreamt of getting out of this life he was forced to lead. On the radio, *More Than a Feeling* by Boston began to play, and the boy had a demonic feeling come over him. He reached over his father's shoulder, grabbed the steering wheel, and aimed their vehicle directly into an oncoming semi-trailer truck; the song continued to play.

(continued)

I never have been a violent person.

I know why my teacher never spoke to my parents about this horrendous tale. My teacher knew I was gay; I am sure of it, in retrospect. I believe he knew I was an imaginative boy screaming within to escape my small town. He knew my story wasn't about harming my family, but an allegory about being trapped in a world I didn't quite grasp; a boy harboring anger about a topic I dared not speak of in those days. And Mr. Moor knew my fascination with the macabre as I devoured Edgar Allan Poe during earlier reading assignments. (Who knew there was a difference between malady and milady? It made all the difference when I read "The Fall Of The House Of Usher.")

After my mom's death, I found this handwritten story in a box of high school papers that she had saved. I assume my parents had read it and never thought I was a killer child. Besides, my parents knew I loved playing my trombone (never a violin).

On a lighter note, for our first assignment in speech class, this same English teacher required each student to memorize anything that was at least a minute long. I chose to speak the first verse and chorus of *Life Is A Rock (But The Radio Rolled Me)* recorded by Reunion. Or, at least, what lyrics I could determine, since in the 1970s there was no cellphone service, at least in my area, to search for actual words.

If you know the song, the verses consist of a quick, rap-like babble of music artists and mumbo-jumbo that was difficult to discern. So, I placed my 45 single on the turntable and changed the RPM to 33⅓ to slow the lyrics down. But even that method was faulty, so I wrote what I thought I had heard and recited that for the assignment. My interpretation was exact in parts, yet also way off base. Today, when I hear this song, I continue to sing the mistaken words I memorized back then.

Did you ever play albums on the wrong turntable speed? I discovered Bad Company albums sound like Dolly Parton on amphetamines when played on 45 RPM.

My Nonmusical Passions

So, who else am I, and why should you care? Will you appreciate my songs by knowing who I am? What is it about me, my passions, and life experiences that influenced my musical tastes, my desire to create lists, and my excessive need to track music? Maybe these facts will give you an idea.

I am a traveler	*Days Are Numbers (The Traveller)* (#32, 1985)
geographer	*All Over The World* (#73, 1980)
vexillologist	*I'll Fly For You* (#49, 1984)
gastronome	*Dinner With Gershwin* (#142, 1988)
cinephile	*If This Was A Movie . .* (#19, 2022)
cruciverbalist	*Head Games* (#49, 1979)
photographer	*Photograph* (#20, 2010)
philatelist	*Signed, Sealed, Delivered (I'm Yours)* (#93, 1977)
list maker	*The Wedding List* (#5, 1981)
birder	*Wonder Of Birds* (#15, 1990)
nature lover	*Nature Boy* (legacy song, 1948, Nat King Cole)

I am a collector of all things, from matchbooks and bottle caps to world miniatures and flags.

I am a wit and punster even if my friends groan. I am a logician in love with *The Logical Song* (#1, 1979), a gregarious loner, a very notional kind of guy, and a dabbler in creative things. And I love word games, especially games related to music. I am a Virgo and a Rat, with blood type B personality traits. A lover of anything new or different in life. A quiet explorer and an astute observer. A citizen of the world.

Overall, I am simply a really happy guy, partly thanks to music. Is it evident that, beyond music, I have a full life?!

Loners encounter music more desperately.

Certainly, two of my passions are entrenched within my year-end lists: travel and movies. Those memorable songs I first heard from a movie or while on *Vacation* (#83, 1982; legacy song, 1962, Connie Francis). Face it, movies provide instant memories whenever the theme song is heard. Savvy readers can surmise when I saw a movie or visited a country merely by where theme songs and foreign titles appear in my lists. It is interesting to me how visual memories, whether from a video bar, a movie theater, or a place one has been, impact and strengthen the love of a song.

I have often wondered if I had to give up any of my three biggest passions—music, travel, and movies—could I? Would I be satisfied to give up music because I could hear songs in movies and on my journeys? Could I give up the other two to have music alone? It is a choice I never want to make.

99 Miles from L.A., 1980

In college, I began to attend gay events in nearby towns. Clandestine events spread by word-of-mouth across the agrarian world of south-central Minnesota's small towns. At my very first event (I was nervous to even go), there was Frederick. He smiled across the room and I knew I had to meet him. I thought of him as my first boyfriend, even if it was a short adventure.

One day, in his dorm in a neighboring city, I learned of his love for Art Garfunkel. I knew of Art, of course, but I never really knew much of his solo career until that day with Frederick. As he cued up more Art Garfunkel albums, I encountered the enchanting song, *99 Miles From L.A.*, and I fell in love. With the song, and with Frederick.

It wasn't long after this moment that I heard Johnny Mathis's version on a greatest hits album I had purchased.

I still remember that time of young love whenever I hear a version of this song. Sometimes I sense I am 99 miles from somewhere even when the song isn't playing.

Los Angeles
CITY LIMIT
POP 3,957,900   ELEV 330

I could talk about music forever.

Anyone who knows me well is aware that I can discuss music all day long to the detriment of other topics. To this day, I am one of those people who peppers conversation with melodic lyrical interjections based on the words being said, when I have nothing else to add. I am an easily distracted guy.

Istanbul, 2019

In 2019 I met a very special friend in Turkey (halfway between our Asian and American homes) to celebrate our birthdays. This was our second trip together; our special days are two weeks apart.

On his birthday night, we went out for a fancy and delicious rooftop dinner before descending to a nearby outdoor bar, the Gusta Pub. After a few cocktails we decided to try a *shisha* (hookah/water pipe) for the first time. We ordered strawberry-melon flavored tobacco and enjoyed the novelty on a lovely night in a beautiful world city. Another Fuckit-List item (i.e., "Fuck it, I gotta try it!") was crossed off my list.

At some point, our bartender surprised us with elaborate alcoholic shots in honor of our birthdays. Gratis. As we downed our shots a song played on the bar's video screen and I was distracted. This happens all the time. I stop everything when a new song excites me. Luckily, I found the song using my phone and planned to purchase it when I got home, only to find it unavailable on CD.

The song was *Never Say Die* by Stealth. It grabbed me immediately with its Bond-esque vibe. Though unknown to me, on that wild night of revelry, this song would become my #1 for 2019. Şerefe!

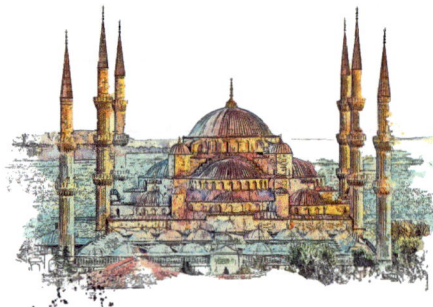

"Who Is Prince?"
and Other Mom Memories, 1984

I bet there are songs that remind you of your parents, especially songs from their album collection. My parents particularly loved Herb Alpert and the Tijuana Brass and Andy Williams. They also purchased many *Reader's Digest* box sets. Basically, "Now That's What I Call Oldies"— pre-sixties oldies, that is.

When it came to TV, we were a CBS family, probably because that was the only channel we received until the communication tower in Godahl was built in the early seventies. While growing up, our family watched many CBS variety shows hosted by Glen Campbell, Carol Burnett, Sonny and Cher, Leslie Uggams, or Tony Orlando and Dawn. I am sure there were others. Through these shows, I was exposed to guest artists and their latest songs. I enjoyed our family TV time.

Later in life, after my father's death, Mom and I shared conversations about music artists she heard, but I mostly remember her love of bluegrass and the wonderful Alison Krauss & Union Station, and how much she enjoyed the song *Children* by Robert Miles. Once, she met Keith Urban at a music festival before he was a huge star. I have the photo and signature to prove it.

Then there are those road trip mixtapes I made for us. I drove and she selected the next CD— mostly country music that fit both our tastes and the many, many songs associated with Route 66, our favorite road trip to take together. The Mother Road was a passion of hers that rubbed off on me.

Yet there is one music moment with Mom that always brings me a smile over all others.

On a June afternoon, I was eating lunch with her at Bridgeman's Ice Cream, the old one on Hennepin Avenue. As we were talking in our booth, my eye caught sight of a white convertible that pulled up out front. In walked his royal purpleness, Prince. This was his hometown, after all.

Without thinking, I grabbed a napkin from the table dispenser, asked the waitress (as they were called then) for a pen, scurried over to him as he stood by the checkout counter, and politely asked for his autograph. He initially seemed a bit put off, but I caught a slight smirk as he signed the napkin. Even in his heeled boots he was shorter than me.

Prince received his chocolate to-go shakes—or were they malts?—and got into his convertible. Apollonia was behind the wheel. It happened so quickly, so unexpectedly, so long ago, that details are blurred. My mind initially exaggerated this memory by turning the vehicle into a white limousine.

As I returned to our booth, I remarked to Mom how cool it was to meet Prince. Her response was, "Who is Prince?" In her defense, it was June 1984, about a month before the release of the **Purple Rain** album and movie. *When Doves Cry* was already a hit. His career was about to skyrocket worldwide.

One day I will part with his autograph. Who wants to purchase a signature?

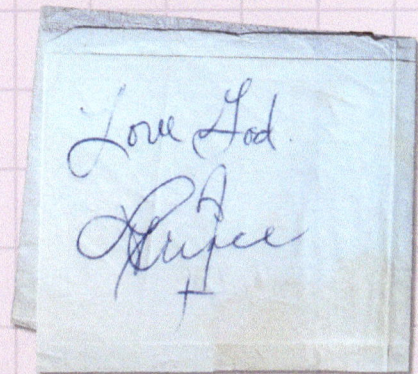

My Musical Tastes

Music is like food—we each have particular tastes.

Each of us has a unique perspective on the music we like. I think it would be difficult for most to explain their distinct musical tastes or why they truly love a particular song.

What immediately draws me to a song? Is it indescribable?
Possibly, but I will try . . .

Current & Past Favorite Artists

In my introductory musings, I presented many of my favorite artists based on their sheer musical fabulousness, their career album releases, and my "single" chart positions for their songs over the years. Needless to say, these artists are represented in my year-end top 101 songs.

Of these artists, Kate Bush is my lifetime favorite—in case you haven't noticed her name mentioned four times so far, outside of my year-end lists; five times now. If you immerse yourself in the phenomenal musical beauty of Kate and her compelling, innovative voice and production, then you may understand where to begin when it comes to my tastes. Her distinctive voice is both operatic and mysterious (albeit, off-putting to some). She opened my eyes to future musical possibilities and influenced many artists that followed. Prior to Kate, my childhood favorites were easily Elton John and the Bee Gees.

It is interesting to note that Madonna has the most appearances in my year-end lists (and, not surprisingly to me, the majority of my favorites by her are not her biggest hits). She's prolific and knows the way around a gorgeous melody.

Maybe knowing my childhood icon artists will help you understand the music I love. In relation to this book, many of my iconic artists' career hits precede 1976, the year I began tracking music. My favorite childhood songs of these artists, and others, are listed in the Artist Cross-Reference section.

I present some of my icons, in no particular order:

**The Beatles   Diana Ross & The Supremes
The Who   The Stylistics   Helen Reddy
Seals & Crofts   Carpenters   Dionne Warwick
Yes   Simon & Garfunkel   The Guess Who
Led Zeppelin   Bread   Crosby, Stills, Nash (& Young)
Doris Day   Marvin Gaye   Chicago
Emerson, Lake & Palmer   Roberta Flack
The Rolling Stones   Andy Williams
The Doobie Brothers   Johnny Mathis
Julie Andrews   Henry Mancini
Sly And The Family Stone   Carole King
Earth, Wind & Fire   The Moody Blues
The Fifth Dimension   Steely Dan
Todd Rundgren   The Association
Dusty Springfield   Herb Alpert
Dolly Parton   Perry Como   Gene Kelly
Neil Diamond   Bad Company   Cher**

I'd be remiss if I didn't give a nod to composers and songwriters I did not yet appreciate or know when I was a child, such as Cole Porter, Hildegard von Bingen, Ennio Morricone, Bach, Satie, Tchaikovsky, Vivaldi, Orff, and the rest of the classical world.

My Favorite Song

Though I can name my favorite artists, it is more difficult to name my favorite song ever. How can you pick only one? And I know people will ask, so, if cornered, I often vacillate between *Summer Breeze* by Seals & Crofts and *Ain't No Sunshine* by Bill Withers. If you ask me another day, my answer might be *Between A Man And A Woman* by Kate Bush, or *I Go Crazy* by Paul Davis. (This latter song is surprisingly ranked at 31 in 1977, which only shows how temporal any ranking of my favorite songs can be. Seriously, I could rework my top 101 songs as often as I rewrite this text!)

Influential Musical Styles

I definitely have a "pop ear" for songs with unique, fresh melodies that range from the most gorgeous, peaceful ballads you have never heard to weird, awesome, frenetic dance hits! There is a better chance that I will love a song if it's "dancey-clappy" (as one friend snarkily describes my music) than I will if it's a mainstream ballad. Perhaps I often like my songs fast, like how I walk. Perchance I'm an introspective guy who needs some fire in his music.

Are you in the Moog for love?

And I have an affinity for songs *In A Minor Key* (#73, 1984) that haunt my soul with potential dread or emptiness, songs of veiled intrigue that exude *Urgent* (#99, 1981) directives with each passing line.

When I started my year-end lists in 1976, I listened to pop, rock (especially psychedelic and prog rock), R&B, country, funk, folk, easy listening, and disco. Of these, disco most invigorated me. Jokingly, I say that my love of disco/dance tunes is the most stereotypically gay thing about me. And though great dance favorites abound in my early listening years, it wasn't the only genre that ruled my charts back then.

The late, late seventies and early eighties brought forth a redux British invasion that quickly became my favorite musical genre—new wave! For me, it remains an exciting era of music with its vast array of fresh sounds and experimental artists. I feel lucky that my young brain and soul matured during this period.

The Minneapolis Sound soon followed, which made this local boy extremely proud and profoundly influenced me and the American music scene. Then, by the late eighties, everything went musically wacko for me.

I wish to clarify one point here before I continue: Though I like many musical styles, as evidenced by the artists found within my year-end lists, personally, I find the need to classify a song or artist into a cramped niche or style very limiting, ill-defined, and wholly unnecessary. If it is a great song, I don't care what genre it is, outside of the need to describe the sound to others. Nonetheless, I will try to encapsulate, in one list, some of the past and ongoing styles which inform my musical taste. Here I go!

ska/reggae   new age   alt-rock   jazz fusion
Celtic fusion   worldbeat   dream pop
nouveau lounge   chant dance   trip hop   Eurodisco
drum & bass   synthpop   darkwave
country pop   goth   Arab pop   technopera
post-punk   grunge   emo   EDM   electronica
house   hip hop   Christian rock   industrial
nü metal   chillwave   Cantopop   neo soul

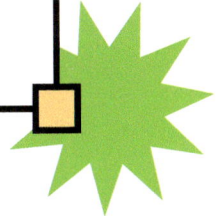

Get the idea? No matter the genre nor its nuanced subname, there is music to love.

As you read earlier, I have an attraction to movie songs, especially James Bond themes, and the attached visual memories these songs bring with them. And I love great instrumentals, whether TV themes or an orchestral opus. I sense that LGBTQ+ artists likely have built-in personal bias with respect to my musical likings. And I have a decidedly western-cultured ear. We each have some biases in life, including in our music preferences.

Some songs fit me perfectly— like a snug, faux-fur earmuff.

An Unscientific Description of a Great Song

What makes a fantastic song? For me, broadly, it is a combination of a catchy (and complex) melody and a memorable chorus with an enticing vocal delivery. But, no matter what, I gotta love *The Voice* (#36, 1982) unless, of course, the song is an instrumental. I ponder which factors might elevate a song to greatness in my esteem, such as whether owning it and hearing it more often makes a difference. Or whether my partiality for certain artists over my lifetime plays a role. I do have preferences with respect to songs by my favorite artists, but I can also be hypercritical when they release new music. Some artists just hit the spot for me.

A great song is four minutes where nothing else matters.

I don't know how to describe my favorite songs. The description could be specific, or more likely generic, for each song. So excuse me as I muse rhapsodic with an arrangement of euphonious inanities to confuse the matter further. (Read it poetically.) I'm excited by:

A fresh voice, a singular voice, divinely pure, lusty, gravelly, growly, desperate, dramatic, or reedy.

A catchy pop sensation, anthems with broad shoulders, downright disco freakouts.

Walls of sound, streets of throbbing cacophony, harmonic gardens wrapped in bubblegum.

Syncopation, offbeat percussion, jiggy, jangly, crunchy, squeaky guitars, Spanish guitars, tubular bells!

Movie themes, a stunning debut, dynamic instrumentals, and remakes that sound brand new.

A bagpipe, rainstick, dulcimer, oboe, oud—dithering with zithers, a Hammond organ any time.

A thoughtful sample, majestic interpolations, and paeans in languages I don't understand.

Vibrato, vocoder, a vocal death drop, ethereal chorales, cæsurae followed by a false ending.

Retro coolness, a street café twist, smoke-filled pacing, or jazzy insouciance late into the night.

A surprise turn by a star, a dense song story, nonsensical ditties, the moment a song goes all weird.

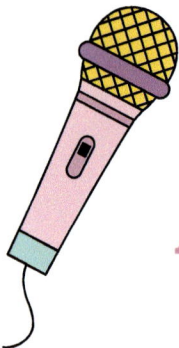

Falsetto canyons, robotic wastelands, whirling arabesques. Hark! I hear a timpani!

Sensual groans, sound effects, a sterile, dry delivery; intonations across octave hills.

Arpeggios on steroids, arcane deep cuts, the susurration of temple bells in an evening breeze.

4AD, ZTT, EMI, A&M, RSO, Rhino—Casablanca, Windham Hill, Nettwerk, Real World, and Island.

Theremin, gourd, pipa, tabla, koto, marimba—water randomly plinking on a tin roof, rusty.

Symphonic swirls, an abrupt klaxon, vocal mayhem, a Darth Synth claiming the multiverse.

An honored songwriter, beloved producers, male/female vocals blended in one band.

Chunky vibes, a killer key change, a clever lyric frolic, or unexpected bridges between eerie refrains.

Breathtaking choruses, extreme segues, hi-fi static, a bamboo flute wafting from somewhere in the fog.

Frisky staccatos in melody meadows, a full-horn battlefield attack—then whistling nothingness fading away.

Wah-wah mutes, luscious layering, cowboy lullabies trapped in a studio nightmare.

Gamelan, steel drums, mouth harp, castanets, or my grandma's washboard in the village parade.

BPM overdrive, a rapturous five-note progression, a song with hooks in need of an earworm.

Hey, there, what's that sound turning all Gregorian chanty on me? Eh? ¡Hey ocarina! ¡Ay!

Enough silliness. Are you confused yet? I still am.

Why does anyone love a song? Why are we drawn to particular sounds? It seems so personal. If *you* had to describe your favorite types of songs . . . could you? How would you explain it to others? Do you ruminate over how a song makes you feel, do you love the lyrics, or a specific note sequence, or does it simply make you want to dance? Or do you love it merely because you can't escape it?

One person's #1 song is another's musical nightmare.

It is odd that lyrics usually don't influence my initial love of a song. Words don't matter if a song sounds great. Songs in foreign languages come to mind. To be honest, lyrics can escape me until it is a favorite song. Yet, there are sharp lyrics and word plays I absolutely adore from the start.

I am one of those people who naturally gravitates to less popular, more eclectic tastes in life, whether it is food, travel, movies, or music. I am a curious guy. Maybe I lean toward melodies that aren't mainstream even though numerous pop hits are strewn across my top 101 lists. I think the more obscure artists and songs deserve their recognition, here, since popular songs and artists have plenty of fans elsewhere.

Despite my peculiar tastes there are times when my #1 weekly song parallels the public psyche and the national and world music charts. Which reminds me of a conversation with an old acquaintance, simplified here:

> **Her:** "I waited in line all night to get concert tickets."
> **Me:** "I would never wait that long for (unnamed megastar)."
> **Her:** "You're in luck because there will *never* be a line for *anything* you're interested in!"

Touché! I wear my individuality proudly, especially when it comes to music.

Why do I love any song or artist? Is it about a specific moment, at that place, at that time of day, with that friend; or that loneliness or certain mood elevating a song to something sublime? Or is it just a damn good song? 'Nuff said.

My World of Music, Mūzika, Egwu, ସଙ୍ଗୀତ, мусикӣ

I feel a great song without knowing the language.

There are great artists around the world to discover, though I prefer certain world-music styles over others. For example, I like the instrumentation and rhythms from southern and eastern Asia and the Middle East more than those from Latin America. Yet, the geographer and traveler in me is proud to say that, outside of Antarctica, there are artists who were born or raised on every continent found in my lists, including the following countries, territories, and special administrative regions:

Algeria
Andorra
Argentina
Aruba
Australia
Austria
Azerbaijan
Bahrain
Barbados
Belarus
Belgium
Bermuda
Brazil
Bulgaria
Cameroon
Canada
Chile
China
Colombia
Côte d'Ivoire
Cuba
Czech Republic
Denmark
Dominican Republic
Egypt
Eritrea
Ethiopia

Finland
France
Georgia
Germany
Greece
Guernsey
Guinea-Bissau
Guyana
Haiti
Hong Kong
Hungary
Iceland
India
Indonesia
Iran
Ireland
Isle Of Man
Israel
Italy
Jamaica
Japan
Jordan
Kenya
Kosovo
Kuwait
Lebanon
Lesotho

Libya
Lithuania
Malaysia
Malta
Mexico
Moldova
Montserrat
Morocco
Netherlands
New Zealand
Nigeria
Norway
Pakistan
Peru
Philippines
Poland
Portugal
Puerto Rico
Romania
Russia
Saint Kitts & Nevis
Saint Vincent & the Grenadines
Senegal
Serbia
Singapore
Slovak Republic

Somalia
South Africa
South Korea
Spain
Sudan
Sweden
Switzerland
Taiwan
Tanzania
Thailand
Tibet
Trinidad & Tobago
Tunisia
Turkey
Ukraine
United Arab Emirates
United Kingdom (England, Scotland, Wales & Northern Ireland)
United States
Uzbekistan
Vietnam
Zambia
Zimbabwe

Then there is The Earth Orchestra (#78, 2021), encompassing 197 musicians from 197 countries. One Band. One World.

This is the perfect moment to recognize the fascinating Yma Sumac who put Peru on my music map! Yma's vocalizations have enchanted me since I was introduced to her, musically not literally. She was Kate Bush or Klaus Nomi before their time.

My Favorite Albums by Year

Before I end this topic, maybe my favorite albums from each year since 1976 will provide more insight into my tastes.

YEAR	ALBUM TITLE	ARTIST
1976	*Dreamboat Annie*	Heart
1977	*Rumours*	Fleetwood Mac
1978	*A Fantasy Love Affair*	Peter Brown
1979	*Candy-O*	The Cars
1980	*The Wall*	Pink Floyd
1981	*Never For Ever*	Kate Bush
1982	*The Dreaming*	Kate Bush
1983	*The Hurting*	Tears For Fears
1984	*It's My Life*	Talk Talk
1985	*Hounds Of Love*	Kate Bush
1986	*The Colour Of Spring*	Talk Talk
1987	*Tango In The Night*	Fleetwood Mac
1988	*Blue Bell Knoll*	Cocteau Twins
1989	*The Sensual World*	Kate Bush
1990	*Heaven Or Las Vegas*	Cocteau Twins
1991	*Cruel Inventions*	Sam Phillips
1992	*Shimmering, Warm And Bright*	Bel Canto
1993	*The Red Shoes*	Kate Bush
1994	*Fumbling Towards Ecstasy*	Sarah McLachlan
1995	*Stone Age (Stone Edge in US)*	Stone Age (Stone Edge)
1996	*Walking Wounded*	Everything But The Girl
1997	*The Great Game*	Brother Sun Sister Moon
1998	*Blue Wonder Powder Milk*	Hooverphonic
1999	*No Angel*	Dido
2000	*Minor Earth Major Sky*	a-ha
2001	*Starcrossed*	Maggie Reilly
2002	*Conjure One*	Conjure One
2003	*Details*	Frou Frou
2004	*Hopes And Fears*	Keane
2005	*Aerial*	Kate Bush
2006	*Eyes Open*	Snow Patrol
2007	*(tie) Out Of The Woods System*	(tie) Tracey Thorn Seal
2008	*Rockferry*	Duffy
2009	*Junior*	Röyksopp

YEAR	ALBUM TITLE	ARTIST
2010	*Believe*	Morgan Page
2011	*Within And Without*	Washed Out
2012	*Give You The Ghost*	Poliça
2013	*Ice On The Dune*	Empire Of The Sun
2014	*After The Disco*	Broken Bells
2015	*Radiant*	Iris
2016	*Aphasia*	Tanya Chua
2017	*Royal Blues*	Dragonette
2018	*My Indigo*	My Indigo
2019	*Morgenstund*	Schiller
2020	*Chromatica*	Lady Gaga
2021	*Californian Soil*	London Grammar
2022	*The Silence In Between*	Bob Moses
2023	*Higher Than Heaven*	Ellie Goulding
2024	*Fake Is The New Dope*	Hooverphonic

The Music Speaks for Me

In some ways I present a rather erratic glimpse of how to describe the songs I love. Yet there are over five thousand songs I present—each one representing an aspect of my tastes—and together, these wonderful songs overshadow my misgivings in this chapter.

Though humans are flawed, there is purity in music.

Việt Nam, 2019

This memory is not so much about a specific song, though three of my #1 songs of 2019 (year-end positions 4, 7, and 12) were known to me from this moment.

I made a visit to a tiny CD/DVD store named *Cửa Hàng Băng Đĩa* in the middle of Ho Chi Minh City (though it is forever Saigon to me). It was incredibly hot and humid on the day I walked to this store that I had discovered online. I often seek new music, especially local artists, when I travel. So I search for record stores around the world. It's not every traveler's priority but it is one of mine.

Though only ten-or-so blocks from my hotel, I had finished my water bottle halfway there and felt dizzy. I sat down before I would faint from the heat. After resting a bit I almost crawled to purchase more fluids nearby and continue to my destination. My body and clothing were drenched in sweat by the time I reached the store after two crazy street crossings along the way; it was a sea of scooters and motorbikes.

> Search *crossing the street in Vietnam* and watch any random video. It looks scary, but it is also exhilarating and an exercise in human trust.

I opened the sliding door of a store roughly the size of my living room and looked at the two elderly owners behind the counter. Initially, their faces stared at my red, soaked visage with a look hovering between horror and confusion. I greeted them with my rudimentary Vietnamese and my huge smile, as they immediately yelled someone's name toward the back of the store. From behind a curtain appeared a girl I presumed to be their granddaughter. She knew English quite well.

I showed her song titles and artists scrawled in Vietnamese that I had seen on my hotel's video channel. She proceeded to search for any songs they had amid their music bins, which I observed as beautiful chaos. Though unable to find my specific songs, she suggested a few recent Vietpop compilations; I purchased these and said my goodbye in Vietnamese as they thanked me. And I returned to the street sauna for my walk back to the hotel, though this time I had more joy in my step and electrolytes in my system.

Near the end of my visit, when my friend and I returned to Saigon, I walked to this store once again with a list of more Vietnamese songs and artists that intrigued me. But this time, when I slid open the door, the grandparents greeted me with welcoming smiles and a happy shout into the back for their granddaughter.

I love these small moments on my travels the most. Even as I type this story, I have joyful tears at remembering their tiny store and my favorite songs from the CDs the granddaughter suggested for me. I suspect I'd love many Vietnamese pop songs if given the exposure. What songs would I discover if I lived in any other country than my own?

A History Lesson: The Creation of My Lists

Music is ancient, innate, and universal.

Before I continue, this chapter and the next (concerning perceived controversies) are perfunctory necessities to satisfy my need to explain myself and my year-end selections. Cross thy T's, and dot thy whatevers . . .

In 1972 or 1973, I was curious to know the titles of songs and their respective performers. And I started to buy 45s and cassettes during these same years, as would any teenager of that age and time.

Around 1974, when I was the quiet janitor of my childhood church, I discovered Casey Kasem's *American Top 40* on a local radio station. The station played the three-hour show every Saturday afternoon, which was the average weekly time it took me to clean the nave, narthex, and social hall. Alas, I was also expected to shovel snow and mow the yard on this salary. I was paid fifty dollars per month.

I would plug in my portable radio to have music while I worked (when I wasn't creating piano ditties in the social hall or changing the drawknobs and couplers to create some cool sounds from the balcony electric organ). Once, the organist walked in on me, sitting on her bench, her approaching steps drowned out by my musical frivolity. It's not like I was paid by the hour.

It was New Year's Eve, 1975, and, unbeknownst to me, the local station played the *American Top 40* year-end countdown from song #100 to #1 of the year. Listening to the countdown on that night, I wondered what my favorites for 1975 would have been. I was fifteen and impressionable.

So, that New Year's Eve I began to write down what could become my favorite songs for 1976 in preparation for determining their year-end ranking.

When 1976 ended, I slowly went through every song I had written down for the prior year, aurally or mentally comparing each song to the others, until I had settled on my favorites in order. Some comparisons were so difficult. Imagine choosing between salted caramel fudge swirl and coconut macadamia ice cream. Now showing at the multiplexes: *Devil Woman* vs. *Evil Woman*. Or, it's a beauty pageant . . . who will win? I found no joy in judging any great song against the others on my list. This process is still no easy feat.

The initial process was too long ago to remember exact details, but I eventually did create my first year-end list. And I've created a list for every year since. Because I wrote down every song I wanted to remember, each year's song tally varied, whether it was 153 songs (1976) or 490 (2011) songs.

As I ranked a song, its details (name, artist, and album title) would be logged in my year-end list; then crossed off that year's ongoing tally of memorable songs I tracked. This process continued until every song was ranked and crossed out. I then tossed those initial tracking sheets. (I have included photo samples below of a tracking sheet along with part of an original year-end list.) Though all songs I documented were ranked, I took the most time and earnestness in determining my top 101. Hence, I only present my year-end 101 in this book. If I had ranked every song I ever wrote down as seriously as I ranked my top 101, it would be a weeks- or months-long effort that life never afforded me, especially during my busiest, wild (or working) years. Beyond the top 101, the importance of a song's placement seemed to carry less relevance, but I tracked every song I loved, nonetheless. To remember.

I placed my 1976 year-end list in a special notebook and created a year design (or logo) because I thought I was a clever, artistic guy. Perhaps I was a bit of a weirdo. (See photo 3 for the cover of my original year-end notebook with my

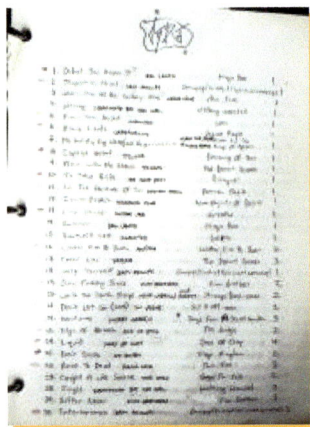

Partial original year-end list

Tracking sheet

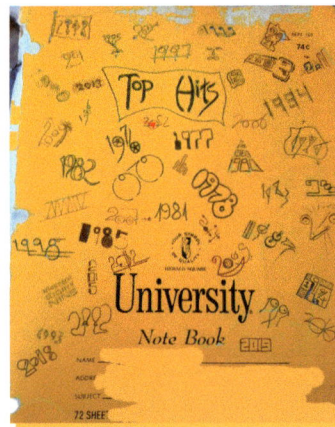

Year-end notebook cover

yearly designs.) These rustic designs are replicated within my year-end lists. A bit imperfect like life, and like me.

When 1977 ended, I repeated this process. And so on to the present day.

My entire process is still done by hand. I like simplicity. (I have said I would never turn into my grandparents, yet here I am! What's an *iPod*?)

I will always have internal dilemmas about my charts and lists. But I present my song lists as they were— as they still are! I am passionate and proud of my choices.

Beyond My Initial Chart Years

Over time I moved the year-end lists to a three-ring binder, using loose-leaf hole-reinforcement stickers to preserve the pages. I now have a second binder after forty-nine years of creating my lists. If I ever have to rescue one thing from my home due to an impending disaster, it would be these binders. Before photos, or other personal items of value, I would save my song lists, knowing that I would remember my music and life memories if my music collection were ever lost or destroyed.

In 1979, I began my own weekly charts of my current favorite forty songs in a new notebook. I used this same notebook (and those that followed) as my diary, tracking things I did that week, movies I saw, dates I went on, events I attended, etc. By tracking my songs weekly, I knew which were in heavy rotation on my stereo system. And then I knew the highest position on my chart that each song reached in preparation for the upcoming year-end list. In October 1993, due to life and time constraints, I began to track only my weekly top ten songs, though I

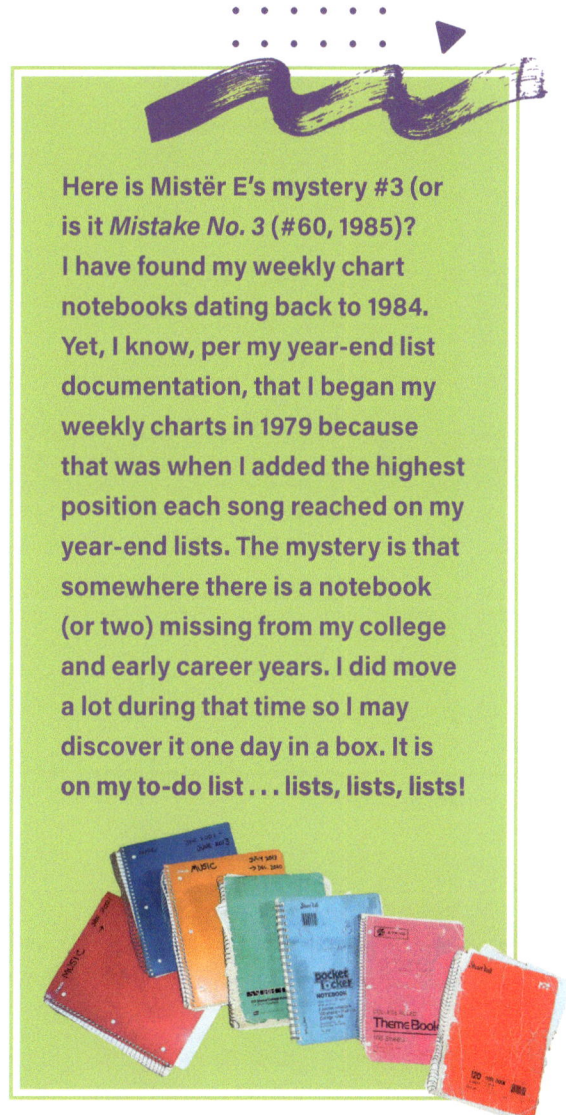

Here is Mistër E's mystery #3 (or is it *Mistake No. 3* (#60, 1985)? I have found my weekly chart notebooks dating back to 1984. Yet, I know, per my year-end list documentation, that I began my weekly charts in 1979 because that was when I added the highest position each song reached on my year-end lists. The mystery is that somewhere there is a notebook (or two) missing from my college and early career years. I did move a lot during that time so I may discover it one day in a box. It is on my to-do list . . . lists, lists, lists!

continued to assign a rough chart "peak position" for those songs that didn't make my weekly top-ten favorites.

Once I began tracking each song's highest position on my weekly charts, the procedure for creating my year-end list became less daunting. This weekly chart ranking also created what became my #1 collection of songs. Often friends hear me say, "This song is a number-one hit for me!" This is why I know this fact. You will find most of my #1 hits occupying the top positions in each year-end list. Some years I had fifteen #1 songs. Another year I may have had twenty-six. My #1 songs range between dance fabulousness to stark, pleading emptiness. A few #1 songs surprised me when they grew on me, slowly moving up my chart.

Some years were especially difficult to decide which *one* song was my overall favorite; other years I readily knew.

Compiling my top 101 songs became an annual January task, depending on required duties or other distractions. I have perfected the process immensely as far as the time it takes. Technological changes over the decades significantly reduced tracking down each song from my music collection and revisiting it in preparation for its ranking. I still try to relisten (when possible) and compare each potential hit against the others, with a fresh ear, before it is officially enshrined in my year-end lists.

The Beauty and Fragility of My Lists

I take my music charts and lists seriously. Throughout my life, I've tried to dedicate one night a week to my current favorite songs and albums. And I dedicate time to research new music, whether by going to record stores and flipping through the racks, hopping between radio stations, checking out new music from the library, viewing music videos, or scouring online music charts. Despite life's busy schedule, I am diligent, proactive, and greedy to find new music. And I feel rather lucky when I discover a great new song or artist incidentally. But there are songs that got away.

One thing to keep in mind as you peruse my top 101 lists: every song was ranked based on the moment the list was created. My mood or stressors of that day, my age and change in musical tastes, my initial emotions and memories about a particular song, radio saturation . . . heck, almost anything may have changed my feelings about a song and therefore the eventual position it landed in my year-end lists.

Music exists to meet each moment.

When I view my year-end rankings, I often think about how subjective they are. So frivolous. So meaningless to anyone other than me. Ephemeral music lists from the depths of one person's mind. Believe me, my ranking was not a science—there was no magical musical formula—though probably, my system has become more refined as each year passes. But now, as I share my silly obsession with the world, I begin to see some historical value to these lists, and maybe, other music freaks will be inspired to find new artists, though I presume some melomaniacs may only find validation of the artists they love within these lists.

I think these lists are an interesting overview of how music has changed in forty-nine years, juxtaposed against how one person and his musical tastes changed over the same time period.

So, there you are! That's how my lists were made.

Karaoke—Hong Kong 2015 / Osaka 2019

I'm an OK singer—a decent baritone and a tenuous tenor depending on the song range and time of day. It was easy to sing in high school and college choirs where my voice could meld within the many. I was often shy singing solo, along with my fear of being center stage, as you learned earlier with my *Born Free* debacle in fifth grade. Karaoke is one of those singing situations that lay one bare for ridicule, so it is not something I commonly or publicly do. I have had past, embarrassing mistakes in my karaoke choices (e.g., *Jackie Blue* by the Ozark Mountain Daredevils—the original OMD, haha). Now, I judiciously select songs where I positively know the beginning note, melody, and words. A few drinks help to relax my nerves and voice.

Out of all the times I've sung karaoke, there are two moments in Asia that I fondly relive in my mind. Karaoke is popular there, and no one knows me on my travels, so who cares how it turns out.

I flew to Hong Kong for my fifth visit in 2015. It has always been one of those places I have an affinity for, like it is a second home. My transpacific flight landed late at night. After my hotel check-in, I rushed to a nearby gay bar (a new one to me) when a local friend texted me to join him. It was after 1:00 a.m. Hong Kong time, by then.

Within minutes of finding my friend in the crowded bar, he passed a mic and said, "You're singing with me, dear." His next song selection was about to start. The song was *Hello* by Adele.

By the first chorus, my friend, in his tipsy and easily distracted state, rose to greet other friends and left me solo. Hello-o! What's happening? Luckily the song had been released a few weeks earlier so I knew the melody and understood the emotion required to respect the song. It was not a disaster for me, having received decent applause from the crowd considering I was a stranger to most and the only white boy in the bar. Not unusual in my travels.

It was a great first evening back in Kowloon and a memorable way to start my latest Hong Kong adventure.

Meanwhile, in April 2019, I went to Osaka, Japan, near the end of *sakura* (cherry blossom) season. One night, I officially met, in person, a social-media friend who introduced me to some of the local gay bars in the *Shinsekai* district of the city. I was intrigued that most of the bars in this area were tiny, accommodating twelve to twenty people, max.

Our last bar that evening was the most curious. My friend led me down a side alley to an elevator and he punched the top floor button. As we waited for the door to open, my friend explained that all five or six floors of this elevator led to a different gay bar. How would I know? Most of the elevator placards were written in Japanese next to the corresponding floor number.

As we entered the top-floor bar, I quickly scanned the tiny space populated by seven patrons and two bar staff and realized that not only was I the sole foreigner, but that at age fifty-eight, I was one of the youngest men there! I knew this was going to be fun. Though tiny, the bar had an entire wall of glass facing the *Tsutenkaku* (Eiffel Tower of Osaka). The changing color schemes of the illuminated tower enhanced the ambience, adding to the magic of the moment.

As with many of the bars that evening, karaoke selections filled this tiny airspace with song, some gorgeous, some not so much. But the energy was exciting. Eventually, I resolved to sing what I supposed was the perfect song: *Merry Christmas Mr. Lawrence – FYI* by Japanese popstar Utada. I chose an English song of hers, speculating that the locals might appreciate my attempt to sing an artist they'd recognize with a melody that is nationally known. You see, Utada's song interpolates Ryuichi Sakamoto's famous theme from the David Bowie movie of the same name. It would take my friend, the bartender, and another patron to eventually find a method to flip the karaoke machine to an English keyboard before my song search was possible. Luckily it was available.

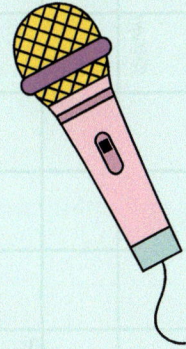

Shortly after I finished, a few of the locals asked me to duet with them on some American pop hits, including the lovely *(They Long To Be) Close To You* by the Carpenters. They were so polite, saying how their English was terrible, yet they sang beautifully with me, the guy who knows very little Japanese! They were too humble.

The night progressed with more song and umeshu (ume plum liqueur).

A few nights later, I escorted my Taiwanese traveling partner and two local friends to the magical elevator, the gateway to the tiny bars. We ascended to the top-floor bar to begin. None of us sang this night; we just enjoyed conversation and the view. As the evening waned, my local friends caught their respective last trains home. Consequently, my travel partner and I rode the elevator to other floors and listened outside each door to see if there was any action to be heard. None. On the third floor, we decided to enter the mystery door despite the lack of sound. It was then when my Taiwanese friend accidentally rediscovered his favorite Osaka bar from his past travels. A bar named Jun. No wonder my friend didn't remember, amid the jumbled streets of Shinsekai, to turn into this certain alleyway, find this elevator, and then press the correct floor button.

Today, I can still see the smiles of the locals, and I cherish their enthusiasm to duet with me.

I feel honored and lucky to experience the world through music; to revel with others when music is our only shared language. The world would be a better place if we all sang together. In perfect harmony. Or not so perfect. Who cares about perfection—at least we'd be laughing.

Year-End List Controversies

I already established that my songs and their rankings are all nebulous, fantastical BS, and really nothing but one person's lifelong obsession. So how can there be controversies over supposed piffle?

I knew some of my limitations as a music listener when I first started my lists. But then, I truly didn't foresee that I would continue ranking songs for the rest of my life. So why should I have concerns about my lists?

Since I am sharing my songs and rankings with the world, I want others to understand my confines and the decisions I made as I created each year's list. Why are songs and artists absent? Why is a song listed in the wrong year? Why so many "double-sided" singles, etc.?

I merely wish to thwart the eventual, online hate and derision by explaining my past and current decisions. There is no need to defend my song choices since, after all, they are the songs I love. I am proud of the songs that made my lists.

This being said, here are my explanations of potential chart "controversies."

The Song Selection

I only know the music I know.

As you review the songs in this book, bear in mind that each year is based on the music of *that* time and the songs I discovered in that particular year. As I aged and bought more music, my aural tastes and musical exposure expanded and continued to evolve. Nevertheless, my musical viewpoint is US-centric.

In the 1970s, my year-end lists are populated with 90 percent popular hits, which are replaced by 80 percent deep cuts and lesser-known artists in my later years. (When I say deep cuts, I really mean my "singles," the songs I would release as singles if *I* made record-industry decisions.) Most of my early song favorites I heard on the radio or from my older brother's albums—they were the only songs I knew!

Conversely, my year-end lists from the 1990s onward are filled with songs I owned and often never heard outside my home. I surrounded myself with the best music to shield me from outside ills.

The more I hear a likeable song, the stronger its favorability becomes to me over time. Rarely do I begin to love a song more if I didn't find it interesting upon first listen. Still, the reverse effect can be true; when a song is overplayed by outside sources, my love may decrease from the saturation. Hence the current state of corporate radio—a huge determiner of chart popularity—is rather stultifying to me. So I must pursue my own music. I am not amused hearing the same twenty songs from uninspired listening formats, replayed and pounded into my brain in daily repetition for months and sometimes years. I exit my car and a certain hit song is playing. After lunch, I return to my vehicle, turn on the radio, and the same song is playing again on the same channel. Rather sad. Possibly lazy.

It is the curse of musical inurement! Those songs we like until they're "played to death." Some of these songs fall lower on my year-end rankings. Yet many of *my* favorite songs I played over and over during the year in which the songs were ranked. Do you remember playing a new song on your turntable or playlist and replaying it a dozen times? Some songs are instant favorites even before the song is halfway through.

Some of my year-end lists are more vibrant and diverse than others. Over various periods of my life, I had less access to new music, less time to listen to the radio, or less money to explore new artists. At times, my life was just too damn busy or complicated to be a perfect music fan. In some years, I never heard hugely popular songs.

A quick shout-out to our musical mentors—those older siblings, friends, and especially parents, who exposed us to music.

I dare pop radio stations to play any of my top-ten songs across the nearly five decades I have been tracking music. Station managers may be surprised by the listener reception. And oldies stations, how about spinning an artist's fifth biggest song instead of the only two you ever play? Variety is the spice of life.

You will find some year-end lists are skewed to repeat artists because I owned the albums and grew to love many songs—especially in years I had little time for outside music. I find some years' lists more lacking in variety. Of course, technology has changed over these forty-nine years of tracking music. Access to music is easier, but I still struggle with the time factor. The library has changed everything for me in the last three decades! I never knew they had albums and CDs until a friend told me. My charts flourished upon this discovery with all the albums I could reserve and explore leisurely at home. No more afternoons spent on a store's listening station. By the way, use and support your local libraries!

I am saying that my year-end lists, no matter how I try, are limited by my music experience and tastes. And that my exposure to songs has varied and expanded over these years. But I must say, each year's top thirty songs are thoughtful and rather tight, groovy, rad, and on fleek no matter which year you review. Pure musical brilliance abounds in those songs.

The Wrong Year

Remember back in 1976 when I began documenting my potential year-end songs? Yes, I have prattled on and on since then. In that very first year when I created my year-end list, I wrote down some songs that debuted in 1975, yet I added them to the pool of songs ranked in 1976. Back then, no one had the Internet to fact-check anything and a person could only go by the date listed on an LP or 45—which I certainly did not confirm when I began compiling songs. I didn't write down every song from 1975, though, when I began my first list; *Sky High* by Jigsaw is on my 1976 year-end list but *Miracles* by Jefferson Starship is not. Yet, both songs are found in the Artist Cross-Reference.

Needless to say, the "wrong year" issue occurs throughout these top 101 lists for various reasons.

- Sometimes a song was released nationally as a single in the following year (or two) after its album release appearance.

- Sometimes songs (and albums) released late in the year were lost during the busy year-end holiday season (which is also my big movie season) and were not added or ranked until the following year when I had time to analyze them. Often these songs weren't even known to me until then. Life always came before fun.

- Sometimes albums or singles were released in the US market in a different year or were never released here at all, and I discovered the song much later.

- And there was my ongoing annual dilemma at the end of each calendar year—the cutoff, my demarcation within my tracked songs list—that determined which songs were ranked in the past year's list or saved for the next. This was a careful decision based on where each song fell or was expected to fall in my weekly top-ten charts as of my cutoff decision date. Therefore, songs from the same album may fall into two different years in relation to my year-end lists.

And now the most controversial reason for a song being listed in the wrong year:

- Occasionally I'm obsessed by a song released in the past, but it became familiar to me years after its release, and it is ranked in my year-end list during the year I initially heard it.

These lost songs were part of my life within the year I fell in love with them. And they ended up in my lists within the "wrong" year for that reason only. This is truly a reflection of what occurs in actual worldwide record sales and airplay charts. The reverse is also true, where one of my favorite charted songs is ranked in my year-end list a year or more before it ever became a national or international hit. There is so much music released each year that anyone can be late in discovery. I think you'd agree.

Here are some real-life examples of songs (and artists) where I was ahead of the game, and some songs that were my hits in years beyond their original release date:

1. Remember when Seal's *Kiss From A Rose* was featured in a certain Batman movie and became a US #1 hit? His song was my #1 song for 1994 and had entered my chart one year before its US pop chart peak.

2. *West End Girls* by Pet Shop Boys is similar for me, though it didn't even make my top 101 list for 1984, the year of its release. Why? Because I had barely heard it that year, even though I had purchased the 12-inch single. I listened to it more the next year. Life again distracted me from my music. By the way, *West End Girls* was a US #1 song in March 1986!

3. In 1983, I purchased the 45 single of Sheriff's *When I'm With You* and it is found in my year-end list that same year, yet the song wasn't a huge US hit until 1989. *

4. Dua Lipa's *Levitating* was the year-end #1 song in the US for the year after the album and single were released (2021) because the song remained on the charts forever. This song ranked in the US top 100 for 2022 also. It is in my 2020 year-end list.

5. Little did I know that Billie Eilish & Khalid released a spare, haunting song, appropriately titled *lovely* in 2018. I became aware of this enchanting song when I heard it from my fourth-floor hotel window one October 2022 night in Lisbon, Portugal. I came out of my shower and didn't have time to find the song using my phone, so I ran outside (fully clothed) and asked the street performers down the block who the artist was in their prior dance routine. It became a #1 song for me in that same year. This delightful song is still in the *Billboard Global 200* chart as 2024 ends. It was a bigger hit outside the US market (where it peaked at #64 on the *Billboard Hot 100*).

6. The incredible Shuggie Otis and his song *Aht Uh Mi Hed* (#26, 2001) and Kreo' and their amazing dance hit *Burn For You* (#28, 2016) were late-charted hits for me. Both songs were released over a decade before I first heard them. As an aside, it wasn't until Shuggie Otis reissued his CD in 2001 that I learned he wrote *Strawberry Letter 23* (#4, 1977). I charted the Brothers Johnson's version in 1977.

7. While writing this book, something remarkable happened to my all-time favorite artist. And it further vindicates my thoughts about this wrong-year "controversy" not being controversial at all. In 2022, a musical miracle occurred for Kate Bush and her wonderful song *Running Up That Hill (A Deal With God)*. It was barely a blip in the US top 40 in 1985, yet a new generation of music fans catapulted it to the #1 position on the world charts in 2022. All because it was featured in the streaming drama *Stranger Things*. And it remained in the US top 10 for five months. Meanwhile, this song will forever remain my #1 one song of 1985. I have the documentation. And I did not add it to my 2022 list. Why punish my 2022 songs by competing for a year-end list position with that powerhouse from my past?

As I finished this book, I finally watched season four of *Stranger Things* only to realize how prominent Kate's song was throughout the season. I am overjoyed by its inclusion and so very happy that *Running Up That Hill (A Deal With God)* grabbed the number-23 position in the 2022 US year-end singles chart.

Even the Grammys tend to nominate artists in the Best New Artist category in years well after their initial album release dates, when they reach fame.

Sophie Ellis-Bextor's *Murder On The Dancefloor* entered the *Billboard Hot 100* in January 2024. What surprised me is that it didn't make my top 101 in 2002. It was ranked at #235.

I could present more examples, but you get the point.

There are wonderful songs I initially hear through a friend, or on a cool lounge mix in a restaurant or bar, without knowing or caring when they were released. If I loved them, I added them to my weekly charts and they ended up on my year-end lists in whichever year it was.

It is obvious that people can only begin to love a song when they are gifted a moment to actually hear it. That being said, these were my songs for the year in which they are listed—whether that's two years or ten years after their initial release dates, or a year or decade before they were national hits. It is what it is. Just enjoy the songs that made my book despite the years in which they are listed.

Remember that David Bowie didn't hit it big in the States on his first try, yet both *Space Oddity* and *Changes* were re-released a few years later to larger success. Wrong year . . . again!

Double Hits

*Imagine Albert without Halsey,
<u>Long Time</u> with no <u>Foreplay</u>.*

*What is <u>Eye In The Sky</u> (or Jock Jams)
without <u>Sirius</u>? Seriously.*

You will find many double hits ranked together in my lists, as explained in my Year-End Lists preface.

Maybe this was my way of cheating to get more songs into my year-end top 101 lists. There were times when I loved too many songs and my weekly chart couldn't hold them all, so I combined unrelated songs by the same artist into a double hit. Heck, they were, and are, my personal charts and lists, so nothing seemed to matter to me except remembering the songs I loved.

My double hits include:

- Actual double-sided releases (e.g., Toni Braxton's *You're Makin' Me High/Let It Flow*, or Queen's *Bicycle Race/Fat Bottomed Girls*)

- The actual B-side of the single (e.g., The Pretenders's *Back On The Chain Gang/My City Was Gone*, or Supertramp's *Goodbye Stranger/Even In The Quietest Moments*)

- Songs coupled with their respective intro, outro, or reprise (e.g., Steve Miller Band's *Space Intro/Fly Like An Eagle*, *Hard To Say I'm Sorry/Get Away* by Chicago, or *The Time Machine (Part 1)/(Part 2)* by Alan Parsons)

- Back-to-back songs that merge seamlessly as one on the album (e.g., *She Smiles/Filmstar* by Mulu, or *You Are The One/Le Disko* by Shiny Toy Guns). I can't listen to one without the other.

- My method to save space on my weekly charts or merely my capricious crazy whims of smashing two or more songs as one combined hit (e.g., my wacky triple threat listing of Pointer Sisters' *Jump (For My Love) / Automatic / I Need You*, or Washed Out's *Reckless Desires / Game Of Chance*). In recent years, I try to avoid unwise "song smashing" but can anyone ever protect me from myself?

In the end, treat each double hit as a bonus in this book. Thank you for understanding my offense of "packing" my charts and my year-end top 101. More songs to acknowledge in the end! And what's wrong with that?

101 Songs

So why list 101 hits each year instead of 100?

When I was a child, I wondered what the next song on the year-end national chart would be, the song that didn't make the cut. So my 101st song each year answers that question. An *amuse-bouche* for you. A song that almost got away.

Songs That Got Away (Part I) — Simmering under My Top 101

As you learned earlier, I tracked songs as I heard them. I wrote down the songs I thought worthy of my weekly top 40 and ranked them in preparation for my year-end list. Among the fifteen thousand or so songs I tracked since 1976, there are artists barely found in this book and some artists aren't represented at all—many amazing artists whose songs never rose to the heights of my year-end top 101 lists, including artists such as:

Jody Watley   Michael Jackson   Def Leppard
The The   Natalie Cole   Roxette
Whitney Houston   George Benson   The Roches
Destiny's Child   Bon Jovi   Paramore
Breathe   Vanessa Williams   J. Geils Band
Van Halen   Martha Wash   Taylor Dayne
Michael Bublé   ZZ Top   Paul Hardcastle
Muse   Jimmy Buffett   "Weird Al" Yankovic
Wilson Phillips   Love And Rockets   The Jets
Billy Ocean   Japan   Billy Squier
Kelly Clarkson   Zap Mama   Eddie Rabbitt
Amy Winehouse   Angelique Kidjo
Emmylou Harris   .38 Special   Luther Vandross
Peter Cetera   INXS   Robert Plant
World Party   Modern Talking   Jimmy Cliff
Information Society   Scritti Politti
Smashing Pumpkins   Pearl Jam   LL Cool J
Yeah Yeah Yeahs   Frank Zappa   Loverboy
Toro y Moi   REO Speedwagon   Basement Jaxx

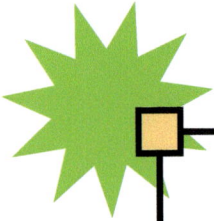

Echo & The Bunnymen   Evanescence
Kaiser Chiefs   Girls' Generation   Bush
Vanessa Carlton   Eminem   Spyro Gyra   Rainbow
Wang Chung   La Bouche   The Chicks
Eros Ramazzotti   Matchbox Twenty
LCD Soundsystem   The Story   Traveling Wilburys
Puddle Of Mudd   Patty Smyth/Scandal
Marcia Griffiths   Public Image Ltd (PiL)
C+C Music Factory   Within Temptation
Asha Bhosle   Andy Lau   Ziggy Marley   Jill Sobule
Sparks   Tim McGraw   2 Unlimited   Robbie Nevil
Franz Ferdinand   Ronnie Milsap   Angela Bofill
Happy Mondays   Patti Austin   The Stranglers

You get the idea. For each artist in my top 101 lists, there are two or more other artists that year who never made the cut.

No matter how many Barry Manilow songs I love, he only appears once in my year-end 101 lists, late in his career, but it was a #1 song for me. Though Destiny's Child is not found in my lists, Beyoncé, Kelly Rowland, and Michelle Williams have solo appearances. Likewise, Fifth Harmony is missing, though Normani and Camila Cabello are represented.

Since my musical taste is not necessarily mainstream, there are many popular favorites and well-known artists across many musical genres not found in my top 101. Because I ranked a vast number of songs beyond my top 101 each year, I included some songs by those artists that may be of interest to others—including a few US #1 hits—to recognize songs that fell farther down on my lists, and to allow comparison between the national musical ethos and my ever-changing tastes over the years. Though I may say I have a "pop ear," my eclectic selection of 101 favorites might belie that in many years.

These extra cuts (and their original rankings) are at the end of each year-end list. I can't stop myself from listing more songs . . .

There are songs that ranked beyond the top 101 in my year-end lists that would be ranked higher if I did my ranking today (e.g., West End Girls by Pet Shop Boys or Bonnie Tyler's Total Eclipse Of The Heart). I've included some of these missing favorites as extra cuts.

There are songs *within* my top 101 that would be much higher today if I redid my rankings, such as *Painted Desert* by Pat Benatar (#92, 1985) and the before-mentioned *I Go Crazy* by Paul Davis. It makes me wonder what I was thinking some years as I made my final lists.

Some songs age differently.

My music is a competitive field between the thousand or so songs I hear or sample every year. I *could* present to you every song I ever wrote down, but my top 101 songs were my focus when creating my lists. Just because a song was ranked at 117 or 390 on my year-end list does not diminish my feelings for it; the song meant enough to me to track it. I have songs attached to great memories, but even *that* factor did not elevate them competitively into my top 101.

To be honest, in the early years of my project, I didn't give instrumentals the attention they deserved. Likewise, I didn't always discover new songs in genres outside my typical listening.

Then again, there are songs I didn't know as well when my year-end lists were finalized. Like all music, we may change our feelings about a song. It seems fondness for some songs may grow over the decades, maybe as an effect of nostalgia and longing for bygone youth.

Time and circumstance let a song bloom anew.

Songs That Got Away (Part II) – Songs Lost, Disliked, or Unknown

I wrote a song, but I forgot the words.

But there are true songs that got away from me. In the Artist Cross-Reference section I have included additional special songs that were not tracked by me. I forgot . . . life was busy . . . time escaped me . . . I'm not superhuman.

The cross-reference guide explains the "unranked" statuses assigned to these types of missing songs:

- Songs that were childhood favorites prior to 1976 (e.g., *Rock The Boat* by The Hues Corporation). My legacy songs, as referred to in this book.

- Songs I did not know when they were released and never charted when I later became aware of them (e.g., *Solsbury Hill* by Peter Gabriel). In my early chart years, I did not often track songs from albums released in prior years (such as the debut and sophomore albums by The B-52s).

- Songs I failed to track though I loved them, and sometimes, owned them! Songs that were easily "top-100" worthy, such as *Funkytown* by Lipps Inc. or *(I Just) Died In Your Arms* by Cutting Crew. Or failing to track any songs from the fantastic 1992 album, *Skin*, by Ephraim Lewis, who died tragically before his talent fully bloomed.

- Songs that got away because, in my early chart years, I was a proper little boy who followed the rules. I didn't write down a song as *my single* if it wasn't released as such by the artist/record label (e.g., *Dogs In The Yard* by Paul McCrane or *Give Me Your Love* by the Babys). I rectify that error in part by including those songs. With music, there are no rules!

- Favorite Christmas and other seasonal songs not found within my year-end lists (e.g., *December Will Be Magic Again* by Kate Bush).

Any song in my top 101 lists could have been replaced by a fantastic song that got away. Some of these missing songs could easily have been a #1 for me.

When a houseplant dies, I assume it hated my music.

We all dig different music, so I try not to disparage others' musical tastes. Music is a deeply personal thing and our personal connection to it is often difficult to convey to others through our words and feelings. We each experience music differently.

Yet, there are moments when we dislike the music a friend is playing; as my friends know, I am honest-without-being-judgmental about songs or artists they love, when I am not particularly wowed. Some music just isn't my sound. On the other hand, I own many artists who are an acquired taste for my friends. I rather love when a friend nixes a #1 song of mine. Like all else in life, our differences in music make the world a better place in ways we can't

> **Unabashedly love the music you love. It's part of you and your pursuit of happiness. Never apologize—you own it.**

imagine. This is the power of music. Embrace your favorites, be proud of your artists, share their messages, and don't be a hater to others and their music.

So, yes, there are many songs not found in my book because they aren't my thing. And I won't dwell on negative thoughts about musical artists and genres not found here. Nor will I dwell on artists' personal lives and other negative energy concerning music. None of us are perfect, so I enjoy the art and forgive the artist.

What is the sound of a song never heard?

There is one more reason some songs or artists are missing from my list; a concern that brews within me but doesn't keep me awake at night . . . *songs I will never hear!* Alas, despite all the hours I spend pursuing music, there are songs I'll never know.

Of course, my lists do not contain songs I never had exposure to. How can one love something they never hear? I ponder this concept when I crave new music, especially during a musical dry spell, and wonder about great songs released around the world. Out there somewhere is beautiful music that you and I may never know. Songs from another continent, in another language; songs from another generation or music format or style unfamiliar to us; songs being played on the next radio channel up the dial.

Oh wait . . . there are always those songs we hear even though we never discover the song title or artist, despite using song-recognition apps or online lyric searches. Do you recall songs you heard at a club or restaurant that you liked, but never discovered the artist or title? I am blessed to know the songs I have heard.

Enough of my so-called controversies. My favorite songs speak for themselves.

How can a song feel so cold, so desperate, so hollow, yet still provide warmth?

Note: Beyond the Artist Cross-Reference, my epilogue contains final, leftover thoughts and my remaining music-memory tales.

Teenage Cassette Years, 1974-1975

Around 1974, my first cassettes, before I switched to LPs, were Mike Oldfield's *Tubular Bells*, Elton John's initial *Greatest Hits* collection, and *Joy* by Isaac Hayes, which I purchased through the RCA Music Service club (which eventually became BMG Music Service).

Often, simultaneously, I enrolled in Columbia House's record club. I remember joining and then quitting both clubs, then enrolling again and again to get even more "free" albums, cassettes, or CDs. As you learned, I was not a rich young man, so I took advantage of all the tricks of these clubs—the secret 'extra LP' box, ordering double-record sets as one freebie, or ordering my first required album (to fulfill my club obligation) at half-price upon reenrolling in the club. I heard tales of friends who got their free albums and then moved with no forwarding address to avoid buying the required additional albums; I never did this because I am an honest man and, more importantly, I desired to re-up again in a year or two. When your name is one-of-a-kind, it is rather difficult to hide within a corporation mailing list, even during the snail-mail years.

I digress, back to cassette chitchat . . . I recall creating horror film "soundtracks" on cassette tapes—squeaking doors, groans and growls, the wind through the trees, loud thuds on the floor, breaking glass, a ball bouncing down the stairs. I also ridiculously loved to tape my favorite commercial jingles directly from the TV. You know, sometimes you just feel like a nut, in life. Other times, I wanted bologna that had a first name, or a special San Francisco treat.

I think back to the radio songs I taped directly from our family's stereo console speaker, sprawled on the carpet in our dining room, replete with various ambient noise intrusions. Often my recordings sadly began a few notes late because the songs weren't announced in advance.

Two particular tape-recording memories stay with me.

I was recording Diana Ross's *Touch Me In The Morning* from the stereo console when Mom began banging a wooden spoon against the rim of a Pyrex mixing bowl as she made dinner. The bowl was probably orange, aqua, or avocado green—popular colors back then.

Or the winter evening I taped Michael Martin Murphey's *Wildfire* as a snowmobile illegally zipped by on our side yard.

> I wonder what happened to those cassettes. Mistër E's final mystery?

To this day, I hear these recordings in my mind and sing the songs with the errant sounds, "touch me in the (pound, clang, clonk) morning . . ." or "they called her wild . . . (vrroooom, zoom) fire."

Artist Cross-Reference

Main artists and groups with an entry in my year-end lists may be searched alphabetically here, along with my favorite songs (and artists) not found in my year-end lists. Song titles are ordered by year of release or the year the song charted for me, along with the year-end position or a designated code assigned to each song.

Additional Songs (Not Found in My Year-End Lists)

Additional favorite songs that were never charted by me are found in this section under the artist's name. These songs are listed with their approximate album or single release year and are assigned a code (instead of a year-end list position) as described here:

P   Pre-1976 songs: My legacy songs—the best of the best of my childhood favorites.

M   Missed songs—the songs that got away: These songs are memorable, post-1975 songs that I forgot to document, or they're songs I failed to chart at the time I became aware of them.

X   Christmas and seasonal favorites not previously charted by me.

T   Favorite TV themes or jingles not previously charted by me.

Naming Formats

In this section, solo artists and some bands (e.g., Miller, Steve, Band) are alphabetized by last name, unless the name is a mononym (e.g., Cher). Some artists whose names appear to be a person are actually the name of the group (e.g., Bob Moses, Tommy Tutone, Bettie Serveert, Eli Young Band, or Sally Shapiro, the latter being both a person and her duo) and are alphabetized by the group name. Some artists who go by a pseudonym may be alphabetized by their full moniker (e.g., Fatboy Slim or Father John Misty are both referenced under "F").

Groups whose names begin with "A" or "The" are alphabetized by the first main word of the group name. Artists whose names begin with a numeral are alphabetized by the spelling of that number. Artists who begin with an abbreviation are alphabetized by the full spelling of the abbreviated word (e.g., Mr. Mister is referenced under Mister; Dr. Hook referenced under Doctor; St. James referenced under Saint).

Some languages (e.g., Vietnamese and Chinese) list the last name first and those artists are alphabetized as such, unless the artist performs using an English naming format.

In the cross-reference, songs containing two or more artists (including many listed as "featured") are referenced separately under each artist with no mention of the other artists that share the same recording unless the song is found only in the cross-reference (P, M, X, or T songs).

Some "featured" artists, who have a sole entry in my book (and who are not necessarily established artists on their own), are not listed in the cross-reference. Refer to the Year-End Lists for full artist information.

Format examples: *Feels* by Calvin Harris, featuring Pharrell Williams, Katy Perry, and Big Sean, is found four times in the cross-reference under each respective artist with its year-end position and corresponding year.

Some duets are split into separate cross-reference entries if they are known solo artists in their own right (e.g., Brandy and Monica have separate listings for *The Boy Is Mine*). Duet groups such as Peaches & Herb, Daryl Hall & John Oates, and England Dan & John Ford Coley are referenced once. Then again, as an example, Simon & Garfunkel are alphabetically listed together as a group and separately for their solo entries.

In some cases, for clarity, I have included a parenthetical last name or other name to distinguish an artist who may have a name similar to other popular artists, especially when the artist is not commonly known in the US or elsewhere.

As much as possible, I provide additional cross-reference recommendations when artists performed under other entries found this book (such as a prior band), though other connections may exist (especially as songwriters and producers—such as Carole King, Sia, Todd Rundgren, Jim Steinman, and Diane Warren—or as artists who were session musicians and backup singers). My suggested recommendations do not necessarily link to artists whose work is sampled within other songs.

From *Spooky* to *Stormy* to *Brandy* to *Candy*
Money, Sunny; Sugar, Sugar; Honey, Honey

Bis to KISS, Rush to Lush, TLC to BTS
Dusty, Daya, Des'ree, Duffy and Duran Duran
KC, k.d., Kelis, Kylie, Katy, Kehlani, Keats and Keane
Yuna, MUNA, Loma, Yola, Marina and Selena

Mono to Bono, Poco to Toto
Meco, Dido, Soho, Kygo, and the Go-Go's
La Roux, Mulu, Le Roux, Lulu, Pru and U2!
Secret Garden, Savage Garden, Soundgarden
Springfield, Oldfield, Black Field, Sense Field

King, Queen, Prince and Princess
Lady Gaga, Lord Huron, MS MR & the rest

Calexico, Chicago, Berlin, Chattahoochee
Texas, Kansas, America, Asia

From the Sundays to *New Moon On Monday*;
from 'Til Tuesday to *Wednesday's Child*

From *Rubberband Girl* to *The Rubberband Man*
From *Tragedy and Mystery* to *Mystery of Love*

From *Abacab* to *Zombie*
and ABBA to the Zombies . . .

All the great music of my life—
every song I could think of—is found here!

Artist Cross-Reference

A

ABBA (See also Agnetha Fältskog; Frida; Murray Head; Barbara Dickson; Elaine Page)

Waterloo	P	1974
Honey, Honey	P	1974
S.O.S.	P	1975
Mamma Mia	17	1976
Fernando	80	1976
Knowing Me, Knowing You	36	1977
Money, Money, Money	69	1977
Dancing Queen	76	1977
The Name Of The Game	14	1978
Take A Chance On Me	89	1978
Does Your Mother Know	88	1979
Voulez-Vous	M	1979
Chiquitita	36	1980
Gimme! Gimme! Gimme! (A Man After Midnight)	83	1980
The Winner Takes It All	45	1981
Super Trouper	80	1981
The Visitors	7	1982
When All Is Said And Done	80	1982
The Day Before You Came	49	1983
Keep An Eye On Dan	27	2021

Abbasi, Yalda

Love And Tears	58	2023

ABC

The Look Of Love	65	1982
Poison Arrow	115	1983
If I Ever Thought You'd Be Lonely	M	1983
Be Near Me	69	1985
The Night You Murdered Love	M	1987
King Without A Crown	M	1987

Abdul, Paula

Cold Hearted	62	1989
Straight Up	77	1989
Dance Like There's No Tomorrow	68	2008

Above & Beyond

Blue Sky Action	30	2015

We're All We Need	42	2015
Bittersweet & Blue	34	2018

Ace

How Long	121	1976

Ace Of Base

All That She Wants	115	1993
Living In Danger	6	1994
Edge Of Heaven	23	1996

Aces, The

Put It On The Line	94	2018

Active Child

Hanging On / Johnny Belinda	77	2011
Feeling Is Gone	4	2014
Subtle	20	2014
Temptation	61	2015
Never Far Away	63	2015
Weightless	78	2020

Adam F

The Tree Knows Everything	27	2009

Adams, Bryan

Heaven	197	1984
Don't Give Up	36	2000

Adams, Oleta (See also Tears For Fears)

Woman In Chains	27	1990
Rhythm Of Life	70	1990
Me And My Big Ideas	7	1996

Adamski (See also Seal)

Killer	243	1992

Adele

Set Fire To The Rain	8	2011
Rolling In The Deep	61	2011
Skyfall	17	2012
Hello	53	2015
I Miss You	9	2016
Water Under The Bridge	85	2016

Adiemus (See also Miriam Stockley)		
Adiemus	45	1996

Adventures, The		
Feel The Raindrops	31	1986
Send My Heart	68	1986
Love In Chains	41	1987
Broken Land	37	1988
You Don't Have To Cry Anymore	77	1988
Scarlet	40	1990
Washington Deceased	79	1990

Adventures Of Stevie V, The		
Dirty Cash (Money Talks)	68	1990

Aerosmith		
Sweet Emotion	P	1975
Dream On	31	1976
Walk This Way	60	1977

Aesop Rock		
None Shall Pass	81	2008

æspa f/ nævis		
Welcome To MY World	14	2023

Africa Express		
Johannesburg	5	2020

Afrojack		
Too Wild	69	2014
Another Life	67	2017
Reach	99	2019

After The Fire		
Der Kommissar	114	1983

Against The Current		
Legends Never Die	28	2023

Aguilera, Christina		
Genie In A Bottle	135	1999
Nobody Wants To Be Lonely	40	2001
Moves Like Jagger	170	2011

a-ha (See also Morten Harket)		
Hunting High And Low	9	1985
Take On Me	52	1985
I've Been Losing You	33	1986
The Sun Always Shines On T.V./Driftwood	41	1986
The Living Daylights	24	1987
Cry Wolf	82	1987
Stay On These Roads	87	1988
Early Morning	99	1991
Locust	40	1993
Cold As Stone	79	1993

Minor Earth Major Sky	3	2000
I Won't Forget Her	55	2000
Summer Moved On	4	2001
The Sun Never Shone That Day	41	2001
Did Anyone Approach You?	2	2002
Lifelines	9	2002
Forever Not Yours	51	2002
Oranges On Appletrees	63	2002
Cannot Hide	89	2002
Celice	12	2006
Don't Do Me Any Favours	61	2006
The Bandstand	5	2009
Sunny Mystery	16	2009
Foot Of The Mountain	37	2009
Butterfly, Butterfly (The Last Hurrah)	19	2010
Forest Fire	80	2015
Summer Rain	97	2022

Air (Air French Band)		
Talisman	123	1999
Playground Love (sung by Gordon Tracks)	113	2000
Alone In Kyoto	19	2003
Cherry Blossom Girl	13	2004
Mer Du Japon / Redhead Girl	63	2007

Airlock		
Drama	77	2003

Air Supply		
All Out Of Love	49	1980
Lost In Love	64	1980
Every Woman In The World	99	1980
Making Love Out Of Nothing At All	118	1983

Akalın, Demet		
Bir Anda Sevmiştim	86	2005

Akon		
Cross That Line	117	2006
The Rain/Never Took The Time	38	2007
I Wanna Love You (I Wanna Fuck You)	101	2007
Troublemaker	29	2009
Tonight	67	2010
One In The Chamber	94	2014

Aksu, Sezen		
Üfle De Söneyim	M	2017
İhanetten Geri Kalan	M	2017

alan 阿兰 (Alan Dawa Dolma)		
久遠の河 (River Of Eternity) (Red Cliff theme)	63	2011

Alborán, Pablo

En Brazos De Ella	36	2013
Seré	77	2013
Carretera y Manta	44	2023

Al B. Sure!

Nite And Day/Nuit Et Jour	60	1988
Prelude To The Garden/The Secret Garden (Sweet Seduction Suite)	116	1990

Alcazar

Crying At The Discoteque	20	2004
I Go Shopping	25	2004
This Is The World We Live In	49	2004
LoveLife	81	2005
Baby	98	2011

Aldean, Jason

Got What I Got	87	2019

Aleka's Attic

Across The Way	50	1991

Alesso

Under Control	117	2014
I Wanna Know	93	2016
Falling	23	2017

Ali, Nadia (See also iiO)

Crash And Burn	22	2009
Fine Print	101	2009
Feels So Good	5	2010
Try	47	2010
Call My Name	88	2011
Carry Me	26	2012
Rolling The Dice	82	2012
Must Be The Love	49	2013

Alice Deejay

Better Off Alone	79	2000

Alice In Chains

No Excuses	49	1994
Heaven Beside You	32	1996

Alikiba

Nakshi Mrembo	72	2012

Alive And Kicking

Tighter, Tighter	P	1970

Alizée

Moi...Lolita	6	2002
J.B.G.	24	2002
Veni Vedi Vici	96	2002
A Contre-Courant	31	2003
L'Alizé	34	2003
Youpidou	92	2003
Par Les Paupières	21	2008
Mademoiselle Juliette	84	2008
Les Collines (Never Leave You)	77	2010
Blonde	89	2014
Charles Est Stone	56	2015

All-American Rejects, The

Can't Take It	36	2005

Allen, Deborah

Baby I Lied	77	1984

Allen, Lily

Back To The Start	38	2009

Allen, Peter

Bi-Coastal	M	1980

Allison, Dot

Colour Me	98	2000
You Can Be Replaced	49	2003

Allman, Gregg (The Allman Brothers)

Midnight Rider	P	1970

Allred, Loren

Never Enough	31	2018

All Saints

Pure Shores	16	2000
Rock Steady	100	2006
Hell No	67	2007

Allure

Show Me The Way	89	2013

Almond, Marc (See also Soft Cell)

She Took My Soul In Istanbul	58	1989
A Lover Spurned	28	1990
The Sea Still Sings	34	1991
Deaths Diary	88	1991
The Days Of Pearly Spencer	12	1992

Alok

Car Keys (Ayla)	1	2024

Alpert, Herb (Herb Alpert & The Tijuana Brass)

Taste Of Honey (w/ The Tijuana Brass)	P	1965
Casino Royale (w/ The Tijuana Brass)	P	1967
This Guy's In Love With You	P	1968
Rise	75	1979

Alpinestars

Snow Patrol (Part 1)/(Part 2)	54	2003

Altın Gün

Yüce Dağ Başında	76	2021

alyona alyona		
Teresa & Maria	75	2024

AM		
It's Been So Long	25	2010

Amber		
One More Night	53	1997
This Is Your Night	109	1997
Sexual (Li Da Di)	51	1999
Object Of Your Desire	33	2000

Ambrosia		
Holdin' On To Yesterday	P	1975
How Much I Feel	83	1978
You're The Only Woman (You & I)	47	1980

Ameerah		
The Sound Of Missing You	20	2009

America		
A Horse With No Name	P	1972
I Need You	P	1972
Ventura Highway	P	1972
Only In Your Heart	P	1973
Tin Man	P	1974
Lonely People	P	1974
Sister Golden Hair	P	1975
Daisy Jane	P	1975
You Can Do Magic	126	1982
The Border	59	1983

Ames, Ed		
My Cup Runneth Over	P	1967

Amina (Annabi)		
Eight O'Clock	86	1999
Dis-Moi Pourquoi	101	1999

Amir		
Carrousel	64	2021

Amos, Tori		
Precious Things	26	1992
Crucify	35	1992
Silent All These Years	95	1992
The Happy Worker / Workers (w/ The Cast of Toys)	57	1993
Take To The Sky	94	1993
God	15	1994
Cornflake Girl	28	1994
Space Dog	61	1994
Caught A Lite Sneeze	27	1996
Blue Skies	47	1997
A Sorta Fairytale	92	2002

Taxi Ride	76	2003
Sweet The Sting / Parasol	88	2005
Bouncing Off Clouds	48	2007
Fire To Your Plain	11	2009
Star Of Wonder / Our New Year	68	2009
Spies	24	2021
Speaking With Trees	61	2021
Addition Of Light Divided (+💡÷)	83	2021
Metal Water Wood	26	2022

Amsterburg, Merrie		
Design	37	2001

Amuro, Namie 安室奈美惠		
Sit! Stay! Wait! Down! / Love Story	49	2014
Alive	57	2014
Let's Go	92	2014

Anastacia		
I'm Outta Love	105	2001
One Day In Your Life	66	2002
Left Outside Alone	25	2005
Sick And Tired	24	2006

Andain		
Beautiful Things	1	2004
Promises	70	2011
Turn Up The Sound	66	2012

Anderson, Deborah		
Into Everything	41	2005

Anderson, Gillian		
Extremis	36	1997

Anderson, Jon (See also Yes; Jon & Vangelis)		
In High Places	24	1984
Easier Said Than Done	135	1986
Top Of The World (The Glass Bead Game)	83	1988
Amor Real	71	1994
Within The Lost World	51	1991

Anderson, Laurie		
Big Science	35	1982
O Superman (For Massenet)	43	1982
Excellent Birds	59	1984

Anderson, Lynn		
Rose Garden	P	1970

Andreone, Leah		
It's Alright, It's OK	86	1996
Mother Tongue	98	1997

Andrews, Julie		
Feed The Birds (Tuppence A Bag)	P	1964
Supercalifragilisticexpialidocious (w/ Dick Van Dyke)	P	1964

The Sound Of Music	P	1965
The Lonely Goatherd	P	1965
My Favorite Things	P	1965
Edelweiss (w/ Christopher Plummer)	P	1965
Whistling Away The Dark (w/ Henry Mancini)	P	1970
angela (Japanese band)		
Calling You	11	2020
Anggun		
Snow On The Sahara	98	1998
A Rose In The Wind	16	1999
My Sensual Mind	29	1999
Une Femme	90	2001
C'est Écrit	63	2005
Sadeness II	74	2016
What We Remember	23	2018
Animals, The (See also Eric Burdon)		
The House Of The Rising Sun	P	1964
Don't Let Me Be Misunderstood	P	1965
Don't Bring Me Down	P	1966
When I Was Young	P	1967
Animotion		
Obsession	M	1985
Anka, Paul		
Puppy Love	P	1960
AnnaGrace		
Let The Feelings Go	51	2009
Annie (Anne Lilia Berge Strand)		
Heartbeat	12	2005
Don't Stop	58	2010
My Love Is Better	86	2010
Dark Hearts	67	2021
ANOHNI (Antony Hegarty)		
Prisoner Of Love	58	2011
Antonia (Iacobescu)		
Call The Police	91	2017
Touch Me	76	2020
ANÚNA		
Winter, Fire & Snow	16	1996
Aoki, Steve		
The White Lotus Theme (Aloha)	101	2022
Nobody	57	2023
Apache 207		
Komet	19	2024

Aphrodite's Child (See also Vangelis; Jon & Vangelis)		
The Four Horsemen	P	1971
apl.de.ap		
Spaceship	96	2010
Apollonia		
Take Me With U	74	1985
Apollo 100		
Joy	P	1972
April Wine		
Just Between You And Me	95	1981
Aqua		
Barbie Girl	63	1997
Arash		
I Adore You	48	2024
Arcade Fire		
Reflektor	129	2013
Archer, Tasmin		
Sleeping Satellite	6	1993
Somebody's Daughter	12	1993
In Your Care	39	1993
Halfway To Heaven	92	1993
Sweet Little Truth	75	1998
Take Care	92	2007
Archies, The		
Sugar, Sugar	P	1969
Architects		
Dying Is Absolutely Safe	70	2021
Arden, Jann		
I Would Die For You	74	1996
Holy Moses	38	1998
Piece Of It All	30	2001
Cherry Popsicle	47	2001
Only You	48	2003
Where No One Knows Me	30	2005
Arena, Tina		
Never (Past Tense)	M	2003
Argent		
Hold Your Head Up	P	1972
Aria		
Orange Meadows	86	2002
Armatrading, Joan		
Love And Affection	M	1976
All The Way From America	M	1980
I'm Lucky	M	1981
Reach Out	21	1987

Did I Make You Up	17	1988
Armstrong, Craig		
This Love	25	1998
Rise	82	1998
Armstrong, Louis		
Hello, Dolly!	P	1964
We've Got All The Time In The World	P	1971
Arnold, Eddy		
Make The World Go Away	P	1965
Artificial Joy Club		
Sick & Beautiful	90	1997
Artist Unknown		
Vocal song from the film *Ashes (Kül)*	58	2024
Art Of Noise, The (See also Anne Dudley)		
Moments In Love	25	1985
One Earth	49	1988
Metaforce	100	1999
Arty		
Must Be The Love	49	2013
Asake		
Olorun	95	2024
Asanee-Wasan อัสนี-วสันต์ โชติกุล		
กรุงเทพมหานคร (Bangkok/Krung Thep Mahanakhon)	16	1989
ยินดีไม่มีปัญหา (Happy, No Problem)	71	1989
Ásgeir		
Going Home	8	2014
Ashcroft, Richard (See also The Verve)		
A Song For The Lovers	38	2000
I Get My Beat	95	2000
Check The Meaning	1	2002
Keys To The World	73	2006
Everybody Needs Somebody To Hurt	101	2016
Ashford & Simpson		
Solid	77	1985
A Si 阿肆		
热爱105°C的你 (Love You At 105°C)	76	2023
Asia (See also Yes; The Buggles; Alan Parsons Project; Emerson, Lake & Palmer)		
Only Time Will Tell	100	1982
Askew, Joy		
From The Lips Of The One I Love	48	1997
A World So Rare	78	1997
Association, The		
Along Comes Mary	P	1966

Cherish	P	1966
Pandora's Golden Heebie Jeebies	P	1966
Windy	P	1967
Never My Love	P	1967
Astley, Jon		
Jane's Getting Serious	100	1987
Astley, Rick		
Never Gonna Give You Up	112	1988
Bring Back The Time	73	2022
Astrid S		
Breathe	39	2022
Just Wanted To Know	31	2023
Astronaut Wife		
Pedestal	45	2001
Are You For Real	42	2003
Late Now	63	2003
ATB		
9 PM (Till I Come)	M	1999
The Summer	50	2001
Love Will Find You	55	2001
Hold You	93	2002
I Don't Wanna Stop	78	2003
Ecstasy	45	2004
Marrakech	97	2004
Justify	49	2007
Could You Believe	46	2010
Where You Are	71	2011
Route 66/Faith	12	2017
Never Without You	35	2017
When It Ends It Starts Again	60	2017
ATC (A Touch Of Class)		
All Around The World (La La La La La)	71	2001
Atcher, Bob, & The Dinning Sisters		
Christmas Island (also version by Andrew Sisters)	X	1945
Atlanta Rhythm Section (See also Classics IV)		
So In To You (So Into You)	38	1977
Imaginary Lover	67	1978
Alien	30	1981
Atlas, Natacha		
Duden	56	1997
Guide Me God	58	2003
When I Close My Eyes	37	2004
Aubele, Federico		
Despertar	91	2005

Audien		
Something Better	72	2015
Auer, Jon (See also The Posies)		
Bottom Of The Bottle / Song Noir	75	2006
Au/Ra		
Panic Room	32	2019
i miss u	13	2020
AURORA		
The Innocent	78	2022
Auty, Peter		
Walking In The Air (also version by Aled Jones)	X	1983
Avener, The		
Castle In The Snow	3	2016
Panama	58	2016
Average White Band		
Pick Up The Pieces	P	1974
Avicii		
Liar Liar	69	2013
Peace Of Mind	2	2019
Axiom Of Choice		
Vâleh	M	1994
Axwell Λ Ingrosso (See also Swedish House Mafia)		
Sun Is Shining	57	2015
Ayanga 阿云嘎		
Into The Wild	86	2021

B

Babble (See also Thompson Twins)		
You Kill Me	83	1994
Love Has No Name	68	1996
Babyface		
Hurt You	72	2014
Babys, The (See also John Waite)		
Isn't It Time	9	1977
Give Me Your Love	M	1977
I'm Falling	M	1977
Silver Dreams	81	1978
Every Time I Think Of You/Head First	33	1979
Back On My Feet Again	40	1980
Turn And Walk Away	81	1981
Bachman-Turner Overdrive (BTO) (See also The Guess Who; Ironhorse)		
Takin' Care Of Business	P	1974
You Ain't Seen Nothing Yet	P	1974

Hey You	P	1975
Backstreet Boys		
Quit Playing Games (With My Heart)	52	1997
Everybody (Backstreet's Back)	153	1998
Show Me The Meaning Of Being Lonely	65	1999
Don't Want You Back	71	1999
Larger Than Life	99	1999
Don't Go Breaking My Heart	65	2018
Bad Company		
Ready For Love	P	1974
Bad Company	P	1974
Feel Like Makin' Love	P	1975
Rock 'N' Roll Fantasy	46	1979
Badfinger		
Come And Get It	P	1970
Day After Day	P	1971
It Don't Come Easy (w/ Ringo Starr)	P	1971
Badly Drawn Boy		
River, Sea, Ocean	49	2002
Baez, Joan		
Diamonds And Rust	P	1975
Bailey Rae, Corinne		
Sister	62	2018
Baker, Anita		
Sweet Love	52	1986
Balin, Marty (See also Jefferson Airplane/Starship)		
Hearts	71	1981
Balligomingo		
Wild Butterfly	18	2002
Purify	69	2002
Lost	82	2002
New Favorite Thing	91	2004
Goodbye	1	2009
Spinning	32	2009
Balmorhea, Clarice Jensen & Lisa Morgenstern		
V	109	2021
Baltimora		
Tarzan Boy	108	1986
Balvin, J		
Ganas De Verte	8	2021
Bananarama (See also Shakespears Sister)		
Cruel Summer	16	1984
Rough Justice / The Wild Life	22	1985
A Trick Of The Night	32	1987
More Than Physical	80	1987

Look On The Floor (Hypnotic Tango)	59	2006
Move In My Direction	81	2006
Feel For You	95	2006
Dance Music	49	2019
Intoxicated	93	2019
Tonight (Bright Light Bright Light Remix)	16	2020
I'm On Fire	38	2020
Brand New	33	2022
Need A Little More Time	75	2022
Band Aid (See also The Boomtown Rats; Midge Ure)		
Do They Know It's Christmas?	19	1985
Banderas		
May This Be Your Last Sorrow	27	1991
The Comfort Of Faith	96	1991
Bangles (See also Susanna Hoffs)		
Walk Like An Egyptian	111	1986
Something To Believe In	76	1989
Single By Choice / Song For A Good Son	83	2003
Banks, Azaelia		
Hypnotic	36	2022
Bao, Noonie		
Dust Clears	24	2014
Baraz, Alina		
Fantasy	75	2016
Bardens, Pete (See also Keats)		
In Dreams	60	1987
Gold	93	1988
Further Than We Know	41	1993
Barenaked Ladies		
One Week	233	1998
You + Me Vs The World	98	2017
Barker, Sophie (See also Zero 7)		
Secret	45	2006
Barnes, Cheryl		
Easy To Be Hard	124	1980
Barrett, Gabby		
I Hope	99	2020
Barry, John, Orchestra		
James Bond Theme (also Monty Norman Orchestra)	P	1962
Bartos, Karl (See also Kraftwerk)		
Atomium	110	2013
Basia		
Time And Tide	48	1988
Cruising For Bruising	21	1990

Like Crazy	28	2018
Basil, Toni		
Mickey	105	1982
Over My Head	19	1984
Bass, Fontella		
Rescue Me	P	1965
Bassey, Shirley		
Goldfinger	P	1965
Diamonds Are Forever	P	1972
History Repeating	50	1999
Bastille (B△STILLE)		
Distorted Light Beam	50	2022
Bat For Lashes		
Kids In The Dark	70	2019
Batiste, Jon		
17th Ward Prelude/Uneasy	9	2023
Bauhaus (See also Peter Murphy)		
Bela Lugosi's Dead	M	1979
Bay City Rollers		
I Only Want To Be With You	35	1976
Rock And Roll Love Letter	94	1976
You Made Me Believe In Magic	78	1977
BBMak		
Ghost Of You And Me	23	2001
Beach Boys, The (See also Carl Wilson)		
I Get Around	P	1964
Don't Worry Baby	P	1964
California Girls	P	1965
Barbara Ann	P	1965
Wouldn't It Be Nice	P	1966
God Only Knows	P	1966
Good Vibrations	P	1966
Bear, Edward		
Last Song	P	1972
Beat, The (The English Beat)		
Mirror In The Bathroom	64	1981
Beatles, The (See also George Harrison; John Lennon; Ringo Starr; Paul McCartney; Wings)		
I Want To Hold Your Hand	P	1964
I Saw Her Standing There	P	1964
Love Me Do/P.S. I Love You	P	1964
And I Love Her	P	1964
Eight Days A Week	P	1965
Ticket To Ride	P	1965
Yesterday	P	1965

We Can Work It Out/Day Tripper	P	1965
You've Got To Hide Your Love Away	P	1965
Eleanor Rigby	P	1966
Penny Lane/Strawberry Fields Forever	P	1966
Michelle	P	1966
In My Life	P	1966
Norwegian Wood (This Bird Has Flown)	P	1966
I Am The Walrus	P	1967
A Day In The Life	P	1967
Magical Mystery Tour	P	1967
Blackbird	P	1968
Dear Prudence	P	1968
While My Guitar Gently Weeps	P	1968
Lady Madonna	P	1968
Glass Onion	P	1968
Get Back	P	1969
Come Together/Something	P	1969
Here Comes The Sun	P	1969
The Long And Winding Road	P	1970
Beautiful South, The		
My Book	61	1991
Beauty's Confusion		
Whirlwind	35	2005
Beck		
Loser	M	1994
Lost Cause	100	2002
Uneventful Days	2	2020
Chemical	22	2020
Beckham, Victoria (See also Spice Girls)		
Let Your Head Go	94	2004
Becky G		
People (sped up+reverb)	38	2023
Bedingfield, Daniel		
Gotta Get Thru This	91	2002
Bedingfield, Natasha		
Soulmate	12	2007
Pocketful Of Sunshine / Angel	43	2008
Bedroom Rockers		
Nothing Else Matters	17	2005
Bee Gees (See also Barry Gibb; Robin Gibb; Andy Gibb)		
New York Mining Disaster 1941 (Have You Seen My Wife, Mr. Jones)	P	1967
Lonely Days	P	1970
Jive Talkin'	P	1975

Nights On Broadway	P	1975
Wind Of Change	P	1975
You Should Be Dancing	9	1976
Fanny (Be Tender With My Love)	28	1976
Love So Right	67	1976
Boogie Child	14	1977
How Deep Is Your Love	56	1977
Night Fever	6	1978
Stayin' Alive	13	1978
Tragedy	19	1979
Spirits (Having Flown)	M	1979
Love You Inside Out	62	1979
E·S·P/E·S·P (Vocal Reprise)	12	1988
The Longest Night	39	1988
Giving Up The Ghost	64	1988
It's My Neighborhood	84	1989
Flesh And Blood	M	1989
Wish You Were Here	84	1990
Haunted House	63	1995
Irresistible Force	4	1997
With My Eyes Closed	61	1997
Man In The Middle	64	2001
This Is Where I Came In	80	2001
Beer, Madison		
Sweet Relief	72	2023
17	59	2024
Beirut		
Spillhaugen	52	2024
Belasco, Pete		
Without Within	72	1998
Bel Canto (See also Anneli Drecker)		
Intravenous	8	1990
A Shoulder To The Wheel	18	1990
Dreaming Girl	52	1990
Birds Of Passage	54	1991
Summer	1	1992
Shimmering, Warm And Bright	4	1992
Spiderdust	14	1992
Waking Will	24	1993
Didn't You Know It?	1	1996
Rumour	14	1996
Freelunch In The Jungle	44	1996
Sleepwalker	72	1996
In Zenith	98	1996
Images	8	2000

The Dinosaur-Slipper-Man	69	2001
Agnus Dei	X	2001
Disappear Club 5	8	2003
Dorothy's Victory	18	2003
You Rock My World Tonight	21	2003
Night Lady	82	2003
Beldar & Prymaat w/ Nan Shaefer		
Conehead Love	101	1993
Belinda (Peregrín)		
Luz Sin Gravedad / See A Little Light (two versions)	64	2007
Bell, Andy (See also Erasure)		
Crazy	6	2006
Love Oneself	68	2006
DHDQ	28	2010
Will You Be There?	54	2010
Fly	1	2016
Belle And Sebastian		
Reclaim The Night	94	2022
Beloved, The		
Deliver Me	M	1996
Belt, Silvester		
Luktelk	56	2024
Benassi, Benny		
Spaceship	96	2010
Beautiful People	57	2011
Benatar, Pat		
We Live For Love	27	1980
Heartbreaker	54	1980
You Better Run	60	1980
Hit Me With Your Best Shot	97	1980
Promises In The Dark	96	1981
Love Is A Battlefield	6	1983
We Belong	33	1984
Painted Desert	92	1985
Bennett, Tony		
Stranger In Paradise	P	1963
The Shadow Of Your Smile	P	1965
Benton, Brook		
Rainy Night In Georgia	P	1970
Bérard, Judith		
Debout Dans Les Flammes	38	1999
Berlin (See also Terri Nunn)		
The Metro	9	1983
Sex (I'm A...)	105	1983

Animal	84	2013
Transcendance	101	2019
Bernhard, Sandra		
Losing Yourself / Everybody's Young	76	1986
Berry, Heidi		
Cradle	39	1992
Follow	46	1993
Bertine		
Apples And Diamonds (Lord-Alge Remix)	35	2000
Abigail	60	2002
Bertrand, Plastic		
Ça Plane Pour Moi	M	1977
Bettie Serveert		
Versace	27	2005
Beyoncé		
Telephone	48	2009
Sweet Dreams	104	2010
Virgo's Groove/Summer Renaissance	98	2022
Bodyguard	50	2024
Beyond 黃家駒		
Goodtime	96	2000
B-52s, The (The B-52's)		
Rock Lobster	M	1979
Planet Claire	M	1979
Private Idaho	M	1980
Dirty Back Road	M	1980
Mesopotamia	15	1982
Deep Sleep	40	1982
Summer Of Love	40	1986
Ain't It A Shame	7	1987
Girl From Ipanema Goes To Greenland	46	1987
Love Shack	160	1989
Channel Z	18	1989
Topaz / Follow Your Bliss	35	1989
Dry County	55	1990
Roam	83	1990
Revolution Earth	51	1992
Juliet Of The Spirits	8	2008
Eyes Wide Open	35	2008
Deviant Ingredient	57	2008
Bích Phương		
Rằng Em Mãi Ở Bên (That You Will Always Be By My Side)	22	2016
Big & Rich		
Wild West Show	82	2004

Save A Horse (Ride A Cowboy)	103	2004
Big Dish, The		
Where Do You Live?	60	1989
Miss America	107	1991
Big Sean		
Feels	115	2017
Easy Lover	48	2022
Bilk, Mr. Acker		
Stranger On The Shore	P	1961
Bird, Andrew		
Lone Didion	20	2022
Bis		
Detour	6	1999
Eurodisco	90	1999
What You're Afraid Of	27	2001
Bishop, Elvin		
Fooled Around And Fell In Love	98	1976
Bitter:Sweet		
The Mating Game	87	2007
Bitter Sweets, The		
What A Lonely Way To Start The Summertime	P	1965
Bizarrap		
Fuerte	96	2024
BJ The Chicago Kid		
Reach	99	2019
Björk		
Ooops	109	1991
Venus As A Boy	55	1993
Jòga	46	1998
Blacc, Aloe		
Liar Liar	69	2013
Black		
Everything Is Coming Up Roses	38	1989
Wonderful Life	57	1989
Hey, I Was Right You Were Wrong!	80	1989
Sweetest Smile	82	1989
Black, Luke		
Samo Mi Se Spava	25	2023
Black, Mary		
Columbus	8	1991
The Shadow	38	1991
Blackbyrds, The		
Walking In Rhythm	P	1975
Black Coffee		

Drive	29	2018
Black Eyed Peas (The) (See also will.i.am; Fergie; apl.de.ap)		
Don't Phunk With My Heart	119	2005
Rock That Body	50	2009
Alive	60	2009
I Gotta Feeling	66	2009
Blackfield		
Lonely Soul	68	2017
Black Grape		
In The Name Of The Father	87	1995
BLACKPINK (See also JENNIE)		
Sour Candy	21	2020
Black Uhuru		
Great Train Robbery	M	1986
Blaenavon		
Alone	78	2018
Blake, Perry		
Sandriam	5	2002
Still Lives	36	2002
blanco, benny		
Eastside	116	2018
lock / unlock	105	2024
Blando, Deborah		
Nanita	53	1995
Blaque		
Mind Of A King	101	2000
3LAU (Blau)		
On My Mind	40	2017
Blessid Union Of Souls		
I Believe	88	1995
Blige, Mary J.		
911	49	2000
Family Affair	60	2001
Tonight	67	2010
Blind Faith (See also Steve Winwood; Eric Clapton)		
Can't Find My Way Home	P	1969
Bliss		
Wish U Were There/Wish U Were Here	64	2006
Blondfire		
Liar Liar	69	2013
Blondie (See also Debbie Harry)		
Heart Of Glass	24	1979
One Way Or Another	64	1979
Atomic	72	1980

Call Me	82	1980
Rapture	19	1981
The Tide Is High	27	1981
Forgive And Forget	73	1999
I Want To Drag You Around	67	2014
A Rose By Any Name	111	2014

Bloodhound Gang

The Bad Touch	142	2000

Blood, Sweat & Tears

You've Made Me So Very Happy	P	1969

Bloom, Bobby

Montego Bay	P	1970

Bloom, Luka

Rescue Mission	22	1990
I Need Love	84	1992

Blue October

Congratulations	105	2006

Blue Öyster Cult

(Don't Fear) The Reaper	2	1976
Deadline	48	1980
Burnin' For You	66	1981
Shooting Shark	62	1984

Blue Room

Cry Like This	76	1987

Blue Skies, Johnny (See Sturgill Simpson)

Blue Swede

Hooked On A Feeling	P	1974

Blue Yonder

House Of Love	94	1987

Blunt, James

No Bravery	25	2006
Out Of My Mind	69	2006
Lose My Number	46	2017
Love Under Pressure	24	2022
Cold Shoulder	61	2023
Beside You	94	2023

Blur (See also Gorillaz; 1 Giant Leap)

Girls & Boys / (Pet Shop Boys Remix)	29	1994

Bob Moses

Keeping Me Alive	51	2016
Inner Light	2	2021
Seen It Coming	8	2022
Believe	40	2022
Love Brand New	72	2022

Bocelli, Andrea

Time To Say Goodbye (Con Te Partirò)	91	1997

BoDeans

Take It Tomorrow	M	1987
I'll Be There (Voodoo)	52	1989

Boden, Brigid

Child On A Cloud	6	1997
Sleeping Beauty	13	1997
Oh How I Cry	37	1997
I Am The Wind	8	2007
Pray	46	2007
Love Is The Journey	59	2007

Bolton, Michael

The Best	39	2010
Murder My Heart	73	2010

Bond

Shine	72	2002

Boney M.

Ma Baker	M	1977

Bonham, Tracy

Anyone Can Lose	44	2006

Bono (See also U2)

In A Lifetime	32	1986
In The Name Of The Father	73	1994

Bonobo

Shadows	67	2022

Bonoff, Karla

Please Be The One	96	1982
Somebody's Eyes	120	1984

Booker T. & The MG's

Green Onions	P	1962

Book Of Love

Tubular Bells/Pretty Boys And Pretty Girls	38	1988

Boomtown Rats, The (See also Band Aid)

I Don't Like Mondays	69	1980

Borges, Susan, & The Broken Singles

Symphony	49	2009
No One Will Ever Love You	92	2009

Bosé, Miguel

Agua Clara	M	1995

Boston

More Than A Feeling	10	1976
Foreplay/Long Time	65	1977

Bourke, Pieter

Meltdown	52	2000

Bowie, David		
Space Oddity	P	1969
Changes	P	1972
Starman	P	1972
The Jean Genie	P	1972
Aladdin Sane (1913-1938-197?)	P	1973
Rebel Rebel	P	1974
Young Americans	P	1975
Fame / Fame '90 (both versions)	P	1975
Wild Is The Wind	P	1975
Golden Years	6	1976
TVC 15	113	1976
D.J.	M	1979
Ashes To Ashes	M	1980
Fashion	24	1981
Cat People (Putting Out Fire)	90	1982
Under Pressure	27	1982
Peace On Earth/Little Drummer Boy (with Bing Crosby)	X	1982
Let's Dance	48	1983
This Is Not America	5	1985
Box Tops, The		
The Letter	P	1967
Boy George (See also Culture Club)		
You Are My Heroin	59	1989
The Crying Game	160	1993
Boy Meets Girl		
Waiting For A Star To Fall	224	1988
Boys Don't Cry		
I Wanna Be A Cowboy	83	1986
Boys Voice		
Healing Broken Hearts	17	1985
Brady, Jesse, Band		
Souvenirs	74	1980
Bram Tchaikovsky		
Girl Of My Dreams	90	1979
Branch, Michelle		
Intro/Are You Happy Now?	50	2003
Brandy		
The Boy Is Mine	29	1998
Full Moon	57	2002
Branigan, Laura		
Gloria	52	1982
Self Control	43	1984
The Lucky One	132	1984

Brass Construction		
Movin'	45	1976
Bravery, The		
An Honest Mistake	66	2005
Braxton, Toni		
You're Makin' Me High/Let It Flow	48	1996
Un-Break My Heart	75	1996
Never Just For A Ring	94	2000
Hurt You	72	2014
Braxton, Traci		
What About Love?	78	2015
Brazilian Girls		
Don't Stop	47	2005
Homme	78	2005
Bread		
Make It With You	P	1970
It Don't Matter To Me	P	1970
Mother Freedom	P	1971
Baby I'm-A Want You	P	1971
Everything I Own	P	1972
Diary	P	1972
The Guitar Man	P	1972
Sweet Surrender	P	1972
Bremers, Beverly		
Don't Say You Don't Remember	P	1971
Brennan, Brídín		
Face To Face	26	2006
Power Of Three	4	2007
Breakdown	71	2007
Brennan, Moya (Maíre Brennan, prior to 2004) (See also Clannad)		
Cé Leis	19	1992
No Easy Way	54	1992
Against The Wind	101	1992
Misty Eyed Adventures	22	1995
Perfect Time	41	1998
The Big Rock	99	1998
Saltwater	28	1999
Whisper To The Wild Water	52	1999
Follow The Word	18	2000
Show Me (Jakatta Mix)	24	2004
Tell Me Now (What You See)	93	2005
Miles And Miles	48	2006
Merry-Go-Round	21	2007

Brick		
Dusic	30	1977
Dazz	54	1977

Brickell, Edie, & New Bohemians		
What I Am	63	1988
Air Of December	48	1989

Bridges, Alicia		
I Love The Night Life (Disco 'Round)	27	1978

Bright Light Bright Light		
An Open Heart	12	2014
Happiness	19	2014
Love Part II	34	2014
Feel It	70	2014
How To Make A Heart	76	2014
Kiss For Kiss	6	2016
Tonight (Bright Light Bright Light Remix)	16	2020
You Make It So Easy, Don't You	50	2020
Love Song	72	2020
These Dreams	7	2021
It's Alright, It's OK	30	2021
Enjoy Youth	35	2024

Brightman, Sarah		
(I Lost My Heart To A) Starship Trooper (with Hot Gossip) / Starship Troopers (two songs, similar titles)	M	1978
Pie Jesu	14	1985
By Now	33	1993
The Second Element/ The Second Element II	66	1993
Rain	M	1995
I Loved You	3	1997
Ghost In The Machinery	58	1997
Time To Say Goodbye (Con Te Partirò)	91	1997
Something In The Air	74	1998
Only An Ocean Away	17	1999
Deliver Me / Eden	21	1999
Tu	40	1999
La Lune/Winter In July	28	2000
Mysterious Days	46	2003
It's A Beautiful Day / Beautiful	59	2003
I've Seen It All	9	2005
I Will Be With You (Where The Lost Ones Go)	54	2007
Fleurs Du Mal	51	2008
Closer	24	2013
7th Heaven	83	2013

	45	2018
Follow Me	45	2018
Fly To Paradise	96	2018

Britti		
Nothing Compares To You	63	2024

Broadfield, Olivia		
Crashing Down	33	2009
Safe	36	2009

Broken Bells (See also Gnarls Barkley; Danger Mouse)		
The Ghost Inside	94	2010
The Changing Lights	1	2014
Holding On For Life	5	2014
After The Disco	17	2014
One Night	27	2022
We're Not In Orbit Yet...	35	2023

Bronski Beat (See also Jimmy Somerville; The Communards)		
Smalltown Boy	4	1984
Ain't Necessarily So	39	1985
Why?	51	1985

Brood, Herman, & His Wild Romance		
Saturdaynight	45	1979

Brooklyn Dreams		
Sad Eyes	44	1977

Brooks, Garth (as Chris Gaines)		
Right Now	107	1999

Brookville (See also Ivy)		
Beautiful View	29	2007
Walking On Moonlight	68	2007

Brothers, Cary		
Here On Earth	47	2009

Brothers Johnson, The		
Get The Funk Out Ma Face	25	1976
I'll Be Good To You	44	1976
Strawberry Letter 23	4	1977
Stomp!	130	1980

Brother Sun Sister Moon (See also Luminous)		
Havana	12	1997
Bangkok	45	1997
Nicosia	71	1997

Brown, Bobby		
My Prerogative	125	1989
Don't Let Me Die	97	2012

Brown, Chris		
No Air	63	2008
Pass Out	84	2010

Beautiful People	57	2011
Zero	34	2016
Under The Influence	121	2022

Brown, Findlay

All That I Have	14	2010

Brown, Foxy

When The Lights Go Out	14	2008

Brown, Jennifer

Tuesday Afternoon	19	2002

Brown, Kane

Different Man	102	2022

Brown, Peter

Do Ya Wanna Get Funky With Me?	43	1977
Dance With Me	53	1978
For Your Love	M	1978
Without Love	M	1978

Brown, Sam

Stop!	67	1989

Brown, V V

Bottles / Back In Time	98	2010

Browne, Jackson

Doctor My Eyes	P	1972
That Girl Could Sing	31	1980
Boulevard	98	1980
Lives In The Balance	77	1986

Brücken, Claudia (See also Propaganda; OneTwo)

Love Oneself	68	2006

Bryan, Luke

You And The Beach / Night One	124	2015
Out Of Nowhere Girl	68	2018

BT

Blue Skies	47	1997
Shame	2	2000
Dreaming	66	2000
Somnambulist (Simply Being Loved)	48	2004
Love Can Kill You	37	2010
In The Air	19	2011
Must Be The Love	49	2013
Always	46	2020
The One To Love You (The Lifelike Mix)	61	2020
No Warning Lights	91	2021

B-Tribe (See also Sacred Spirits/Indigo Spirit; Classical Spirit)

You Won't See Me Cry	50	1994
Nadie Entiende	97	1994

Que Mala Vida	28	1995
Nanita	53	1995
La Guapa	89	1998

BTS (See also Jungkook; j-hope)

Black Swan (Japanese Version)	58	2020
작은 것들을 위한 시 (Boy With Luv)	100	2019
Who	5	2021

Bucketheads, The

The Bomb! (These Sounds Fall Into My Mind)	M	1995

Buckingham, Lindsey (See also Fleetwood Mac)

Trouble	47	1982
Go Insane	58	1984
Street Of Dreams	70	1992
In My World	84	2017

Buckinghams, The

Kind Of A Drag	P	1966
Don't You Care	P	1967

Buffett, Jimmy

Come Monday	P	1974

Buffalo Springfield (See also Loggins & Messina; Crosby, Stills, Nash & Young; Neil Young; Stephen Stills; Poco)

For What It's Worth (Stop, Hey What's That Sound)	P	1967

Bugg, Jake

Indigo Blue	1	2017
The Love We're Hoping For	11	2017
Lost	14	2021
Lonely Hour	25	2021
Rabbit Hole	43	2021

Buggles, The (See also Asia; Yes)

Video Killed The Radio Star	23	1980

Bunton, Emma (Emma) (See also Spice Girls)

Free Me / (Dr. Octavo Mix)	96	2005
Baby Please Don't Stop	48	2019

Burdon, Eric (See also The Animals)

Spill The Wine	P	1970

Busface

Circles (Just My Good Time)	96	2007

Bush, Kate

Wuthering Heights	63	1978
The Man With The Child In His Eyes	M	1978
Games Without Frontiers	2	1980
Wow / Hammer Horror	33	1980
Babooshka	3	1981

The Wedding List	5	1981
Sat In Your Lap	26	1982
Night Of The Swallow	M	1982
Get Out Of My House	M	1982
The Dreaming	1	1983
There Goes A Tenner	21	1983
Suspended In Gaffa/Ne T'en Fui Pas	30	1983
December Will Be Magic Again	X	1983
Running Up That Hill (A Deal With God)	1	1985
Experiment IV	2	1986
Cloudbusting	5	1986
Mother Stands For Comfort / The Big Sky	12	1986
Watching You Without Me	21	1986
Don't Give Up	28	1986
Be Kind To My Mistakes	2	1988
This Woman's Work	6	1988
The Sensual World	3	1989
Between A Man And A Woman	1	1990
Never Be Mine	3	1990
Heads We're Dancing	38	1990
Sister And Brother	80	1990
The Fog	56	1991
Something Good	91	1992
Big Stripey Lie	3	1993
Constellation Of The Heart	17	1993
And So Is Love	20	1993
Lily	34	1993
Rubberband Girl	43	1993
How To Be Invisible	5	2005
King Of The Mountain	19	2005
Somewhere In Between	14	2006
Nocturn/Aerial	28	2006
π	38	2006
Wild Man	18	2011
Flower Of The Mountain / Song Of Solomon (2011)	62	2011
Tawny Moon	41	2016
Butthole Surfers		
The Shame Of Life	26	2002
Byrds, The (See also McGuinn, Clark & Hillman; Firefall; Crosby, Stills & Nash)		
Turn! Turn! Turn! (To Everything There Is A Season)	P	1965
Eight Miles High	P	1966
Byrne, David (See also The Talking Heads)		
America Is Waiting/Mea Culpa (w/ Brian Eno)	M	1981

God's Child (Baila Conmigo)	9	1995
Eleven Days	99	2010
Byrne & Kelly		
Land Of A Thousand Dreams	43	2016

C

Cab, Cris		
Liar Liar	26	2014
Cabello, Camila		
Crying In The Club	31	2017
Cry For Me	51	2020
HE KNOWS	102	2024
Caesars		
Jerk It Out	85	2005
Cage, John		
4'33"	P	1952
Cahen, Fabien		
La Passion	83	2008
Caiola, Al, and His Orchestra		
Bonanza	T	1961
Cake		
No Phone	81	2004
Caldera, Junior		
What You Get	97	2010
Caldwell, Bobby		
What You Won't Do For Love	91	1979
Coming Down From Love	85	1980
Calexico		
Quattro (World Drifts In)	30	2003
Two Silver Trees	97	2009
Call, The		
I Still Believe	131	1990
C AllStar		
The Queen (后會無期) f/ GiGi Leung (梁詠琪)	40	2016
Buy Car Buy House (上車咒)	73	2016
CamelPhat		
Panic Room	32	2019
Higher	30	2024
Cameo		
Word Up	69	1986
Cameron, Dove		
Use Me (Brutal Hearts)	102	2023
Camouflage		
Love Is A Shield	113	1990
Campbell, Glen		

By The Time I Get To Phoenix	P	1967
Wichita Lineman	P	1968
Dreams Of The Everyday Housewife	P	1968
Galveston	P	1969
Where's The Playground Susie	P	1969

Candyflip
Redhills Road	43	1991

Cannons
Hurricane	14	2022
Purple Sun	71	2022
Loving You	54	2023

Cantrell, Blu
Hit 'Em Up Style (Oops!)	122	2001
So Blu	46	2002

Capercaillie (See also Sharon Shannon)
Stinging Rain	91	1995
Black Fields	6	1996
Hi Rim Bo	42	1996
Claire In Heaven	8	1997
Níl Sí I nGrá	40	1997
Shelter	17	1998
The Tree	76	1998
Beautiful Wasteland	83	1998
Tighinn Air a'Mhuir Am Fear A Phosas Mi	14	2001
Truth Calling	72	2001

Capital Cities
Safe And Sound	99	2013
Gatekeeper Julie	106	2018

Captain & Tennille
Love Will Keep Us Together	P	1975
The Way I Want To Touch You	P	1975
Shop Around	56	1976
Lonely Nights (Angel Face)	83	1976
You Never Done It Like That	46	1978

Cara, Irene
Fame	118	1980
Flashdance...What A Feeling	77	1983

Cardigans, The
My Favourite Game	57	1998
Erase/Rewind	8	1999

Carey, Mariah
When You Believe	120	1999
Petals	178	2000

Carlisle, Belinda (See also Go-Go's)
Circle In The Sand	51	1988

Carlton, Larry
The Theme From Hill Street Blues	106	1981

Carmen, Eric (See also The Raspberries)
All By Myself	85	1976
She Did It	100	1977

Carnes, Kim
You're A Part Of Me	33	1978
More Love	84	1980
Bette Davis Eyes	29	1981
Draw Of The Cards	61	1981
Mistaken Identity	75	1981
Does It Make You Remember	106	1983

Carolina Liar
Better Alone	6	2009

Carpenter, Sabrina
Fast Times	104	2022

Carpenters
(They Long To Be) Close To You	P	1970
We've Only Just Begun	P	1970
Merry Christmas, Darling	X	1970
Superstar/Bless The Beasts And Children	P	1971
For All We Know	P	1971
Let Me Be The One	P	1971
Goodbye To Love	P	1972
Hurting Each Other	P	1972
It's Going To Take Some Time	P	1972
Yesterday Once More	P	1973
Solitaire	P	1973

Carr, Vikki
It Must Be Him	P	1967

Cars, The (See also Benjamin Orr; The New Cars)
Just What I Needed	97	1978
Let's Go	11	1979
Good Times Roll/All Mixed Up	18	1979
Touch And Go	50	1980
Double Life	93	1980
Since You're Gone	84	1982
Drive	40	1984
Why Can't I Have You	65	1985
I'm Not The One	46	1986

Carson, Lori
Pure	27	1995
Gun	96	1995

Carter, Aaron
Fool's Gold	43	2017

Carter, Charlene		
I Couldn't Say No	56	1983
Carter, Valerie		
Change In Luck	M	1978
Carthy, Eliza		
Wildwood	24	2001
Train Song	10	2002
Beautiful Girl	29	2002
Casablancas, Julian		
Instant Crush	28	2013
Cascada		
Evacuate The Dancefloor	121	2009
Cash, Johnny		
I've Been Everywhere	P	1966
(Ghost) Riders In The Sky	M	1979
Cash, Rosanne		
Seven Year Ache	116	1981
Price Of The Fire	107	1988
I Want A Cure	70	1991
The Only Thing Worth Fighting For	112	2018
Cash Cash		
Finest Hour	56	2018
Cassie		
Me & U	82	2006
cassö		
Prada	23	2023
Castaways, The		
Liar, Liar	P	1965
Cast of HAIR		
Walking In Space (movie version)	M	1979
Catherine Wheel		
I Want To Touch You	64	1992
Black Metallic	80	1992
Cat Power		
I've Been Thinking	38	2005
Ruin	96	2012
Cause & Effect (See also Solsun; Whitewaits)		
She Said	18	1994
Inside Out	58	1994
It's Over Now	60	1994
Stone Girl	98	1994
She's So Gone	38	2002
Real?	48	2002
Into The Light	22	2003
Sunrise	68	2003

Stay	18	2004
Happy?	13	2010
This Is Who I Am	43	2010
Happiness Is Alien	14	2011
Shine	96	2011
Cautious Clay		
Agreeable	89	2021
Cavell, Paige		
Tears	78	2024
C-BooL		
Fire In My Head	71	2019
Celeste		
Tonight Tonight	84	2021
Ceredwen		
Beltain – Beltane	23	2000
Y Bryn Gwyn – The White Hall	51	2000
Chad & Jeremy		
A Summer Song	P	1964
Chad Valley		
Now That I'm Real (How Does It Feel?)	39	2011
I Owe You This	54	2012
Chainsmokers, The		
New York City	8	2017
Paris	82	2017
Side Effects	6	2018
Hope	64	2019
Solo Mission	12	2022
Chairlift (See also Caroline Polachek)		
Ghost Tonight	18	2012
Wrong Opinion	37	2012
Chali 2na		
Face Of Danger	15	2013
Chan, Eason 陳奕迅		
阿貓阿狗 (Cat & Dog)	38	2014
Chan, Jackie		
Endless Love I/II (神话) (美麗的神話 I/II)	72	2008
Chance, Greyson		
Summertrain	50	2011
Chandra, Sheila (See also Monsoon)		
Village Girl	M	1984
Strange Minaret	125	1991
Chanson		
Don't Hold Back	99	1979

Chao, Manu		
Bongo Bong/Je Ne T'Aime Plus	14	1999
Chapin, Harry		
Taxi	P	1972
Cat's In The Cradle	P	1974
Sequel	88	1980
Chapman, Tracy		
Fast Car	15	1988
Talkin' Bout A Revolution	52	1988
Crossroads	43	1989
For My Lover	54	1989
This Time	30	1990
Born To Fight	43	1990
Wedding Song	1	2000
Unsung Psalm	17	2000
It's OK	40	2000
Charlatans, The (The Charlatans UK)		
The Only One I Know	41	1990
Then	4	1991
You're Not Very Well	73	1991
(No One) Not Even The Rain	97	1992
Come In Number 21	68	1994
I Never Want An Easy Life If Me And He Were Ever To Get There	88	1994
Muddy Ground	15	2007
City Of The Dead	93	2007
Charli XCX (Charli xcx)		
I Love It	104	2013
Constant Repeat	35	2022
Chasez, JC (See also *NSYNC)		
Somnambulist (Simply Being Loved)	48	2004
Come To Me	62	2004
Châu Khải Phong		
Còn Là Gì Của Nhau (What's Left Of Each Other)	7	2019
Ngắm Hoa Lệ Rơi (Watch The Flowers Fall)	79	2019
Chavez, Ingrid		
Heartbeat (Tainaki Kaiki II: returning to the womb)	67	1992
Cheap Trick		
Dream Police	61	1979
I Want You To Want Me	109	1979
Voices	67	1980
Everything Works If You Let It	92	1980
Stop This Game	69	1981

Cheb Mami		
Desert Rose	54	2000
Chen Hui-Ting 陳惠婷		
Last Night On Mars	34	2017
Skyscraper (摩天大樓)	80	2017
Tomorrow's Party	16	2018
Cheng, Sammi 鄭秀文		
插曲 (Episode/Chaqu)	29	2000
發熱發亮 (Shining Bright/Hot And Bright)	53	2000
Cher (See also Sonny & Cher)		
Bang Bang (My Baby Shot Me Down)	P	1966
Gypsys, Tramps & Thieves	P	1971
The Way Of Love	P	1972
Living In A House Divided	P	1972
Half-Breed	P	1973
Dark Lady	P	1974
One By One	121	1996
Believe	49	1998
Taxi Taxi	67	1999
The Music's No Good Without You	42	2002
A Different Kind Of Love Song	99	2002
Cheri		
Working Girl	110	1983
Cherrelle		
Artificial Heart	95	1986
Saturday Love	57	1986
High Priority	105	1987
Cherry, Neneh		
I've Got U Under My Skin	98	1990
Chesney, Kenny		
Somewhere With You	4	2011
One Lonely Island	17	2024
Thinkin' Bout	76	2024
Chic (See also Nile Rodgers)		
Le Freak	24	1978
Dance, Dance, Dance (Yowsah, Yowsah, Yowsah)	52	1978
I Want Your Love	59	1979
Chicago		
25 Or 6 To 4 (1986 version also)	P	1970
Beginnings/Colour My World	P	1971
Just You 'N' Me	P	1973
Feelin' Stronger Every Day	P	1973
(I've Been) Searchin' So Long	P	1974
Wishing You Were Here	P	1974

Old Days	P	1975
If You Leave Me Now	40	1976
Baby, What A Big Surprise	53	1977
Hard To Say I'm Sorry/Get Away	14	1982
Hard Habit To Break	31	1984

Chicane
Saltwater	28	1999
Don't Give Up	36	2000
Autumn Tactics	86	2000
Stoned In Love	87	2008

Chicks, The (The Dixie Chicks)
March March	107	2020

Chiffons, The
One Fine Day	P	1963

Childs, Toni
Dreamer	16	1988
House Of Hope	32	1991
Lay Down Your Pain	30	1994
Predator	70	1994

Chi-Lites, The
Oh Girl	P	1972

Chilliwack
My Girl (Gone, Gone, Gone)	42	1981

Chimera
Let Me Be Around	47	1996
Tiago	73	1996
Catch Me	93	1996

China Crisis
Christian	M	1982
Docklands/Forever I And I	M	1982
Wishful Thinking	1	1984
Working With Fire And Steel / Hanna Hanna	25	1984
Tragedy And Mystery	91	1984
Black Man Ray	84	1985
King In A Catholic Style	98	1985
Gift Of Freedom	51	1986
Hampton Beach	48	1987
Arizona Sky	68	1987
St. Saviour Square	10	1989
Diary Of A Hollow Horse	21	1989

Chloë (Agnew) (from Celtic Woman)
The Last Rose Of Summer/Walking In The Air	X	2002

Chloe x Halle
Wolf At Your Door	26	2020
Galaxy	52	2020

Chou, Jay 周杰倫
本草綱目 (Herbalist Manual)	97	2006
夜的第七章 (Twilight's Chapter Seven)	20	2007
四季列車 (Four Seasons Train)	50	2013
Intro/Greatest Works Of Art (最偉大的作品)	82	2022

Chow, Dominic 周啓生
太胡鬧 (Too Mischievous)	130	1992

Christians, The
I Found Out	76	1990

Christie, Lou
Lightnin' Strikes	P	1965

Christine And The Queens
Paradis Perdus	111	2015
Damn, Dis-Moi (Girlfriend)	39	2018
Full of Life	108	2023

Christy, Lauren
Walk This Earth Alone	12	1998
Boomerang Bang	55	1998

Chromeo
Night By Night	66	2011

Chua, Tanya 蔡健雅
Strange Species (異類的同類)	12	2016
Aphasia (失語者)	14	2016
One Carat (一克拉)	42	2016
Best Way To Die (活著是最好的死亡)	49	2016
Can I Help You Sir? (先生有事嗎?)	77	2016
Breakdown	33	2021
Bluebirds	53	2021
Into The Wild	86	2021

Chumbawamba
Tubthumping	18	1997
Amnesia	60	1998
Jacob's Ladder	71	2003
One Way Or The Other	35	2004
Don't Pass Go	84	2004

Church, The (See also Hex)
Under The Milky Way	54	1988
Ripple	38	1992

Church, Charlotte
Let's Be Alone	97	2007

CHVRCHΞS (Chvrches)
Science/Visions	125	2013

Ciara
Thinkin Bout You	106	2019

Cielo y Tierra		
Nuestra Única Ilusíon	1	1997
Los Cuatro Elementos	23	1997

Cigarettes After Sex		
Baby Blue Movie	4	2024

The Cinematic Orchestra f/ Lou Rhodes		
Crimson Skies	9	2011

Citizen Cope		
Son's Gonna Rise	21	2005

City And Colour		
Two Coins	11	2013
Imagination	81	2019

City Boy		
5-7-0-5 (5.7.0.5.)	56	1978
The Day The Earth Caught Fire	25	1979

Clannad (See also Maíre/Moya Brennan; Enya)		
Theme From Harry's Game	M	1983
Newgrange	M	1983
Coinleach Glas An Fhómhair/I See Red	M	1983
Strange Land	M	1984
Now Is Here	M	1984
The Wild Cry	17	1986
In A Lifetime	32	1986
Closer To Your Heart	50	1986
Something To Believe In	10	1988
Sirius	22	1988
Turning Tide	73	1988
Many Roads	92	1988
The Hunter	29	1990
World Of Difference	57	1990
A Dream In The Night (The Angel & The Soldier Boy)	21	1991
The Poison Glen	29	1992
Why Worry?	32	1992
Rí Na Cruinne	96	1992
I Will Find You (Theme From 'The Last Of The Mohicans')	51	1993
Banba Óir	60	1993
There For You	93	1993
From Your Heart	5	1996
Farewell Love	15	1996
Seanchas	43	1996
Of This Land	5	1998
An Gleann	11	1998
Let Me See	61	1998

What Will I Do?	95	1999
Brave Enough	20	2013
The Song In Your Heart	48	2013

Clapton, Eric (See also The Yardbirds; Cream; Blind Faith; Derek And The Dominoes)		
Let It Rain	P	1972
Another Ticket	31	1981

Claptone		
Alone	78	2018
Cruising (So They Say)	57	2018
Under The Moon	69	2018
Just A Ghost	12	2021
Satellite	11	2022
Fade Away	41	2022

Clark, The Dave, Five		
Because	P	1964

Clark, Petula		
Downtown	P	1964
My Love	P	1965

Clark, Roy		
Yesterday, When I Was Young	P	1969

Clash, The (See also Mick Jones)		
Train In Vain (Stand By Me)	56	1980
Rock The Casbah	63	1982

Classical Spirit (See also B-Tribe; Sacred Spirit/Indigo Spirit)		
Gloria Deo Patri	43	2003

Classics IV		
Spooky	P	1967
Stormy	P	1967
Traces	P	1969

Clean Bandit		
Dust Clears	24	2014
Extraordinary	97	2014
Solo	53	2018
Baby	89	2019

Climax		
Precious And Few	P	1972

Climax Blues Band		
Couldn't Get It Right	7	1977
Gotta Have More Love	67	1981

Cline, Patsy		
Walkin' After Midnight	P	1957
I Fall To Pieces	P	1961
Crazy	P	1961

Strange	P	1962
Tra Le La Le La Triangle	P	1963

Clinic

Come Into Our Room	56	2003

Clooney, Rosemary

Come On-A My House	P	1951
Mambo Italiano	P	1954
Sway	P	1954

Club Cheval

Young Rich And Radical	30	2016

Club Dogo f/ Arisa

Fragili	74	2014

Club Nouveau (See also Timex Social Club)

Why You Treat Me So Bad	26	1987

Cocker, Joe

You Are So Beautiful	P	1975

Cocteau Twins (See also Elizabeth Fraser; This Mortal Coil; Snowbird)

Aikea-Guinea	M	1984
Aloysius	M	1984
Ivo / Pandora (for Cindy)	36	1985
Quisquose	46	1985
How To Bring A Blush To The Snow	37	1986
Pink Orange Red	85	1986
The Itchy Glowbo Blow	5	1988
Carolyn's Fingers	43	1988
Blue Bell Knoll	1	1989
Watchlar	6	1990
Road, River And Rail	2	1991
Pitch The Baby	24	1991
Frou-Frou Foxes In Midsummer Fires	33	1991
Fifty-Fifty Clown	41	1992
Know Who You Are At Every Age	5	1993
Theft, And Wandering Around Lost	14	1993
Summerhead	100	1994
Seekers Who Are Lovers	60	1996
The Amusement Park (娛樂場) (w/ Faye Wong (王菲))	M	1997

Coldplay

Yellow	58	2001
God Put A Smile Upon Your Face	22	2002
Don't Panic	43	2002
White Shadows	2	2005
Low	29	2005
Adventure Of A Lifetime	46	2015

Cole, Cheryl (Cheryl) (See also Girls Aloud)

3 Words	8	2010
Happy Hour	33	2010
Rain On Me	51	2010
Yeah Yeah	1	2012

Cole, Lloyd

Downtown	106	1990

Cole, Nat "King"

(Get Your Kicks On) Route 66	P	1946
Nature Boy	P	1948
Mona Lisa	P	1950
Unforgettable	P	1952
Those Lazy-Hazy-Crazy Days Of Summer	P	1963

Cole, Paula / Paula Cole Band

Saturn Girl	4	1994
Chiaroscuro	10	1994
Happy Home	59	1994
I Am So Ordinary	69	1994
Where Have All The Cowboys Gone?	3	1996
Road To Dead	26	1996
Feelin' Love	9	1997
I Don't Want To Wait	101	1997
I Believe In Love (Paula Cole Band)	12	1999
Amen (Paula Cole Band)	41	1999
Calling All Saviors	29	2024

Colette

What's Wrong With Being Lonely	58	2005

Collective Soul

The World I Know	39	1995
December	61	1995

Collins, Edwyn

A Girl Like You	2	1995
Sometimes Always Never	91	2019

Collins, Judy

Both Sides Now	P	1968
Running For My Life	M	1980
Aberdeen / The Weight	105	2016

Collins, Phil (See also Genesis)

In The Air Tonight	1	1981
I Missed Again	93	1981
Another Day In Paradise	19	1989

Colour Of Memory, The

Always With Me	17	1995
Rigmarole	24	1995
The Grace	95	1995

Colvin, Shawn

Steady On	62	1990
The Dead Of The Night	11	1991
Shotgun Down The Avalanche	26	1991
Sunny Came Home	43	1997

Commodores (See also Lionel Richie)

Sweet Love	76	1976
Brick House	41	1977
Easy	98	1977
Sail On	69	1979
Lady (You Bring Me Up)	101	1981
Night Shift	91	1985

Common

Everywhere	56	2009

Communards, The (See also Jimmy Somerville; Bronski Beat)

Disenchanted	11	1987
So Cold The Night	54	1987
For A Friend	18	1988
Tomorrow	25	1988
Hold On Tight	56	1988

Como, Perry

Catch A Falling Star	P	1957
Seattle	P	1969
It's Impossible	P	1970

Company B

Fascinated	37	1987

Comsat Angels, The (The C.S. Angels)

Independence Day	81	1984
Island Heart	101	1984
I'm Falling	99	1985
The Cutting Edge	3	1987
You'll Never Know	74	1987
Shiva Descending	42	1993
Always Near	47	1993

Concrete Blonde

Everybody Knows	39	1990
Tomorrow, Wendy	37	1991

Conjure One (See also Delerium)

Damascus/Center Of The Sun	3	2002
Manic Star	20	2003
Tears From The Moon	29	2003
Make A Wish	38	2003
Sleep	53	2003
Endless Dream	7	2005

I Believe	49	2005
One Word	72	2005
Extraordinary Way	42	2006
Forever Lost	43	2006
Face The Music	72	2006
Like Ice	48	2010
I Dream In Colour	48	2011
Still Holding On	52	2014
Kill The Fear	95	2018

Conniff, Ray, And The Singers

Somewhere, My Love	P	1966

Connors, Norman

You Are My Starship	87	1976

Conti, Bill

Gonna Fly Now (Theme From "Rocky")	66	1977

Cook, Elizabeth

Perfect Girls Of Pop	94	2020

Cooke, Sam

You Send Me	P	1957
Cupid	P	1960

Coolidge, Rita

(Your Love Has Lifted Me) Higher And Higher	94	1977
You	99	1978

Coolio

Gangsta's Paradise	83	1995

Cooper, Alice

(I'm) Eighteen	P	1971
School's Out	P	1972
Only Women Bleed (Only Women)	P	1975
Clones (We're All)	29	1980

Copeland

Should You Return	26	2008

Coppola, Imani

Legend Of A Cowgirl	102	1997

Cornelius Brothers & Sister Rose

Treat Her Like A Lady	P	1971
Too Late To Turn Back Now	P	1972

Cornell, Chris (See also Soundgarden)

Long Gone	90	2009

Corrs, The

Erin Shore (Traditional Intro)/Forgiven Not Forgotten	70	1996
No Good For Me	34	1998
Only When I Sleep	71	1998
Baby Be Brave/Silver Strand	38	2004

Black Is The Colour	21	2006
I Do What I Like	36	2016

Corsten, Ferry

Let You Go	36	2012
Wounded	10	2022

Costello, Elvis / Elvis Costello & The Attractions

Watching The Detectives	M	1978
Accidents Will Happen	M	1979
Man Out Of Time	128	1982
Beyond Belief	M	1982
Everyday I Write The Book	88	1983
The Only Flame In Town	169	1985
Adrian (Eurythmics f/ Elvis Costello)	25	1986
So Like Candy (Elvis Costello)	65	1991

Cotton, Gene

Before My Heart Finds Out	10	1978
You're A Part Of Me	33	1978
Like A Sunday In Salem (The Amos & Andy Song)	18	1978

Cotton, Josie

Johnny, Are You Queer?	103	1982
See The New Hong Kong	40	2011
All I Can See Is The Face Of Bruce Lee	76	2011

Coulais, Bruno

Return Of The Cranes	101	2003

Couleé, Shea, & Gess f/ Mykki Blanco

Collide	80	2020

Cousins, Tina

Live & Breathe	45	2000
Rip It Up	77	2006

Cousteau

Talking To Myself	40	2003

Cowboy Junkies

Sweet Jane	103	1989
A Common Disaster	101	1996

Cracknell, Sarah (See also Saint Etienne)

Goldie	80	2000

Cranberries, The

Pretty	13	1993
I Still Do	18	1993
Waltzing Back	23	1993
Not Sorry	31	1993
Linger	72	1993
Put Me Down	90	1993
Zombie	8	1994

Ode To My Family	75	1994
Ridiculous Thoughts	34	1995
The Icicle Melts	49	1995
Disappointment	69	1995
Hollywood	87	1996
Catch Me If You Can	47	2019

Crash Test Dummies

Mmm Mmm Mmm Mmm	55	1994

Craven, Beverley

I Listen To The Rain	M	1990

Crawford, Randy

Street Life (w/ The Crusaders)	M	1979
Don't Wanna Be Normal	29	1986
Gettin' Away With Murder	164	1987

Crawler

Stone Cold Sober	23	1977

Crazy Town (See also Shifty Shellshock)

Butterfly	86	2001

Cream (See also Eric Clapton; Blind Faith)

Strange Brew	P	1967
White Room	P	1968
Badge	P	1969

Croce, Jim

Operator (That's Not The Way It Feels)	P	1972
Time In A Bottle	P	1973

Crookes, Joy

19th Floor	2	2022
Feet Don't Fail Me Now	15	2022

Crosby, Bing

Peace On Earth/Little Drummer Boy (with David Bowie)	X	1982

Crosby, Stills & Nash / Crosby, Stills, Nash & Young (See also Neil Young; Stephen Stills; Buffalo Springfield; The Byrds)

Suite: Judy Blue Eyes	P	1969
Long Time Gone	P	1969
Woodstock (with Neil Young)	P	1970
Ohio (with Neil Young)	P	1970
Carry On/Questions	P	1970
To The Last Whale: Critical Mass/Wind On The Water	P	1975
Cathedral	M	1977
Just A Song Before I Go	136	1977
I Give You Give Blind	M	1977
Dark Star	M	1977

Cross, Christopher		
Sailing	9	1980
Ride Like The Wind	65	1980
Arthur's Theme (Best That You Can Do)	85	1981
Think Of Laura	88	1984
Crow, Sheryl		
What I Can Do For You	72	1994
My Favorite Mistake	90	1998
Try Not To Remember	27	2008
Evolution	86	2024
Crowded House (See also Split Enz; Neil Finn; Tim Finn; Finn Brothers)		
World Where You Live	59	1986
Hole In The River	17	1987
Don't Dream It's Over	79	1987
I Feel Possessed	82	1988
Into Temptation	27	1989
Chocolate Cake	101	1991
Four Seasons In One Day	57	1992
Whispers And Moans / Fall At Your Feet	71	1992
Private Universe	34	1994
Archer's Arrows	32	2010
Cruise, Julee		
Into The Night	88	1990
Cruise Control		
No Condom, No Sex	51	1989
Crusaders, The		
Street Life (w/ Randy Crawford)	M	1979
Crush		
Penthouse Girl, Basement Boy	100	1998
Cruz, Taio		
Higher	65	2010
Crystal Castles vs. Health		
Crimewave	76	2008
Crystal Method, The		
Grace	3	2014
Cuff Links, The		
Tracy	P	1969
Culture Club (See also Boy George)		
Do You Really Want To Hurt Me	52	1983
Mistake No. 3	60	1985
Cummings, Burton (See also The Guess Who)		
Stand Tall	113	1977
Cure, The		
Charlotte Sometimes	M	1981

Love Song	37	1989
Fascination Street	85	1989
Prayers For Rain	88	1989
Purple Haze	63	1994
Curiosity Killed The Cat		
Misfit	87	1987
Curry, Tim		
Sweet Transvestite	P	1975
Curtin, Hoyt		
(Meet) The Flintstones (w/ Joseph Barbera, William Hanna)	T	1961
The Jetsons	T	1962
Jonny Quest Main Theme	T	1966
Curtis, Sonny		
Love Is All Around (Mary Tyler Moore Theme)	T	1970
Curve		
Coast Is Clear	45	1992
Faît Accompli	81	1992
Crystal	87	1994
Beyond Reach	52	1998
Cut Copy		
Strangers In The Wind	34	2008
Tied To The Weather	85	2018
Cutting Crew		
(I Just) Died In Your Arms	M	1987
Cyrus, Miley		
Don't Call Me Angel (Charlie's Angels)	55	2019
Nothing Breaks Like A Heart	122	2019
Midnight Sky	7	2020
Prisoner	37	2021
Cyrus, Noah		
I Just Want A Lover	100	2023

D

Daecolm		
I Adore You	48	2024
Daft Punk		
One More Time	54	2001
Harder, Better, Faster, Stronger	94	2001
Instant Crush	28	2013
Within	37	2013
The Game Of Love	41	2013
Get Lucky	64	2013
Starboy	7	2016

D'Agostino, Gigi		
I'll Fly With You (L'Amour Toujours) (Bla Bla Bla)	110	2001
Daigle, Lauren		
Still Rolling Stones	99	2018
Daily, E.G.		
Mind Over Matter	158	1987
Dalcan, Dominique		
Rose	20	1998
Daltrey, Roger (See also The Who)		
Without Your Love	80	1980
Free Me	86	1980
Dâm-Funk		
Damn, Dis-Moi (Girlfriend)	39	2018
Damian & London Symphony Orchestra		
Queen Of Night	100	2005
Damon('s), Liz, Orient Express		
1900 Yesterday	P	1970
Dandy Warhols, The		
We Used To Be Friends	88	2003
Danger Mouse (See also Gnarls Barkley; Broken Bells)		
Season's Trees	95	2011
Turn The Light	3	2019
Danity Kane (See also Dawn Richard)		
Damaged	50	2008
Bad Girl	90	2008
Dao Dezi (See also Deep Forest)		
Kokerikero	6	1995
Ti Eliz Iza	32	1995
La Jument De Mishao	52	1996
D'Arby, Terence Trent (Sananda Maitreya)		
Sign Your Name	113	1988
Delicate	24	1994
Supermodel Sandwich	15	1995
Darude		
Sandstorm	M	1999
David, Craig		
Fill Me In	111	2001
Walking Away	54	2002
6 Of 1 Thing	66	2008
Hot Stuff (Let's Dance)	86	2008
My First Love	39	2009
Davine		
Cheveux Noirs	74	2018
Davis, Paul		
I Go Crazy	31	1977

Do Right	52	1980
Davis, Skeeter		
The End Of The World	P	1963
Dawes		
I Can't Think About It Now	94	2015
Dax, Danielle		
The Living And Their Stillborn	28	1991
Day, Doris		
Secret Love	P	1953
By The Light Of The Silvery Moon	P	1953
Que Sera, Sera (Whatever Will Be, Will Be)	P	1956
Any Way The Wind Blows	P	1960
Sentimental Journey	P	1964
Daya		
Bad Girl	21	2021
Daye, Lucky		
Fade Away	56	2020
D-Block Europe		
Prada	23	2023
dc Talk		
Consume Me	33	1999
Dead Can Dance (See also Lisa Gerrard; Brendan Perry)		
Mother Tongue	66	1989
Spirit	41	1991
Bird	73	1992
American Dreaming	96	1994
Nierika	91	1996
Amnesia	68	2012
Dead Man's Bones		
Pa Pa Power	128	2023
deadmau5		
I Remember	3	2008
Move For Me	38	2008
Ice Age (deadmau5 Remix)	90	2014
Dean, Ester		
Another Life	67	2017
Dean And The Weenies		
Fuck You	89	1989
Death Cab For Cutie (See also The Postal Service)		
Soul Meets Body	51	2005
Black Sun	26	2015
Before The Bombs	95	2019
DeBarge, El		
Prelude To The Garden/The Secret Garden (Sweet Seduction Suite)	116	1990

DeBurgh, Chris		
Sight And Touch	116	1985
Decemberists, The		
The Engine Driver	22	2005
Don't Go To The Woods	104	2024
Dee, Kiki		
I've Got The Music In Me	P	1974
Don't Go Breaking My Heart	19	1976
Chicago	90	1977
Deep Dish		
Sergio's Theme	60	2005
Say Hello	84	2005
Deep Forest (See also Dao Dezi)		
Deep Forest	49	1993
Boheme	48	1995
Marta's Song	62	1995
While The Earth Sleeps	20	1996
Endangered Species (Galleon Remix)	61	2002
Bedi	60	2013
Deep Purple		
Smoke On The Water	P	1973
Dees, Rick, & His Cast Of Idiots		
Disco Duck	99	1976
DeFranco Family f/ Tony DeFranco		
Heartbeat – It's A Lovebeat	P	1973
Delegates, The		
Convention '72	P	1972
Delerium (See also Conjure One; Fauxliage)		
Silence	1	1998
Euphoria (Firefly)	44	1998
Enchanted	74	1999
Heaven's Earth	57	2000
Fallen Icons	36	2001
Daylight	56	2001
Innocente	101	2001
Truly	1	2003
After All	24	2003
Run For It	61	2003
Touched	22	2004
Fallen	40	2004
Paris	99	2004
Fleeting Instant	55	2006
Dust In Gravity	60	2010
Consciousness Of Love	35	2012
Days Turn Into Nights	29	2013

Ray	41	2015
Blue Fires	32	2016
Stay	65	2017
Coast To Coast	36	2023
Delfonics, The		
Didn't I (Blow Your Mind)	P	1970
Dell-Vikings, The		
Come Go With Me	P	1957
Del Rey, Lana		
Blue Jeans	64	2012
Cola	21	2013
Summertime Sadness (Cedric Gervais Mix)	70	2013
West Coast	60	2014
Music To Watch Boys To	67	2015
Lust For Life	28	2017
Love	101	2017
Doin' Time	27	2019
Don't Call Me Angel (Charlie's Angels)	55	2019
Đen		
Ta Cứ Đi Cùng Nhau (Let's Go Together)	25	2019
Denver, John		
Take Me Home Country Roads	P	1971
Rocky Mountain High	P	1972
Annie's Song	P	1974
I'm Sorry/Calypso	P	1975
Fly Away	P	1975
Deodato		
Also Sprach Zarathrustra (2001)	P	1973
Depeche Mode (See also Erasure; Yazoo; Martin L Gore)		
Everything Counts	M	1983
Lie To Me	68	1985
People Are People	107	1985
Blasphemous Rumours / It's Called A Heart	70	1986
A Question Of Time / A Question Of Lust	98	1986
Never Let Me Down Again/Pleasure, Little Treasure	15	1987
Stripped	49	1987
Strangelove	96	1987
The Things You Said	41	1988
Behind The Wheel/Route 66	125	1988
Personal Jesus	44	1989
Enjoy The Silence	24	1990
Policy Of Truth	86	1990
Walking In My Shoes	45	1993

I Feel You	88	1993
It's No Good	10	1997
Home	80	1997
Uselink/Useless	45	1998
Freelove	46	2001
Dream On	65	2001
I Feel Loved	67	2001
Precious	44	2005

Depp, Lily-Rose
One Of The Girls	107	2024

Derek And The Dominos (See also Eric Clapton)
Layla	P	1971

Derringer, Rick
Rock And Roll, Hoochie Koo	P	1974

Derulo, Jason
Breathing	11	2012
Cheyenne	32	2015
Saturday/Sunday	98	2023
Don't Go Nowhere	106	2024

Des'ree
Delicate	24	1994
You Gotta Be	42	1994

Dessa
The Man I Knew	74	2013
What If I'm Not Ready	32	2024

DeTiger, Blu
Intro To Everything / Expensive Money	77	2024
Disappearing	108	2024

Devo
Whip It	34	1980
Working In A Coal Mine	70	1981
Let Me Tickle Your Fancy	89	1982

Devonsquare
If You Could See Me Now	53	1993

DeVorzon, Barry, & Perry Botkin, Jr.
Nadia's Theme (The Young And The Restless)	M	1976

Diab, Amr
Al Malak El Barea الملاك البريء	M	1998
Tamally Ma'ak تملي معاك	M	2008

Diablo, Don
Survive	90	2019

Diamond, Neil
Solitary Man	P	1966
Shilo	P	1968

Sweet Caroline (Good Times Never Seemed So Good)	P	1969
Cracklin' Rosie	P	1970
Longfellow Serenade	P	1974
America	88	1981

Dickson, Barbara
I Know Him So Well	40	1985

Dico, Tina (See also Zero 7)
Sinners And Saints	17	2006
Head Shop	27	2006
Losing	62	2006
My Mirror / Use Me	96	2006

Dido (See also Faithless)
Hunter	11	1999
Don't Think Of Me	19	1999
Here With Me	42	1999
My Lover's Gone	43	1999
My Life	43	2000
Slide	46	2000
Sand In My Shoes	17	2003
Stoned	14	2004
Don't Believe In Love	65	2008
Go Dreaming	19	2013
End Of Night	39	2013
NYC	7	2014
Take You Home	13	2019
Hurricanes	21	2019
Fly To You	42	2024

Diesel
Sausalito Summernight	92	1981

Dieselle
DJ (The Magic Key)	25	2016

Digby, Marié
Love With A Stranger	16	2010

Digital Farm Animals x Shaun Frank x Dragonette (See also Dragonette)
Tokyo Nights	24	2018

Dion, Céline
Refuse To Dance	33	1994
Falling Into You	14	1997
My Heart Will Go On	152	1998
A New Day Has Come	97	2002
Reveal	5	2003
Somebody Loves Somebody	46	2013
Tu Sauras	45	2016
Flying On My Own	76	2019

Diplo		
Hey Baby	25	2017
Use Me (Brutal Hearts)	102	2023

Dire Straits		
Skateaway	49	1981

Dirty Harry (Amazonica)		
Makin Me Crazy	56	2006

Dirty Heads		
Oxygen	73	2017

Dirty Vegas		
Days Go By	50	2002
Ghosts	101	2002
Walk Into The Sun	46	2005
A Million Ways	70	2005
Roses	74	2005
Changes	74	2011
21st Century	94	2011

Disclosure		
BOSS	118	2016

Disco Biscuits		
Loose Change/On Time	78	2010

Dishwalla		
Counting Blue Cars	89	1996

Dissidenten		
Cairo By Night	85	1990

Ditto, Beth (See also Gossip)		
I Wrote The Book	55	2011
A Rose By Any Name	111	2014

Dixie Cups, The		
Chapel Of Love	P	1964

Django Django		
Introduction/Hail Bop	96	2013
Beam Me Up	51	2018
Dead Machine	73	2023

DJ Dado		
X-Files	M	1996

DJ Encore f/ Engelina		
I See Right Through To You	37	2002
Out There	7	2003

DJ Shadow		
Our Pathetic Age	52	2019

DJ Snake		
Good Day	93	2017
No More	96	2019
Try Me	70	2020

DNA		
Rusted Pipe (Tom's Mix)	16	1990

DNCE (See also Jonas Brothers, Nick Jonas, Joe Jonas)		
Cake By The Ocean	91	2016

Dobson, Fefe		
Intro/Ghosts	83	2011

Dr. Calculus		
Full Of Love (1986 version – "Perfume From Spain")	61	1988

Dr. Dre		
California Love	106	1996

Dr. Hook (& The Medicine Show)		
Only Sixteen	59	1976
Sharing The Night Together	50	1978

Doi Todd, Mia		
Growing Pains	55	2003
Digital	73	2003

Doja Cat		
Say So	103	2020
In Your Eyes (2021 remix)	105	2021

Dolby, Thomas		
She Blinded Me With Science/One Of Our Submarines	10	1983
Europa And The Pirate Twins	34	1983
Screen Kiss	2	1984
Don't Turn Away	89	1987
My Brain Is Like A Sieve	44	1988
Neon Sisters	48	1993
Quantum Mechanic	41	1995
Nothing New Under The Sun	38	2011

Don, Stefflon		
Instruction	78	2017

Donaghy, Siobhan (Siobhán) (See also Sugababes)		
Halcyon Days	18	2007
Medevac	69	2007

Donalds, Andru		
Heart Of Stone	M	1997

Donaldson, Bo, And The Heywoods		
Billy, Don't Be A Hero	P	1974
Who Do You Think You Are	P	1974

Donovan		
Sunshine Superman	P	1966
Mellow Yellow	P	1966
Season Of The Witch	P	1966

Doobie Brothers, The (See also Michael McDonald; Patrick Simmons)		
Long Train Runnin'	P	1973
Black Water	P	1974
Another Park, Another Sunday	P	1974
I Cheat The Hangman	P	1975
Takin' It To The Streets	33	1976
It Keeps You Runnin'	82	1977

Doors, The (See also Jim Morrison)		
Light My Fire	P	1967
People Are Strange	P	1967
Hello, I Love You	P	1968
Riders Of The Storm	P	1971

Double		
The Captain Of Her Heart	26	1986

Douglas, Carl		
Kung Fu Fighting	P	1974

Dover, Connie		
Laddie, Lie Near Me	27	1997

Dovlatov, Ilkin		
Özünlə Apar	23	2024

Dragonette (See also Digital Farm Animals)		
Body 2 Body	18	2017
Love Can't Touch Me Now	29	2017
Darth Vader	36	2017
Future Ghost	3	2018
Tokyo Nights	24	2018
Twennies	68	2022

Drake		
Hotline Bling	130	2015
Passionfruit	50	2017

Dream, The (The-Dream)		
Long Gone	7	2013

Dream Academy, The		
Life In A Northern Town	45	1985
The Love Parade	35	1986
Indian Summer	73	1987
Power To Believe	46	1988
In The Hands Of Love	58	1988
Love	67	1991
It'll Never Happen Again	83	1991

Dreaming In Stereo		
Sea Dreams/Misery Loves Companies	81	2010

Drecker, Anneli (See also Bel Canto; Röyksopp)		
Becoming More Like God	62	1994

It's All Here	13	2003
All I Know	39	2003
Tundra (Mánaiga)	52	2003
You Don't Have To Change	8	2006
Stop This	23	2006
Vision One	8	2009
Sun-Wave	85	2017

DuBois, Ja'Net		
Movin' On Up (Theme From "The Jeffersons")	T	1975

Duby, Heather		
Judith	85	2001

Duck Sauce		
Barbra Streisand	59	2011

Dudearella		
Top Of The World	45	1999

Dudley, Anne (See also The Art Of Noise)		
Wishing On A Star	77	2000

Duffy		
Stepping Stone	2	2008
Mercy	71	2008
Rain On Your Parade	2	2009
My Boy	22	2011
Whole Lot Of Love	90	2016

Duffy, Stephen 'Tin Tin' (See also The Lilac Time)		
Kiss Me	76	1985

Dulfer, Candy		
Lily Was Here	77	1991

Dum Dum Girls		
Rimbaud Eyes	93	2014

Dumont, Duke		
Ocean Drive	1	2015
The Fear	17	2020
Nightcrawler	65	2021
Something On My Mind	3	2023

Dundas, David		
Jeans On	49	1976

Duran Duran (See also Simon Le Bon)		
New Moon On Monday	84	1984
Union Of The Snake	87	1984
Save A Prayer	13	1985
A View To Kill	37	1985
Skin Trade	98	1987
All She Wants Is	121	1989
Come Undone	11	1993

Ordinary World	37	1993
Out Of My Mind	32	1997
Taste The Summer	55	2004
(Reach For The) Sunrise	57	2004
Still Breathing	23	2005
Finest Hour	61	2005
She's Too Much	80	2008
Leave A Light On	73	2011
Give It All Up	77	2021
Danse Macabre	80	2023
Durutti Column, The		
Messidor/Sketch For Dawn II	M	1981
Dusky		
Swansea	15	2017
Dylan, Bob		
Subterranean Homesick Blues	P	1965
Lay Lady Lay	P	1969
Tangled Up In Blue	P	1975

E

Eagles (See also Don Henley; Glenn Frey; Joe Walsh; Don Felder; Poco)		
Witchy Woman	P	1972
Best Of My Love	P	1974
One Of These Nights	P	1975
Take It To The Limit	62	1976
Life In The Fast Lane	20	1977
Hotel California	39	1977
Heartache Tonight	82	1979
I Can't Tell You Why	13	1980
Earth Orchestra, The		
Out N Back	78	2021
Earth, Wind & Fire		
Shining Star	P	1975
That's The Way Of The World	P	1975
Getaway	M	1976
Serpentine Fire	106	1978
September	92	1979
Boogie Wonderland	116	1979
Easton, Sheena		
For Your Eyes Only	6	1981
You Could Have Been With Me	5	1982
When He Shines	99	1982
U Got The Look	85	1987
Echoes		
Human	43	2022

Echosmith		
Cool Kids	114	2014
Cracked	33	2020
Stuck	86	2020
God Only Knows (Timbaland Remix)	11	2021
Edelman, Randy		
Can't It All Be Love	57	1977
Edge, The (See also U2)		
Heroine (Theme From "Captive")	28	1987
Edison Lighthouse		
Love Grows (Where My Rosemary Goes)	P	1970
Edmunds, Dave		
Girls Talk	65	1979
Efron, Zac		
Rewrite The Stars	114	2018
Egan, Walter		
Hot Summer Nights	11	1978
Magnet And Steel	59	1978
Eiffel 65		
Move Your Body	14	2000
Blue (Da Ba Dee)	67	2000
Losing You	32	2002
I DJ With The Fire	59	2002
Living In My City (Theme From The Turin Winter Olympic Games 2006)	13	2005
Eighth Wonder		
I'm Not Scared/J'ai Pas Peur	32	1989
808 State		
Ooops	109	1991
Eilish, Billie		
lovely	5	2022
Birds Of A Feather	112	2024
Einaudi, Ludovico		
Low Mist Var. 2 (Day One) / (Day Six)	38	2021
Ekko, Mikky		
Subtle	20	2014
Elastica		
Connection	115	1995
2:1	42	1997
Elderbrook		
Numb	77	2020
Inner Light	2	2021
Eldredge, Brett		
Cycles	111	2017
Electric Guest		
Troubleman	38	2012

Song	Pos	Year
Awake	45	2012
This Head I Hold	80	2012
Basic	59	2020
Electric Light Orchestra (ELO)		
Can't Get It Out Of My Head	P	1974
Evil Woman	22	1976
Strange Magic	73	1976
Do Ya (also by The Move, 1972)	26	1977
Telephone Line	40	1977
Livin' Thing	50	1977
Sweet Talkin' Woman	48	1978
Mr. Blue Sky	51	1978
Turn To Stone	65	1978
Don't Bring Me Down	80	1979
All Over The World	73	1980
Xanadu	141	1980
Without Someone	11	1988
Sorrow About To Fall	33	1988
Electronic (See also New Order; The Smiths)		
Getting Away With It	67	1990
Get The Message	42	1991
Idiot Country	60	1991
Disappointed	242	1992
Elias, Jonathan		
Follow In My Footsteps	29	1991
Within The Lost World	51	1991
The Chant Movement	69	1991
Eliot		
All I'm Made Of	80	2006
Elissa راسيلا		
Tesada'a Bemeen (قدصت نيمب) (Who Do You Believe In?)	17	2015
Eli Young Band		
How Quickly You Forget	140	2012
Elliman, Yvonne		
I Don't Know How To Love Him	P	1971
If I Can't Have You	115	1978
Elliot, Mama Cass (See also The Mamas & The Papas)		
Dream A Little Dream Of Me (w/ The Mamas & The Papas)	P	1968
Make Your Own Kind Of Music	P	1969
Elliott, Missy ("Misdemeanor")		
Bad Girl	90	2008
Ellis, Shirley		
The Nitty Gritty	P	1963
The Name Game	P	1964
Ellis-Bextor, Sophie		
Get Over You	40	2002
Murder On The Dancefloor	235	2002
Move This Mountain	3	2003
Sparkle	62	2003
Nowhere Without You	78	2004
Circles (Just My Good Time) (as Mademoiselle E.B.)	96	2007
Starlight	29	2011
Revolution	89	2011
El Roman, Rafet		
Bana Sen Lazımsın	3	2005
Emerson, Toby		
Rapture	97	2008
Emerson, Lake & Palmer (ELP) (See also Asia)		
From The Beginning	P	1972
Hoedown	P	1972
Still...You Turn Me On	P	1973
I Believe In Father Christmas	X	1977
EMF		
Unbelievable	111	1991
Eminem		
Without Me	132	2002
Emotions, The		
Best Of My Love	80	1977
Boogie Wonderland	116	1979
Empire Of The Sun (See also PNAU; Luke Steele)		
We Are The People	3	2009
Walking On A Dream	77	2009
Lux/DNA	2	2013
Awakening	8	2013
I'll Be Around	16	2013
Celebrate	25	2013
High And Low	109	2016
There's No Need	32	2017
Digital Life	45	2017
Changes	18	2024
Television	99	2024
Encanto Cast (Carolina Gaitán, Mauro Castillo, Adassa, Rhenzy Feliz, Diane Guerrero, Stephanie Beatriz)		
We Don't Talk About Bruno	110	2022
England Dan & John Ford Coley		
I'd Really Love To See You Tonight	42	1976
Nights Are Forever Without You	50	1976

Soldier In The Rain	M	1977
Love Is The Answer	9	1979
Dowdy Ferry Road	M	1979

Enigma (See also Sandra)

Mea Culpa	9	1991
Sadeness Part I	14	1991
Age Of Loneliness (Carly's Song)	21	1993
Return To Innocence	47	1994
Beyond The Invisible	82	1996
T.N.T. For The Brain	84	1997
Look Of Today	100	2003
Sadeness Part II	74	2016

Enisa

Fool 4 U	101	2024

Eno, Brian

America Is Waiting/Mea Culpa (w/ David Byrne)	M	1981

Enriquez, Jocelyn

Do You Miss Me	118	1997

En Vogue

Hold On	90	1990
Don't Let Go (Love)	21	1996
Bring Back The Time	73	2022

Envy Of None (See also Rush)

Dumb	52	2022

Enya (See also Clannad)

Orinoco Flow (Sail Away)	2	1989
Cursum Perficio	15	1989
Storms In Africa	99	1989
Caribbean Blue	5	1992
Afer Ventus	49	1992
Book Of Days	78	1992
Athair Ar Neamh	56	1996
Only Time	56	2000
May It Be	113	2002
Trains And Winter Rains	79	2008
The Humming	82	2015
Echoes In Rain	96	2015

Equinox

Bones	52	2018

Era (+eRa+)

Ameno	18	1999
Enae Volare (Mezzo)	55	1999
Omen Sore	78	2001
Something Exciting	63	2018
7 Seconds	97	2018

Erasure (See also Depeche Mode; Yazoo; Andy Bell)

Oh L'Amour	63	1987
Sometimes	71	1987
Chains Of Love	24	1988
Ship Of Fools	53	1988
Victim Of Love	97	1988
A Little Respect	49	1989
You Surround Me	42	1990
Too Darn Hot	72	1991
Love To Hate You	76	1991
In My Arms	46	1997
A Whole Lotta Love Run Riot	53	2011
Make It Wonderful	33	2013
There'll Be No Tomorrow!	71	2013
Gaudete	94	2013
Dead Of Night	73	2014

Eric B. & Rakim

Friends (Jody Watley f/ Eric B. & Rakim)	144	1989

Erivo, Cynthia

What In The World	133	2015

Eruption f/ Precious Wilson

I Can't Stand The Rain	15	1978

Essex, David

Rock On	P	1973

Estefan, Gloria

I See Your Smile	135	1993
Make Me Say Yes	63	2012

Estelle

American Boy	108	2008

Esthero

That Girl	59	1999
Can You Feel It	10	2010

Etana

August Town	92	2011

Etheridge, Melissa

Dance Without Sleeping	9	1993
Into The Dark	15	2000
This Human Chain	59	2019

Etro Anime

Let It Go	46	2004

Euphoria

Sinners And Saints	17	2006
Anyone Can Lose	44	2006

Europe

The Final Countdown	M	1986

Eurythmics (See also Annie Lennox; David A. Stewart; Platinum Weird)

Sweet Dreams (Are Made Of This)	8	1983
Love Is A Stranger	80	1983
Here Comes The Rain Again	6	1984
Who's That Girl?	18	1984
Julia	4	1985
Would I Lie To You?	35	1985
There Must Be An Angel (Playing With My Heart)	57	1985
Adrian	25	1986
It's Alright (Baby's Coming Back)	47	1986
Beethoven (I Love To Listen To)	14	1988
You Have Placed A Chill In My Heart	74	1988
Don't Ask Me Why	69	1989
You Hurt Me (And I Hate You)	73	1990

Everlast

Ends	97	1999
What It's Like	113	1999

Everly Brothers, The

All I Have To Do Is Dream	P	1958
Crying In The Rain	P	1962

Everything But The Girl (See also Tracey Thorn)

Never Could Have Been Worse	15	1985
Frost And Fire	33	1985
Apron Strings	66	1988
Imagining America	23	1990
Driving	54	1990
Missing / (Todd Terry Mix)	3	1995
Wrong	4	1996
Single	28	1996
Before Today	62	1996
Walking Wounded	39	1997
Flipside	85	1997
Five Fathoms	44	1999
Temperamental	32	2000
Forever	24	2023
Run A Red Light	37	2023

Evonne (Hsu) 許慧欣

謎 (Mystery)	74	2006

Exile

Kiss You All Over	73	1978

Exposé

Seasons Change	84	1988

Eye To Eye (See also Marshall Hain)

Nice Girls	25	1982

EZI

DaNcing in a RoOm	54	2018

F

Faces (See also Small Faces; Rod Stewart)

(I Know) I'm Losing You	P	1971

Fagen, Donald (See also Steely Dan)

I.G.Y. (What A Beautiful World)	81	1982

Fahl, Mary (See also October Project)

In The Great Unknown	94	2003

Fahree

Özünlə Apar	23	2024

Faith, Paloma

Til I'm Done	79	2018
How You Leave A Man	46	2024

Faith, Percy

The Theme From "A Summer Place"	P	1960

Faithless (See also Dido; 1 Giant Leap)

Addictive	16	2003

Faith No More

Epic	M	1990

Falco

Der Kommissar	114	1983
Rock Me Amadeus	136	1986

Fall Out Boy (See also Patrick Stump)

My Songs Know What You Did In The Dark (Light Em Up)	82	2013

Faltermeyer, Harold

Axel F	101	1985

Fältskog, Agnetha (See also ABBA)

Can't Shake Loose	81	1983
The Last Time	72	1990

Faniello, Fabrizio

Just 4 Christmas	54	2006

Fantasia

So Much To Prove	91	2013

Far☆East Movement

Rocketeer	10	2011
Don't Look Now	49	2011
Do It In The AM	72	2011

Farmer, Mylène

Optimistique-Moi	95	2002
Fuck Them All	14	2005
Peut-Être Toi	16	2005
Porno Graphique	42	2005
Appelle Mon Numéro	47	2008

Looking For My Name	96	2009
Oui Mais... Non	28	2011
Elle A Dit	35	2013
Love Dance	45	2013
Monkey Me	55	2013
Stolen Car	66	2016
N'Oublie Pas	72	2018
Farnham, John (See also Little River Band)		
You're The Voice	114	1990
Farris, Dionne		
I Know	99	1995
FAST BOY		
Good Life	85	2023
Wave	72	2024
Fatboy Slim		
Right Here, Right Now	133	1999
Eleven Days	99	2010
Father John Misty		
Young Lady	100	2013
The Next 20th Century	4	2022
Fauxliage (See also Delerium; Leigh Nash)		
All The World	79	2007
Fay, Kalyn		
Judadatla Tsisqwa (Spotted Bird)	82	2023
FC/Kahuna		
Hayling	36	2003
Feelabeelia		
In The Middle Of The Night	22	1986
Oxygen	39	1986
Feeling, The		
Sewn	61	2007
Feist		
My Moon My Man	114	2007
Felder, Don (See also Eagles)		
Heavy Metal (Takin' A Ride)	97	1981
Feldt, Sam		
Gold	56	2019
Felt		
Primitive Painters	104	1988
Fem2Fem		
Charmed	101	1994
Animus	78	1995
Where Did Love Go	84	1995
Fenton, George / Jonas Gwangwa		
Cry Freedom	21	1988

Fergie (See also Black Eyed Peas)		
Glamorous	151	2006
Ferguson, Jay		
Shakedown Cruise	57	1979
Ferguson, Maynard		
Gonna Fly Now (Theme From "Rocky")	67	1977
Ferguson, Rebecca		
Love	8	2019
Ferrante & Teicher		
Exodus	P	1960
Midnight Cowboy	P	1969
Ferras		
Don't Give Up	59	2008
Ferrell, Will		
Double Trouble (Tiësto's Euro 90's Tribute Mix)	92	2020
Husavik (My Hometown)	34	2020
Ferry, Bryan (See also Roxy Music)		
Don't Stop The Dance	42	1985
Slave To Love	47	1985
Help Me	6	1986
Is Your Love Strong Enough?/Windswept	16	1986
The Right Stuff	20	1987
Kiss And Tell	29	1988
Limbo	59	1988
I Put A Spell On You	68	1993
Gemini Moon	85	1994
Don't Want To Know	95	1994
You Can Dance	69	2010
Driving Me Wild	58	2014
One Night Stand	34	2015
Loop De Li	43	2015
Fiasco, Lupe		
Daydreamin'	105	2007
5th Dimension, The		
Up – Up And Away	P	1967
Stoned Soul Picnic	P	1968
Aquarius/Let The Sunshine In (The Flesh Failures)	P	1969
Wedding Bell Blues	P	1969
One Less Bell To Answer	P	1970
Love's Lines, Angles And Rhymes	P	1971
(Last Night) I Didn't Get To Sleep At All	P	1972
Filatov & Karas		
Au Au	33	2019

Fil Bo Riva		
I Like You	51	2024
Filter		
Take A Picture	87	2000
Fine Young Cannibals		
Johnny Come Home	30	1986
Ever Fallen In Love	29	1987
She Drives Me Crazy	25	1989
Good Thing	53	1989
Since You've Been Gone	64	1997
Finger Eleven		
Window Song	88	2007
Finn, Neil (See also Split Enz; Crowded House; Finn Brothers)		
Sinner	92	1998
Chameleon Days	88	2017
Finn, Tim (See also Split Enz; Finn Brothers; Crowded House)		
In A Minor Key	73	1984
No Thunder, No Fire, No Rain	19	1988
Carve You In Marble	45	1988
Finn Brothers (See also Split Enz; Neil Finn; Tim Finn; Crowded House)		
Only Talking Sense	19	1996
Suffer Never	29	1996
Fiona, Melanie		
Give It To Me Right	87	2010
Firefall		
You Are The Woman	72	1976
Livin' Ain't Livin'	75	1976
Just Remember I Love You	84	1977
Strange Way	62	1978
So Long	71	1978
Goodbye, I Love You	76	1979
Headed For A Fall	57	1980
First Class		
Beach Baby	P	1974
First Kiss		
I'll Be True	94	1996
Fischerspooner		
Just Let Go	92	2005
The Best Revenge	78	2009
Fisher		
Breakable	70	1998
Fisher, Tricia Leigh		
Empty Beach	74	1990

Fitz And The Tantrums		
MoneyGrabber	68	2011
The Walker	100	2014
Five Blobs, The		
The Blob	P	1958
Five For Fighting		
Superman (It's Not Easy)	124	2001
Policeman's Xmas Party	X	2006
Five Man Electrical Band		
Signs	P	1971
5 Seconds Of Summer		
Easier	9	2019
Thin White Lies	91	2020
Five Stairsteps, The		
O-o-h Child	P	1970
Fixx, The		
Saved By Zero	22	1983
One Thing Leads To Another	36	1983
I Will	90	1985
Want That Life	100	2004
FKA twigs		
Measure Of A Man	23	2022
Flack, Roberta		
Where Is The Love (w/ Donny Hathaway)	P	1972
Killing Me Softly With His Song	P	1973
Feel Like Makin' Love	P	1974
Making Love / I'm The One	6	1982
Flaming Lips, The		
Do You Realize??	139	2004
Marching The Hate Machines (Into The Sun)	101	2005
Flamin' Oh's		
I Remember Romance	129	1980
Fleetwood Mac (See also Lindsey Buckingham; Stevie Nicks; Christine McVie; Bob Welch)		
Bare Trees	P	1972
Rhiannon (Will You Ever Win)	11	1976
Say You Love Me	34	1976
Over My Head	54	1976
Dreams	2	1977
You Make Loving Fun	12	1977
Go Your Own Way	34	1977
Don't Stop	74	1977
Tusk	37	1979
Brown Eyes	M	1979
Sara	6	1980

Sisters Of The Moon	18	1980
Fireflies	59	1981
Gypsy	50	1982
Love In Store	37	1983
Little Lies	9	1987
Big Love	81	1987
Seven Wonders	99	1987
Tango In The Night	85	1988
Everywhere	96	1988
Behind The Mask	26	1990
In The Back Of My Mind	44	1990
Make Me A Mask	22	1993
Smile At You	33	2003
Peacekeeper	37	2003
Silver Girl	85	2003
Fleming, Renée		
No One's Gonna Love You	91	2010
Fletcher		
Holiday	16	2022
Flight Of The Conchords		
Inner City Pressure	36	2008
Flock Of Seagulls, A		
I Ran (So Far Away)	17	1982
Space Age Love Song	53	1982
Wishing (If I Had A Photograph Of You)	12	1983
Nightmares	58	1983
The More You Live, The More You Love	35	1984
The Story Of A Young Heart	43	1985
Florence + The Machine (See also Florence Welch)		
Howl	36	2010
Only If For A Night	21	2012
My Love	22	2022
Flo Rida		
Good Feeling	127	2012
Flowers, Brandon (See also The Killers)		
I Can Change	5	2015
Can't Deny My Love	19	2015
Flowers, Mike, Pops (The Mike Flowers Pops)		
Wonderwall	37	1995
Flume		
Sirens	104	2023
Flying Lizards, The (See also Marshall Hain)		
Money (That's What I Want)	59	1980
Flying Machine, The		
Smile A Little Smile For Me	P	1969

Focus		
Hocus Pocus	P	1973
Fogelberg, Dan		
The Power Of Gold	64	1978
There's A Place In The World For A Gambler	75	1978
Heart Hotels	76	1980
Same Old Lang Syne	2	1981
Hard To Say	60	1981
Ever On	97	1990
Foghat		
Fool For The City	70	1976
Folk Implosion		
Natural One	19	1995
Fonseca		
Cómo Te Extraño	12	2009
ABCDario	12	2012
Fonsi, Luis		
Baby	89	2019
Foo Fighters		
Everlong	93	1997
Fordham, Julia		
Happy Ever After	115	1989
Foreigner		
Cold As Ice	18	1977
Feels Like The First Time	47	1977
Double Vision	79	1978
Head Games	49	1979
Waiting For A Girl Like You	10	1981
Urgent	99	1981
I Want To Know What Love Is	78	1985
Forestella 레스텔라		
Legends Never Die	28	2023
Forest For The Trees		
Dream	89	1997
Planet Unknown	79	1998
for KING & COUNTRY		
God Only Knows / Timbaland Remix (two versions)	11	2021
Forster, Mark		
Genug	17	2023
Foster, David		
Love Theme From St. Elmo's Fire ("Just For A Moment," vocal version with Donny Gerrard & Amy Holland)	150	1985

Foster The People		
Don't Stop (Color On The Walls)	34	2011
Pumped Up Kicks	100	2011
Lost In Space	44	2024
Fountains Of Wayne (See also Ivy)		
Traffic And Weather	58	2007
Four Aces, The		
Love Is A Many-Splendored Thing	P	1955
4 Non Blondes		
What's Up	77	1993
Four Seasons, The (The 4 Seasons) (See also Frankie Valli)		
Big Girls Don't Cry	P	1962
Let's Hang On!	P	1965
Who Loves You	P	1975
December, 1963 (Oh, What A Night)	27	1976
Four Tet		
Crawl, End Crawl	98	2008
Skater	90	2024
Four Tops, The		
Baby I Need Your Loving	P	1964
I Can't Help Myself (Sugar Pie Honey Bunch)	P	1965
Reach Out I'll Be There	P	1966
Standing In The Shadows Of Love	P	1966
River Deep – Mountain High (w/ The Supremes)	P	1970
Fox, Cass (Cassandra)		
Touch Me	6	2008
Daddy Dear	29	2008
Foxboro Hot Tubs		
Dark Side Of Night	61	2008
Foxes		
Sister Ray	100	2022
Foxy		
Get Off	36	1978
Fragma		
Toca's Miracle (w/ Coco Star)	M	2000
Frampton, Peter		
Do You Feel Like We Do	20	1976
Show Me The Way	63	1976
I'm In You	49	1977
Signed, Sealed, Delivered (I'm Yours)	93	1977
I Can't Stand It No More	84	1979
Francis, Connie		
Who's Sorry Now	P	1958

Where The Boys Are	P	1961
Vacation	P	1962
Follow The Boys	P	1963
Frangoulis, Mario		
Night Wants To Forget	96	2003
Franke & The Knockouts		
Sweetheart	102	1981
Frankie Goes To Hollywood		
The Power Of Love/bang...	31	1985
Franklin, Aretha		
Respect	P	1967
Chain Of Fools	P	1967
Eleanor Rigby	P	1969
You're All I Need To Get By	P	1971
Spanish Harlem	P	1971
Until You Come Back To Me (That's What I'm Gonna Do)	P	1973
Who's Zoomin' Who	119	1985
Save Me	11	2010
Franklin, Kirk		
Stomp	22	1997
Frankmusik		
Gotta Boyfriend?	90	2010
Do It In The AM	72	2011
Wrecking Ball	41	2012
Franks, Michael		
Your Secret's Safe With Me	M	1985
Fraser, Brooke		
Love, Where Is Your Fire?	98	2009
Fraser, Elizabeth (See also Cocteau Twins; Sun's Signature)		
Primitive Painters	104	1988
This Love	25	1998
Teardrop	19	1998
Fred, John, & His Playboy Band		
Judy In Disguise (With Glasses)	P	1967
Fredericks, Chloe		
Can't Make You Love Me	96	2022
Free		
All Right Now	P	1970
Freeez		
I.O.U.	188	1983
Freelove, Laurie		
Heaven On Earth	20	1991
Smells Like Truth	63	1991
O My Heart	61	1992

Frehley, Ace (See also KISS)		
New York Groove	41	1979
Freur		
Doot-Doot	61	1984
Frey, Glenn (See also Eagles)		
You Belong To The City	75	1985
Frida (Anni-Frid Lyngstad) (See also ABBA)		
I Know Something's Going On	64	1983
Threnody	M	1983
Vem Kommer Såra Vem Ikväll (Anni-Frid Lyngstad)	85	1998
Friday, Gavin		
I Want To Live	74	1993
Where In The World?	83	1993
In The Name Of The Father	73	1994
Friedman, Dean		
Ariel	27	1977
Friends Of Distinction, The		
Grazing In The Grass	P	1969
Love Or Let Me Be Lonely	P	1969
Frost, Max		
Nice And Slow	39	2014
Frost, Max, And The Troopers		
Shape Of Things To Come	P	1968
Frou Frou (See also Imogen Heap)		
Let Go	6	2003
Psychobabble	11	2003
Must Be Dreaming	35	2003
Holding Out For A Hero	44	2004
Furtado, Nelly		
All Good Things (Come To An End)	70	2006
Love Bites	94	2024
Fury In The Slaughterhouse		
Every Generation Got Its Own Disease	38	1994
Fused		
Twisted/Twisted (Reprise)	77	2002
Future		
Rollin	55	2017
Double Fantasy	71	2023
We Still Don't Trust You	26	2024
Fuzzbox (We've Got a Fuzzbox and We're Gonna Use It!!)		
International Rescue	M	1989

G

Gabriel, Peter (See also Genesis)		
Solsbury Hill	M	1977
Games Without Frontiers	2	1980
I Don't Remember	76	1981
Shock The Monkey	54	1982
The Rhythm Of The Heat	47	1983
I Have The Touch	67	1983
This Is The Picture (Excellent Birds)	59	1984
Don't Give Up	28	1986
Sledgehammer	38	1986
In Your Eyes	54	1986
Big Time	45	1987
The Feeling Begins	64	1989
Shaking The Tree	79	1989
Steam	53	1992
Digging In The Dirt	74	1992
Lovetown	64	1994
While The Earth Sleeps	20	1996
A.I.	5	2017
Road To Joy (Bright-Side Mix)	114	2024
Gaines, Jeffrey		
Hero In Me	92	1992
Gainsbourg, Charlotte		
5:55/AF607105	65	2007
Deadly Valentine	26	2018
Sylvia Says	98	2018
Gainsbourg, Serge		
Bonnie And Clyde (w/ Brigitte Bardot)	P	1968
Je T'Aime… Moi Non Plus (w/ Jane Birkin)	P	1969
Gala		
Graduale	66	1999
Gala (Rizzatto)		
Freed From Desire	34	1997
Galantis		
Peanut Butter Jelly	84	2015
Fool 4 U	101	2024
Galimatias		
Fantasy	75	2016
Gallagher('s), Noel, High Flying Birds		
Think Of A Number / (Pet Shop Boys Magic Eye 12" remix)	6	2023
Gallery		
Nice To Be With You	P	1972
Gano, Gordon		
Only The Lonely	16	1997
Gap Band, The		
Early In The Morning	M	1982
You Dropped A Bomb On Me	M	1982

Garbage		
Queer	77	1995
Stupid Girl	77	1996
You Look So Fine	95	1998
The World Is Not Enough	76	1999
Androgyny	95	2001
Cherry Lips (Go Baby Go!)	73	2002
This City Will Kill You	66	2021

Gardiner, Paul (See also Gary Numan + Tubeway Army)		
Stormtrooper In Drag (w/ Gary Numan)	M	1981

Garfunkel, Art (See also Simon & Garfunkel)		
All I Know	P	1973
I Believe (When I Fall In Love It Will Be Forever)	P	1975
99 Miles From L.A.	P	1975
Breakaway	148	1976
Bright Eyes	167	1979
Scissors Cut	M	1981
A Heart In New York	56	1981

Garibay		
I Need You	52	2017
Phone Down	43	2020

Garland, Judy		
Have Yourself A Merry Little Christmas	X	1944

Garnet Crow		
Maboroshi (まぼろし) (Phantom)	22	2007

Garrix, Martin		
Scared To Be Lonely	7	2017
Ocean	84	2018
So Far Away	5	2018
Summer Days	62	2019

Gaye, Marvin		
How Sweet It Is To Be Loved By You	P	1964
I Heard It Through The Grapevine	P	1968
Ain't Nothing Like The Real Thing (w/ Tammi Terrell)	P	1968
You're All I Need To Get By (w/ Tammi Terrell)	P	1968
What's Going On	P	1971
Let's Get It On	P	1973
I Want You	M	1976
Got To Give It Up (Pt. 1)	19	1977
Sexual Healing	74	1983

Gayle, Crystal		
Ready For The Times To Get Better	129	1978

	151	1983
You And I	151	1983

Gaynor, Gloria		
Honey Bee	P	1974
Never Can Say Goodbye	P	1974
I Will Survive	16	1979

G-Dragon 지드래곤		
Window (창문)	59	2018

G.E.M.		
Young Man & Sea	89	2023

Genesis (See also Phil Collins; Peter Gabriel; Mike + The Mechanics)		
Follow You, Follow Me	7	1978
Turn It On Again	32	1980
Misunderstanding	104	1980
No Reply At All	98	1981
Man On The Corner	28	1982
Paperlate/You Might Recall	68	1982
abacab	88	1982
Mama	51	1983
Land Of Confusion	43	1987

Gerrard, Lisa (See also Dead Can Dance)		
Meltdown	52	2000

Gerry And The Pacemakers		
Don't Let The Sun Catch You Crying	P	1964

Gesaffelstein		
Lost In The Fire	80	2019

Getz, Stan		
The Girl From Ipanema (w/ Astrud Gilberto)	P	1964

G Girls (Alexandra Stan, Lori, Antonia & INNA) (See also Antonia (Iacobascu); INNA)		
Call The Police	91	2017

Ghost, Amanda		
Absolution	24	1997

Ghostland		
Guide Me God	58	2003

Giant Steps		
(The World Don't Need) Another Lover	88	1988

Gibb, Andy		
I Just Want To Be Your Everything	1	1977
Shadow Dancing	3	1978
(Love Is) Thicker Than Water	20	1978
An Everlasting Love	39	1978
(Our Love) Don't Throw It All Away	55	1978
Desire	35	1980
Time Is Time	38	1981

Me (Without You)	58	1981
Gibb, Barry (See also Bee Gees)		
Guilty	114	1980
What Kind Of Fool	11	1981
Underworld	78	2008
In The Now	70	2016
Gibb, Robin (See also Bee Gees)		
Boys Do Fall In Love	48	1984
Lonely Night In NY	86	2006
Beth Gibbons (See also Portishead)		
Whispering Love	127	2024
Gibbons, John		
Would I Lie To You	69	2017
Gibbs, Terri		
Somebody's Knockin'	113	1981
Gibson, Debbie		
Foolish Beat	76	1988
Gil, Gilberto		
Rafazenda	67	1996
Gilbert, Brantley		
Bro Code	89	2017
Gilberto, Astrud		
The Girl From Ipanema (w/ Stan Getz)	P	1964
Gilberto, Bebel		
Batucada	97	1996
Gilder, Nick		
Here Comes The Night	58	1978
Hot Child In The City	93	1978
Gill, Alan		
Letter To Brezhnev Theme	87	1986
Gina G		
Ooh Aah... Just A Little Bit	164	1997
Gin Blossoms		
Found Out About You	119	1994
Gingold, Hermione, & The Biddys		
Pick-A-Little, Talk-A-Little	P	1962
girli		
2 Year Itch	121	2024
Girlpool		
Lie Love Lullaby	32	2022
Girls Aloud (See also Cheryl Cole)		
Life Got Cold	16	2004
Something Kinda Ooooh	66	2007
Girls' Generation		
Dancing Queen	M	2012
One Last Time	M	2017
Gjon's Tears		
Répondez-Moi	32	2021
Glass, Philip		
Powaqqatsi	90	1988
Glass Animals		
Domestic Bliss	108	2020
A Tear In Space (Airlock)	36	2024
Glee Club, The		
Take You There	65	1994
Gnarls Barkley (See also Danger Mouse; Broken Bells; Cee Lo Green)		
Crazy	94	2006
gnash		
i hate u, i love u	72	2016
Go_A (Ґоу_Ей)		
SHUM	57	2021
Godley & Creme (See also 10cc)		
Cry	23	1985
God's Property		
Stomp	22	1997
Godwin, Peter		
The Art Of Love	102	1984
Go-Go's (The) (See also Belinda Carlisle; Jane Wiedlin)		
This Town	M	1981
Our Lips Are Sealed	21	1982
Vacation	83	1982
We Got The Beat	114	1982
Gold, Andrew (See also Wax)		
Lonely Boy	63	1977
Thank You For Being A Friend	80	1978
Gold Fields		
Closest I Could Get	30	2013
Dark Again	58	2013
Golden, Pamela		
If This Is Love	3	1992
Lisa Of The Wind	17	1992
Golden Earring		
Radar Love	P	1974
Golden Palominos, The		
Pure	27	1995
Gun	96	1995
Goldfrapp (See also Alison Goldfrapp)		
Hunt	85	2010
Everything Is Never Enough	90	2017

Goldfrapp, Alison (See also Goldfrapp)		
Impossible	55	2022
Goldsmith, Jerry		
Theme From The Waltons	T	1972
Barnaby Jones	T	1973
Ave Satani	69	1976
Gomez, Selena (Selena Gomez & The Scene)		
Love You Like A Love Song (& The Scene)	85	2011
Stars Dance	61	2013
The Heart Wants What It Wants	53	2014
Me & The Rhythm	89	2015
Dance Again	79	2020
Gomm, Ian		
Hold On	4	1979
Good Charlotte		
All Black	16	2007
Goodrem, Delta		
Bare Hands	22	2008
Believe Again	57	2009
Goodrum, Randy		
Silhouette	61	1986
Gordon, Nina		
Tonight And The Rest Of My Life	13	2000
Gore, Lesley		
It's My Party	P	1963
You Don't Own Me	P	1963
Gore, Martin L. (See also Depeche Mode)		
Compulsion	12	1989
Never Turn Your Back On Mother Earth	72	1989
In A Manner Of Speaking	33	1990
Gore, Michael		
Theme From "Terms Of Endearment"	92	1984
Gorillaz (See also Blur; 1 Giant Leap)		
Clint Eastwood	98	2001
Feel Good Inc	62	2005
Silent Running	70	2023
Gossip (See also Beth Ditto)		
Casualties Of War	5	2012
Involved	86	2012
Perfect World	101	2012
Turn The Card Slowly	65	2024
Gotan Project		
Panamericana	165	2010
Gotye		
State Of The Art	2	2012

Somebody That I Used To Know	95	2012
Heart's A Mess	51	2013
Goulding, Ellie		
Starry Eyed	7	2011
Lights	11	2011
Under The Sheets	20	2011
Animal	56	2011
Hanging On	7	2012
Little Dreams	48	2012
Human	71	2012
Under Control	14	2013
Ritual	22	2013
Only You	38	2013
Stay Awake	42	2013
My Blood	52	2013
Burn	92	2013
Outside	62	2014
Love Me Like You Do	23	2015
On My Mind	52	2015
Hollow Crown	62	2020
Flux/Brightest Blue	97	2020
Easy Lover	48	2022
Higher Than Heaven	7	2023
Temptation	15	2023
Intuition	20	2023
Cure For Love	26	2023
Like A Saviour	34	2023
Midnight Dreams	40	2023
Free	103	2024
Goulet, Robert		
The Impossible Dream	P	1969
Grace (See also Oakenfold)		
Don't Call Me (You're Not Mine)	19	1997
If I Could Fly	28	1997
Not Over Yet	50	1997
Grace Pool		
Paint The Ending	79	1991
Graffiti6		
Annie You Save Me	40	2012
Stone In My Heart	76	2012
Grande, Ariana		
Love Me Harder	22	2014
no tears left to cry	58	2018
Don't Call Me Angel (Charlie's Angels)	55	2019
we can't be friends (wait for your love)	117	2024

Grand National		
Talk Amongst Yourselves / (Sasha Involver Remix)	74	2004

Grant, Eddy		
Electric Avenue	183	1983

Grashüpfer (Grasshopper) 草蜢		
So Sad	34	1992

Grass Roots, The		
Let's Live For Today	P	1967
Temptation Eyes	P	1970
Sooner Or Later	P	1971

Gray, Dobie		
Drift Away	P	1973

Gray, Macy		
Caligula	108	2000

Green, Al		
Let's Stay Together	P	1971

Green, CeeLo (Cee Lo) (See also Gnarls Barkley)		
Bright Lights Bigger City	51	2011

Green Day		
Boulevard Of Broken Dreams	138	2004

Greene, Jessy		
Hidden Track (the sky above, the earth below me) (bonus song #12)	63	2004

Grey, Skylar		
Room For Happiness	79	2012

Grey Eye Glances		
Days To Dust	48	2000
Snow	58	2000
Close Your Eyes	14	2003

Grimes		
Flesh Without Blood	18	2016
Easily	54	2016
Violence	55	2020
Fly To You	42	2024

Groban, Josh		
Now Or Never	7	2007
You Are Loved (Don't Give Up)	13	2007
Machine	35	2007
The World We Knew (Over And Over)	35	2020

Groove Armada		
History	7	2010
Just For Tonight	29	2010

Gross, Henry		
Shannon	23	1976

G-Spliff		
At The End Of Time	53	2007
What'd I Do Wrong?	56	2007

Guaraldi, Vince, Trio		
Linus And Lucy / Christmas Time Is Here	X	1964

Guarini, Justin		
Inner Child	70	2003

Gucci Mane		
Survive	90	2019

Guðnadóttir, Hildur		
Leaving	93	2023

Guess Who, The (See also Bachman-Turner Overdrive; Burton Cummings; Ironhorse)		
These Eyes	P	1969
Undun/Laughing	P	1969
No Time	P	1969
Hand Me Down World	P	1970
No Sugar Tonight/New Mother Nature	P	1970

Guetta, David		
Love Is Gone	101	2008
It's The Way You Love Me	31	2009
When Love Takes Over	89	2009
Lovers On The Sun	32	2014
Yesterday	81	2014
Dangerous	10	2015
Another Life	67	2017
So Far Away	5	2018
Drive	29	2018
Make It To Heaven (Rework)	23	2020
I'm Good (Blue)	113	2022
Family Affair (Dance For Me) (remix of Mary J. Blige single from 2001)	M	2022
Saturday/Sunday	98	2023

Guidry, Greg		
Goin' Down	85	1982

Gundelach		
Fjernsynet	3	2020

Gurvitz, Adrian		
Classic	62	1982

Guster		
Satellite	34	2006

Guthrie, Gwen		
Ain't Nothin' Goin' On But The Rent	53	1986
What Can You Do For Me	58	1993

Gyptian

Drive Me Crazy	72	2010

H

Hadley, Tony (See also Spandau Ballet)

Out Of The Blue	72	2000

Hagen, Nina

New York / NY	80	1984

HAIM

Days Are Gone	62	2013
Forever	68	2013
Falling	95	2013
Pray To God	4	2015

Haircut One Hundred (See also Nick Heyward)

Love Plus One	82	1982

Hal

Extremis	36	1997

Haley (Haley Gibby)

I Remember	3	2008
Move For Me	38	2008
This Is How It Goes (Kaskade's Grand Club Edit)	76	2009
Llove	42	2011

Hall, Daryl, & John Oates

When The Morning Comes	P	1974
She's Gone	57	1976
Sara Smile	95	1976
Rich Girl	29	1977
Back Together Again	51	1977
Why Do Lovers (Break Each Other's Heart?)	64	1977
How Does It Feel To Be Back	44	1980
You've Lost That Lovin' Feeling	51	1980
Wait For Me	55	1980
You Make My Dreams	87	1981
Your Imagination	33	1982
Maneater	59	1982
I Can't Go For That (No Can Do)	66	1982
One On One	73	1983
Family Man	100	1983
Out Of Touch	78	1984

Hall, Juanita

Bali Ha'i (South Pacific movie version)	P	1958

Halsey

Eyes Closed	6	2017
Alone	54	2017
Now Or Never	79	2017
Without Me	110	2018
Eastside	116	2018
작은 것들을 위한 시 (Boy With Luv)	100	2019
I Am Not A Woman, I'm A God	46	2021

Hamilton, Joe Frank & Reynolds

Don't Pull Your Love	P	1971
Fallin' In Love	P	1975
Winners And Losers	P	1975

Hammer, Jan

Crockett's Theme (Miami Vice)	T	1986

Hammond, Albert

It Never Rains In Southern California	P	1972

Hancock, Herbie

Rockit	M	1983
Machine	35	2007

Handsome Boy Modeling School

I've Been Thinking	38	2005

Hanno, Yoshihiro

海上花 Flowers Of Shanghai: Theme Song	54	1998

Happenings, The

See You In September	P	1966

Hardcastle, Paul

19	176	1985
Rainforest	M	1985

Hard-Fi

Cash Machine	6	2005
Move On Now	2	2006
The King	3	2007
We Need Love	5	2007
Watch Me Fall Apart	78	2007
Fire In The House	34	2012

Hardwell

Written In Reverse	27	2014

Harket, Morten (See also a-ha)

Keep The Sun Away	14	2012
Just Believe It	23	2012
Burn Money Burn	84	2012

Harmer, Sarah

Greeting Card Aisle	76	2004

Harper, Ben

Morning Yearning	19	2006

Harris, Calvin

Sweet Nothing	89	2012
Outside	62	2014
Blame	101	2014

Pray To God	4	2015
How Deep Is Your Love	9	2015
This Is What You Came For	76	2016
Rollin	55	2017
Feels	115	2017
Promises	9	2018
One Kiss	11	2018
Desire	92	2023
Body Moving	39	2024
Free	103	2024
Harris, Richard		
MacArthur Park	P	1968
Harrison, George (See also The Beatles)		
What Is Life	P	1971
Give Me Love (Give Me Peace On Earth)	P	1973
Crackerbox Palace	95	1977
Harry, Debbie (Deborah) (See also Blondie)		
In Love With Love	62	1988
Liar, Liar	70	1988
He Is So	93	1990
No Talking Just Head	59	1996
Hart, Corey		
It Ain't Enough	44	1984
Sunglasses At Night	55	1984
Never Surrender	85	1985
Eurasian Eyes	43	1986
Harvey, PJ		
Down By The Water	47	1995
I Inside The Old I Dying	69	2023
Hathaway, Donny		
Where Is The Love (w/ Roberta Flack)	P	1972
And Then There's Maude (Maude Theme)	T	1972
Havnevik, Kate		
Not Fair	50	2007
Kaleidoscope	89	2007
Hawkins, Screamin' Jay		
I Put A Spell On You	P	1956
Hawkshaw, Kirsty (See also Opus III)		
Dreaming	66	2000
Just Be Me	32	2006
Fleeting Instant	55	2006
Hayes, Darren (See also Savage Garden)		
A Conversation With God	81	2007
Step Into The Light	45	2008
Hayes, Isaac		
Theme From Shaft	P	1971

Hayla		
Shiver	53	2024
Hayward, Justin (See also The Moody Blues)		
Forever Autumn	21	1978
Haza, Ofra		
Im Nin'Alu	42	1988
Galbi	20	1989
Shaday	56	1989
Daw Da Hiya	86	1992
Love Song (Dr. Lunatic's Keemovision)	47	1998
Show Me	41	2000
Ahava	78	2000
Mysterious Days	46	2003
Head, Murray		
Superstar	P	1971
Bangkok/One Night In Bangkok	10	1985
Head And The Heart, The		
Paradigm	86	2022
Heads, The		
No Talking Just Head	59	1996
Only The Lonely	16	1997
Heap, Imogen (See also Frou Frou)		
Have You Got It In You?	10	2005
Clear The Area	33	2005
Hide And Seek	55	2005
Closing In	37	2006
Headlock	60	2006
Congratulations	105	2006
Glittering Cloud (Locusts)	37	2007
It's Better To Have Loved	75	2007
First Train Home	72	2009
Minds Without Fear	43	2014
Lifeline	75	2014
Heart		
Crazy On You	4	1976
Magic Man	24	1976
Barracuda	22	1977
Straight On	60	1978
Dog & Butterfly	58	1979
Magazine	89	1979
What About Love	67	1985
These Dreams	60	1986
Nobody Home	78	1986
There's The Girl	71	1988
Heart Throbs, The		
Dreamtime	82	1990

She's In A Trance	97	1991
Winter Came Too Soon	52	1992
Hooligan	55	1992
Tiny Feet	98	1992
Heatwave		
Boogie Nights	5	1977
The Groove Line	1	1978
Always And Forever	41	1978
The Star Of A Story	M	1978
Heaven 17		
Let Me Go	24	1983
Heavy D & The Boyz		
Now That We Found Love	M	1991
Hebb, Bobby		
Sunny	P	1966
Hedges, Michael		
All Along The Watchtower	M	1985
Hefti, Neal		
Batman Theme	T	1966
The Odd Couple (w/ Sammy Cahn)	T	1968
Heil, Jerry		
Teresa & Maria	75	2024
Heldens, Oliver		
The Right Song	114	2016
10 Out Of 10	48	2023
Helicopter Girl		
Don't Come Around Here	141	2001
It Doesn't Get Much Better Than This	9	2008
Angel City	13	2008
Rivermouth	40	2008
Giants Building Giants	62	2008
Susan's Industry	24	2009
Henderson, Ella		
REACT	75	2023
Hendrix, Jimi		
Foxey Lady	P	1967
Hendryx, Nona (See also Labelle)		
I Sweat (Going Through The Motions)	105	1984
Henley, Don (See also Eagles)		
The Boys Of Summer	18	1985
New York Minute	69	1990
Heppner		
I Feel You	15	2005
Dream Of You	53	2005
H.E.R.		
Convince Me Otherwise	23	2021

Hermanos Gutiérrez		
Low Sun	14	2024
Herrmann, Bernard		
The Twilight Zone	T	1960
Hest, Ari		
Aberdeen / The Weight	105	2016
Hewitt, Emma		
Foolish Boy	M	2012
Only Love	13	2016
No Warning Lights	91	2021
Hex (See also The Church)		
Antelope	23	1991
Hollywood In Winter	68	1991
Hey Violet		
Guys My Age	27	2017
Where Have You Been (All My Night)	58	2017
Heyward, Nick (See also Haircut One Hundred)		
You're My World	M	1988
Tell Me Why	28	1989
H Factor		
The Hurt Stays Home	89	1990
Hill, Faith		
This Kiss	114	1999
A Baby Changes Everything	49	2008
Hilson, Keri		
The Way I Are	1	2007
Return The Favor	17	2009
Don't Look Now	49	2011
Himmelman, Peter		
Name	46	1990
Hinder		
Far From Home	55	2009
Hiroshima		
One Wish	M	1985
Hirsch, Beth		
One Fine Day	2	2003
Enjoy Youth	35	2024
Ho, Don (with the Ali'is)		
Tiny Bubbles	P	1966
Beautiful Kauai	P	1966
Hồ Gia Hùng		
Thay Thế (Replace)	12	2019
Hodgson, Roger (See also Supertramp)		
Desert Love	30	1988
Hoffs, Susanna (See also Bangles)		
Follow In My Footsteps	29	1991

It's Lonely Out Here	62	1991

Hogan, Brooke

Strip	40	2009

Hole

Doll Parts	79	1994

Holland, Amy

How Do I Survive	70	1980
Love Theme From St. Elmo's Fire (vocal version, "Just For A Moment")	M	1985

Holland, Nicky

Ladykiller	50	1992
Nobody's Girl	79	1997

Hollies, The (See also Crosby, Stills & Nash)

Bus Stop	P	1966
I Can't Let Go	P	1966
Long Cool Woman (In A Black Dress)	P	1972
The Air That I Breathe	P	1974

Holmes, Rupert

Him	75	1980

Holy Ghost!

Slow Motion	52	2011
Wait & See	64	2011
I Wanna Be Your Hand	98	2013

Hoobastank

Tears Of Yesterday	18	2009

Hooverphonic

2Wicky	21	1997
Club Montepulciano	6	1998
Revolver	15	1998
Inhaler	26	1998
Eden	37	1998
Lung	63	1999
Electro Shock Faders	87	1999
Out Of Sight	4	2000
Mad About You	39	2000
Jacky Cane	89	2000
Everytime We Live Together We Die A Bit More	21	2001
The Magnificent Tree	53	2001
Sometimes	58	2002
Human Interest	75	2003
Wake Up	41	2006
We All Float	99	2006
Gentle Storm	23	2008
Expedition Impossible	39	2008
Norwegian Skies	16	2011

One Two Three	32	2011
Amalfi	37	2014
Badaboum	10	2016
Hiding In A Song	17	2016
Deep Forest	53	2016
I Like The Way I Dance	98	2016
Romantic	16	2019
Uptight	24	2019
Belgium In The Rain	44	2021
The Wrong Place	55	2021
Hidden Stories	101	2021
And Then I Found You	5	2024
Two Wrongs Right	16	2024
The Best Day Of Our Life	60	2024

Hopkin, Mary

Those Were The Days	P	1968

Horan, Niall (See also One Direction)

On The Loose	94	2017
Nice To Meet Ya	94	2019

Horne, Lena

Stormy Weather	P	1943

Hornsby, Bruce, And The Range

The Way It Is	112	1986
Something To Believe In	10	1988

Hot Butter

Popcorn	P	1972

Hot Chip

Flutes	69	2012
Miss The Bliss	29	2022
The Evil That Men Do	142	2022

Hot Chocolate

Rumours	P	1973
You Sexy Thing	18	1976
So You Win Again	124	1977
Every 1's A Winner	28	1979

Houston, Thelma

Don't Leave Me This Way	96	1977

Houston, Whitney

When You Believe	120	1999

Howard, James Newton

The Hanging Tree (Rebel Remix)	60	2015

How To Destroy Angels

Ice Age (deadmau5 Remix)	90	2014

How To Dress Well

Cold Nites	97	2013

H

Hsin, Winnie 辛曉琪 (Xin Xiaoqi)		
煙 (The Smoke)	32	1998
Hubert Kah		
Machine Gun (Welcome, Machine Gun)	63	1990
It's Me, Cathy (Follow My Heart)	77	1990
Hues Corporation, The		
Rock The Boat	P	1974
Hugel		
I Adore You	48	2024
Human League, The		
Don't You Want Me	23	1982
Love Action (I Believe In Love)	79	1982
Mirror Man	16	1983
(Keep Feeling) Fascination	25	1983
Life On Your Own	47	1984
Louise	63	1984
The Lebanon	68	1984
Human	42	1986
Are You Ever Coming Back?	78	1987
The Stars Are Going Out	15	1991
Rebound	40	1991
Filling Up With Heaven	30	1995
One Man In My Heart	82	1995
All I Ever Wanted	28	2001
Never Let Me Go	43	2011
Human Touch		
Promise Not To Fall	92	2018
Hurts		
Wonderful Life	18	2010
Sunday	21	2011
Better Than Love	45	2011
Exile	72	2013
Kaleidoscope	6	2015
Ready To Go	72	2017
White Horses	39	2020
Slave To Your Love	49	2020
Voices	65	2020
HUSH (陳品赫)		
Toy Boy (身體會說話)	47	2023
Husky Rescue		
Summertime Cowboy	106	2005
Hyland, Brian		
Gypsy Woman	P	1970

I

Ian, Janis		
At Seventeen	P	1975
Icehouse		
We Can Get Together	83	1981
Icehouse	13	1982
Hey' Little Girl	13	1983
Great Southern Land / Street Café	45	1983
Love In Motion	23	1984
Don't Believe Anymore	48	1985
No Promises	4	1986
Paradise	7	1986
The Kingdom	1	1987
Angel Street	4	1987
Cross The Border	66	1987
Man Of Colours	13	1988
Ice Spice		
Karma (2023 mix)	130	2022
Icicle Works		
Birds Fly (Whisper To A Scream)	207	1984
Icona Pop		
I Love It	104	2013
Ides Of March, The		
Vehicle	P	1970
Idol, Billy		
Hot In The City	108	1982
White Wedding	123	1983
Eyes Without A Face	39	1984
Sweet Sixteen	104	1987
Iglesias, Enrique		
Be With You	114	2000
Love To See You Cry	23	2002
Love And Pain	74	2024
iiO (See also Nadia Ali)		
Rapture (Tastes So Sweet)	13	2002
At The End	86	2003
Is It Love	5	2006
Kiss You (Bailey Edit)	30	2006
All I Need	12	2011
It'll Be Like	37	2011
Holiday	84	2011
Illumination (Richard Souther)		
The Fire Of The Spirit (O Ignis Spiritus Paracliti)	26	1997

Tree Of Wonders (O Vos Felices Radices)/ [Sanctus]	66	1997

Imany

Don't Be So Shy	80	2016

Imbruglia, Natalie

Leave Me Alone	63	1998
Torn	112	1998
Sunlight	84	2002

Impressions, The

Gypsy Woman	P	1961

Incubus

Drive	5	2001
Here In My Room	27	2004
Love Hurts	26	2007

Indeep

The Record Keeps Spinning	89	1984

india.arie

Worthy/What If	36	2019

Indians, The

Look Up To The Sky	41	1994

Indigo Girls

Closer To Fine	100	1989
I'll Give You My Skin	49	1991

Indila

Love Story	14	2015
Mini World	27	2015
Carrousel	64	2021

Ingram, James

Prelude To The Garden/The Secret Garden (Sweet Seduction Suite)	116	1990

In-Grid

You Promised Me (Tu Es Foutu)	39	2004

Ingrosso, Benjamin

Man On The Moon	97	2021

INNA (See also G Girls)

Say It With Your Body	83	2017
Call The Police	91	2017

Inner City

Good Life	50	1989
It Could Be	67	2020

Innocence Mission, The

Black Sheep Wall	2	1990
Clear To You	10	1990
Wonder Of Birds	15	1990
And Hiding Away	45	1991

Beginning The World	37	1992
That Was Another Country	50	1995

Inspiral Carpets

Commercial Rain	92	1990
Two Worlds Collide	97	1993

INXS

Need You Tonight	132	1987
The Strangest Party (These Are The Times)	113	1995
Elegantly Wasted	117	1997

Iona

Everything Changes	53	1996
Wisdom	57	1996

Iris

Annie, Would I Lie To You	7	2002
You're The Answer	25	2003
Whatever	41	2003
Sorrow Expert	89	2003
It Generates	28	2005
Lands Of Fire	45	2005
Hell's Coming With Me	98	2006
Closer To Real	75	2010
Rewired	7	2015
Another Way	20	2015
Wayseer	90	2015
Joy Kill	14	2020
Speak Out	30	2020
Third Strike	95	2020

Iris, Donnie

Ah! Leah!	43	1981

Ironhorse (See also The Guess Who; Bachman-Turner Overdrive)

Sweet Lui-Louise	42	1979

Irrepressible, Jamie

I Had This Thing	82	2014

Isaak, Chris

Lie To Me	16	1987
Suspicion Of Love	67	1988
You Owe Me Some Kind Of Love	91	1988
Wicked Game	6	1989
Don't Make Me Dream About You	92	1989
Blue Spanish Sky	65	1990
Can't Do A Thing (To Stop Me)	59	1993
Shadows In A Mirror	55	1995
Graduation Day	79	1995

Please	77	1999
Reverie	59	2016

Isham, Mark
Pittsburgh, 1901 (Theme From "Mrs. Soffel")	M	2006

Isley Brothers, The
That Lady (Part 1)	P	1973

Ivy (See also Fountains Of Wayne; Brookville)
Thinking About You	59	2005
How's Never	75	2011

J

Jacks, Terry
Seasons In The Sun	P	1974

Jackson, Janet
Nasty	117	1986
Runaway	111	1995
What About	8	1998
Velvet Rope / Rope Burn	23	1998

Jackson, Jermaine (See also Jackson 5)
Let Me Tickle Your Fancy	89	1982

Jackson, Joe
Is She Really Going Out With Him?	30	1979
It's Different For Girls	1	1980
Steppin' Out	42	1982
Breaking Us In Two	50	1983
Left Of Center	10	1986
Discipline	98	1989
Glamour And Pain	87	2001

Jackson, Michael (See also Jackson 5)
Ben	P	1972
Billie Jean	125	1983
Beat It	179	1983

Jackson, Randy
Dance Like There's No Tomorrow	68	2008

Jackson, Wanda
Busted	114	2011

Jackson 5 (The Jacksons) (See also Michael Jackson; Jermaine Jackson)
ABC	P	1970
I'll Be There	P	1970
Never Can Say Goodbye	P	1971
Dancing Machine	P	1974
Enjoy Yourself (The Jacksons)	128	1976

Jaehn, Felix
Ain't Nobody (Loves Me Better)	66	2015
Love On Myself	10	2020

Jaggerz, The
The Rapper	P	1970

Jain
Makeba	72	2019

Jakatta
One Fine Day	2	2003
My Vision	12	2003
Home Away From You	23	2003
Show Me (Jakatta Mix)	24	2004

James
Born Of Frustration	112	1992

James, Etta
At Last	P	1961
Good Feeling	127	2012

James, Jessie
Burn It Up	24	2010

James, Jim
Same Old Lie	26	2017
Hide In Plain Sight	75	2017

James, Rick (& The Stone City Band) (See also Mary Jane Girls)
You And I	77	1978
Super Freak (Pt. 1)	M	1981

James, Samantha
Waves Of Change	74	2010

James, Tommy,& The Shondells
Hanky Panky	P	1966
I Think We're Alone Now	P	1967
Crimson And Clover	P	1968
Crystal Blue Persuasion	P	1969
Draggin' The Line (Tommy James, solo)	P	1971

James Gang, The (See also Joe Walsh; Eagles)
Walk Away	P	1971

Jamies, The
Summertime, Summertime	P	1958

Jamiroquai
Alright	99	1997

Japanese Breakfast
Machinist	22	2018
Diving Woman / Here Come The Tubular Bells	75	2018

Jarosz, Sarah
Columbus & 89th	98	2024

Jarre, Jean-Michel
Oxygène (Part IV)	M	1977
Brick England	33	2016

Here For You	64	2016
Jarreau, Al		
L Is For Lover	101	1987
Jars Of Clay		
Liquid	24	1996
Flood	34	1996
Crazy Times	29	1997
Fade To Grey	33	1998
Jay & The Americans		
This Magic Moment	P	1968
Jayhawks, The		
Waiting For The Sun	172	1992
Jay-Z		
No Church In The Wild	93	2011
Jazz, Maxi (See also Faithless)		
My Culture	65	2003
Jean, Wyclef		
911	49	2000
Hips Don't Lie	143	2006
Jean-Baptiste		
Spaceship	96	2010
Jefferson Airplane / Jefferson Starship (Starship) (See also Marty Balin)		
White Rabbit (Jefferson Airplane)	P	1967
Today (Jefferson Airplane)	P	1967
Miracles	P	1975
With Your Love	52	1976
Jane	87	1979
Stranger	47	1981
Find Your Way Back	48	1981
No Way Out	64	1984
Jellyfish		
Bedspring Kiss	53	1991
The King Is Half-Undressed	80	1991
Jem		
24	3	2004
They	58	2004
How Would You Like It	55	2008
JENNIE (Jennie Kim) (See also BLACKPINK)		
One Of The Girls	107	2024
Jepsen, Carly Rae		
Summer Love	66	2020
Beach House	95	2022
Come Over	99	2023
Put It To Rest	40	2024

JES		
Where You Are	17	2010
Unleash The Beat	23	2010
Such A Long Time / Lovesong	79	2010
Show Me The Way	89	2013
Stay	65	2017
Just Believe	67	2023
Jessica 6		
White Horse	2	2011
Prisoner Of Love	58	2011
Jesus Jones		
Right Here Right Now	131	1991
Jethro Tull		
Living In The Past	P	1969
Bungle In The Jungle	P	1974
Skating Away (On The Thin Ice Of The New Day)	P	1974
The Whistler	89	1977
Jewel		
Who Will Save Your Soul	69	1996
Foolish Games	54	1997
Leave The Lights On / Intuition	91	2003
Jewel, Johnny		
Windswept	34	2019
j-hope (See also BTS)		
lock / unlock	105	2024
Jia Peng Fang 贾鹏芳		
Silent Moon	M	1998
Jigsaw		
Sky High	43	1976
Joan As Police Woman		
The Love Has Got To Me	100	2021
Joe		
Get To Know Me	41	2007
Losing	6	2012
Joel, Billy		
She's Always A Woman	47	1978
Movin' Out (Anthony's Song)	85	1978
Only The Good Die Young	86	1978
Sometimes A Fantasy	62	1980
It's Still Rock And Roll To Me	94	1980
Allentown	69	1983
We Didn't Start The Fire	70	1989
Johanson, Jay-Jay		
Automatic Lover	73	2004

John, Elton		
Your Song	P	1970
Friends	P	1970
Tiny Dancer	P	1971
Madman Across The Water	P	1971
Rocket Man (I Think It's Going To Be A Long Long Time)	P	1972
Daniel	P	1972
Crocodile Rock	P	1972
Someone Saved My Life Tonight	P	1974
Philadelphia Freedom	P	1974
Bad Blood (Neil Sedeka w/ Elton)	P	1975
Don't Go Breaking My Heart	19	1976
Funeral For A Friend/Love Lies Bleeding	21	1976
Island Girl	86	1976
Bite Your Lip (Get up and dance!)	73	1977
Reverie/Song For Guy	M	1978
Fanfare/Chloe	9	1981
Nobody Wins	53	1981
Blue Eyes	51	1982
Empty Garden (Hey Hey Johnny)	60	1982
A Word In Spanish	75	1988
I Don't Want To Go On With You Like That	102	1988
Sacrifice	78	1990
Believe	114	1995
Karmatron	3	2012
Good Morning To The Night	28	2012
Sine From Above	27	2020
Cold Heart (PNAU Remix) / (Claptone Remix)	26	2021

John, Robert		
The Lion Sleeps Tonight	M	1972

Johnny Hates Jazz		
Shattered Dreams	72	1988
Don't Let It End This Way	96	1989
Magnetized	23	2013
You Belong To You	87	2013

Johns, Sammy		
Chevy Van	P	1975

Johnson, Andreas		
Glorious / (NUM Remix)	1	2001
Breathing	79	2001

Johnson, Michael		
Almost Like Being In Love	29	1978
Sailing Without A Sail/When You Come Home	70	1979

Johnston, Zoë		
We're All We Need	42	2015

Joi		
Oh My People	88	1999

Joli, France		
Come To Me	103	1979

Jon & Vangelis (See also Jon Anderson; Vangelis; Yes; Aphrodite's Child)		
I Hear You Now	M	1979
The Friends Of Mr. Cairo	4	1981
I'll Find My Way Home	1	1982
He Is Sailing	83	1983
Wisdom Chain	36	1992
Money	48	1992
Be A Good Friend Of Mine	59	1992

Jonas, Joe (See also Jonas Brothers; DNCE)		
Not Alone	31	2022

Jonas, Nick (See also Jonas Brothers)		
Jealous	85	2014
Find You	18	2018
Right Now	77	2018
Heights / (Chill Version)	45	2021
This Is Heaven	82	2021

Jonas Brothers (See also Nick Jonas; Joe Jonas; DNCE)		
Only Human	14	2019
Every Single Time	35	2019

Jones, Donell		
What's Next	54	2011

Jones, Grace		
Private Life	M	1980
Walking In The Rain	64	1982
I've Seen That Face Before (Libertango)	M	1982
My Jamaican Guy	53	1983
Nipple To The Bottle	99	1983
Slave To The Rhythm	73	1986
I'm Not Perfect (But I'm Perfect For You)	69	1987
The Chant Movement	69	1991
Corporate Cannibal	100	2008
Williams' Blood	100	2009
Ooh La La	52	2023

Jones, Howard		
New Song	26	1984
Things Can Only Get Better	118	1985
Eagle Will Fly Again	96	2016
The One To Love You (The Lifelike Mix)	61	2020

Jones, Jack		
The Impossible Dream	P	1966
Love Boat Theme	T	1977

Jones, Jax		
You Don't Know Me	22	2017
Instruction	78	2017
Breathe	44	2018
Play	39	2019
i miss u	13	2020
Cruel	45	2020

Jones, Mick (See also The Clash)		
Reboot The Mission	122	2012

Jones, Norah		
Season's Trees	95	2011

Jones, Oran "Juice"		
The Rain	128	1986

Jones, Quincy		
Stuff Like That	126	1978
Prelude To The Garden/The Secret Garden (Sweet Seduction Suite)	116	1990

Jones, Rickie Lee		
We Belong Together	58	1982
Pirates (So Long Lonely Avenue)	61	1982
It Must Be Love	61	1985

Jones, Steve		
Pleasure And Pain	61	1987

Jones, Tom		
It's Not Unusual	P	1965
Thunderball	P	1965
Daughter Of Darkness	P	1970
I (Who Have Nothing)	P	1970
She's A Lady	P	1971
Something In The Air	74	1998
Stoned In Love	87	2008

Jordan, Marc		
This Independence	72	1987
Soldier Of Fortune	68	1988
I Ching	100	1988

Journey (See also Steve Perry)		
Lovin', Touchin', Squeezin'	74	1979
Walks Like A Lady	66	1980
Good Morning Girl/Stay Awhile	71	1980
Don't Stop Believin'	12	1981
Who's Crying Now	15	1981
The Party's Over (Hopelessly In Love)	21	1981
Still They Ride	37	1982
Open Arms	101	1982
Send Her My Love	7	1983
After The Fall	92	1983
Separate Ways (Worlds Apart)	129	1983
Girl Can't Help It	81	1986

Juanes		
Es Por Ti	129	2002
Mayo	1	2023

Judybats, The		
Woman In The Garden	5	1991
She Lives (In A Time Of Her Own)	95	1991
My Dead Friend	7	1993
Incredible Bittersweet	61	1993
Being Simple	89	1993

Jungkook (Jung Kook) (See also BTS)		
Somebody	8	2024

Jungle		
Dry Your Tears/Keep Moving	51	2021

Jungle Brothers, The		
I Get A Kick	94	1991

Junip		
Line Of Fire	88	2013

Junkie XL		
A Little Less Conversation (Elvis VS JXL Remix, 2002)	P	1968
Angels	75	2004
Broken	20	2005

Junkilla		
Without You	17	2019

Justice		
On'n'On	111	2012
Neverender	85	2024

JVKE (Jake)		
Fool 4 U	101	2024

K

Kahn, Madeline		
I'm Tired	P	1974

Kajagoogoo (See also Limahl)		
Too Shy	65	1983

Kamoze, Ini		
Here Comes The Hotstepper	67	1994

Kansas		
Carry On Wayward Son	77	1977

Dust In The Wind	88	1978

Karen O

Turn The Light	3	2019

Karol G

Sola Es Mejor	54	2022

Kaskade

Steppin' Out	23	2004
Be Still	9	2006
The X	93	2006
Stars Align	25	2007
I Remember	3	2008
Let's Begin	10	2008
Move For Me	38	2008
This Is How It Goes (Kaskade's Grand Club Edit)	76	2009
Human Reactor	64	2010
Llove	42	2011
Lessons In Love	10	2012
Room For Happiness	79	2012
Missing You	54	2013
In Common (Kaskade Remix)	8	2016

Katy B

Katy On A Mission	41	2011

Katydids

The Boy Who's Never Found	44	1991

Kavinsky

Nightcall	23	2011
Blizzard / Grand Canyon	101	2013

Kaylif, Layla

Conflict Junkie	9	2000
Shakespeare In Love	27	2000
The Sweetest Find	64	2000

KC And The Sunshine Band

Get Down Tonight	P	1975
(Shake, Shake, Shake) Shake Your Booty	14	1976
That's The Way (I Like It)	37	1976
Keep It Comin' Love	8	1977
I'm Your Boogie Man	28	1977
Wrap Your Arms Around Me	43	1978
Boogie Shoes	96	1978
Please Don't Go	13	1979

Keane

Your Eyes Open	11	2004
Untitled 1 / Sunshine	33	2004
We Might As Well Be Strangers	47	2004
Somewhere Only We Know	90	2004
Nothing In My Way	18	2006
Is It Any Wonder?	29	2006
Spiralling	74	2008
Your Love	26	2010
Clear Skies	40	2010
The Boys	75	2012
I'm Not Leaving	67	2019

Keats (See also Alan Parsons Project; Pete Bardens; Pilot; The Zombies)

Walking On Ice	58	1986
Avalanche	M	1986

Kehlani

Done For Me	76	2018

Keith

98.6	P	1966

Kelis

Dandelion	97	2001
Spaceship	96	2010

Kelley, Charles

Dancing Around It	81	2016

Kelly, R.

Do What U Want	14	2014

Kelly, Tori

Coffee	118	2019

Kenna

Spiral	1	2006

Kenny G

Songbird	165	1987

Kenya Grace

Strangers	60	2023

Kershaw, Nik

Wouldn't It Be Good	7	1984

Kesha (Ke$ha)

TiK ToK	109	2010
Love Into The Light	85	2013
Something To Believe In/Eat The Acid	10	2023

Keys, Alicia

Fallin'	59	2001
In Common / (Kaskade Remix)	8	2016
Time Machine	63	2020
Underdog	90	2020

Khaled (Cheb Khaled)

Aïcha	100	1997

Khalid

Rollin	55	2017

Silence	87	2017
Ocean	84	2018
Eastside	116	2018
Hundred	78	2019
lovely	5	2022
Not Alone	31	2022
Where You Go	95	2023
Khan, Chaka (See also Rufus)		
Tell Me Something Good	117	1976
Ain't Nobody	224	1984
Hello Happiness	66	2019
Immortal Queen	70	2024
Khia		
My Neck, My Back (Lick It)	M	2002
Khởi My		
Người Lạ Thoáng Qua (Glimpse Of Strangers)	37	2019
Kid Cudi		
Young Lady	100	2013
Kidman, Nicole		
Hindi Sad Diamonds	89	2001
Kiesza		
Hideaway	119	2014
We Are Strong	102	2017
Love Me With Your Lie	59	2021
Dancing And Crying	87	2024
Kihn, Greg, Band		
The Breakup Song (They Don't Write 'Em)	26	1981
Jeopardy	86	1983
Killers, The (See also Brandon Flowers)		
Somebody Told Me	101	2004
Killing Joke		
Love Like Blood	28	1985
Kills, The		
Kingdom Come	83	2024
Kim, Andy		
Rock Me Gently	P	1974
Kim Hee-Seon 김희선		
Endless Love I/II (神话) (美麗的神話 I/II)	72	2008
Kimbra		
Somebody That I Used To Know	95	2012
Good Intent	42	2012
King		
Love & Pride	121	1985

King, Ben E.		
I (Who Have Nothing)	P	1963
King, Carole		
So Far Away	P	1971
It's Too Late/I Feel The Earth Move	P	1971
Sweet Seasons	P	1972
Corazón	P	1973
Believe In Humanity	P	1973
Jazzman	P	1974
King, Evelyn "Champagne"		
Shame	69	1978
Love Come Down (Evelyn King)	94	1983
King Harvest		
Dancing In The Moonlight	P	1972
Kings, The		
Switchin' To Glide/This Beat Goes On	39	1980
Kingsmen, The		
Louie Louie	P	1963
Kings Of Convenience		
I'd Rather Dance With You	43	2004
Kinks, The		
You Really Got Me	P	1964
Tired Of Waiting For You	P	1965
Sunny Afternoon	P	1966
Lola	P	1970
(Wish I Could Fly Like) Superman	M	1979
KISS (See also Ace Frehley; Paul Stanley)		
Beth	71	1976
Rock And Roll All Nite	91	1976
Calling Dr. Love	55	1977
Rocket Ride	100	1978
I Was Made For Lovin' You	43	1979
A World Without Heroes	75	1982
Kitchens Of Distinction		
Drive That Fast	91	1991
Kitt, Eartha		
C'est Si Bon	P	1953
Santa Baby	X	1953
Where Is My Man?	84	1983
Kiwanuka, Michael		
Floating Parade	37	2024
Klangkarussell		
Netzwerk (Falls Like Rain)	71	2014
Klaxons		
Golden Skans	34	2007

K

Kleerup		
With Every Heartbeat	30	2009
History	59	2009
KLF, The		
3 A.M. Eternal	124	1991
Kloser, Luka		
One More Time	65	2022
Klymaxx		
The Men All Pause	105	1985
Knack, The		
My Sharona	12	1979
Knight, Gladys, & The Pips		
Midnight Train To Georgia	P	1973
Neither One Of Us (Wants To Be The First To Say Goodbye)	P	1973
Knoblock, Fred		
Why Not Me	22	1980
Knocks, The		
Dancing With Myself	100	2016
Knux, The		
I See Stars	35	2011
Koma, Matthew		
Spectrum	79	2013
Written In Reverse	27	2014
Kool & The Gang		
Hollywood Swinging	P	1974
Summer Madness	P	1975
Tonight	34	1984
Cherish	110	1985
Let's Party	87	2023
Heaven's Gift	38	2024
Korgis, The		
Everybody's Got To Learn Sometime	5	1980
Kosheen		
Hungry	4	2002
Catch	20	2002
Cover	35	2002
Wasting My Time	26	2003
Crawling	66	2003
Coming Home	52	2004
Little Boy	88	2004
Chances	9	2007
Damage	24	2007
Overkill	32	2007
Like A Book	90	2007
Tightly	25	2012

Waste	58	2012
Get A New One	75	2013
Save Your Tears	64	2014
Kraftwerk (See also Karl Bartos)		
Autobahn	P	1975
Pocket Calculator	97	1982
Tour De France	137	1984
Krauss, Alison (& Union Station)		
So Long So Wrong (& Union Station)	77	1997
You Will Be My Ain True Love	71	2004
My Poor Old Heart (& Union Station)	77	2005
Kravitz, Lenny		
If I Could Fall In Love	139	2002
Kreo'		
Burn For You	28	2016
Kreviazuk, Chantal		
Blue	9	1999
Krewella		
Broken Record	26	2016
Kristine W		
Fly Again	64	2004
K-391		
Ignite	83	2018
Kubb		
Remain	31	2007
If I Can't Have You	52	2007
Kudai		
Déjame Gritar	76	2007
Kula Shaker		
Tattva	95	1997
Kungs		
Substitution	90	2023
Kwan, Shirley		
So Sad	34	1992
Kygo		
Firestone	39	2015
This Town	21	2018
Riding Shotgun	35	2018
You're The Best Thing About Me	101	2018

L

Labelle (See also Patti LaBelle; Nona Hendryx)		
Lady Marmalade	P	1975
LaBelle, Patti (See also Labelle)		
New Attitude	101	1985
Oh, People	63	1986

Lacuna Coil		
Within Me	91	2006
Lady Antebellum (Lady A)		
Need You Now	89	2010
Something Better	72	2015
Army	61	2017
Lady Gaga		
Just Dance	77	2008
So Happy I Could Die	4	2009
Poker Face	15	2009
I Like It Rough	45	2009
Telephone	48	2009
Bad Romance	145	2009
Monster	27	2010
Murder My Heart	73	2010
Electric Chapel	27	2011
Heavy Metal Lover	44	2011
Judas	82	2011
Applause	12	2013
Do What U Want	14	2014
ARTPOP	42	2014
Donatella/Fashion!	59	2014
The Cure	92	2017
Why Did You Do That?	61	2018
Hair Body Face	82	2018
Heal Me	30	2019
Enigma/Replay	1	2020
Chromatica I/Alice	8	2020
Chromatica II/911	15	2020
Babylon	20	2020
Sour Candy	21	2020
Chromatica III/Sine From Above	27	2020
Stupid Love	54	2020
Die With A Smile	89	2024
Ladyhawke		
Dusk Till Dawn	7	2009
Magic	26	2009
Love Don't Live Here	99	2009
My Love	58	2021
Walk Away	88	2021
Ladytron		
Destroy Everything You Touch	34	2005
Mirage	46	2011
City Of Angels	42	2023
La Grange, Kyla		
Cut Your Teeth	67	2016

Laid Back		
White Horse	142	1984
Laing, Shona		
Soviet Snow	105	1988
Lake		
Time Bomb	83	1977
Lamar, Kendrick		
Pray For Me	119	2018
Mirror	76	2022
Lamb		
Gabriel	83	2005
Lamb, Annabel		
Inside Of My Head	52	1984
Dream Boy	66	1984
Lambchop		
Low Ambition	51	2004
Lambert, Adam		
Whataya Want From Me	53	2009
Mad World	86	2009
Chokehold	16	2012
Broken English	24	2012
Outlaws Of Love	51	2012
Things I Didn't Say	35	2015
Ghost Town	83	2015
Overglow	26	2019
Superpower	84	2019
Roses	44	2020
Lamond, Mary Jane		
Sleepy Maggie	86	1998
Land Of The Loops		
Multi-Family Garage Sale	65	1997
Lane, Reni		
Never Stop	66	2010
lang, k.d.		
Constant Craving	25	1992
Calling All Angels	106	1992
Lifted By Love	82	1994
Lange		
Fireflies	77	2014
Larkin Poe		
Banks Of Allatoona	16	2016
La Roux		
In For The Kill	79	2009
Tutti Frutti	103	2015
Larrieux, Amel		
Dear To Me	65	2004

Larson, Nicolette		
Lotta Love	50	1979
Larsson, Zara		
One Mississippi	33	2017
La's, The		
There She Goes	74	1991
Las Ketchup		
Aserejé [The Ketchup Song (Hey Hah)]	118	2002
Last, James, Band		
The Seduction (Love Theme)	14	1980
LaTour		
Following You	90	1994
Lauper, Cyndi		
Time After Time	13	1984
She Bop	50	1984
All Through The Night	85	1984
True Colors	123	1986
I Drove All Night	81	1989
Fall Into Your Dreams	30	1997
Sisters Of Avalon	67	1997
Into The Nightlife	11	2008
Raging Storm / Lay Me Down	60	2008
Eleven Days	99	2010
Laurence, Duncan		
Someone Else	62	2021
Arcade	68	2021
Lauv		
Who	5	2021
Molly In Mexico	84	2022
LaVette, Bettye		
The Last Goodbye	99	2022
Lawrence, Jennifer		
The Hanging Tree (Rebel Remix)	60	2015
Lawrence, Steve		
Go Away Little Girl	P	1963
Lawrence, Vicki		
The Night The Lights Went Out In Georgia	P	1973
Lay, Omah		
People (sped up+reverb)	38	2023
League Of Legends		
Legends Never Die	28	2023
Leaves		
Crazy	51	2003
LeBlanc & Carr		
Falling	70	1978

Le Bon, Simon (See also Duran Duran)		
Follow In My Footsteps	29	1991
Ledé. Kiana		
Where You Go	95	2023
Ledisi		
Give You More	107	2017
Led Zeppelin		
Immigrant Song	P	1970
Stairway To Heaven	P	1971
D'yer Mak'er	P	1973
The Rain Song	P	1973
Kashmir	P	1975
Bron-Yr-Aur	P	1975
Lee, Brenda		
I'm Sorry	P	1960
Lee, Peggy		
Fever	P	1958
Big Spender	P	1966
Lee, Tommy		
Makin Me Crazy	56	2006
Legend, John		
Who Did That To You?	127	2013
Give You More	107	2017
Legere, Phoebe		
Marilyn Monroe	56	1990
Legrand, Michel		
Brian's Song	P	1972
Leguizamo, John		
Hindi Sad Diamonds	89	2001
LEILAH		
Prada (i like it)	3	2022
Lemaitre		
Polygon Dust	78	2014
Lemonade Mouth Cast		
Determinate / Breakthrough	78	2011
Le Mystère Des Voix Bulgares		
Bulgarian Rhapsody	M	1992
Lenka		
You Will Be Mine	3	2011
Here To Stay	101	2011
Lennon, John (See also The Beatles; Yoko Ono)		
Imagine (John Lennon/Plastic Ono Band)	P	1971
#9 Dream	P	1974
Lennon, Julian		
Too Late For Goodbyes	95	1985

Stick Around	88	1986

Lennox, Annie (See also Eurythmics)

Stay By Me	58	1992
Money Can't Buy It	66	1992
Why	94	1992
What Can You Do For Me	58	1993
Love Song For A Vampire / Little Bird	78	1993
No More "I Love You's"	21	1995
Don't Let It Bring You Down	57	1995
A Thousand Beautiful Things	57	2003
Coloured Bedspread	47	2007

LeRoux (Louisiana's LeRoux)

Nobody Said It Was Easy (Lookin' For The Lights)	70	1982

Les Deux Love Orchestra

The Moth & The Flame	24	2008
Overtures To Ecstasy/Ecstasy	28	2008

Lesiëm

Humilitas	44	2003
Fides	60	2003

Lettermen, The

Hurt So Bad	P	1969

Letters To Cleo

Here And Now	26	1995

Levan, Ivy

Who Can You Trust	22	2015

Level 42

Something About You	49	1986
Physical Presence	101	1986
Leaving Me Now	19	1987
It's Over	51	1987
Lessons In Love	65	1987

Lewis, Barbara

Hello Stranger	P	1963

Lewis, Donna

Without Love	96	1996
I Love You Always Forever	128	1996

Lewis. Ephraim

Skin	M	1992
It Can't Be Forever	M	1992
Hold On	M	1992
World Between Us	M	1992

Lewis, Gary, And The Playboys

This Diamond Ring	P	1965

Lewis, SG

One More	4	2021

Rosner's Interlude/Chemicals	87	2021
Heartbreak On The Dancefloor	18	2021
Call On Me	69	2022
Holding On	12	2023
Intro/Infatuation	18	2023
Another Life	30	2023
Love Bites	94	2024

LFO

Erase Her	43	2001
Dandelion	97	2001

Li, Lykke

Late Night Prelude/Late Night Feelings	22	2019

Lia, Orsa

I Never Said I Love You	104	1979

Libera

Salva Me	63	2001

Libianca

People / (sped up+reverb)	38	2023

Lifehouse

Mesmerized	103	2007

Lightfoot, Gordon

Song For A Winter's Night	X	1967
If You Could Read My Mind	P	1970
Sundown	P	1974
The Wreck Of The Edmund Fitzgerald	127	1976

Lightning Seeds, The

Pure	71	1990

Lights

Prodigal Daughter	66	2022

Like Mike

Hey Baby	25	2017

Lilac Time, The (See also Stephen 'Tin Tin' Duffy)

Rockland	61	1989
The Lost Girl In The Midnight Sun	51	1990

Lil Jon

Yeah! (Usher f/ Lil Jon & Ludacris)	M	2004

Lilly Wood & The Prick

Prayer In C (Robin Schulz Mix)	41	2014

Lil Nas X

STAR WALKIN' (League Of Legends Worlds Anthem)	49	2023
HE KNOWS	102	2024

Lil Wayne

Let It Rock	58	2008
Uneasy	9	2023

Lil Yachty		
The Paradigm	84	2024
Limahl (See also Kajagoogoo)		
Never Ending Story	88	1985
Lind, Bob		
Elusive Butterfly	P	1965
Lindenberg, Udo		
Komet	19	2024
Lindsay, Mark (See also The Raiders)		
Arizona	P	1969
Linh Cáo		
Ta Cứ Đi Cùng Nhau (Let's Go Together)	25	2019
Linkin Park		
In The End	70	2001
Pushing Me Away	84	2001
Numb	113	2003
Lipa, Dua		
Scared To Be Lonely	7	2017
New Rules	59	2017
One Kiss	11	2018
Hallucinate	9	2020
Levitating	85	2020
Cold Heart (PNAU Remix) / (Claptone Remix)	26	2021
Prisoner	37	2021
Love Again	115	2021
Dance The Night	119	2023
Houdini	34	2024
Illusion	81	2024
Lipps, Inc.		
Funkytown	M	1980
lisahall		
Is This Real?	36	1999
Lisa Lisa & Cult Jam w/ Full Force		
All Cried Out	131	1986
Lissie		
The Longest Road / (deadmau5 Vocal Remix)	1	2008
Fight For You	2	2010
Believe / Strange Condition	30	2010
In Sleep	61	2010
When I'm Alone	17	2011
Further Away (Romance Police)	27	2013
Can't Take It Back	30	2014
The Habit	45	2014
Open Heart	33	2015

Don't You Give Up On Me	29	2016
Little Anthony And The Imperials		
Goin' Out Of My Head	P	1964
Hurt So Bad	P	1964
Little Boots		
Stuck On Repeat	28	2009
Hearts Collide	34	2009
Symmetry	62	2009
New In Town	70	2009
Magical / Mathematics	93	2009
All For You	17	2013
Confusion	34	2013
Broken Record	40	2013
Get Things Done	8	2015
Paradise	71	2015
Silver Balloons	17	2022
Nothing Ever Changes	28	2022
Little Dragon		
Fortune	80	2010
Little Eva		
The Loco-Motion	P	1962
Little River Band (See also John Farnham)		
Curiosity (Killed The Cat)	P	1975
It's A Long Way There	81	1976
Help Is On Its Way	13	1977
Lonesome Loser/Shut Down Turn Off	71	1979
The Night Owls	78	1981
You're Driving Me Out Of My Mind	43	1983
Liu, Sara		
RU WO	18	2019
Līve		
Pain Lies On The Riverside	100	1992
Selling The Drama	22	1994
Livingston, Jerry, & Mack David		
Surfside 6	T	1960
Lizzo		
About Damn Time	95	2022
LL Cool J		
Doin It	146	1996
Lloyd, Dennis		
Nevermind	64	2018
Lobo		
Don't Expect Me To Be Your Friend	P	1972
Loeb, Lisa, & Nine Stories		
Stay (I Missed You)	35	1994

Do You Sleep?	59	1995
Lo-Fang		
Intro/Animal Urges	98	2014
Loggins, Dave		
Please Come To Boston	P	1974
Loggins, Kenny (See also Loggins & Messina)		
Whenever I Call You "Friend"	108	1978
I'm Alright (Theme From "Caddyshack")	25	1980
Loggins & Messina (See also Kenny Loggins; Buffalo Springfield; Poco)		
Angry Eyes	P	1972
Lo Moon		
The Right Thing	12	2018
This Is It	33	2018
Intro/Carried Away	74	2022
Connecticut	6	2024
London, Julie		
Cry Me A River	P	1955
London, Theophilus		
Last Name London	107	2011
Love Is Real	39	2012
Londonbeat		
I've Been Thinking About You	173	1991
London Grammar		
Non Believer	2	2018
Leave The War With Me	30	2018
Call Your Friends	3	2021
How Does It Feel	6	2021
Missing	15	2021
Intro/Californian Soil	56	2021
House	21	2024
Higher	30	2024
Lone Bellow, The		
Deeper In The Water	64	2017
Lonely Island, The (See also Justin Timberlake)		
Motherlover	94	2009
Lonestar		
Amazed	137	2000
Looking Glass		
Brandy (You're A Fine Girl)	P	1972
Jimmy Loves Mary-Anne	P	1973
Lopez, Jennifer		
If You Had My Love	98	1999
(Can't Believe) This Is Me	90	2005
On The Floor	145	2011

Emotions	96	2014
Lopez, Trini		
If I Had A Hammer	P	1963
Lorde		
Green Light	121	2017
Lord Huron		
Drops In The Lake	1	2021
The Moon Doesn't Mind/Mine Forever	54	2021
Long Lost	79	2021
Loreen		
Euphoria	M	2012
Los Bravos		
Black Is Black / (Black Is Black '86 Remix)	P	1966
Los Del Rio		
Macarena / (Bayside Boys Mix)	86	1995
Lost, Ben		
Jump The Next Train	29	2023
Lostboy! AKA Jim Kerr (See also Simple Minds)		
Bulletproof Heart	52	2010
Lost Frequencies		
Are You With Me	87	2015
Lostprophets		
Sway	34	2004
Lovato, Demi		
Instruction	78	2017
Solo	53	2018
In The Mirror	25	2020
Love		
Signed D.C.	P	1966
Love And Kisses		
Thank God It's Friday	82	1978
Love And Money		
Strange Kind Of Love	23	1989
Walk The Last Mile	65	1989
Shape Of Things To Come	53	1990
Lovefoxxx		
Nightcall	23	2011
lovelytheband		
Drive	29	2020
Loverboy		
When It's Over	74	1982
Love Spirals Downwards		
Illusory Me	2	1993
And The Wood Comes Into Leaf	38	1993
Write In Water	45	1995

Above The Lone	31	1997
Madras	94	1997
El Pedregal	M	1997
By Your Side	93	1998
Love Spit Love (See also The Psychedelic Furs)		
Am I Wrong	45	1994
Love Unlimited (See also Barry White; Love Unlimited Orchestra)		
Walkin' In The Rain With The One I Love	P	1972
Love Unlimited Orchestra (See also Barry White; Love Unlimited)		
Love's Theme	P	1973
Lovich, Lene		
Lucky Number	M	1978
New Toy	107	1981
Never Never Land	67	1982
Hold On To Love	48	1990
Lovin' Spoonful (See also John Sebastian)		
Do You Believe In Magic	P	1965
Daydream	P	1965
Summer In The City	P	1966
Low		
Just Like Christmas	X	1999
Low, Gary		
You Are A Danger	76	1983
Lowe, Nick		
Cruel To Be Kind	14	1979
LP		
Lost On You / (Swanky Tunes & Going Deeper Remix)	19	2017
Other People	48	2017
N'Oublié Pas	72	2018
Lucero		
Pull Me Close Don't Let Go	85	2021
Lucid		
Stay With Me Till Dawn	16	2006
Ludacris		
Yeah! (Usher f/ Lil Jon & Ludacris)	M	2004
Glamorous	151	2006
Lulu		
To Sir With Love	P	1967
The Man With The Golden Gun	P	1974
Luminous (See also Brother Sun Sister Moon)		
Hummingbirds	21	2002
Lunascape		
Mindstalking	68	2005
Outside	31	2008
Burden Of Beauty	56	2008
Lunn, John		
100 Years Of Downton	98	2019
Lush (See also Sing-Sing)		
Sweetness And Light	75	1991
Untogether	8	1992
For Love	30	1992
Light From A Dead Star	37	1994
Never-Never	39	1994
L.V.		
Gangsta's Paradise	83	1995
Lynch, Dustin		
Why We Call Each Other	14	2018
Back On It	19	2018
Killed The Cowboy	91	2023
Lynch, Ray		
Celestial Soda Pop	M	1984
Lynn, Cheryl		
Got To Be Real	35	1979
Lynyrd Skynyrd		
Tuesday's Gone	P	1973
Free Bird	119	1976
Lytle, Jason		
Tomorrow's Started	29	2012
Lyttle, Kevin		
Turn Me On	120	2004

M

M		
Pop Muzik	68	1979
Mabel		
Don't Call Me Up	113	2019
Macdonald, Amy		
This Is The Life	117	2008
MacDonald, Laurel		
A Wing And A Prayer	69	1999
MacIsaac, Ashley		
Sleepy Maggie	86	1998
Macklemore		
Summer Days	62	2019
Mad Cobra		
Cobrastyle	33	2008
Madeon		
Stay Awake	42	2013

M

Madison Avenue

Don't Call Me Baby	50	2000

Madonna

Holiday/Everybody	75	1983
Borderline	96	1984
Into The Groove	16	1985
Crazy For You	56	1985
Angel	63	1985
Live To Tell	13	1986
Papa Don't Preach	80	1986
The Look Of Love	40	1988
Oh Father	9	1989
Like A Prayer	127	1989
Justify My Love	37	1990
Dear Jessie / Till Death Do Us Part	95	1990
Vogue	101	1990
This Used To Be My Playground	21	1992
Bad Girl	8	1993
In This Life / Why's It So Hard	44	1993
Secret	31	1994
I'll Remember (Theme From "With Honors")	109	1994
Human Nature	18	1995
You'll See	54	1995
Sanctuary	74	1995
Love Tried To Welcome Me	75	1995
Take A Bow	117	1995
Sky Fits Heaven	13	1998
Ray Of Light	22	1998
Frozen	28	1998
Nothing Really Matters	39	1998
Skin	64	1998
The Power Of Good-Bye/To Have And Not To Hold	68	1998
Beautiful Stranger	10	1999
Be Careful (Cuidado Con Mi Corazón)	23	1999
Time Stood Still	44	2000
Impressive Instant	20	2001
Amazing	52	2001
Nobody's Perfect / Gone	57	2001
Die Another Day	16	2002
Hollywood	45	2003
Nothing Fails	84	2003
I'm So Stupid	98	2003
Hung Up	26	2005
How High/Isaac	7	2006
Sorry	31	2006
Jump	53	2006
Miles Away	4	2008
Devil Wouldn't Recognize You	12	2008
4 Minutes	37	2008
Give It 2 Me	69	2008
Celebration	108	2009
Girl Gone Wild	22	2012
Beautiful Killer	31	2012
Some Girls	43	2012
Give Me All Your Luvin'	81	2012
Masterpiece	100	2012
HeartBreakCity	28	2015
Inside Out	45	2015
Ghosttown	98	2015
Living For Love	101	2015
Dark Ballet/God Control	75	2019
Frozen On Fire / Frozen	58	2022

Magdalena Bay

Disappearing	108	2024
True Blue Interlude/Image	129	2024

Magic Wands

Crystals	74	2012

Magna Canta

Agnus Dei	98	2004

Magnetic Fields, The

I Thought You Were My Boyfriend	6	2004

Mai, Ella

Pieces	25	2022

Mai Tai

History	21	1985

Main Ingredient, The

Everybody Plays The Fool	P	1972

Majid Jordan

Waves Of Blue	29	2021

Mako

Smoke Filled Room	86	2016
Legends Never Die	28	2023

Mamas & The Papas, The (See also Mama Cass Elliot)

Monday, Monday	P	1966
California Dreamin'	P	1966
Go Where You Wanna Go	P	1966

Manchester, Melissa

Midnight Blue	P	1975
Just Too Many People	P	1975

Pretty Girls	M	1979
You Should Hear How She Talks About You	118	1982

Mancini, Henry

Peter Gunn Theme	P	1959
Moon River	P	1961
Baby Elephant Walk	P	1962
Experiment In Terror	P	1962
Charade	P	1963
The Pink Panther Theme	P	1964
Love Theme From Romeo And Juliet	P	1969
Whistling Away The Dark (w/ Julie Andrews)	P	1970
(Theme From) Love Story	P	1971

Mandalay

This Life	37	2000
Insensible	8	2002

Mandel, Johnny, & Michael Altman

Suicide Is Painless (Song from "M*A*S*H")	T	1970

Mandrell, Barbara

(If Loving You Is Wrong) I Don't Want To Be Right	73	1979

Manfred Mann / Manfred Mann's Earth Band

Do Wah Diddy Diddy	P	1964
Blinded By The Light (Manfred Mann's Earth Band)	17	1977
Spirit In The Night (Manfred Mann's Earth Band)	102	1977
Runner (Manfred Mann's Earth Band)	79	1984

Mangeshkar, Lata / Sonu Nigam

Do Pal	82	2005

Manhattan Transfer, The

Boy From New York City	90	1981

Manilow, Barry

It's A Miracle	P	1975
New York City Rhythm	P	1975
American Bandstand	T	1975
Could It Be Magic	M	1976
Copacabana (At The Copa)	137	1978
Some Kind Of Friend	M	1983
Wine Song	6	2011

Mann, Aimee (See also 'Til Tuesday)

I Should've Known	65	1993
Jacob Marley's Chain	75	1993
Say Anything	98	1993
That's Just What You Are	56	1995
All Over Now	79	1996

Mannequin Pussy

I Don't Know You	122	2024

Mannheim Steamroller

Above The Northern Lights	16	2008

Mansell, Clint

Rebirth / Invocation	91	2022

Mansionair

Est./Alibi	22	2021
Mirror Me	87	2022

Mansun

Mansun's Only Love Song	53	1998

Mantovani And His Orchestra

Main Theme From Exodus (Ari's Theme)	P	1960
Ebb Tide	P	1966

Manufacture

As The End Draws Near	46	1996

Man Without Country

Sordid Affair	48	2014
Laws Of Motion	50	2015
Sweet Harmony	74	2015
Breathe	39	2022

Marcomé

Yéku	49	1997

Marcy Playground

Sex And Candy	96	1997

Mardones, Benny

Into The Night	8	1980

Maria (Lumiere)

Lonely	28	2004
I Give, You Take	68	2004

Marillion

Kayleigh	44	1985

Marina (Diamandas) (And The Diamonds)

Karma	15	2019
True	23	2019
Baby	89	2019
Emotional Machine	19	2020

Markowitz, Richard

The Wild Wild West	T	1965

Marks, Larry

Scooby-Doo, Where Are You?	T	1969

Marley, Bob, & The Wailers

Get Up, Stand Up	P	1973
Three Little Birds	M	1977
Jamming	M	1977
Is This Love	M	1978

Marley, Skip		
Chained To The Rhythm	14	2017

Marlin, Lene		
Unforgivable Sinner	26	2000
Sitting Down Here	73	2000
Where I'm Headed	83	2000

Marmalade, The		
Reflections Of My Life	P	1970

Maroon 5		
Woman	110	2004
Moves Like Jagger	170	2011
One More Night	57	2012
Animals	86	2014
This Summer's Gonna Hurt Like A Motherfucker	129	2015
Convince Me Otherwise	23	2021

Mars, Bruno		
Moonshine	76	2013
Die With A Smile	89	2024

Mars, Charlie		
Gather The Horses	92	2004

Marshall, Amanda		
Beautiful Goodbye	M	1995

Marshall, Jack		
Theme From The Munsters	T	1964

Marshall Hain (See also Eye To Eye; The Flying Lizards)		
Dancing In The City	27	1979

Marshmello		
Silence	87	2017

Martha & The Vandellas		
Dancing In The Street	P	1964

Martika		
Toy Soldiers	74	1989
Love... Thy Will Be Done	84	1991

Martin, Billie Ray		
Your Loving Arms	101	1998

Martin, Charlotte		
Stromata	76	2006

Martin, Dean		
That's Amore	P	1953
Sway	P	1954

Martin, John		
Don't You Worry Child	98	2012

Martin, Moon		
Rolene	55	1979

Martin, Ricky		
Be Careful (Cuidado Con Mi Corazón)	23	1999
Nobody Wants To Be Lonely	40	2001
Falta Amor	31	2020

Martin, Sam		
Lovers On The Sun	32	2014
Dangerous	10	2015

Martin, Tino		
Zij Weet Het	54	2019

Martinez, Melanie		
Soap	55	2016
Pity Party	89	2016

Marx, Richard		
Hazard	111	1992
Fool's Game	73	1997
Whatever We Started	21	2014
Beautiful Goodbye	16	2015

Mary Jane Girls (See also Rick James)		
In My House	72	1985

Mase		
If You Want Me	26	1999

Masekela, Hugh		
Grazing In The Grass	P	1968

Mason, Dave (See also Traffic)		
We Just Disagree	75	1977

Massey, Curt		
Petticoat Junction	T	1963

Massive Attack (See also Tricky)		
Safe From Harm	3	1991
Three	10	1995
Protection	51	1995
Teardrop	19	1998
What Your Soul Sings	81	2003

Mathis, Johnny		
Chances Are	P	1957
When Sunny Gets Blue	P	1957
It's Not For Me To Say	P	1957
Wild Is The Wind	P	1957
Gina	P	1962
Too Much, Too Little, Too Late (w/ Deniece Williams)	M	1978
The Last Time I Felt Like This (w/ Jane Olivor)	M	1979

Matsutoya, Yumi 松任谷 由実		
Sentimental Route 16 (Kanashimi No Route 16/哀しみのルート16)	M	2007

Matthews, Dave, Band		
What Would You Say	65	1995
The Best Of What's Around	97	1995

Matthews, Eric		
Fanfare	100	1996

Mauriat, Paul, & His Orchestra		
Love Is Blue	P	1968

Max, Ava		
The Motto	41	2021
Last Night On Earth	27	2023
Car Keys (Ayla)	1	2024

Maya, Edward, & Vika Jigulina		
Stereo Love	33	2011

Mayday		
Eternal Summer	M	2013

Mayer, John		
Heartbreak Warfare	125	2010
New Light	71	2018

McBride, Martina		
Good Bye	99	2000

McCall, C. W.		
Convoy	74	1976

McCartney, Jesse		
Feelin' You	114	2006

McCartney, Paul (& Wings) (See also Wings; The Beatles)		
Another Day	P	1971
Uncle Albert/Admiral Halsey (Paul & Linda McCartney)	P	1971
My Love (Paul McCartney & Wings)	P	1973
Live And Let Die (Paul McCartney & Wings)	P	1973
Jet (Paul McCartney & Wings)	P	1974
Band On The Run (Paul McCartney & Wings)	P	1974
Listen To What The Man Said (Paul McCartney & Wings)	P	1975
Coming Up (Live At Glasgow)/Coming Up (Paul McCartney & Wings)	30	1980
Où Est Le Soleil	M	1989

McCluskey, Angela (See also Télépopmusik)		
Tell Me Why	45	2010
In The Air	19	2011

McCombs, Cass		
Bum Bum Bum	17	2017

McCoy, Travie		
Higher	65	2010

Superbad (11:34)	92	2010
Yeah Yeah	1	2012

McCrae, George		
Rock Your Baby	P	1974

McCrane, Paul		
Dogs In The Yard	M	1980

McDonald, Michael (See also The Doobie Brothers)		
I Keep Forgettin' (Every Time You're Near)	71	1982
Good Friends	56	1986
Bittersweet	67	2024

McElderry, Joe		
Love Is War	8	2012

McEntire, Reba (Reba)		
I Wouldn't Wanna Be You	76	1994
Mary, Did You Know?	X	1999
Maggie Creek Road	61	2009
Storm In A Shot Glass	97	2019

McFadden, Brian		
Everybody's Someone	27	2007

McFerrin, Bobby		
Common Threads / Sweet In The Mornin'	43	1992

McGovern, Maureen		
The Morning After	P	1973

McGraw, Tim		
Angel Boy	108	2001

McGuinn, Clark & Hillman (See also the Byrds)		
Don't You Write Her Off	72	1979

MC Hammer		
Addams Groove	210	1991

McKee, Bonnie		
Riding Shotgun	35	2018
Lonely For You	6	2020

McKennitt, Loreena		
The Old Ways	10	1992
All Souls Night	15	1992
The Bonny Swans	52	1994
The Mummers' Dance	3	1998

McKenzie, Bob & Doug		
The Twelve Days Of Christmas	X	1981

McLachlan, Sarah		
Vox	11	1989
Out Of The Shadows	24	1989
Steaming	31	1990
Into The Fire	16	1992
Black	90	1992

Plenty	2	1994
Possession	3	1994
Fear	17	1994
Hold On	23	1994
Wait	44	1994
Elsewhere	56	1994
As The End Draws Near	46	1996
Sweet Surrender	5	1997
Building A Mystery	15	1997
Black & White	35	1997
Silence	1	1998
Adia	132	1998
Song For A Winter's Night	X	2002
Fallen	97	2003
Monsters	61	2014

McLaren, Malcolm

Madam Butterfly (Un Bel di Vedremo)	82	1985
Waltz Darling (w/ the Bootzilla Orchestra)	58	1990
Who The Hell Is Sonia Rykiel?	58	1995
About Her	96	2004

McLean, Don

American Pie	P	1971
Vincent (Starry, Starry Night)	P	1972

MC Lyte

Keep On, Keepin' On	65	1996

McMorrow, James Vincent

Planes In The Sky	90	2021

McPhee, Katharine

Keep Drivin'	88	2010

McRae, Tate

You	95	2021
greedy	111	2023

McTeague, Tricia

Miracle	17	2021
Guardian Angel	48	2021
What Have We Got	16	2023
Space	88	2023

McVie, Christine

In My World	84	2017

Meat Loaf

Paradise By The Dashboard Light: I. Paradise II. Let Me Sleep On It III. Praying For The End Of Time	76	1978

Meco

Star Wars Theme/Cantina Band	10	1977
Theme From Close Encounters	17	1978
Lapti Nek	M	1983

Medeiros, Glenn

Nothing's Gonna Change My Love For You	M	1987

Medina

First Time	60	2018

Meeky Rosie

Forever	72	2007

Meester, Leighton

Entitled	51	2015

M83

Kim & Jessie	52	2008
Go!	23	2016

Meissner, Stan

One Chance	91	1987

Mēl & Kim

Respectable	70	1987

Melanie C (See also Spice Girls)

Blame It On Me	72	2021

Mellencamp, John (John Cougar)

I Need A Lover (John Cougar)	53	1979
Ain't Even Done With The Night (John Cougar)	77	1981
Last Chance	85	1993

Melua, Katie

Blame It On The Moon	83	2004

Melvin, Harold, & The Blue Notes

The Love I Lost	P	1973

Men At Work

Down Under	16	1982
Who Can It Be Now?	56	1982
Overkill	66	1983
Be Good Johnny	93	1983

Mendes, Sérgio, & Brasil '66

Mas Que Nada	P	1966
The Look Of Love	P	1968
The Fool On The Hill	P	1968

Men Without Hats

The Safety Dance	39	1983
On Tuesday	50	1988

Menzel, Idina

I Stand	91	2008
Funny Kind Of Lonely	78	2023

Merchant, Natalie

Carnival	25	1995

Merchants Of Venus		
You Can't Fool That Girl	89	1991
Metheny, Pat, Group		
This Is Not America	5	1985
Métisse		
Boom Boom Ba	100	2000
Metric		
Gold Guns Girls	44	2009
Metro Boomin		
Borrowed Love	40	2019
Creepin'	65	2023
We Still Don't Trust You	26	2024
MFSB		
TSOP (The Sound Of Philadelphia) (w/ the Three Degrees)	P	1974
MGMT		
Electric Feel	122	2008
She Works Out Too Much	70	2018
M.I.A.		
Jimmy	60	2007
Give Me All Your Luvin'	81	2012
Michael, George (See also Wham!)		
Careless Whisper	7	1985
Father Figure	23	1988
Hand To Mouth / Monkey	36	1988
Jesus To A Child	85	1996
Flawless (Go To The City)	67	2004
This Is How (We Want To Get High)	28	2020
Michele, Chrisette		
Number One	31	2011
Snow	112	2013
Mickey & Sylvia		
Love Is Strange	P	1957
Midi Maxi & Efti		
Ragga Steady	16	1994
Midlake		
Head Home	85	2007
Acts Of Man	50	2010
The Old And The Young	25	2014
It's Going Down	28	2014
Provider/Provider Reprise	56	2014
Midler, Bette		
Do You Want To Dance?	P	1972
Boogie Woogie Bugle Boy	P	1973
The Rose	37	1980
My Mother's Eyes	22	1981

Moonlight Dancing	M	1990
Midnight Star		
No Parking (On The Dance Floor) / Freak-A-Zoid	231	1984
Midway State, The		
Atlantic	36	2011
Lightning	97	2011
Mighty Lemon Drops, The		
Where Do We Go From Heaven	50	1990
Mika		
Relax, Take It Easy	57	2007
Mike + The Mechanics (See also Genesis)		
Silent Running (On Dangerous Ground)	116	1986
Miles, John		
Highfly	101	1976
Miles, Robert		
Children	39	1996
Fable	63	1996
Everyday Life	56	1998
Freedom	69	1998
REACT	75	2023
Miles-Kingston, Paul		
Pie Jesu	14	1985
Milky Chance		
Synchronize	101	2023
Milla (Jovovich)		
Clock	81	1994
Miller, Steve, Band		
Quicksilver Girl	P	1968
The Joker	P	1973
Rock'n Me	3	1976
Take The Money And Run	78	1976
Space Intro/Fly Like An Eagle	42	1977
Swingtown	81	1977
Jet Airliner	87	1977
Abracadabra	186	1982
I Want To Make The World Turn Around	44	1987
Miller, Tor		
Carter & Cash	47	2020
Mills, Frank		
Music Box Dancer	96	1979
Milo Greene		
Runaway Kind	110	2020
Milsap, Ronnie		
Stranger In My House	M	1983

M

MinaCelentano		
Se Mi Ami Davvero	64	2022

Minaj, Nicki		
Give Me All Your Luvin'	81	2012
Ganja Burns	46	2018
Say So	103	2020
Last Time I Saw You	7	2024

Mindbenders, The (w/ Wayne Fontana)		
Game Of Love	P	1965

Ministry		
Revenge	119	1984
(Everyday Is) Halloween/All Day	66	1985

Minnelli, Liza		
Don't Drop Bombs	29	1989
If There Was Love	36	1990
I Want You Now	91	1990

Minogue, Dannii		
'Cos You're Beautiful	79	2014
100 Degrees	20	2016

Minogue, Kylie (Kylie)		
Surrender	M	1994
Confide In Me	M	1994
On A Night Like This	59	2000
Light Years	18	2001
Butterfly	74	2001
Can't Get You Out Of My Head	12	2002
Love Affair	17	2002
Come Into My World	98	2002
Slow	114	2003
Red Blooded Woman	69	2004
Promises	87	2004
Sensitized	30	2008
Speakerphone	41	2008
No More Rain	82	2008
Aphrodite	6	2010
Everything Is Beautiful	15	2010
Higher	65	2010
Get Outta My Way	71	2010
Timebomb	33	2012
Fine	16	2014
Million Miles	50	2014
Right Here, Right Now	58	2015
100 Degrees	20	2016
Raining Glitter	81	2018
Say Something	41	2020

	87	2020
Supernova	87	2020
A Second To Midnight	94	2021
Voices	5	2023
10 Out Of 10	48	2023
Tension	50	2023
Padam Padam	68	2023
My Oh My	43	2024
Someone For Me	80	2024

Miracles, The (See also Smokey Robinson)		
Shop Around	P	1960
Going To A Go-Go	P	1965
The Tracks Of My Tears	P	1965
More Love (Smokey Robinson & The Miracles)	P	1967
Love Machine (Part 1)	8	1976

Missing Persons		
Destination Unknown	39	1982
Words	55	1982

Mission, The (The Mission UK)		
Butterfly On A Wheel	47	1990

Mis-Teeq		
Scandalous	77	2004

Mr. Mister		
Broken Wings	64	1985
Kyrie	109	1986

Mr. Probz		
Waves	115	2014

Mr. Siro		
Càng Níu Giữ Càng Dễ Mất (The More You Hold, The More You Lose)	4	2019

Mitchell, Joni		
Big Yellow Taxi	P	1970
Woodstock	P	1970
You Turn Me On, I'm A Radio	P	1972
Help Me	P	1974
Free Man In Paris	P	1974
Good Friends	56	1986
Impossible Dreamer	64	1986
The Windfall (Everything For Nothing)	6	1991
Sex Kills	46	1994

Mitsou		
Les Naufragés	2	1999

Mizzy, Vic		
The Addams Family (Main Theme)	T	1964
Green Acres	T	1965

M

MK (Marc Kinchen)		
17	90	2018
MNEK		
Not Ashamed	47	2024
Moa, Anika		
Good In My Head	88	2002
Moby		
Honey / Natural Blues	92	1999
Porcelain	105	2000
Very	97	2005
Looking For My Name	96	2009
One Last Time	89	2020
Wild Flame	71	2024
Mocedades		
Eres Tú (Touch The Wind)	P	1974
Modern Archetypes		
Mussels	87	2011
Modern English		
I Melt With You	71	1983
Moist		
Machine Punch Through	80	1995
Mok, Karen 莫文蔚		
海上花 Flowers Of Shanghai: Theme Song	54	1998
Molchat Doma		
Черные Цветы (Chernye Cvety)	93	2024
Moloko		
Fun For Me	31	1998
Sing It Back	83	1999
The Time Is Now	76	2001
Familiar Feeling	53	2004
Monáe, Janelle		
Haute/Ooh La La/Lipstick Lover	52	2023
Money, Eddie		
Two Tickets To Paradise	42	1978
Baby Hold On	78	1978
Get A Move On	48	1979
Monica		
The Boy Is Mine	29	1998
Monkees, The		
(Theme From) The Monkees	P	1966
Last Train To Clarksville	P	1966
I'm A Believer/(I'm Not Your) Steppin' Stone	P	1966
Pleasant Valley Sunday	P	1967
Daydream Believer	P	1967

D. W. Washburn	P	1968
Mono		
Life In Mono	36	1998
Silicone	91	1998
Mono Mind (See also Roxette)		
Save Me A Place	16	2017
I Found My Soul At Marvingate	7	2018
Couldn't Believe My Luck	44	2019
Away Away Away/In Control	50	2019
Stranger On A Bus	60	2019
Best Way To Travel	77	2019
Monro, Matt		
From Russia With Love	P	1963
Born Free	P	1966
Monsoon (See also Sheila Chandra)		
Ever So Lonely	M	1983
MONSTA X 몬스타엑스		
Who Do U Love?	69	2021
Montana, French		
Unforgettable	9	2017
Who Do U Love?	69	2021
Montenegro, Hugo (& his orchestra)		
I Dream Of Jeannie (Jeannie) (Hugo Montenegro & Buddy Kaye)	P	1966
The Good, The Bad And The Ugly	P	1968
Montez, Chris		
Call Me	P	1966
Moodorama		
Mindless Moments	30	2000
Moodswings		
Together As One (Luminous)	97	1997
Moody Blues, The (See also Justin Hayward)		
Tuesday Afternoon (Forever Afternoon)	P	1968
The Story In Your Eyes	P	1971
Nights In White Satin	P	1972
Isn't Life Strange	P	1972
The Voice	32	1981
Blue World	163	1984
Moon Seven Times, The		
Miranda	86	1993
Moor, Andy		
Leave Your World Behind	99	2012
Moore, Mae		
Bohemia	82	1993
Pieces Of Clay	78	1994

Here	81	1995
Genuine	101	1995
Moore, Mandy		
In My Pocket	88	2001
In Real Life	103	2022
Moore, Tim		
Second Avenue	211	1978
Moos		
Au Nom De La Rose	93	1999
Morales, David		
How Would U Feel	44	2016
Morcheeba (See also Skye; Skye | Ross)		
Moog Island/The Music That We Hear (1998) (two versions)	37	1996
Never An Easy Way	59	1997
Fear And Love	16	1998
The Sea	50	1998
Let Me See	67	1998
Friction	77	1998
Shallow End	10	2000
Rome Wasn't Built In A Day	76	2000
Aqualung	27	2002
Otherwise	28	2002
Antidote	32	2005
Wonders Never Cease	64	2005
Enjoy The Ride	17	2008
Blue Chair	70	2008
Gained The World	88	2008
Even Though	34	2010
Face Of Danger	15	2013
Hypnotized	18	2014
Paris Sur Mer	40	2018
It's Summertime	100	2018
The Edge Of The World	49	2021
Morissette, Alanis		
You Learn	16	1995
You Oughta Know	20	1995
Hand In My Pocket	31	1995
One	60	1999
You Owe Me Nothing In Return	83	2002
Edge Of Evolution	73	2012
Morningwood		
Ride The Lights	52	2006
Moroder, Giorgio		
Chase	6	1979
(Theme From) Midnight Express	M	1979

I Do This For You	3	2015
Right Here, Right Now	58	2015
74 Is The New 24	65	2015
Lichtjahre	37	2020
Morricone, Ennio		
The Good, The Bad And The Ugly	P	1966
Le Marginal	M	1983
Gabriel's Oboe / The Mission	M	1986
Frantic	128	1988
Morris, Gary		
100% Chance Of Rain	163	1986
Plain Brown Wrapper	58	1987
Morris, Maren		
Kingdom Of One	64	2020
Morrison, Jim (See also The Doors)		
The Chant Movement	69	1991
Morrison, Mark		
Crazy (D-Influence Mix)	86	1997
Return Of The Mack	110	1997
Morrison, Van		
Brown Eyed Girl	P	1967
Moondance	P	1970
Morrissey (See also The Smiths)		
Suedehead	7	1988
Everyday Is Like Sunday	69	1988
November Spawned A Monster	7	1990
Tomorrow	22	1992
The More You Ignore Me, The Closer I Get	84	1994
MORTEN		
Make It To Heaven (Rework)	23	2020
Moss, Jessy		
Pick A Card	9	2003
Motels, The		
Only The Lonely	94	1982
Suddenly Last Summer	130	1983
Remember The Nights	75	1984
Shame	54	1985
Mott The Hoople		
All The Young Dudes	P	1972
Mounsey, Paul		
Stranger In A Strange Land	95	1996
Mousse T. vs. Hot 'n' Juicy		
Horny	62	1999
Moyet, Alison (See also Yazoo)		
Blow Wind Blow	8	1987
Sleep Like Breathing	81	1988

M

It Won't Be Long	58	1991
Never Too Late	40	1992
Getting Into Something	53	1994
Horizon Flame	1	2013
Remind Yourself	3	2013
Changeling	63	2013
Lover, Go	4	2017
I Germinate	81	2017
Mraz, Jason		
Miracle	82	2019
MS MR		
Hurricane	93	2013
Leave Me Alone	69	2015
M-22		
First Time	60	2018
Mui, Anita 梅艷芳		
Rouge (胭脂扣 Yin Ji Kau)	M	1987
Muldaur, Maria		
Midnight At The Oasis	P	1974
Mulu		
She Smiles/Filmstar	9	1998
Pussycat	97	1998
Mumba, Samantha		
Gotta Tell You	88	2000
MUNA		
After	39	2017
So Special	70	2017
Mura Masa		
Prada (i like it)	3	2022
Murphey, Michael Martin		
Wildfire	P	1975
Murphy, Brittany		
Faster Kill Pussycat	79	2006
Murphy, Eddie		
Party All The Time	96	1985
Murphy, Peter (See also Bauhaus)		
Indigo Eyes	78	1988
All Night Long	68	1989
A Strange Kind Of Love	19	1990
Cuts You Up	35	1990
Keep Me From Harm	9	1992
You're So Close	72	1992
The Sweetest Drop	77	1992
Sails Wave Goodbye	85	1995

Murphy, Walter, & The Big Apple Band		
A Fifth Of Beethoven	16	1976
Murray, Anne		
Snowbird	P	1970
Danny's Song	P	1973
Musgraves, Kacey		
High Horse	17	2018
All Is Found	18	2020
Justified	74	2021
If This Was A Movie..	19	2022
Cardinal	49	2024
Mvula, Laura		
You Work For Me	M	2015
Myers, Billie		
Tell Me	21	1998
My Indigo (Sharon Den Adel)		
Indian Summer	13	2018
Black Velvet Sun	37	2018
Where Is My Love	42	2018
My Indigo	50	2018
Myles, Alannah		
Black Velvet	100	1990
My Morning Jacket		
The Day Is Coming	81	2011

N

Nails, The		
88 Lines About 44 Women	M	1984
Naked And Famous, The		
Higher	65	2016
Naked Eyes		
Promises, Promises	40	1983
When The Lights Go Out	12	1984
Naranjo, Mónica		
Eva	82	2009
Nas		
Get To Know Me	41	2007
Nash, Johnny		
I Can See Clearly Now	P	1972
Nash, Leigh (See also Sixpence None The Richer; Fauxliage)		
Innocente	101	2001
Run For It	61	2003
Natalia Kills		
Zombie	99	2011

Naté, Ultra		
Free	197	1998
Desire	146	2001

National, The		
Oblivions	114	2019

Naughty Boy		
La La La	6	2014

Nazareth		
Love Hurts	48	1976

NdegéOcello, Me'Shell		
Leviticus: Faggot	58	1996

N'Dour, Youssou		
Shaking The Tree	79	1989
Diabaram	102	1991
No More	56	1992

Neighbourhood, The		
Cry Baby	92	2015

Neiked		
Sexual	47	2017

Nelly		
Gone	103	2011

Nelson, Phyllis		
I Like You	62	1986

Nemesis Rising		
Number One In Heaven	51	2007

Neon Trees		
Lessons In Love (All Day, All Night)	10	2012

N*E*R*D (See also Pharrell Williams)		
Provider (Zero 7 Mix)	116	2003

Nero, Peter		
Theme From "Summer Of '42"	P	1971

Nesbitt, Nina		
Sweet Dreams & Dynamite	90	2022

New Cars, The (See also The Cars)		
Warm	112	2006

New England		
Don't Ever Wanna Lose Ya	34	1979

New Kids On The Block (NKOTB)		
Bring Back The Time	73	2022

Newley, Anthony		
Talk To The Animals	P	1967

Newman, John		
Tribute	91	2014
Blame	101	2014
Give Me Your Love	57	2016

Newman, Randy		
Theme From "The Natural"	98	1984

Newman, Thomas		
Six Feet Under Theme	45	2002

New Order (See also Electronic)		
Blue Monday	38	1983
True Faith (The Morning Sun)	22	1987
Let's Go (Nothing For Me)	93	1995
Crystal	44	2001
Someone Like You	62	2002
Dracula's Castle	31	2005
Tutti Frutti	103	2015

New Pornographers, The		
Myriad Harbour	86	2007
High Ticket Attractions	71	2017

New Radicals		
Gotta Stay High	32	1999

New Riders Of The Purple Sage		
Till I Met You	M	1977
Llywelyn	M	1977

New Seekers, The (See also The Seekers)		
I'd Like To Teach The World To Sing (In Perfect Harmony)	P	1971

Newton, Juice		
Heart Of The Night	57	1983

Newton-John, Olivia		
If Not For You	P	1971
I Honestly Love You	P	1974
Fly Away	P	1975
Have You Never Been Mellow	P	1975
Summer Nights	30	1978
Deeper Than The Night	81	1979
A Little More Love	115	1979
Magic	24	1980
Suddenly	95	1980
Xanadu	141	1980
Physical	86	1981
Twist Of Fate	63	1983
Soul Kiss	M	1985

New Vaudeville Band, The		
Winchester Cathedral	P	1966

New York City		
I'm Doin' Fine Now	P	1973

Ne-Yo		
The Best	39	2010

Nguyễn Trọng Tài x San Ji x Double X		
Hongkong1	92	2019
Nicholas, Grant		
Broken	20	2005
Nickelback		
Tidal Wave	117	2022
Nicks, Stevie (See also Fleetwood Mac)		
Whenever I Call You "Friend"	108	1978
Stop Draggin' My Heart Around/Kind Of Woman	36	1981
Edge Of Seventeen (Just Like The White Winged Dove)	92	1982
Stand Back	46	1983
If Anyone Falls	89	1983
Nightbird	71	1984
Trouble In Shangri-La	91	2001
The Lighthouse	124	2024
NICKTHEREAL 周湯豪		
什麼都不必說– (2022 Remix) (Don't Have To Say A Thing)	47	2022
Nico & Vinz		
I Wanna Know	93	2016
Nicola (Alexandru)		
Don't Break My Heart	87	2005
Nightingale, Maxine		
Right Back Where We Started From	29	1976
Night VI, The		
Thinking Of You	2	2014
Niki & The Dove		
DJ, Ease My Mind	88	2012
Nilsson		
Without Her	P	1967
Everybody's Talkin'	P	1968
Coconut	P	1971
Without You	P	1971
Me And My Arrow	P	1971
Jump Into The Fire	P	1971
Spaceman	P	1972
You're Breakin' My Heart	P	1972
Nine Inch Nails		
Closer	89	1994
1975, The		
Somebody Else	38	2016
Bagsy Not In Net	68	2020
98°		
Dizzy	93	2000

No Part Of You	66	2013
9 Ways To Sunday		
The Means Becomes The End	18	1991
Nirvana		
Smells Like Teen Spirit	85	1991
Come As You Are	134	1992
Lithium	181	1992
About A Girl	105	1994
Nneka		
Heartbeat	101	2010
No Doubt (See also Gwen Stefani)		
Don't Speak	25	1996
Making Out	30	2002
It's My Life	67	2003
Noel (Pagan)		
Silent Morning	84	1987
No Guidnce		
Is It A Crime?	97	2023
Nomad		
With You	42	2000
Nomi, Klaus		
Total Eclipse	M	1981
Wasting My Time	M	1981
Normani		
Dancing With A Stranger	5	2019
Northern Light		
Minnesota	P	1975
Northern State		
Better Already / Sucka Mofo	95	2007
Nothing But Thieves		
Something On My Mind	3	2023
Nova, Heather		
Not Only Human	49	1999
I'm Alive	85	1999
Love Will Find You	55	2001
*NSYNC (See also Justin Timberlake; JC Chasez)		
I Want You Back	113	1998
Bye Bye Bye	81	2000
Bringin' Da Noise	84	2000
Numan, Gary (+ Tubeway Army)		
Are 'Friends' Electric? (+ Tubeway Army)	2	1979
Cars	20	1980
Complex	26	1980
I Die: You Die	40	1981
Stormtrooper In Drag (w/ Paul Gardiner)	M	1981

Night Talk	87	1982
Change Your Mind	29	1985
Your Fascination	71	1986
Strange Charm	5	1987
My Breathing	23	1987
New Thing From London Town	67	1987
Voix	22	1989
Respect	36	1989
The Angel Wars/Absolution	43	1998
Dominion Day	48	1998
Dead Heaven	78	1998
Angels	75	2004
Here For You	64	2016
Swansea	15	2017
Nunn, Terri (See also Berlin)		
89 Lines	73	1993
Nu Shooz		
I Can't Wait	96	1986
Nymphia Wind		
Queen Of Wind	137	2024
Nzau, Sofiya		
Mwaki	110	2024

O

Oakenfold (Paul Oakenfold) (See also Grace)		
Starry Eyed Surprise (w/ Shifty Shellshock)	M	2002
The Way I Feel	71	2006
Faster Kill Pussycat	79	2006
Celebration	108	2009
Pray For Me (Paul Oakenfold)	1	2022
Hypnotic (Paul Oakenfold)	36	2022
Oasis		
Wonderwall	37	1995
Ocean, Frank		
No Church In The Wild	93	2011
Oceania		
Kotahitanga (Union)	63	2000
Pukaea (The Trumpet)	74	2000
OceanLab		
On A Good Day	52	2009
O'Connell, Finneas (FINNEAS)		
Vengeance	79	2022
O'Connor, Sinéad (Shuhada' Sadaqat)		
Heroine (Theme From "Captive")	28	1987
Feel So Different	20	1990

Nothing Compares 2 U	49	1990
Visions Of You	24	1992
Success Has Made A Failure Of Our Home	88	1992
Germaine/Fire On Babylon	11	1994
You Made Me The Thief Of Your Heart	20	1994
'Til I Whisper U Something	62	2001
Tears From The Moon	29	2003
Guide Me God	58	2003
What Your Soul Sings	81	2003
October Project (See also Mary Fahl)		
Take Me As I Am	13	1994
Bury My Lovely	36	1994
Be My Hero	54	1994
Wall Of Silence	74	1994
Sunday Morning Yellow Sky	13	1995
Something More Than This	46	1995
O'Day, Alan		
Undercover Angel	15	1977
ODESZA		
A Moment Apart	88	2018
The Last Goodbye	99	2022
O'Donis, Colby		
Just Dance	77	2008
Odyssey		
Native New Yorker	49	1978
Ofenbach		
Be Mine	66	2017
Offa Rex		
The Queen Of Hearts	76	2017
Off Broadway usa		
Stay In Time	21	1980
Of Monsters And Men		
Human	36	2015
Vulture, Vulture	53	2019
O'Hearn, Patrick		
Sky Juice	136	1987
Rain Maker	M	1987
Reunion	20	1988
Glory For Tomorrow	M	1988
The Stroll	75	1989
Chattahoochee Field Day	12	1990
Devils Lake	47	1991
Ohio Players		
Fire	P	1974
Sweet Sticky Thing	P	1975
Love Rollercoaster	38	1976

Oh Land		
Sun Of A Gun	86	2011
Renaissance Girls	99	2014
070 Shake		
Come Back Home	18	2022
Frozen	58	2022
Escapism	59	2023
Ohta, Herb		
Song For Anna (Chanson D'Anna)	P	1974
Oh Wonder		
All We Do	55	2015
O'Jays, The		
Back Stabbers	P	1972
For The Love Of Money	P	1974
I Love Music	120	1976
Oladokun, Joy		
i see america	13	2023
Sorry Isn't Good Enough	39	2023
Spotlight	79	2023
Old Dominion		
Some Horses	73	2024
Oldfield, Mike		
Tubular Bells / Tubular Bells Part One	P	1973
In Dulci Jubilo	X	1975
I'm Guilty	M	1979
Sheba	M	1980
Family Man	2	1982
Five Miles Out	11	1982
Talk About Your Life	3	1984
Foreign Affair	11	1984
In High Places	24	1984
To France	37	1984
Jungle Gardenia	M	1984
Pran's Theme / Good News	M	1984
Islands	112	1987
North Point	1	1988
The Time Has Come	55	1988
Earth Moving	9	1990
Innocent	64	1990
Altered State/Maya Gold	80	1993
Oceania/Only Time Will Tell	71	1996
Crystal Clear	83	1996
In The Beginning/Let There Be Light	99	1996
The Voyager	69	1997
Man In The Rain	84	1998

The Source Of Secrets	25	1999
Muse / Cochise	30	1999
Enigmatism	25	2000
The Doge's Palace	34	2000
Mastermind	47	2000
To Be Free	71	2002
Surfing	65	2005
Closer	24	2013
Chariots	84	2014
Olive		
You're Not Alone	128	1997
Smile	5	2000
Push	75	2000
Oliver		
Good Morning Starshine	P	1969
Olivor, Jane		
The Last Time I Felt Like This (w/ Johnny Mathis)	M	1979
OMC		
On The Run	65	1998
Omotayo, Adeleye		
Silent Running	70	2023
Ondar		
Tuva Groove	7	1999
O'Neal, Alexander		
Saturday Love	57	1986
Criticize	59	1987
One Direction (See also Harry Styles; Niall Horan; Liam Payne; ZAYN; Louis Tomlinson)		
What A Feeling	73	2015
1 Giant Leap (See also Blur; Gorillaz; Faithless)		
My Culture	65	2003
OneRepublic (See also Ryan Tedder)		
Apologize	39	2007
A.I.	5	2017
Onetwo (See also Claudia Brücken; Propaganda; Orchestral Manoeuvres In The Dark)		
Home (Tonight)	74	2007
One 2 Many		
Downtown	101	1989
In My Heart	81	1990
Ono, Yoko (See also John Lennon)		
Walking On Thin Ice	M	1981
Opus III (See also Kirsty Hawkshaw)		
It's A Fine Day	87	1992
When You Made The Mountain	93	1994

Dreaming Of Now	42	1995
Ora, Rita		
R.I.P. / Roc The Life	137	2014
Orbison, Roy		
Crying	P	1961
Dream Baby (How Long Must I Dream)	P	1962
Blue Bayou	P	1963
She's A Mystery To Me	128	1989
Orbit, William		
Dice	2	2004
Spiral	1	2006
Orbital		
The Box	81	1996
Hummingbirds	21	2002
Orchestral Manoeuvres In The Dark (OMD) (See also Onetwo)		
Almost	3	1982
Souvenir	24	1982
Enola Gay / Stanlow	29	1982
Joan Of Arc (Maid Of Orleans)	41	1982
Julia's Song	M	1982
Genetic Engineering	3	1983
Talking Loud And Clear	41	1984
Locomotion	46	1984
Secret	41	1985
So In Love	53	1985
Never Turn Away	79	1985
Women III	18	1986
(Forever) Live And Die	19	1986
La Femme Accident	86	1986
Apollo XI	13	1991
Very Close To Far Away	85	2000
Save Me	11	2010
Pulse	30	2011
The Future, The Past, And Forever After	90	2011
Final Song	67	2013
Art Eats Art	42	2017
Anthropocene	53	2023
Organized Noize		
Set It Off	33	1996
Orhan, Mahmut		
Forgive Me	30	2022
Orlando, Tony, & Dawn / Dawn		
Candida (Dawn)	P	1970
Knock Three Times (Dawn)	P	1970
Summer Sand (Dawn)	P	1970
Say, Has Anybody Seen My Sweet Gypsy Rose (Dawn f/ Tony Orlando)	P	1973
Orleans		
Dance With Me	P	1975
Still The One	41	1976
Orr, Benjamin (See also The Cars)		
Stay The Night	40	1987
Orrall, Robert Ellis		
I Couldn't Say No	56	1983
Orton, Beth (See also Finlay Quaye)		
Stars All Seem To Weep	64	1999
Stolen Car	94	1999
Anywhere	52	2002
Dice	2	2004
Orzabal, Roland (See also Tears For Fears)		
Bullets For Brains	10	2001
Low Life	17	2001
Ticket To The World	48	2001
Snowdrop	70	2002
Hypnoculture	78	2002
Osborne, Jeffrey		
Love Power	113	1987
Osborne, Joan		
Crazy Baby	8	1995
St. Teresa	12	1995
Ladder	40	1995
One Of Us	64	1995
Osbourne, Kelly		
One Word (Chris Cox Remix)	1	2005
O'Sullivan, Gilbert		
Alone Again (Naturally)	P	1972
Clair	P	1972
Get Down	P	1973
Other Ones, The		
Holiday	77	1987
Otis, Shuggie		
Aht Uh Mi Hed	26	2001
O-Town		
Liquid Dreams	249	2000
Otyken		
Altay	91	2024
Our Daughter's Wedding		
Target For Life	30	1982
Auto Music	41	1983

Outfield, The		
Voices Of Babylon	83	1989

Outkast		
Ms. Jackson	104	2001

Over The Rhine		
Jacksie	4	1993
I've Been Slipping	28	1993
Rhapsodie	62	1993
Within Without	25	1994
Give Me Strength	8	2001
The World Can Wait	75	2001

Owl City (Adam Young)		
Alive	27	2012

Ozark Mountain Daredevils		
Jackie Blue	P	1975

Ozcan, Ummet		
Altay	91	2024

Özen, Gökhan		
Benim İçin N'Apadın	40	2005

O-Zone		
Dragostea Din Tei (Numa Numa / Ma Ya Hi)	76	2005

Ozuna		
Stars	32	2023

P

Pablo Cruise		
A Place In The Sun	88	1977
Whatcha Gonna Do?	106	1977
Don't Want To Live Without It	72	1978

Pachelbel, Johann		
Canon In D Major (Ordinary People Theme) (adapted by Marvin Hamlisch)	M	1980

Padilla, José		
Something	75	2002

Page, Elaine		
I Know Him So Well	40	1985

Page, Morgan		
The Longest Road / (deadmau5 Vocal Remix)	1	2008
Fight For You	2	2010
Traces Remain	3	2010
In The Dark	9	2010
Believe / Strange Condition	30	2010
Tell Me Why	45	2010
In The Air	19	2011
Video	15	2012
Carry Me	26	2012
Body Work	60	2012
The Actor	87	2012
Against The World	36	2014
Safe Till Tomorrow	12	2015
Trigger	21	2015
Open Heart	33	2015
Wounded	10	2022
Come Right Back	45	2024

Paige, Jennifer		
Crush	42	1998

Palmer, Robert		
I Didn't Mean To Turn You On	74	1986
Addicted To Love	100	1986
Early In The Morning	91	1989

Paloalto		
The World Outside	32	2004

Paper Lace		
The Night Chicago Died	P	1974

Parachute Club, The		
Innuendo	M	1984

PARIS (See PVRIS)		

Paris Sisters, The		
I Love How You Love Me	P	1961

Parker, Kevin		
Summer Breaking/Daffodils	18	2015

Parks, Arlo		
Too Good	107	2021

Parliament		
Flash Light	4	1978

Parsons, Alan (Alan Parsons Project, 1976-1987) (See also Asia; Keats; Andrew Powell)		
(The System Of) Doctor Tarr And Professor Fether	M	1976
I Wouldn't Want To Be Like You	21	1977
Breakdown	M	1977
Voyager/What Goes Up...	40	1978
Damned If I Do	32	1979
Time	16	1981
Games People Play	33	1981
The Turn Of A Friendly Card (Part One) / (Part Two)	M	1981
Sirius/Eye In The Sky	18	1982
Old And Wise	61	1983
Psychobabble	91	1983
You Don't Believe	56	1984

Prime Time	82	1984
Days Are Numbers (The Traveller)	32	1985
Light Of The World	72	1986
Standing On Higher Ground / Inside Looking Out	75	1987
La Sagrada Familia	106	1987
Mr Time	91	1993
Too Close To The Sun	35	1996
Press Rewind	56	1999
The Time Machine (Part 1)/(Part 2)	31	2000
Out Of The Blue	72	2000
We Play The Game	29	2004
One Note Symphony	28	2019
Miracle	82	2019
Halos	81	2022
Parton, Dolly		
Jolene / (Destructo Remix, 2021)	P	1974
The Bargain Store	P	1975
9 To 5	57	1981
Hard Candy Christmas	X	1982
Potential New Boyfriend	127	1983
9 To 5 vs. Eple	M	2003
God Only Knows	11	2021
Bittersweet	67	2024
Partridge Family, The		
The Partridge Family (Come On Get Happy)	T	1970
I Think I Love You	P	1970
PARTYNEXTDOOR		
East Liberty	79	2015
Paul, Billy		
Me And Mrs. Jones	P	1972
Pausini, Laura		
Volveré Junto A Ti	87	2002
Io Sí (Seen)	60	2021
Paxton, Larry		
Cowboy's Dream/All The Pretty Horses (Medley)	82	2001
Payne, Freda		
Band Of Gold	P	1970
Payne, Liam (See also One Direction)		
Tell Your Friends	96	2020
Payola$		
Eyes Of A Stranger	35	1983
Peaches & Herb		
Shake Your Groove Thing	110	1979

Pearce, Carly		
Hummingbird	138	2024
Pebbles		
Mercedes Boy	65	1988
Girlfriend	114	1988
Peniston, CeCe		
Finally	179	1992
People In Planes		
If You Talk Too Much (My Head Will Explode)	50	2006
Perretta, Julian		
On The Line	47	2018
Substitution	90	2023
Perry, Brendan (See also Dead Can Dance)		
Wintersun	126	2011
Perry, Jarell		
Win	15	2014
First Time	66	2014
Perry, Katy		
Teenage Dream	62	2010
Circle The Drain	26	2011
Walking On Air	53	2013
Spiritual	13	2014
Rise	35	2016
Chained To The Rhythm	14	2017
Déjà Vu	49	2017
Bigger Than Me	77	2017
Witness	95	2017
Feels	115	2017
365	38	2019
Perry, Mike		
The Ocean	82	2016
Perry, Steve (See also Journey)		
Foolish Heart	81	1985
Peter And Gordon		
A World Without Love	P	1964
Peter Bjorn And John		
Satellite	11	2022
Peter, Paul & Mary (See also Paul Stookey)		
Lemon Tree	P	1962
If I Had A Hammer (The Hammer Song)	P	1962
I Dig Rock And Roll Music	P	1967
Leaving On A Jet Plane	P	1969
Petit Biscuit		
Sunset Lover	98	2020

Petras, Kim

Claws	62	2023

Pet Shop Boys (See also Neil Tennant)

West End Girls	123	1984
Love Comes Quickly	8	1986
Opportunities (Let's Make Lots Of Money)	48	1986
What Have I Done To Deserve This?	10	1987
It's A Sin	55	1987
King's Cross	3	1988
Rent	8	1988
Heart	47	1988
I'm Not Scared	8	1989
It's Alright	97	1989
This Must Be The Place I Waited Years To Leave	10	1991
Being Boring	25	1991
How Can You Expect To Be Taken Seriously?	86	1991
Can You Forgive Her?	27	1993
Dreaming Of The Queen	52	1993
Absolutely Fabulous	66	1994
Decadence	66	1995
To Step Aside	10	1996
Before	36	1996
Discoteca/Single	41	1996
Happiness Is An Option	24	1999
Vampires	62	2000
Closer To Heaven	68	2000
Here	41	2002
Break 4 Love	94	2002
Miracles	4	2004
Numb	15	2006
I'm With Stupid	22	2006
Twentieth Century	57	2006
Integral	67	2006
Love Etc.	13	2009
More Than A Dream	58	2009
The Way It Used To Be	84	2009
Together	60	2011
A Face Like That	44	2012
Leaving	65	2012
Hell	86	2013
Brick England	33	2016
Burn	50	2016
In Bits	84	2016

Dreamland	75	2020
Think Of A Number (Pet Shop Boys Magic Eye 12" remix)	6	2023
Feel	61	2024

Petty, Tom, And The Heartbreakers

Breakdown	28	1978
Refugee	81	1980
Don't Do Me Like That	90	1980
Stop Draggin' My Heart Around	36	1981
A Woman In Love (It's Not Me)	41	1981
Don't Come Around Here No More	62	1985
A Face In The Crowd (Tom Petty)	94	1990

Phair, Liz

Never Said	91	1994
Whip-Smart	92	1995

Phan Mạnh Quỳnh

Người Khác (Others)	19	2019
Miền Gian Khổ (Endless Hardships) / Nhạt (Light)	49	2022

Phantogram

Fall In Love	95	2014

Phantom Planet

Turn Smile Shift Repeat	31	2002

Phantoms

Just A Feeling	3	2017

Phillips, Sam

Holding On To The Earth	13	1990
Tripping Over Gravity	7	1991
Now I Can't Find The Door	90	1991
Raised On Promises	18	1992
Standing Still	63	1992
Same Changes	14	1994
Same Rain	32	1994
Slapstick Heart	2	1996
Help Yourself	18	1996
Entertainmen	30	1996

Phish

Bouncing Around The Room	43	1995

Phoenix

Everything Is Everything	17	2004
(You Can't Blame It On) Anybody/ Congratulations	71	2005
Ti Amo	99	2017
Alpha Zulu	6	2022

Pickett, Bobby "Boris", And The Cryptkickers

Monster Mash	P	1962

Pickett, Wilson		
In The Midnight Hour	P	1965
Land Of 1000 Dances	P	1966
Pierces, The		
Boring	10	2007
You'll Be Mine	13	2011
Pigalle, Anne		
Hé! Stranger	105	1986
Pilgrimage		
Campus Stella/Field Of Stars	10	1998
Pilgrimage	24	1998
Dark Skies	51	1998
Pilot (See also Keats)		
Magic	P	1974
Pinback		
Fortress	125	2005
P!NK		
(Hey Why) Miss You Sometimes	73	2019
Pink('s), Ariel, Haunted Graffiti		
Can't Hear My Eyes	31	2010
Pink Floyd		
Money	P	1973
Time	P	1973
Us And Them	P	1974
Wish You Were Here	P	1975
Another Brick In The Wall Part II	10	1980
Run Like Hell/Don't Leave Me Now	63	1980
Pink Martini		
Let's Never Stop Falling In Love / Lilly	98	2005
Pitbull		
DJ Got Us Fallin' In Love	42	2010
On The Floor	145	2011
We Are Strong	102	2017
Pitney, Gene		
Town Without Pity	P	1961
Placebo		
Scene Of The Crime	120	2013
Plastic Toy		
Try Me	70	2020
Platinum Weird (See also David A. Stewart; Dave Stewart & The Spiritual Cowboys; Eurythmics)		
Will You Be Around	78	2006
Platt, Ben		
Chasing You	81	2021
Platten, Rachel		
Unfolding	66	2024

Platters, The		
Smoke Gets In Your Eyes	P	1958
Player		
Baby Come Back	32	1978
Prisoner Of Your Love	101	1978
PlayRadioPlay! (Analog Rebellion)		
Forgiveness, The Enviable Trait	88	2009
Pluma, Peso		
Igual Que Un Ángel	33	2024
Plumb		
Damaged	24	2000
Stranded	71	2000
P.M. Dawn		
I'd Die Without You	118	1993
PNAU (See also Empire Of The Sun)		
Karmatron	3	2012
Good Morning To The Night	28	2012
Nothing In The World	15	2018
In My Head	25	2018
Go Bang	32	2018
Stars	32	2023
Poco (See also Buffalo Springfield; Loggins & Messina; Eagles)		
Indian Summer	11	1977
Crazy Love	52	1979
Heart Of The Night	95	1979
Poe		
Angry Johnny	40	1996
Trigger Happy Jack (Drive By A Go-Go)	104	1996
Exploration B/Haunted	83	2001
Damascus/Center Of The Sun	3	2002
Make A Wish	38	2003
Pointer Sisters		
Yes We Can Can	P	1973
How Long (Betcha Got A Chick On The Side)	P	1975
Happiness	94	1979
He's So Shy	105	1980
Jump (For My Love) / Automatic / I Need You	95	1984
Polachek, Caroline (See also Chairlift)		
You And I	15	2011
Sirens	104	2023
Butterfly Net	15	2024
Fly To You	42	2024

Poliça		
Dark Star	4	2012
Form	32	2012
Fist Teeth Money	77	2012
Chain My Name	13	2013
Spilling Lines	46	2014
Lime Habit	48	2016
Agree	38	2018
Alive	38	2022

Police, The (See also Sting)		
Message In A Bottle	21	1979
Roxanne	26	1979
Walking On The Moon	42	1980
Every Little Thing She Does Is Magic	7	1981
Don't Stand So Close To Me	14	1981
De Do Do Do, De Da Da Da	17	1981
Secret Journey / Invisible Sun	38	1982
Spirits In The Material World	44	1982
Every Breath You Take	17	1983
King Of Pain	26	1983
Synchronicity II	96	1983
Wrapped Around Your Finger	29	1984

PollyAnna		
Nobody	57	2023

Pontes, Dulce		
Ondeia (Água)	32	2001

Pop, Iggy		
Daw Da Hiya	86	1992

Pop Etc (POP ETC)		
Keep It For Your Own	55	2012

Pop Will Eat Itself		
X Y & Zee	140	1991

Porter, Billy		
Not Ashamed	47	2024

Portishead (See also Beth Gibbons)		
Sour Times (Nobody Loves Me)	5	1994
Roads	1	1995
Only You	72	1997

Portnoy, Gary		
Where Everybody Knows Your Name (The Theme From "Cheers")	82	1983

Posies, The (See also Jon Auer)		
It's Great To Be Here Again!	56	2005
Conversations	89	2005

Post, Mike		
The Rockford Files	P	1975
The Theme From Hill Street Blues	106	1981
Law & Order / "dun dun"	T	1990

Post Malone		
Otherside	107	2018
Circles	46	2019

Postal Service, The (See also Death Cab For Cutie; Rilo Kiley)		
The District Sleeps Alone Tonight	109	2004

Potter, Grace		
Hot To The Touch	95	2015

Powell, Andrew (See also Alan Parsons Project)		
Ladyhawke (Main Title)	M	1985

Praise (See also Miriam Stockley)		
Easy Way Out	1	1993
Chinatown	10	1993
Brand New Day	69	1993
So Cold	81	1993

Pray For Rain		
Chinese Choppers / Off The Boat / Burning Room / Taxi To Heaven (selections from "Sid And Nancy")	M	1986

Prefab Sprout		
Bonny / Goodbye Lucille #1	34	1986
When Love Breaks Down	93	1986
Knock On Wood	63	1989
Machine Gun Ibiza	5	1990
Doo-Wop In Harlem	22	1991
Scarlet Nights	55	1991

Presets, The		
This Boy's In Love	73	2009

Presley, Elvis		
Blue Christmas	X	1957
It's Now Or Never	P	1960
Can't Help Falling In Love	P	1961
Viva Las Vegas	P	1964
Go East, Young Man	P	1965
So Close, Yet So Far (From Paradise)	P	1965
A Little Less Conversation / (Elvis VS JXL Remix, 2002)	P	1968
In The Ghetto	P	1969
Suspicious Minds	P	1969
Kentucky Rain	P	1970

Presley, Lisa Marie		
S.O.B.	104	2003

You Ain't Seen Nothin' Yet	56	2012

Preston, Billy

Outa-Space	P	1972
Will It Go Round In Circles	P	1973
Nothing From Nothing	P	1973
With You I'm Born Again	7	1980

Preston, Robert

Gary, Indiana	P	1962
Seventy Six Trombones	P	1962

Pretenders, The

Brass In Pocket (I'm Special)	15	1980
Talk Of The Town	94	1981
Back On The Chain Gang/My City Was Gone	101	1983
2000 Miles	X	1983
Show Me	116	1984
Hymn To Her	122	1987
If There Was A Man	94	1988
Born For A Purpose	1	1991

Price, Kate

The Labyrinth	100	1995

Pride, Charley

Kiss An Angel Good Mornin'	P	1971

Priest, Maxi

Close To You	45	1990

Prince (The Artist Formerly Known As Prince)

Little Red Corvette	90	1983
When Doves Cry (with The Revolution)	21	1984
I Would Die 4 U (with The Revolution)	141	1984
Take Me With U	74	1985
Pop Life (with The Revolution)	89	1985
Raspberry Beret/She's Always In My Hair (with The Revolution)	102	1985
Mountains (with The Revolution)	91	1986
Sign '☮' The Times	13	1987
U Got The Look	85	1987
Anna Stesia	90	1989
Thieves In The Temple	118	1990

Prince Royce

Te Perdiste Mi Amor	106	2013

Princess

Say I'm Your No. 1	11	1985

Propaganda (See also Claudia Brücken; Onetwo)

Duel	38	1985
ρ – Machinery (p:Machinery)	94	1986

Your Wildlife	11	1990
Vicious Circle	61	1990

Propellerheads

History Repeating	50	1999

Prophet Omega

An Area Big Enough To Do It In	30	2004

Pru

Aaroma Of A Man	29	2001

Prydz, Eric

Generate	59	2015

Psychedelic Furs, The (See also Love Spit Love)

Love My Way	M	1983
The Ghost In You/Heartbeat	93	1984
Heaven	100	1984
There's A World	31	1991
Don't Be A Girl	64	1991

Public Service Broadcasting

E.V.A. / The Race For Space	56	2016

Puckett, Gary, And The Union Gap

Woman, Woman	P	1967
Lady Willpower	P	1968

Pure Prairie League

Amie	P	1975

Purple Disco Machine

Hypnotized	48	2020
In The Dark	9	2022
About Damn Time (Purple Disco Machine Remix)	95	2022
Something On My Mind	3	2023
Paradise	51	2023
Substitution	90	2023

Pussycat Dolls, The (See also Nicole Scherzinger)

Don't Cha	113	2005
Beep (f/ will.i.am)	M	2006
Jai Ho! (You Are My Destiny) (f/ Nicole Scherzinger)	119	2008

Puth, Charlie

Attention	51	2017
Done For Me	76	2018
I Hope	99	2020

PVRIS (PARIS)

Wish You Well	13	2021
Anywhere But Here/Headlights	4	2023

Q

Q

Dancin' Man	48	1977

Q-Feel

Dancing In Heaven (Orbital Be-Bop)	192	1983

Qntal

Ecce Gratum (Club Mix)	94	2005

Quarterflash

Harden My Heart	31	1982
Take Me To Heart	87	1983

Quaye, Finley

Dice	2	2004

Queen

Killer Queen	P	1975
You're My Best Friend	30	1976
Bohemian Rhapsody	58	1976
Somebody To Love	101	1977
We Will Rock You/We Are The Champions	91	1978
Bicycle Race/Fat Bottomed Girls	94	1978
Another One Bites The Dust	19	1980
Crazy Little Thing Called Love	111	1980
Flash (Flash's Theme)	M	1981
Under Pressure	27	1982

Queen Latifah

Set It Off	33	1996
Cue The Rain	119	2009

? And The Mysterians

96 Tears	P	1966

R

Rabbitt, Eddie

Suspicions	137	1979
You And I	151	1983

Radio Dept., The

Swedish Guns	41	2017

Radiohead

Everything In Its Right Place	136	2001

Raf

Wave	72	2024

Rafferty, Gerry (See also Stealers Wheel)

Right Down The Line	34	1978
Baker Street	90	1978
Home And Dry	31	1979
Get It Right Next Time	47	1979

Rahman, A. R.

Jai Ho / Jai Ho! (You Are My Destiny)	119	2008

Raichel, The Idan, Project

Bo'ee (Come With Me)	70	2007

Raiders, The (Paul Revere & The Raiders) (See also Mark Lindsay)

Indian Reservation (The Lament Of The Cherokee Reservation Indian)	P	1971

Railway Children, The

Every Beat Of The Heart	81	1991

Raise The Dragon

The Blue Hour	121	1984

Raitt, Bonnie

You're Gonna Get What's Coming	54	1979
Luck Of The Draw	132	1991

Ram Jam

Black Betty	97	1977

Raman, Susheela

What Silence Said	89	2006

Rare Bird

Passing Through	P	1974

Rare Earth

I Know I'm Losing You	P	1970
I Just Want To Celebrate	P	1971
Warm Ride	74	1978

Raspberries, The (See also Eric Carmen)

Go All The Way	P	1972

Rauhofer, Peter

Break 4 Love	94	2002

Ravenscroft, Thurl

You're A Mean One, Mr. Grinch	X	1966

Raveonettes, The

Heart Of Stone	63	2010
Observations	53	2012

Ray, Don

Got To Have Loving	19	1978

Ray, Jimmy

Are You Jimmy Ray?	81	1998

Raydio (Ray Parker, Jr.)

Jack And Jill	54	1978
You Can't Change That	85	1979

RAYE

You Don't Know Me	22	2017
Make It To Heaven (Rework)	23	2020
Regardless	20	2021
Natalie Don't	42	2021

Prada	23	2023
Escapism	59	2023
Black Mascara	84	2023
Rayne, Blake		
Your Love's Keepin' Me Tonight	55	2014
Rea, Chris		
Fool (If You Think It's Over)	84	1978
I Can Hear Your Heartbeat	22	1984
All Summer Long	27	1985
On The Beach	41	1989
Looking For The Summer	171	1991
Reader, Eddi		
Nobody Lives Without Love	49	1996
Ready For The World		
Love You Down	27	1987
Ready Set, The		
First	19	2016
Reagan, Lisa		
À L'infini (Remix)	44	2008
Real Estate		
You Are Here	100	2024
Real Life		
Send Me An Angel / Send Me An Angel '89	76	1984
Real McCoy		
Another Night	89	1995
Rebo, Max, Band		
Lapti Nek (also version by Meco)	M	1983
Redbone		
Come And Get Your Love	P	1974
Redding, Otis		
(Sittin' On) The Dock Of The Bay	P	1968
Reddy, Helen		
I Am Woman	P	1972
Peaceful	P	1973
Leave Me Alone (Ruby Red Dress)	P	1973
Angie Baby	P	1974
Ain't No Way To Treat A Lady	P	1975
Emotion	P	1975
Red Hot Chili Peppers		
Breaking The Girl	85	1992
Soul To Squeeze	95	1993
My Friends	72	1995
Californication	68	1999
The Getaway	78	2016

Rednex		
Cotton Eye Joe	67	1995
Red Rider		
Lunatic Fringe	M	1981
Red Rockers		
China	97	1983
Reed, Lou		
Walk On The Wild Side	P	1973
Reeves, Jim		
Welcome To My World	P	1964
Re-Flex		
The Politics Of Dancing	69	1984
Regard (DJ Regard)		
You	95	2021
Rehab		
Bottles&Cans	21	2009
Reilly, Maggie (See also Mike Oldfield)		
In The Heat Of The Night/Elena	11	1997
Torn Between Lovers	55	1997
All That My Heart Can Hold	1	1999
Don't Wanna Lose	22	1999
Everytime We Touch ('98)	54	1999
Talking To Myself	2	2001
Adelena	16	2001
Replay	51	2001
Memories	77	2001
Humilitas	44	2003
Fides	60	2003
All Things Are Quite Silent | Forever	46	2006
Fifth Moon	69	2009
Stars At Night	31	2013
Break Of Day	31	2014
I'm With You Now	4	2020
Don't Look Back	24	2020
The Dream Is Over	60	2020
Enchantment	40	2021
Somewhere In Time	75	2021
Reinhart, Haley		
Liar	61	2012
R.E.M. (See also Michael Stipe)		
The One I Love	52	1987
Orange Crush	33	1989
World Leader Pretend	45	1989
Texarkana	16	1991
Losing My Religion	52	1991

Radio Song	121	1991
Ignoreland	11	1992
Sweetness Follows	27	1992
Bang And Blame	9	1994
I Don't Sleep, I Dream	43	1994
Crush With Eyeliner	52	1995
Leave	76	1996
Rembrandts, The		
Just The Way It Is, Baby	99	1990
Remi, Salaam		
One In The Chamber	94	2014
Rent Cast		
Seasons Of Love (movie version)	135	2005
REO Speedwagon		
One Lonely Night	127	1985
Replacements, The		
Here Comes A Regular	122	1986
Republica		
Ready To Go	31	1996
Drop Dead Gorgeous	25	1997
Don't You Ever	82	1997
Res		
Golden Boys	35	2001
Restless Heart		
I'll Still Be Loving You	93	1987
Reunion		
Life Is A Rock (But The Radio Rolled Me)	P	1974
Rexha, Bebe		
Yesterday	81	2014
Sacrifice	16	2021
I'm Good (Blue)	113	2022
Stars	32	2023
Heart Wants What It Wants	33	2023
Miracle Man	86	2023
My Oh My	43	2024
Reynolds, Debbie		
Tammy	P	1957
Rhodes, Happy		
When The Rain Came Down	M	1987
Words Weren't Made For Cowards	7	1992
Feed The Fire	13	1992
Phobos	33	1992
Out Like A Lamb	25	1993
I Cannot Go On	29	1993
Closer	35	1993

Runners	64	1993
Collective Heart	7	1994
Hold Me	19	1994
Ray (Back From The Offworld)	66	1998
Rhye		
Phoenix	66	2018
Black Rain	71	2021
Rhythm Heritage		
Theme From S.W.A.T.	61	1976
Baretta's Theme ("Keep Your Eye On The Sparrow")	82	1976
Rich, Charlie		
Behind Closed Doors	P	1973
The Most Beautiful Girl	P	1973
Richard, Cliff		
Devil Woman	1	1976
Carrie	3	1980
We Don't Talk Anymore	45	1980
Dreamin'	61	1980
Suddenly	95	1980
A Little In Love	100	1981
Richard, Dawn (See also Danity Kane)		
Intro (In The Hearts Tonight)/Return Of A Queen	78	2013
Quiet In A World Full Of Noise	111	2024
Richey, Kim		
Come Around	20	1999
Richie, Lionel (See also Commodores)		
Endless Love	50	1981
Hello	54	1984
Ridings, Freya		
I'd Bet	19	2023
Righteous Brothers, The		
You've Lost That Lovin' Feelin'	P	1964
Unchained Melody	P	1965
(You're My) Soul And Inspiration	P	1966
Rihanna		
Rehab	62	2007
Photograph	20	2010
Only Girl (In The World)	112	2010
S&M	65	2011
Diamonds	67	2012
Towards The Sun	37	2015
This Is What You Came For	76	2016
Rilo Kiley (See also The Postal Service)		
Dreamworld	77	2007

Rimes, LeAnn		
Everybody's Someone	27	2007
Doesn't Everybody	23	2009
Grace	3	2014

Ringside		
Struggle	54	2005
Tired Of Being Sorry (aka Spanishfaster)	57	2005

Riperton, Minnie		
Lovin' You	P	1975

Ritchie Family, The		
Best Disco In Town	97	1976

Rivers, Johnny		
Secret Agent Man	P	1966
Summer Rain	P	1967
Rockin' Pneumonia – Boogie Woogie Flu	P	1972

Roan		
Let's Begin	10	2008

Roberts, Sam, Band		
The Hands Of Love	116	2014

Robertson, Robbie		
Ghost Dance (& The Red Road Ensemble)	60	1995
Unbound	4	1998
Salvation Adagio	79	2024

Robinson, Porter		
Polygon Dust	78	2014

Robinson, Smokey (See also The Miracles)		
Cruisin'	M	1979
How You Make Me Feel	56	2023

Robinson, Tom		
Atmospherics (Listen To The Radio)	73	1982

Robinson, Vicki Sue		
Turn The Beat Around	51	1976

Robyn (See also Röyksopp)		
Cobrastyle (Press Trigger)	33	2008
With Every Heartbeat	30	2009
The Girl And The Robot	85	2009
Dancing On My Own	105	2010
Monument / (T.I.E. Version) (two versions)	29	2014
Do It Again	44	2014
Got To Work It Out	44	2015
Honey	48	2018
Because It's In The Music	80	2018
Send To Robin Immediately	6	2019
Missing U	20	2019

Roches, The		
Face Down At Folk City	M	1985

Roc Project, The		
Never (Past Tense)	M	2003

Rodgers, Nile (See also Chic)		
Give Me Your Love	57	2016
Roses	44	2020
One More	4	2021
lock / unlock	105	2024

Rodrigo y Gabriela		
Ixtapa/Stairway To Heaven	82	2007

Roe, Tommy		
Dizzy	P	1969

Roger (Troutman)		
Boom! There She Was	108	1987
California Love	106	1996

Rogers, Kenny		
Just Dropped In (To See What Condition My Condition Was In) (Kenny Rogers And The First Edition)	P	1968
Lady	28	1980

Rogue Wave		
Sightlines	111	2007

Rolling Stones, The		
As Tears Go By	P	1965
Under My Thumb	P	1966
Gimme Shelter	P	1966
Paint It, Black	P	1966
Ruby Tuesday	P	1967
She's A Rainbow	P	1967
Sympathy For The Devil	P	1968
You Can't Always Get What You Want	P	1969
Angie	P	1974
Miss You	25	1978
Shattered	36	1979
Emotional Rescue	46	1980
She's So Cold	101	1980
If I Was A Dancer (Dance, Pt. 2)	M	1981
Heaven	M	1981

Romantics, The		
Talking In Your Sleep	72	1983

Romeo Void		
Never Say Never	131	1982
A Girl In Trouble (Is A Temporary Thing)	8	1984

Ronettes, The		
Be My Baby	P	1963

Ro Nova		
What Have We Got	16	2023

Ronson, Mark		
Summer Breaking/Daffodils	18	2015
Late Night Prelude/Late Night Feelings	22	2019
Nothing Breaks Like A Heart	122	2019

Ronstadt, Linda		
Long Long Time	P	1970
You're No Good	P	1974
Tracks Of My Tears	P	1975
When Will I Be Loved	P	1975
It's So Easy	33	1977
Someone To Lay Down Beside Me	99	1977
Hurt So Bad	68	1980
The Ways Of Love	129	1990
War Of Man	62	1992
Winter Light	X	1993
Heartbeats Accelerating	113	1994

Rosales, Melanie		
What You Really Want	99	1984

Rose, David, And His Orchestra		
The Stripper	P	1962

Rose, Eliza		
Body Moving	39	2024

Rosebuds, The		
Life Like	14	2009
Waiting For You	47	2011

Rose Royce		
Wishing On A Star	M	1978
Love Don't Live Here Anymore	3	1979

Ross, Diana (See also The Supremes)		
Ain't No Mountain High Enough	P	1970
Remember Me	P	1970
Touch Me In The Morning	P	1973
Love Hangover	36	1976
Theme From Mahogany (Do You Know Where You're Going To)	89	1976
I Thought It Took A Little Time (But Today I Fell In Love)	M	1976
Upside Down	136	1980
Endless Love	50	1981
Muscles	57	1982
Swept Away	60	1984
Missing You	97	1985

Ross, Rick (RICK RO$$)		
Cross That Line	117	2006

Rossum, Emmy		
Don't Stop Now	20	2008
Slow Me Down	92	2008

Rothberg, Patti		
Inside	66	1996

Roudette, Marlon		
Body Language	54	2015
When The Beat Drops Out	62	2015

Rowland, Kelly		
Better Without You	99	2007
It's The Way You Love Me	31	2009
When Love Takes Over	89	2009
Commander	41	2010
Gone	103	2011

Roxette (See also Mono Mind)		
The Look	161	1989
It Must Have Been Love	146	1990

Roxy Music (See also Bryan Ferry)		
Dance Away	M	1979
Avalon	M	1982
More Than This	11	1983

Royal & The Serpent		
Inner Gold	92	2024

Röyksopp (See also Robyn; Anneli Drecker; Susanne Sundfør)		
Remind Me	10	2003
Poor Leno	69	2003
9 To 5 vs. Eple	M	2003
What Else Is There?	8	2005
Only This Moment	33	2006
Follow My Ruin	58	2006
Vision One	8	2009
This Must Be It	25	2009
The Girl And The Robot	85	2009
Monument / (T.I.E. Version) (two versions)	29	2014
Do It Again	44	2014
Sordid Affair	48	2014
I Had This Thing	82	2014
Save Me	38	2015
Skulls	47	2015
Thank You	70	2015
Never Ever	62	2016
The Ladder	7	2022
Breathe	39	2022
Let's Get It Right	45	2022
Impossible	55	2022

Oh, Lover	88	2022
Stay Awhile	11	2023
Just Wanted To Know	31	2023
Rozalla		
Everybody's Free (To Feel Good)	141	1992
Look No Further	76	1995
RubberBand 最新派台歌		
Gotta Go!	87	2016
Rubicon		
I'm Gonna Take Care Of Everything	139	1978
Ruby And The Romantics		
Our Day Will Come	P	1963
Rudimental		
Bloodstream (Rudimental Remix)	9	2014
Regardless	20	2021
Rudolf, Kevin		
Let It Rock	58	2008
Ruff Endz		
No More	92	2000
Rufus featuring Chaka Khan (See also Chaka Khan)		
Tell Me Something Good	117	1976
Ain't Nobody	224	1984
Rüfüs Du Sol		
Eyes	65	2019
No Place	86	2019
On My Knees	73	2021
Inhale/Music Is Better	28	2024
RUNAGROUND		
Chase You Down	61	2016
Rundgren, Todd (See also TR-i; Utopia; The New Cars)		
I Saw The Light	P	1972
Hello It's Me	P	1973
Good Vibrations	88	1976
Can We Still Be Friends	12	1978
Change Myself	164	1991
Fiction	56	2017
Runga, Bic		
Sway	75	1999
RuPaul		
Sissy That Walk	83	2014
Rush (See also Envy Of None)		
The Spirit Of Radio	77	1980
Limelight	39	1981
Tom Sawyer	73	1981
New World Man	76	1982

Rushen, Patrice		
Forget Me Nots	M	1982
Russell, Brenda		
Piano In The Dark	156	1988
Russell, Leon		
Lady Blue	P	1975
Ryan, Kate		
Magical Love	15	2003
The Rain	50	2004
Love Or Lust	28	2007
Ella Elle L'a	53	2008
L.I.L.Y.	93	2008
Madness	4	2013
Walk To The Beat	32	2013
Gold	56	2019
Wild Eyes	81	2020
RyanDan		
Tears Of An Angel	43	2009
Like The Sun	67	2009

S

Saban, Maya		
I've Seen It All	9	2005
I Miss You	99	2005
Sacred Spirits / Sacred Spirit / Indigo Spirit (See also Classical Spirit; B-Tribe)		
Dawa (the cradlesong)	7	1995
Yeha-Noha (wishes of happiness & prosperity)	98	1995
Culture Clash (Indigo Spirit)	81	1999
Dela Dela (Sacred Spirit)	15	2001
Land Of Promise (Sacred Spirit)	100	2001
Sade (Sade Adu)		
Hang On To Your Love	26	1985
Smooth Operator	30	1985
The Sweetest Taboo	15	1986
Never As Good As The First Time	79	1986
Nothing Can Come Between Us	34	1988
Paradise	101	1988
Pearls	15	1993
Feel No Pain	71	1993
Every Word	7	2000
Immigrant	39	2001
King Of Sorrow	92	2001
Soldier Of Love	53	2010
Love Is Found	80	2011

Safina, Alessandro		
Luna (Only You)	6	2001
Safran, Natalia, & Mick Jaroszyk		
All I Feel Is You	68	2014
Sagoo, Bally		
Teri Akhiyan	33	1997
Saint Etienne (See also Sarah Cracknell)		
Avenue	63	1993
Urban Clearway	26	1994
On The Shore	86	1994
After Hebden	97	2017
St. James, Rebecca		
Lamb Of God	81	2002
SAINt JHN		
Roses (Imanbek Remix)	83	2020
St. Paul & The Broken Bones		
City Federal Building	103	2023
St. Vincent		
Hell Is Near	69	2024
Saisse, Philippe		
Film Noir	88	1998
Sakamoto, Kyu		
Sukiyaki	P	1963
Sakamoto, Ryuichi (See also Yellow Magic Orchestra)		
Merry Christmas, Mr. Lawrence	M	1983
Diabaram	102	1991
Heartbeat (Tainai Kaiki II) - returning to the womb	67	1992
Same Dream, Same Destination	57	1994
Minamata Piano Theme	59	2022
Saleh, Dua		
want	88	2024
Saliva		
Famous Monsters	28	2003
Sally Shapiro		
Time To Let Go	36	2007
Miracle	63	2009
Save Your Love	71	2009
If It Doesn't Rain	26	2013
All My Life	65	2013
Why Did I Say Goodbye	62	2022
Salsoul Orchestra, The		
Nice 'N' Naasty	47	1976
Salt Ashes		
Somebody	5	2016

Wilderness	52	2016
Mad Girl	37	2022
I'm Not Scared To Die	43	2023
Salt-N-Pepa		
Stomp (featuring Salt)	22	1997
Bring Back The Time	73	2022
Sam & Dave		
Hold On! I'm A Comin'	P	1966
Sam F f/ Sophie Rose		
Limitless	63	2017
Sandal, Mustafa		
Yamah Tövbeler	24	2005
Sandé, Emeli		
Extraordinary Being	41	2019
Human	74	2019
Survive	90	2019
Sandén, Molly (My Marianne)		
Husavik (My Hometown)	34	2020
Double Trouble (Tiësto's Euro 90's Tribute Mix)	92	2020
Sandpipers, The		
Come Saturday Morning	P	1969
Sandra (Cretu) (See also Enigma)		
(I'll Never Be) Maria Magdalena	24	1985
In The Heat Of The Night	M	1985
Secret Land	17	1989
We'll Be Together	39	1989
When The Rain Doesn't Come	68	1992
Son Of A Time Machine	18	1998
Perfect Touch	34	2002
Forgive Me	44	2002
Such A Shame	53	2002
Casino Royale / Sleep (two versions)	43	2007
What Is It About Me	55	2007
R U Feeling Me	46	2009
What If	65	2009
Tête À Tête	75	2009
Between Me & The Moon	59	2012
Sandro		
Running	82	2020
Sanford-Townsend Band		
Smoke From A Distant Fire	91	1977
Sang, Samantha		
Emotion	87	1978
You Keep Me Dancing	98	1978

Santa Esmeralda f/ Leroy Gomez		
Don't Let Me Be Misunderstood	5	1978
Santana		
Evil Ways	P	1969
Black Magic Woman/Gypsy Queen	P	1970
Oye Cómo Va	P	1970
She's Not There	68	1977
Winning	68	1981
Smooth	119	1999
Breathing Underwater	98	2021
Santaolalla, Gustavo		
De Usuahia Al A Quiaca	95	2005
Santigold (Santogold)		
Before The Fire	31	2016
Walking In A Circle	79	2016
Santo & Johnny		
Sleep Walk	P	1959
Sasha (Welsh DJ)		
Talk Amongst Yourselves (Sasha Involver Remix)	74	2004
Corvette/Shelter	4	2016
Sasha Alexander (Sascha Schmitz)		
Let Me Be The One	31	2001
Saszan		
Remedium	32	2020
Savage Garden (See also Darren Hayes)		
To The Moon And Back	2	1997
Carry On Dancing	20	1997
I Want You/Tears Of Pearls	57	1997
Truly Madly Deeply	123	1997
You Can Still Be Free	70	2000
Sayer, Leo		
You Make Me Feel Like Dancing	35	1977
How Much Love	37	1977
When I Need You	70	1977
Living In A Fantasy	74	1981
Say Lou Lou		
Nightcrawler	65	2021
Scaggs, Boz		
It's Over	100	1976
Lido Shuffle	85	1977
Look What You've Done To Me	87	1980
Scars On 45		
Insecurity	9	2012
My Eyes Are Still Bright	2	2015

Scherzinger, Nicole (See also Pussycat Dolls)		
Jai Ho! (You Are My Destiny)	119	2008
Power's Out	30	2012
Schifrin, Lalo		
Mission: Impossible	P	1967
Schiller (Christopher von Deylen)		
I've Seen It All (two versions)	9	2005
I Feel You	15	2005
Desire	37	2005
Dream Of You	53	2005
I Miss You / Mittelerde (Middle Earth)	99	2005
Miles And Miles	48	2006
Die Nacht...Du Bist Nicht Allein	65	2006
Sehnsucht	5	2008
Let Me Love You	54	2008
Try	47	2010
Let It Rise	56	2010
Playing With Madness	59	2010
I Will Follow You	100	2010
Sunday Version 02	1	2011
Alive	27	2012
Ultramarin	90	2012
Epic Shores	5	2013
Sonne	10	2013
Desert Empire	56	2013
Only Love	13	2016
Once Upon A Time I / Once Upon A Time II	63	2016
Sweet Symphony (My Heart Beats Again)	88	2016
Love	8	2019
Dreamcatcher	42	2019
In Between	51	2019
Lichtjahre	37	2020
Miracle	17	2021
Guardian Angel	48	2021
Dark Sun	51	2022
What Have We Got	16	2023
Ein Morgen Im August/Love And Tears	58	2023
Space	88	2023
Heaven Can Wait (Christopher von Deylen)	57	2024
Schilling, Peter		
Major Tom (Coming Home)	44	1983
Schnell Fenster (See also Split Enz)		
Whisper	87	1990
School Of Seven Bells (SVIIB)		
Show Me Love	47	2012

Missing You	54	2013
Music Takes Me	37	2016
On My Heart	60	2016
Ablaze	94	2016
Schulz, Robin		
Prayer In C (Robin Schulz Mix)	41	2014
Sugar	88	2015
Right Now	77	2018
Schwartz, Sherwood		
The Ballad Of Gilligan's Isle (w/ George Wyle, The Wellingtons)	T	1964
The Brady Bunch (w/ Frank De Vol, The Brady Six)	T	1971
Scissor Sisters (See also Jake Shears)		
Lovers In The Backseat	8	2004
Tits On The Radio	10	2004
Comfortably Numb	56	2004
The Other Side	4	2006
Sex And Violence	1	2010
Night Life	35	2010
Harder You Get	55	2010
Something Like This	70	2010
Inevitable	52	2012
Scorpions		
Still Loving You	148	1984
Scott, Calum		
If Our Love Is Wrong	55	2018
Love On Myself	10	2020
Scott, Jill		
Daydreamin'	105	2007
Scott, Lisbeth		
Veni Redemptor Gentium	13	2001
Beg	72	2003
Grace	90	2006
Script, The		
We Cry	81	2009
Scripture		
Words Needed	37	1999
Scritti Politti		
Boom! There She Was	108	1987
Seal		
Crazy	46	1991
Killer	243	1992
Kiss From A Rose	1	1994
Newborn Friend	21	1994
Prayer For The Dying	40	1994
Human Beings	2	1998
State Of Grace	27	1999
Lost My Faith	31	1999
Excerpt From	34	1999
Loneliest Star	4	2003
My Vision	12	2003
Waiting For You	27	2003
Amazing	14	2007
The Right Life	18	2008
If It's In My Mind, It's On My Face	48	2008
Loaded	67	2008
If I'm Any Closer	21	2010
Weight Of My Mistakes	22	2010
Life On The Dancefloor	68	2015
Daylight Saving	2	2016
Padded Cell	11	2016
Let Yourself	15	2016
Just A Ghost	12	2021
Seals & Crofts		
Summer Breeze (also 2004 remix by Supreme Beings Of Leisure)	P	1972
Diamond Girl	P	1973
Hummingbird	P	1973
We May Never Pass This Way (Again)	P	1973
King Of Nothing	P	1974
Get Closer	66	1976
Searchers, The		
Love Potion Number Nine	P	1964
Sebastian		
The Way I Are	1	2007
Can You Feel It	10	2010
Sebastian, John (See also Lovin' Spoonful)		
Welcome Back	84	1976
Sebestyén, Márta		
Marta's Song	62	1995
Secada, Jon		
Just Another Day	147	1992
Secret Garden		
Nocturne	22	1996
Prayer	78	1999
Sleepsong	80	2005
Sedaka, Neil		
Calendar Girl	P	1960
Breaking Up Is Hard To Do	P	1962
Laughter In The Rain	P	1974
Bad Blood (f/ Elton John)	P	1975

Seeb (SEEB)		
Breathe	30	2017
Sweet Dreams & Dynamite	90	2022
Seekers, The (See also The New Seekers)		
Georgy Girl	P	1966
Seger, Bob (& The Silver Bullet Band)		
Turn The Page	P	1973
You'll Accomp'ny Me (& The Silver Bullet Band)	96	1980
Seger, Shea		
Clutch	38	2001
Selena		
God's Child (Baila Conmigo)	9	1995
Captive Heart	8	1996
Semisonic		
Never You Mind	73	1998
Secret Smile	80	1999
She's Got My Number	66	2001
Bed	93	2001
Sennek		
A Matter Of Time	10	2018
Sense Field		
Save Yourself	56	2002
Seungri 승리		
할말 있어요 (Gotta Talk To U)	11	2014
You Hoooo!!!	35	2014
Ignite	83	2018
SEVENTEEN 세븐틴		
Ash	81	2023
707		
I Could Be Good For You	53	1980
Sewell, Conrad		
Firestone	39	2015
Sex, Love & Water	86	2018
Shabaz		
Caravan	14	2002
Shadowfax		
Kindred Spirits	93	1985
Shakespears Sister (See also Bananarama)		
The Trouble With Andre	121	1992
Shakira		
Sombra De Tí	53	1999
Octavo Día	58	1999
Whenever, Wherever / Suerte (Whenever, Wherever)	42	2001
Ready For The Good Times	74	2002

Hips Don't Lie	143	2006
La Fuerte	96	2024
Shangri-Las, The		
I Can Never Go Home Anymore	P	1962
Remember (Walking In The Sand)	P	1964
Shannon		
Let The Music Play	74	1984
Shannon, Sharon (See also Capercaillie)		
Cavan Potholes	88	1996
Shao Rong 邵容		
Bamboo Dance	80	2002
Shapeshifters, The (Shape:UK)		
You Never Know	35	2006
Shapplin, Emma		
Discovering Yourself	3	1999
Nothing Wrong	76	2010
The Hours On The Fields	5	2011
Sharp, Dee Dee		
Mashed Potato Time	P	1962
Sharpe, Bill		
Change Your Mind	29	1985
New Thing From London Town	67	1987
Shears, Jake (See also Scissor Sisters)		
Kiss For Kiss	6	2016
Voices	5	2023
Sheeran, Ed		
Bloodstream / (Rudimental Remix)	9	2014
Shape Of You	96	2017
Bad Habits	47	2021
Sheik, Duncan		
In The Absence Of Sun	11	1996
She Runs Away	50	1996
Barely Breathing	92	1996
Wishful Thinking	35	1998
Life's What You Make It	79	2011
Shelley, Pete		
Need A Minit	97	1987
Shelton, Blake		
Different Man	102	2022
Sheppard, T.G.		
I Loved 'Em Every One	91	1981
Sherbs (Sherbet)		
No Turning Back	124	1981
Sheriff		
When I'm With You	33	1983

Sherman, Bobby		
Seattle	P	1969
Easy Come, Easy Go	P	1970
Julie, Do Ya Love Me	P	1970
She Wants Revenge		
These Things	101	2006
Shifty Shellshock		
Starry Eyed Surprise (w/ Oakenfold)	M	2002
Shiny Toy Guns		
You Are The One/Le Disko	83	2006
Starts With One	98	2007
Shirelles, The		
Soldier Boy	P	1962
Shocking Blue		
Venus	P	1969
Shontelle		
Cold Cold Summer	54	2009
Perfect Nightmare	91	2011
Shooting Star		
Last Chance	79	1980
Flesh And Blood	65	1981
Hollywood	69	1982
Shungudzo		
Come On Back	89	2018
Sia (See also Zero 7)		
This Fine Social Scene	84	2006
Clap Your Hands	68	2010
Dusk Till Dawn	125	2018
Towards The Sun	2	2024
Immortal Queen	70	2024
Siberry, Jane		
Seven Steps To The Wall	67	1986
One More Colour	97	1986
The White Tent The Raft	98	1988
Bound By The Beauty	93	1989
Calling All Angels	106	1992
Temple	70	1993
Sail Across The Water	84	1993
Sickick		
Frozen On Fire	58	2022
Sigala		
Give Me Your Love	57	2016
Silvetti (Bebu Silvetti)		
Spring Rain (Lluvia De Primavera)	131	1977

Silver		
Wham Bam (Shang-A-Lang)	46	1976
Silver Convention		
Fly, Robin, Fly	26	1976
Get Up And Boogie (That's Right)	53	1976
Simmons, Patrick (See also The Doobie Brothers)		
So Wrong	M	1983
Simon, Carly		
That's The Way I've Always Heard It Should Be	P	1971
You're So Vain	P	1972
We Have No Secrets	P	1972
Haven't Got Time For The Pain	P	1974
Attitude Dancing	P	1975
Nobody Does It Better	115	1977
You Belong To Me	57	1978
Why	4	1982
Touched By The Sun	80	1994
Simon, Paul		
Kodachrome	P	1973
50 Ways To Leave Your Lover	P	1975
Simon & Garfunkel (See also Paul Simon; Art Garfunkel)		
The Sound Of Silence	P	1965
Mrs. Robinson	P	1968
El Condor Pasa (If I Could)	P	1970
America	P	1972
My Little Town	P	1975
Simone, Nina		
I Put A Spell On You	P	1965
To Be Young, Gifted And Black	P	1969
Simple Minds (See also Lostboy! AKA Jim Kerr)		
Promised You A Miracle	20	1983
New Gold Dream (81-82-83-84)	27	1983
Someone Somewhere In Summertime	32	1983
Glittering Prize	55	1983
Don't You (Forget About Me)	58	1985
Alive And Kicking	71	1985
All The Things She Said	89	1986
This Is Your Land	46	1989
Intro/Banging On The Door	12	1991
See The Lights	48	1991
Real Life	57	1991
Hypnotised	29	1995
If I Had Wings	40	1998

Song For The Tribes	96	1998
Sleeping Girl	90	2003
Different World (Taormina.Me)	87	2006
Graffiti Soul	64	2009
Moscow Underground	74	2009
Light Travels	91	2009
Honest Town	77	2015

Simply Red

Holding Back The Years	11	1986
The Right Thing	25	1987
Suffer	47	1987
Maybe Someday...	86	1987
I'm Gonna Lose You	4	1988
It's Only Love	42	1989
Sunrise	59	2004
Shades 22	20	2024

Simpson, Sturgill (Johnny Blue Skies)

Use Me (Brutal Hearts)	102	2023

Sinatra, Frank

Strangers In The Night	P	1966
Somethin' Stupid (Frank & Nancy Sinatra)	P	1967
My Way	P	1969

Sinatra, Nancy

These Boots Are Made For Walkin'	P	1966
Sugar Town	P	1966
You Only Live Twice	P	1967
Somethin' Stupid (Frank & Nancy Sinatra)	P	1967

Sinclar, Bob, & Tonino Speciale

I Believe	41	2018

Singh, Talvin

Jaan	76	1997

Singing Nun, The

Dominique	P	1963

Sing-Sing (See also Lush)

A Kind Of Love	25	2008
A Modern Girl	89	2008

Siouxsie And The Banshees

Cities In Dust	82	1986

Sister Sledge (See also Kathy Sledge)

We Are Family	7	1979

Sisters Of Mercy, The

More	82	1991

Sivan, Troye

Take Yourself Home	88	2020
You	95	2021

Sixpence None The Richer (See also Leigh Nash; Fauxliage)

Breathe	102	1999

Skye (Edwards) (See also Morcheeba; Skye│Ross)

Love Show	51	2006
Every Little Lie	19	2012
Featherlight	46	2012
High Life	18	2013

Skye│Ross

Light Of Gold	71	2016

Skyliners, The

Since I Don't Have You	P	1959

Sledge, Kathy (See also Sister Sledge)

Freedom	69	1998

Sleeping Lions

Sound Of My Heart	72	1984

Sloan, Sasha (Sasha Alex Sloan)

This Town	21	2018

Slowdive

alife	11	2024

Sly & The Family Stone

Dance To The Music	P	1968
Everyday People	P	1968
Hot Fun In The Summertime	P	1969
Thank You Falettinme Be Mice Elf Agin/ Everybody Is A Star	P	1970

Sly Fox

Let's Go All The Way	65	1986

Small Faces

Itchycoo Park	P	1967

Smashing Pumpkins

Landslide	110	1994

Smash Mouth

Walkin' On The Sun	74	1997

Smile (Smile.dk)

Butterfly	130	2000

Smith, Caitlyn

House Of Cards	68	2019

Smith, Jenifer

Mesa Drive	70	1997

Smith, Kendra

Interlude Dirigible/Valley Of The Morning Sun	73	1995

Smith, Mindy

Hard To Know	60	2004

Smith, O. C.

Little Green Apples	P	1968

Smith, Patti (Patti Smith Group)		
Because The Night	26	1978
Frederick	10	1979
Dancing Barefoot	M	1979
It Takes Time (Patti Smith & Fred Smith)	46	1992
Smith, Rex		
You Take My Breath Away	101	1979
Smith, Sam		
La La La	6	2014
Writing's On The Wall	40	2015
Promises	9	2018
Dancing With A Stranger	5	2019
How Do You Sleep?	61	2019
Diamonds	74	2020
Hurting Interlude/Lose You	55	2023
Desire	92	2023
Smith, Will		
Men In Black	92	1997
Smithereens, The		
In A Lonely Place	M	1986
Cut Flowers	25	1990
A Girl Like You	112	1990
Anywhere You Are	82	1992
Smiths, The (See also Morrissey; Electronic)		
This Charming Man	86	1984
What Difference Does It Make?	90	1984
Reel Around The Fountain	97	1984
Stop Me If You Think You've Heard This One Before	147	1984
How Soon Is Now?	2	1985
Some Girls Are Bigger Than Others	45	1986
There Is A Light That Never Goes Out	M	1986
Oscillate Wildly	2	1987
Bigmouth Strikes Again	92	1987
Last Night I Dreamt That Somebody Loved Me	32	1988
Smyth, B.		
Leggo	81	2013
Snap!		
Rhythm Is A Dancer	130	1993
Sneaker		
More Than Just The Two Of Us	86	1982
Sneaker Pimps		
6 Underground	7	1997
Sniff 'n' The Tears		
Driver's Seat	5	1979

New Lines On Love	93	1979
Snoop Dogg		
I Wanna Love You (I Wanna Fuck You)	101	2007
Awake	97	2015
Snow, Miike		
Paddling Out	92	2012
Change Your Mind	20	2018
Snow, Phoebe		
Poetry Man	P	1975
Snowbird (See also Cocteau Twins; This Mortal Coil)		
I Heard The Owl Call My Name	23	2014
Snow Patrol		
Somewhere A Clock Is Ticking	7	2004
Ways & Means	80	2004
Run	89	2004
Shut Your Eyes	3	2006
Make This Go On Forever	20	2006
Set The Fire To The Third Bar	39	2006
Take Back The City	73	2008
The Lightning Strike: (i) What If This Storm Ends?	96	2008
Lifeboats	19	2009
If There's A Rocket Tie Me To It	80	2009
Fallen Empires	49	2012
The Weight Of Love	78	2012
Years That Fall	31	2024
SOFI TUKKER		
Forgive Me	30	2022
Soft Cell (See also Marc Almond)		
Tainted Love/Where Did Our Love Go	12	1982
Soho		
Hippychick	75	1990
Solar Twins		
Nightfall	25	2001
Earthbound	34	2001
Alleluias	81	2001
Soleil, Stella (Sister Soleil)		
Red (Sister Soleil)	84	1999
Runaway Crush	22	2001
Imperfect	33	2001
Angel Face	68	2001
Solsun (See also Cause & Effect)		
The Only Ones?	27	2018
The Science Of Dust/Siren Call	49	2018
Solveig, Martin		
Places	20	2017

Somerville, Jimmy (See also Bronski Beat; The Communards)		
Don't Know What To Do (Without You)	4	1990
Heaven Here On Earth (With Your Love)	17	1990
Perfect Day	96	1990
Coming	19	1993
Heartbeat	33	1995
By Your Side	38	1995
A Dream Gone Wrong	44	1995
Too Much Of A Good Thing	68	1995
Dark Sky	62	1998
Someday Soon	82	1999
Here I Am	96	1999
Could It Be Love	50	2005
Hearts	48	2015
Something Corporate		
Me And The Moon	85	2004
Sonic Dream Collective		
Don't Go Breaking My Heart	75	1997
Sonic Youth		
Superstar	27	1994
Sonique		
It Feels So Good	11	2000
Move Closer	19	2000
I Put A Spell On You	97	2000
Alive	41	2004
Sonny & Cher (See also Cher)		
I Got You Babe	P	1965
The Beat Goes On	P	1967
Sophie And The Giants		
Hypnotized	48	2020
In The Dark	9	2022
Paradise	51	2023
S.O.S. Band, The		
Take Your Time (Do It Right) Part 1	M	1980
Just Be Good To Me	163	1983
Soul Family Sensation		
The Sheffield Song	30	1991
Soul II Soul f/ Caron Wheeler		
Back To Life	95	1989
Soundgarden (See also Chris Cornell)		
Black Hole Sun	92	1994
Souther, J.D.		
Her Town Too	63	1981
Space		
Female Of The Species	68	1997

Spain		
Born To Love Her	12	2001
Spandau Ballet (See also Tony Hadley)		
True	15	1983
Gold	15	1984
Only When You Leave	45	1984
I'll Fly For You	49	1984
Spanky And Our Gang		
Sunday Will Never Be The Same	P	1967
Sparks		
(When I Kiss You) I Hear Charlie Parker Playing	107	1995
Not That Well-Defined	114	2023
Sparks, Jordin		
No Air	63	2008
S.O.S. (Let The Music Play)	95	2009
Sparro, Sam		
Black & Gold	120	2008
You Make It So Easy, Don't You	50	2020
Spears, Britney		
...Baby One More Time	48	1999
Oops! . . . I Did It Again	117	2000
Toxic	103	2003
Gimme More	45	2007
Unusual You	41	2009
3	125	2009
Scream & Shout	90	2013
Mind Your Business	133	2023
Spencer, The Jeremy, Band		
Cool Breeze	15	1979
Spice Girls (See also Emma Bunton; Melanie C; Victoria Beckham)		
Wannabe	44	1997
Mama	114	1997
Viva Forever	80	1998
SpiceHouse		
Baby, I Know That You Know	92	2006
Spider		
New Romance (It's A Mystery)	38	1980
Spinners, The		
It's A Shame	P	1970
I'll Be Around	P	1972
Could It Be I'm Falling In Love	P	1972
One Of A Kind (Love Affair)	P	1973
Then Came You (w/ Dionne Warwicke)	P	1974

"They Just Can't Stop It" The (Games People Play)	P	1975
The Rubberband Man	77	1976
Spiral Staircase		
More Today Than Yesterday	P	1969
Spirit Of Eden, The		
The Dreaming/Fionnghuala	27	1998
Sleep With The Ancients	79	1999
Spirit Of The West		
Bone Of Contention	78	1996
Spiteri, Sharleen (See also Texas)		
Melody	94	2008
Split Enz (See also Finn Brothers; Crowded House; Tim Finn; Neil Finn; Schnell Fenster)		
One Step Ahead	13	1981
Hard Act To Follow	18	1981
I Got You	34	1981
History Never Repeats	37	1981
Ghost Girl	M	1981
Pioneer/Six Months In A Leaky Boat	22	1982
Dirty Creature	34	1982
Giant Heartbeat	46	1982
Message To My Girl	36	1984
Our Day	59	1985
Springfield, Dusty		
I Only Want To Be With You	P	1964
Wishin' And Hopin'	P	1964
The Look Of Love	P	1967
Son-Of-A Preacher Man	P	1968
I Close My Eyes And Count To Ten	P	1968
The Windmills Of Your Mind	P	1969
What Have I Done To Deserve This?	10	1987
Nothing Has Been Proved	5	1989
Springfield, Rick		
Jesse's Girl	55	1981
Don't Talk To Strangers	91	1982
Springsteen, Bruce		
I'm On Fire	86	1985
Squeeze		
Tempted	28	1981
Satisfied	78	1991
Stacey Q		
Two Of Hearts	90	1986
Stafford, Jim		
Spiders & Snakes	P	1973

Staind		
It's Been Awhile	11	2001
Stallion		
Old Fashioned Boy (You're The One)	58	1977
Stampeders		
Sweet City Woman	P	1971
Stanley, Pamala		
Coming Out Of Hiding	28	1984
Stanley, Paul (See also KISS)		
I Will Be With You (Where The Lost Ones Go)	54	2007
Staple Singers, The		
I'll Take You There	P	1973
Let's Do It Again	64	1976
Star, Coco		
I Need A Miracle	M	1996
Star, Jeffree		
Get Away With Murder	83	2010
Starbuck		
Moonlight Feels Right	39	1976
Starclub		
World Keeps Turning	67	1993
The Answer	96	1993
s t a r g a z e		
Agree	38	2018
Starland Vocal Band		
Afternoon Delight	68	1976
Lovin' You With My Eyes	100	1980
Starr, Ayra		
People (sped up+reverb)	38	2023
Starr, Edwin		
War	P	1970
Starr, Ringo (See also The Beatles)		
It Don't Come Easy	P	1971
Photograph	P	1973
Laughable	100	2017
Starz		
Cherry Baby	45	1977
State Of Grace (Paul Schwartz)		
Veni Redemptor Gentium	13	2001
Christe Redemptor	84	2007
Staves, The		
Devotion	115	2022
Stealers Wheel (See also Gerry Rafferty)		
Stuck In The Middle With You	P	1973

Stealing Sheep		
Dead Machine	73	2023
Stealth		
Never Say Die	1	2019
Steam		
Na Na Hey Hey Kiss Him Goodbye	P	1969
Steele, Jevetta		
Calling You	99	1988
Steele, Luke (See also Empire Of The Sun)		
Looking 4 Myself	70	2012
Steely Dan (See also Donald Fagen)		
Do It Again	P	1972
Reelin' In The Years	P	1973
Rikki Don't Lose That Number	P	1974
The Fez/Don't Take Me Alive	M	1976
FM (No Static At All)	35	1978
Peg	104	1978
Stefani, Gwen (See also No Doubt)		
Four In The Morning	73	2007
You're My Favorite	24	2016
Steinman, Jim		
Rock And Roll Dreams Come Through	79	1981
Steppenwolf		
Born To Be Wild	P	1968
Magic Carpet Ride	P	1968
Stereo MC's		
Ground Level	30	1993
Playing With Fire	99	1993
Stereophonics		
Maybe Tomorrow	47	2003
Stevens, Cat (Yusuf Islam)		
Wild World	P	1971
Moonshadow	P	1971
Morning Has Broken	P	1972
Oh Very Young	P	1974
(Remember The Days Of The) Old Schoolyard	72	1977
Stevens, Ray		
Everything Is Beautiful	P	1970
The Streak	P	1974
Stevens, Sufjan		
Mystery Of Love	93	2018
Run Away With Me	69	2020
Stewart, Al		
Year Of The Cat	62	1977

On The Border	137	1977
Time Passages	31	1978
Song On The Radio	67	1979
Midnight Rocks (Al Stewart & Shot In The Dark)	78	1980
Bad Reputation	27	1988
Stewart, Amii		
Knock On Wood	63	1979
Friends	73	1985
Stewart, Dave, & Barbara Gaskin		
(I Know) I'm Losing You	38	1987
Do We See The Light Of Day	34	1989
Levi Stubbs' Tears	34	1990
Subterranean Homesick Blues	35	1991
Stewart, David A. (See also Eurythmics; Platinum Weird)		
Mr Reed (Dave Stewart & The Spiritual Cowboys)	36	1991
Lily Was Here	77	1991
Stewart, John		
Gold	17	1979
Midnight Wind	29	1979
Lost Her In The Sun	41	1980
Price Of The Fire	107	1988
Dealing With The Night	93	1992
Stewart, Rod (See also Faces)		
(I Know) I'm Losing You	P	1971
Tonight's The Night (Gonna Be Alright)	79	1976
The Killing Of Georgie (Part I And II)	52	1977
The First Cut Is The Deepest	61	1977
Do Ya Think I'm Sexy?	78	1979
Passion	103	1981
Human	61	2001
Don't Come Around Here	141	2001
Stills, Stephen (Manassas) (See also Crosby, Stills & Nash)		
It Doesn't Matter	P	1972
Sting (See also The Police)		
Fortress Around Your Heart	83	1985
We Work The Black Seam	24	1986
Russians / I Burn For You	55	1986
We'll Be Together	53	1987
Be Still My Beating Heart	35	1988
Fragil / Fragile	86	1988
Why Should I Cry For You?	100	1991
Shape Of My Heart	54	1993

A Thousand Years	91	1999
Desert Rose	54	2000
You Will Be My Ain True Love	71	2004
Power's Out	30	2012
Stolen Car	66	2016

Stipe, Michael (See also R.E.M.)

I'll Give You My Skin	49	1991
Sun / Punk Club	96	2001

Stirling, Lindsay

Kintsugi	27	2024
Eye Of The Untold Her	41	2024
Unfolding	66	2024
Inner Gold	92	2024

Stockley, Miriam (See also Praise; Adiemus)

Adiemus	45	1996
Brave New World	60	2000
Forever My Heart	69	2000
Wishing On A Star	77	2000

Stone Age (Stone Edge)

Sellet	4	1995
Kalon Mari (Marie's Heart)	11	1995
Zo Laret (It Is Said)	38	1996
Maureen Maguire	5	1999
Maribrengaël	15	1999
Podour Bihan	89	1999
Shame To Humanity	61	2022
Rozenn An Dro	70	2022

Stonebolt

I Will Still Love You	37	1978

StoneBridge

Put 'Em High	95	2016

Stone Sour

Bother	64	2002

Stone Temple Pilots

Creep	107	1993
Big Empty	99	1994
Trippin' On A Hole In A Paper Heart	102	1996

Stookey, Paul (See also Peter, Paul & Mary)

Wedding Song (There Is Love)	P	1971

Stories

Brother Louie	P	1973

Stratton, Casey

For Reasons Unexplained	5	2004
Blood	15	2004
The Dead Sea	21	2004
Ocean	70	2004

The House Of Jupiter	93	2004
Maybe For A Minute	13	2006
Opaline	36	2006
Sacrifice	40	2007

Strawberry Alarm Clock

Incense And Peppermints	P	1967

Streisand, Barbra

People	P	1964
Jingle Bells?	X	1967
I Wonder As I Wander	X	1967
Don't Rain On My Parade	P	1968
On A Clear Day (You Can See Forever)	P	1970
Stoney End	P	1970
The Way We Were	P	1973
All In Love Is Fair	P	1974
My Heart Belongs To Me	105	1977
Love Theme From "Eyes Of Laura Mars" (Prisoner)	68	1978
No More Tears (Enough Is Enough)	66	1979
The Main Event/Fight	83	1979
Woman In Love	17	1980
Guilty	114	1980
What Kind Of Fool	11	1981
Promises	46	1981
Memory	32	1982
Comin' In And Out Of Your Life	72	1982
Don't Lie To Me	45	2019

STRFKR

I Don't Want To See	111	2013
Budapest	80	2021
interspace 3/Chizzlers	116	2024

Strix Q

Boyss	12	1980

Stromae

L'Enfer	93	2022

Stuart, Marty

Cowboy's Dream/All The Pretty Horses (Medley)	82	2001

Stump, Patrick (See also Fall Out Boy)

Summer Days	62	2019

Style Council, The

My Ever Changing Moods	65	1984
Waiting	6	1987

Styles, Harry (See also One Direction)

Golden	100	2020
As It Was	129	2022

Stylistics, The		
You Are Everything	P	1971
People Make The World Go Round	P	1972
You Make Me Feel Brand New	P	1974
Styx		
Lady	P	1974
Come Sail Away	86	1977
Babe	22	1979
Why Me	89	1980
The Best Of Times	62	1981
Too Much Time On My Hands	89	1981
Subramaniam, L.		
Salaam Bombay!	94	1989
Suburbs, The		
Music For Boys	M	1981
Walk Out!	39	2021
You Ruined The World For Me Now	106	2021
Subwoolfer		
Give That Wolf A Banana	13	2022
Suede (London Suede)		
Attitude	42	2004
Sugababes (See also Siobhan Donaghy)		
Freak Like Me	90	2002
Spiral	1	2006
Sugarcult		
Counting Stars / Destination Anywhere	79	2004
Sugarloaf		
Green-Eyed Lady	P	1970
Don't Call Us, We'll Call You (f/ Jerry Corbetta)	P	1974
Sullivan, Jazmine		
Stanley	31	2015
Sultan & Ned Shepard (Sultan + Shepard)		
In The Air	19	2011
Call My Name	88	2011
Sumac, Yma		
Babalu	P	1952
Xtabay (Lure Of The Unknown Love)	P	1955
Summer, Donna		
Love To Love You Baby	32	1976
Could It Be Magic	M	1976
I Feel Love	6	1977
Bad Girls	44	1979
Hot Stuff	56	1979
No More Tears (Enough Is Enough)	66	1979

On The Radio/There Will Always Be A You	58	1980
State Of Independence	93	1982
Love Is In Control (Finger On The Trigger)	111	1982
She Works Hard For The Money	133	1983
Dinner With Gershwin	142	1988
Fame (The Game)	15	2008
Summit, John		
Human	43	2022
Shiver	53	2024
Tears	78	2024
Sundays, The		
Here's Where The Story Ends	14	1990
Sundfør, Susanne		
Save Me	38	2015
Never Ever	62	2016
Oh, Lover	88	2022
Stay Awhile	11	2023
Sun's Signature (See also Elizabeth Fraser; Cocteau Twins)		
Bluedusk	80	2022
Super Idol		
热爱105°C的你 (Love You At 105°C)	76	2023
Supertramp (See also Roger Hodgson)		
Give A Little Bit	3	1977
The Logical Song	1	1979
Take The Long Way Home / Breakfast In America	8	1979
Goodbye Stranger/Even In The Quietest Moments	79	1979
It's Raining Again	85	1983
Supreme Beings Of Leisure		
Never The Same	61	2000
Rock And A Hard Place	11	2002
Give Up	87	2003
Supremes, The (Diana Ross And The Supremes) (See also Diana Ross)		
Where Did Our Love Go	P	1964
Stop! In The Name Of Love	P	1965
I Hear A Symphony	P	1965
You Keep Me Hangin' On	P	1966
You Can't Hurry Love	P	1966
Love Is Like An Itching In My Heart	P	1966
Reflections (Diana Ross And The Supremes)	P	1967
Love Child (Diana Ross And The Supremes)	P	1968

Someday We'll Be Together (Diana Ross And The Supremes)	P	1969
River Deep – Mountain High (w/ The Four Tops)	P	1970
Nathan Jones	P	1971

Swae Lee
Unforgettable	9	2017
Borrowed Love	40	2019

Swayze, Patrick
She's Like The Wind	35	1987

Swedish House Mafia (See also Axwell Λ Ingrosso)
Don't You Worry Child	98	2012
Moth To A Flame	99	2021

Sweet
Little Willy	P	1973
Fox On The Run	65	1976
Love Is Like Oxygen	92	1978

Sweet, Kelly
We Are One	19	2007

Sweet, Matthew
Daylight	56	2001

Sweet Rush
Troublemaker	29	2009

Swift, Taylor
Cardigan	93	2020
Lavender Haze	63	2022
Anti-Hero	92	2022
Karma	130	2022

Swims, Teddy
The Door	12	2024

Swindell, Cole
Never Say Never	83	2022

Swing Out Sister
Communion	M	1987
Surrender	9	1988

Switch Disco
REACT	75	2023

Switchfoot
Dare You To Move	131	2002

Sylvers, The
Boogie Fever	7	1976
High School Dance	46	1977
Hot Line	79	1977

Sylvester
Dance (Disco Heat)	170	1978

Sylvia
Nobody	M	1982

Sylvian, David
Orpheus	79	1988
Heartbeat (Tainai Kaiki II) - returning to the womb	67	1992

Syreeta (Wright)
With You I'm Born Again	7	1980

T

Taeyeon 김태연 (Kim Taeyeon)
I	46	2016
Siren	60	2022

Take That (See also Robbie Williams)
Back For Good	70	1995
Rule The World	19	2008

Talking Heads (See also Tom Tom Club; David Byrne)
Psycho Killer	M	1978
Take Me To The River	40	1979
Life During Wartime (This Ain't No Party . . . This Ain't No Disco . . . This Ain't No Foolin' Around)	122	1979
Burning Down The House	95	1983
And She Was	87	1985

Talk Talk
Talk Talk	45	1982
Today	5	1983
Candy	28	1983
Such A Shame	5	1984
Dum Dum Girl	10	1984
It's My Life	14	1984
Tomorrow Started	M	1984
I Don't Believe In You	1	1986
Life's What You Make It	3	1986
Give It Up	14	1986
Happiness Is Easy	34	1987
Living In Another World	39	1987
Inheritance	26	1988
Eden	31	1989
I Believe In You	40	1989
Ascension Day	39	1991

Tame Impala
Sundown Syndrome	115	2010
Tomorrow (Kali Uchis f/ Tame Impala)	M	2018
Neverender	85	2024

Tamperer, The, f/ Maya		
Feel It	59	1998
Tangerine Dream		
Love On A Real Train	M	1983
Cat Scan	95	1988
Mothers Of Rain	55	1989
Running Out Of Time / One For The Books	M	1989
Tanghetto		
Montevideo	M	2003
Tapia de Veer, Cristobal		
The White Lotus Theme (Renaissance) (Kabumi Remix / Tiësto Remix) / (Aloha)	101	2022
T-ara 티아라		
넘버나인 (No. 9)	40	2014
Tarkan		
Şimarik	65	2000
Bu Gece	90	2000
Taste Of Honey, A		
Boogie Oogie Oogie	9	1978
Sukiyaki	52	1981
t.A.T.u.		
All The Things She Said	32	2003
Show Me Love	93	2003
Dangerous And Moving (Intro)/All About Us	75	2005
Craving (I Only Want What I Can't Have)	40	2006
Fly On The Wall	44	2010
Taupin, Bernie		
Citizen Jane	56	1987
Tavares		
Whodunit	108	1977
Taylor, James		
Fire And Rain	P	1970
You've Got A Friend	P	1971
Mexico	P	1975
Your Smiling Face	59	1977
Up On The Roof	23	1979
Her Town Too	63	1981
Taylor, Johnnie		
Disco Lady	93	1976
Taylor, Koko		
Up In Flames	32	1990
Taylor, R. Dean		
Indiana Wants Me	P	1970
Taylor-Stanley, Julia		
Brave New World	60	2000

Tears For Fears (See also Roland Orzabal; Oleta Adams)		
Pale Shelter (You Don't Give Me Love)	2	1983
Mad World	4	1983
Change	14	1983
Suffer The Children	70	1984
Everybody Wants To Rule The World	3	1985
Head Over Heels	6	1985
Shout	20	1985
I Believe	27	1986
Mothers Talk/Sea Song	99	1986
Sowing The Seeds Of Love	4	1989
Woman In Chains	27	1990
Laid So Low (Tears Roll Down) / Tears Roll Down	31	1992
Elemental	16	1993
Fish Out Of Water	32	1993
Goodnight Song	50	1993
New Star	77	1994
Raoul And The Kings Of Spain	14	1995
Me And My Big Ideas/Los Reyes Católicos (Reprise)	7	1996
Humdrum And Humble	51	1996
Secrets	80	1996
Falling Down	90	1996
Quiet Ones	26	2004
I Love You But I'm Lost	53	2017
The Tipping Point	50	2021
Let It All Evolve	44	2022
My Demons	56	2022
Tedder, Ryan (See also OneRepublic)		
The Way I Feel	71	2006
Rocketeer	10	2011
Teddybears		
Cobrastyle	33	2008
Teenage Fanclub		
Born Under A Good Sign	128	2005
Tegan And Sara		
Video	15	2012
Body Work	60	2012
I Was A Fool	6	2013
Faint Of Heart	69	2016
Hold My Breath Until I Die	57	2019
Hello, I'm Right Here	36	2020
Télépopmusik (See also Angela McCluskey)		
Breathe	47	2002

Into Everything	41	2005

Telling, The

World On A Wing	26	1993
Guardian Angel	36	1993

Temper Trap, The

Thick As Thieves	83	2016

Temples

Afterlife	25	2024

Tempo, Nino, & April Stevens

Deep Purple	P	1963

Temposhark

It's Better To Have Loved	75	2007

Temptations, The

My Girl	P	1965
(I Know) I'm Losing You	P	1966
Get Ready	P	1966
Just My Imagination (Running Away With Me)	P	1971
Papa Was A Rollin' Stone	P	1972

10cc (See also Godley & Creme; Wax)

I'm Not In Love	P	1975
I'm Mandy Fly Me	M	1976
The Things We Do For Love	24	1977
Dreadlock Holiday	8	1978

Teng, Vienna

Hope On Fire	61	2004

Tennant, Neil (See also Pet Shop Boys; Electronic)

Getting Away With It	67	1990
No Regrets	46	1999

Tennis

Let's Make A Mistake Tonight	66	2023
Forbidden Doors	83	2023

Ten Years After

I'd Love To Change The World	P	1971

Terrell, Tammi

Ain't Nothing Like The Real Thing (w/ Marvin Gaye)	P	1968
You're All I Need To Get By (w/ Marvin Gaye)	P	1968

Texas (See also Sharleen Spiteri)

Black Eyed Boy	7	1998
The Hush	39	1999
Saint	47	1999
Summer Son	57	1999
In Our Lifetime	61	1999
When We Are Together	82	2000
Inner Smile	70	2003
Careful What You Wish For	54	2004

Get Down Tonight	10	2006
What About Us	11	2006
Can't Resist	66	2006
The Conversation	44	2013
Can't Control	13	2017
It Was Up To You	24	2017
Falling	93	2021

Teya & Salena

Who The Hell Is Edgar?	77	2023

Thalía

Te Perdiste Mi Amor	106	2013

Thames, Hudson

Drive It Like You Stole It	99	2016

Thanh Hưng

Yêu Khác Thương Hại (Love Others Pity)	85	2019

These Modern Socks

Worry Free Lifestyle	85	2008

They Might Be Giants

I'm Impressed	80	2007

Thievery Corporation

Lebanese Blonde	99	2001
The Time We Lost Our Way	43	2005
Marching The Hate Machines (Into The Sun)	101	2005

Thin Lizzy

The Boys Are Back In Town	55	1976

Thirsk, Kristy

Heaven's Earth	57	2000
Ray	41	2015

Thirty Seconds To Mars

Stuck	55	2024

This Mortal Coil (See also Cocteau Twins; Snowbird)

Alone/Mama K(2)	64	1987

This Picture

Step Up	6	1992

Thomas, B.J.

Hooked On A Feeling	P	1968

Thomas, Rob

Smooth	119	1999
This Is How A Heart Breaks	79	2005

Thomas, Timmy

Why Can't We Live Together	P	1972

Thompson, Chris

I Will Be With You (Where The Lost Ones Go)	54	2007

Thompson, Julie

My Paradise	11	2015

Your Secret's Safe	29	2015
Thompson, Linda		
Take Me On The Subway	84	1986
Thompson Twins (See also Babble)		
Lies	29	1983
Love On Your Side	70	1983
Hold Me Now	9	1984
Doctor! Doctor!	42	1984
Sister Of Mercy / The Gap	53	1984
Lay Your Hands On Me	100	1985
Nothing In Common	75	1986
Strange Jane	69	1992
The Invisible Man/The Saint	75	1992
Thorn, Tracey (See also Everything But The Girl)		
Protection	51	1995
Falling Off A Log	2	2007
A-Z	6	2007
Get Around To It	23	2007
The Tree Knows Everything	27	2009
Kentish Town	12	2010
Why Does The Wind?	82	2010
Smoke	1	2018
Sister	62	2018
Thorpe, Billy		
Children Of The Sun	60	1979
Thousand Points Of Night, A (Don Was)		
Read My Lips	114	1993
Three Degrees, The		
When Will I See You Again	P	1974
TSOP (The Sound Of Philadelphia) (w/ MFSB)	P	1974
Get Me (sampled from Here I Am, 1975)	95	2004
Three Dog Night		
One	P	1969
Eli's Coming	P	1969
Easy To Be Hard	P	1969
Out In The Country	P	1970
Liar	P	1971
An Old Fashioned Love Song	P	1971
Black & White	P	1972
Pieces Of April	P	1972
3LAU (See Blau)		
3 Mustaphas 3		
Awara Hoon	59	1990
Thunderball		
On The Sly	79	2002

Thunderclap Newman		
Something In The Air	P	1969
T.I.		
My Love	100	2007
Tiësto		
Sweet Misery	12	2004
Just Be	32	2006
Here On Earth/Always Near	47	2009
Written In Reverse	27	2014
Footprints	47	2014
The Right Song	114	2016
Double Trouble (Tiësto's Euro 90's Tribute Mix)	92	2020
The Motto	41	2021
The White Lotus Theme (Renaissance) (Tiësto Remix)	101	2022
I'd Bet	19	2023
Learn 2 Love	46	2023
Tijoux, Ana		
Hypnotized	18	2014
Tikaram, Tanita		
Twist In My Sobriety	7	1989
For All These Years	87	1989
'Til Tuesday (See also Aimee Mann)		
Voices Carry	55	1985
What About Love	36	1986
Coming Up Close	88	1987
Timbaland		
The Way I Are	1	2007
Apologize	39	2007
Bombay (f/ Amar & Jim Beanz)	M	2007
4 Minutes	37	2008
Return The Favor	17	2009
Can You Feel It	10	2010
God Only Knows (Timbaland Remix)	11	2021
Timberlake, Justin (See also *NSYNC; The Lonely Island)		
What Goes Around...Comes Around	94	2007
My Love	100	2007
4 Minutes	37	2008
Motherlover	94	2009
Drown	54	2024
Timex Social Club (See also Club Nouveau)		
Rumors	106	1986
Tinashe		
Joyride	87	2018

Ting Tings, The		
We Walk	112	2008
One By One	85	2012
Do It Again	99	2015
Tinie Tempah		
Hanging On	7	2012
Tiromancino		
Due Destini	4	2005
Muovo Le Ali Di Nuovo	52	2005
Angoli Di Cielo	11	2007
L'Alba Di Domani	42	2007
Mai Saputo Il Tuo Nome	63	2014
Piccoli Miracoli	44	2017
TLC		
What About Your Friends	76	1993
Waterfalls	103	1995
To, Alex 杜德伟 (Du De Wei)		
救你 (Save You)	14	1998
Toad The Wet Sprocket		
Something's Always Wrong	12	1994
Fall Down	48	1994
Todmobile		
Voodooman	65	2002
Tokens, The		
The Lion Sleeps Tonight	P	1961
Tokyo Tea Room		
If You Love Her	13	2024
Tomlinson, Louis (See also One Direction)		
Kill My Mind	73	2020
Tommy Tutone		
867-5309/Jenny	77	1982
Tomorrow X Together 투모로우바이투게더 (+OMORROW X +OGETHER)		
날씨를 잃어버렸어 (We Lost The Summer)	31	2021
Tom Tom Club (See also The Talking Heads)		
Genius Of Love	20	1982
Wordy Rappinghood	48	1982
The Man With The 4-Way Hips	68	1983
Suboceana	47	1989
Tonic		
If You Could Only See	51	1997
Too Much Joy		
Crush Story	93	1991
Topic		
I Adore You	48	2024
Topley-Bird, Martina		
I Still Feel	69	2005
Everywhere	56	2009
Tornados, The (The Tornadoes)		
Telstar	P	1962
Torrini, Emilíana		
To Be Free	22	2000
Wednesday's Child	9	2001
Total		
If You Want Me	26	1999
Toto		
Georgy Porgy	39	1979
Hold The Line	86	1979
99	11	1980
If It's The Last Night	72	1981
Rosanna	95	1982
Africa	23	1983
Toto Coelo (Total Coelo)		
I Eat Cannibals	136	1983
Milk From The Coconut (Part 1)	219	1983
Touch And Go		
Straight To...Number One	3	2001
Tove Lo		
Talking Body	91	2015
Scars	39	2016
Give It All Up	77	2021
How Long	21	2022
2 Die 4	53	2022
Call On Me	69	2022
My Oh My	43	2024
Love Bites	94	2024
Towa Tei		
Batucada	97	1996
Townshend, Pete (See also The Who)		
Let My Love Open The Door	4	1980
A Little Is Enough	16	1980
Toys, The		
A Lover's Concerto	P	1965
T'Pau		
Heart And Soul	62	1987
Traffic (See also Dave Mason; Steve Winwood)		
Dear Mr. Fantasy	P	1967
Trancendental		
Hamam/Istanbul Uyurken (Hamam Trance Version)	35	1999

Trans-Siberian Orchestra		
Christmas Eve/Sarajevo 12/24	X	1996
Trans X		
Living On Video	182	1983
Trash Can Sinatras, The		
Obscurity Knocks	92	1991
Travolta, John		
Let Her In	92	1976
Summer Nights	30	1978
T. Rex		
Bang A Gong (Get It On)	P	1972
TR-i (Todd Rundgren) (See also Todd Rundgren)		
Property	87	1993
Tricky (See also Massive Attack)		
Bonnie & Clyde	57	2013
Trilogía		
Todo Por Ti	60	1997
Trịnh Đình Quang		
Nếu Em Còn Tồn Tại (If I'm Still Alive)	58	2019
Triumph		
Hold On	38	1979
Troggs, The		
Love Is All Around	P	1968
TR/ST		
Dark Day	97	2024
True, Andrea, Connection		
More, More, More	12	1976
N.Y., You Got Me Dancing	16	1977
What's Your Name, What's Your Number	61	1978
Tsai, Jolin		
Gentlewomen	67	2018
Womxnly	88	2019
Tubes, The		
Don't Touch Me There	125	1976
Prime Time	M	1979
Don't Want To Wait Anymore	23	1981
She's A Beauty	126	1983
Tunstall, KT		
The Mountain	11	2019
Tu Phace		
On Time	78	2010
Turner, Laura		
Soul Deep	31	2004
Turner, Tina		
What's Love Got To Do With It	113	1984

We Don't Need Another Hero (Thunderdome)	12	1985
Private Dancer	49	1985
In Your Wildest Dreams	87	1997
Something Beautiful (2023 version)	62	2024
Turtles, The		
Happy Together	P	1967
You Showed Me	P	1969
TV On The Radio		
Happy Idiot	88	2014
Twain, Shania		
You're Still The One	94	1998
Number One	74	2023
12 Girls Band 女子十二楽坊		
Freedom (自由)	M	2001
Dunhuang (敦煌)	M	2005
Twenty One Pilots		
Paladin Shift	3	2024
21 Savage		
Creepin'	65	2023
Twin Shadow		
I Owe You This	54	2012
When The Lights Turn Out	100	2015
Twista		
Get Me	95	2004
2 Chainz		
Leggo	81	2013
Two Door Cinema Club		
Ordinary	97	2016
Talk	69	2019
2 Live Crew, The		
Me So Horny	M	1989
2manydjs (Soulwax)		
9 To 5 vs. Eple (w/ Destiny's Child sample)	M	2003
Two Nice Girls		
Only Today	23	1992
Princess Of Power	89	1992
2Pac (Tupac Shakur)		
California Love	106	1996
Tycoon		
Such A Woman/How Long (Can We Go On)	20	1979
tyDi		
Just Believe	67	2023
Tyler, Bonnie		
Total Eclipse Of The Heart	103	1983

Islands	112	1987
Tyler, The Creator		
Castaway	31	2019
Tzuke, Judie		
Stay With Me Till Dawn	16	2006
Enjoy The Ride	17	2008
Blue Chair	70	2008
Like The Sun (RyanDan w/ Bailey & Judie Tzuke)	67	2009

U

UB40		
Red Red Wine	83	1984
Always There	83	1997
Uchis, Kali		
Tomorrow (f/ Tame Impala)	M	2018
Blue	2	2023
Moonlight	64	2023
Igual Que Un Ángel	33	2024
Uh Huh Her		
Covered	46	2008
Common Reaction	10	2009
Same High	49	2010
Philosophy	69	2011
Many Colors	13	2012
Marstorm	62	2012
Innocence	10	2014
Hustle Me	65	2014
Shiiine	80	2014
Ullman, Tracey		
They Don't Know	30	1984
Ultravox (See also Midge Ure; Visage)		
The Voice	36	1982
Reap The Wild Wind	31	1983
Hymn	78	1983
Lament	20	1984
Dancing With Tears In My Eyes	27	1984
Same Old Story	83	1987
Perfecting The Art Of Common Ground	71	1995
Brilliant	83	2012
Under The Influence Of Giants		
Mama's Room	30	2007
Underwood, Carrie		
The Fighter	92	2016
Undisputed Truth, The		
Smiling Faces Sometimes	P	1971

Unheilig		
Sonne	10	2013
Unit 4 + 2		
Concrete And Clay	P	1965
UNKLE		
Looking For The Rain	57	2017
Urban, Keith		
The Fighter	92	2016
Gemini	113	2018
Ure, Midge (See also Ultravox; Visage; Band Aid)		
If I Was	20	1986
She Cried	92	1986
Hell To Heaven	14	1989
Just For You	78	1989
Dear God	86	1989
Sister And Brother	80	1990
Live Forever	13	1996
Breathe	55	1996
Trail Of Tears	64	1996
Personal Heaven	64	2008
Let It Rise	56	2010
Are We Connected	51	2014
Urge Overkill		
Take A Walk	51	1994
U.S. Girls		
4 American Dollars	42	2020
So Typically Now	21	2023
Us3		
Cantaloop (Flip Fantasia)	104	1994
Usher		
Yeah! (f/ Lil Jon & Ludacris)	M	2004
What's Your Name	111	2008
OMG	4	2010
DJ Got Us Fallin' In Love	42	2010
Looking 4 Myself	70	2012
Scream	91	2012
Usmanova, Yulduz		
Tsche Mischod	90	1995
Utada 宇多田 ヒカル (Hikaru Utada)		
Exodus '04	73	2005
Merry Christmas Mr. Lawrence – FYI	9	2009
Shittosaserubeki Jinsei (嫉妬されるべき 人生, A Life to Be Envied)	8	2018
Play A Love Song	73	2018

Utah Saints		
Something Good	91	1992
What Can You Do For Me	58	1993
Solution	100	1993
B777	7	2001
Massive / Sun / Punk Club	96	2001

Utopia (See also Todd Rundgren; TR-i; The New Cars)		
Set Me Free	91	1980

Uttara-Kuru		
Tsugaru	15	2002

U2 (See also Bono; The Edge)		
I Will Follow	20	1981
Tomorrow/October	25	1981
Gloria	10	1982
New Year's Day	18	1983
Two Hearts Beat As One	54	1983
Sunday Bloody Sunday	60	1983
Pride (In The Name Of Love)	17	1984
I Still Haven't Found What I'm Looking For	42	1987
With Or Without You	50	1987
Zoo Station	60	1992
Until The End Of The World	83	1992
Numb	56	1993
Hold Me, Thrill Me, Kiss Me, Kill Me	94	1995
Staring At The Sun	62	1997
Electrical Storm	67	2002
The Hands That Built America (Theme From "Gangs Of New York")	76	2002
Ordinary Love	33	2014
You're The Best Thing About Me	101	2018

Valens, Ritchie		
Donna/La Bamba	P	1958

Valeriya		
There I'll Be	42	2008
Where Are You?	95	2008
No One / Out Of Control	99	2008

Valli, Frankie (See also The Four Seasons)		
Can't Take My Eyes Off You	P	1967
My Eyes Adored You	P	1974
Our Day Will Come	P	1975
December, 1963 (Oh, What A Night)	27	1976
Grease	22	1978

van Buuren, Armin		
Feels So Good	5	2010
Take A Moment	95	2010
Sunny Days	21	2017
I Need You	52	2017
Sex, Love & Water	86	2018
Lonely For You	6	2020
Phone Down	43	2020
Always	46	2020
It Could Be	67	2020
Runaway	84	2020

van de Wal, Marian		
La Mirada Interior	88	2006

Vandi, Despina		
Sunday Version 02	1	2011

van Doorn, Sander		
Rolling The Dice	82	2012

van Dyk, Paul		
Time Of Our Lives	86	2004

Van Dyke, Dick		
Chim Chim Cher-ee (w/ Julie Andrews)	P	1964

Vanessa-Mae		
Velvet Rope	23	1998

Vangelis (See also Jon & Vangelis; Aphrodite's Child)		
Chung Kuo	M	1979
Chariots Of Fire – Titles	9	1982
Love Theme/Blade Runner (End Titles)	M	1982
Mask: Movement 2	66	1986
The Will Of The Wind	13	1989
Rotation's Logic	66	1990
Good To See You	19	1991
Side Streets	59	1991
Losing Sleep (Still, My Heart)	61	1996
Spanish Harbour	88	1997

Vanity Fare		
Early In The Morning	P	1969

Vannelli, Gino		
Hurts To Be In Love	106	1985
Wild Horses	114	1987

Vanotek		
Love Is Gone	63	2019

VanWarmer, Randy		
Just When I Needed You Most	98	1979

Vapors, The		
Turning Japanese	161	1980

Vaughan, Rhydian 鳳小岳		
Pumpkin Man南瓜超人	126	2023

Vaughan, Sarah		
Whatever Lola Wants	P	1955
Vaughn, Billy, & His Orchestra		
A Swingin' Safari	P	1962
Vaults		
One Last Night	25	2015
Védís		
Thoughts	68	2002
Vee, Bobby		
Run To Him	P	1961
The Night Has A Thousand Eyes	P	1962
Vega, Suzanne		
Left Of Center	10	1986
Solitude Standing	33	1987
Luka	57	1987
Gypsy/Wooden Horse (Caspar Hauser's Song)	89	1988
Rusted Pipe / Rusted Pipe (Tom's Mix)	16	1990
Pilgrimage	66	1991
Big Space/Predictions	87	1991
99.9F°	28	1992
Blood Makes Noise	44	1992
In Liverpool	47	1992
Casual Match	12	1996
Birth-Day (Love Made Real)	54	1996
World Before Columbus	41	1997
Penitent	49	2001
It Makes Me Wonder	55	2002
Vegas, Dimitri		
Hey Baby	25	2017
The White Lotus Theme (Aloha)	101	2022
Vela, Rosie		
Magic Smile	9	1986
Interlude	18	1987
Sunday	30	1987
Fool's Paradise	31	1987
Velasquez, Jaci		
Child Of Mine (I Have Come)	30	1998
You're Not There	19	2001
Velvet Cash		
Pray For Me	1	2022
Hypnotic	36	2022
Ventures, The		
Walk – Don't Run / Walk, Don't Run '64	P	1960
Hawaii Five-O	P	1968

Venus Hum		
Montana	80	2003
Hummingbirds	9	2004
Venuti, Mario		
Ventre Della Città	54	2014
Il Tramonto	87	2014
Verve, The (See also Richard Ashcroft)		
Bittersweet Symphony	58	1998
This Time	70	1999
Verve Pipe, The		
Photograph	84	1996
Vesna		
My Sister's Crown	96	2023
Vieha, Mark / Keith Reinhard		
Big Mac Song	T	1975
Viers, Laura		
Freedom Feeling	96	2021
Village People		
5 O'Clock In The Morning	M	1982
Vinton, Bobby		
Blue Velvet	P	1963
Blue On Blue	P	1963
Mr. Lonely	P	1964
Visage (See also Midge Ure; Ultravox)		
Fade To Grey	M	1980
Vision / Vision II		
Vision (O Euchari In Leta Via)	5	1995
Praise For The Mother (O Virga Ac Diadema)	23	1995
Eye Goes Blind (Aya) (Vision II)	38	1997
Vitamin Z		
Burning Flame	94	1985
Angela	44	1986
Don't Wait For Me	60	1990
Vittoria And The Hyde Park		
Burn Down The Summer	2	2017
Voegele, Kate		
Burning The Harbor	24	2011
Vogues, The		
Five O'Clock World	P	1966
Voice Of The Beehive		
Monsters And Angels	98	1991
Voicestra		
Sweet In The Mornin'	43	1992
Vollenweider, Andreas		
Book Of Roses	79	1992

von Deylen, Christopher (See Schiller)		
Voudouris, Roger		
Get Used To It	77	1979

W

Wainwright, Martha		
Set The Fire To The Third Bar	39	2006
Waite, John (See also The Babys)		
Missing You	67	1984
Waitresses, The		
I Know What Boys Like	78	1982
Christmas Wrapping	X	1982
Walker, Alan		
Faded / (Restrung Remix)	21	2016
Alone	74	2017
Ignite	83	2018
Diamond Heart	43	2019
Man On The Moon	97	2021
Walker Brothers, The		
Make It Easy On Yourself	P	1965
The Sun Ain't Gonna Shine (Anymore)	P	1966
Wallen, Morgan		
Sunrise	41	2023
Wallflowers, The		
Closer To You	99	2003
Reboot The Mission	122	2012
Wall Of Voodoo		
Mexican Radio	165	1983
Walsh, Joe (See also The James Gang; Eagles)		
Rocky Mountain Way	P	1973
Life's Been Good	45	1978
Wanderlust		
I Walked	36	1995
Wang, Billie 比莉 (Billie)		
什麼都不必說– (2022 Remix) (Don't Have To Say A Thing)	47	2022
Wang Chung		
Dance Hall Days	118	1984
Wanted, The		
Chasing The Sun	93	2012
War		
Spill The Wine	P	1970
All Day Music	P	1971
The Cisco Kid	P	1973
Why Can't We Be Friends?	P	1975

Low Rider	P	1975
Ward, Anita		
Ring My Bell	201	1979
Ware, Jessie		
In Your Eyes	19	2021
Save A Kiss	28	2021
The Kill/Remember Where You Are	36	2021
Begin Again	22	2023
Free Yourself	45	2023
Warnes, Jennifer		
First We Take Manhattan	36	1987
War On Drugs, The		
I Don't Wanna Wait	92	2021
Warpaint		
New Song	27	2016
Warwick, Dionne (Dionne Warwicke)		
Don't Make Me Over	P	1962
Anyone Who Had A Heart	P	1963
Walk On By	P	1964
Trains And Boats And Planes	P	1966
I Just Don't Know What To Do With Myself	P	1966
What The World Needs Now Is Love	P	1966
Alfie	P	1967
The Windows Of The World	P	1967
I Say A Little Prayer	P	1967
(Theme From) Valley Of The Dolls	P	1968
Do You Know The Way To San Jose	P	1968
(There's) Always Something There To Remind Me	P	1968
Promises, Promises	P	1968
I'll Never Fall In Love Again	P	1969
This Girl's In Love With You	P	1969
Then Came You (w/ Spinners) (listed as Dionne Warwicke)	P	1974
Love Power	113	1987
Washed Out		
You And I	15	2011
Far Away	25	2011
Straight Back	50	2012
All I Know	47	2013
It All Feels Right	73	2013
Hard To Say Goodbye	86	2017
Reckless Desires / Game Of Chance	53	2020
Hide	101	2020
Wait On You	68	2024

Waterlillies		
She Must Be In Love	M	1994

Waters, Crystal		
Gypsy Woman (She's Homeless) (La Da Dee La Da Da)	71	1991
100% Pure Love	M	1994

Watley, Jody		
Still A Thrill	124	1987
Don't You Want Me	123	1988
Friends (f/ Eric B. & Rakim)	144	1989

Wax (Wax UK) (See also Andrew Gold; 10cc)		
Only A Visitor	23	1986

Way Out West		
Diamond Dust	4	2018
Running Away	91	2018

Wayquay		
Navigate	81	1997

Weekend Players		
I'll Be There	64	2003
Jericho	74	2003

Weeknd, The		
Wicked Games	9	2013
Tears In The Rain	80	2013
Love Me Harder	22	2014
Where You Belong	15	2015
Earned It (Fifty Shades Of Grey)	49	2015
Can't Feel My Face	76	2015
Starboy	7	2016
Rockin'	108	2016
Secrets	10	2017
Lust For Life	28	2017
Love To Lay	38	2017
Party Monster	62	2017
Pray For Me	119	2018
Lost In The Fire	80	2019
Heartless	83	2019
Blinding Lights	12	2020
In Your Eyes / (2021 remix w/ Doja Cat)	105	2020
Take My Breath	63	2021
Moth To A Flame	99	2021
How Do I Make You Love Me?	42	2022
Is There Someone Else?	46	2022
Less Than Zero	57	2022
Creepin'	65	2023
Double Fantasy	71	2023

	26	2024
We Still Don't Trust You	26	2024
One Of The Girls	107	2024

Weepies, The		
River From The Sky	64	2015
Does Not Bear Repeating	93	2015

Weezer		
Byzantine	116	2019

Weisberg, Tim		
The Power Of Gold	64	1978

Weissberg, Eric, & Steve Mandell		
Dueling Banjos	P	1973

Welch, Bob (See also Fleetwood Mac)		
Sentimental Lady	32	1977
Hot Love, Cold World	95	1978

Welch, Florence (See also Florence + The Machine)		
Sweet Nothing	89	2012

Wellington, Danaé		
Wild Flame	71	2024

Welsh, Laura		
Cold Front	81	2015

Wendy And Lisa (See also Prince & The Revolution)		
Waterfall	95	1987

Wes (Madiko)		
Alane	87	1998

West, Kanye (Ye)		
American Boy	108	2008
Heartless	123	2009
No Church In The Wild	93	2011

Westenra, Hayley		
Across The Universe Of Time	19	2004
You Are Water	49	2006
Prayer	63	2006

West India Company		
Ave Maria (Om Ganesha)	80	1985

West Indian Girl		
Miles From Monterey	39	2005
What Are You Afraid Of	48	2005

Weyes Blood		
Butterfly Net	15	2024

Whack, Tierra		
DIFFICULT	10	2024

Wham! (See also George Michael)		
Wake Me Up Before You Go-Go	160	1984
Careless Whisper (Wham! f/ George Michael)	7	1985

Everything She Wants	34	1985
Last Christmas	X	1986

White, Barry (See also Love Unlimited; Love Unlimited Orchestra)

Never, Never Gonna Give Ya Up	P	1973
Can't Get Enough Of Your Love, Babe	P	1974
It's Ecstasy When You Lay Down Next To Me	25	1977
Prelude To The Garden/The Secret Garden (Sweet Seduction Suite)	116	1990
In Your Wildest Dreams	87	1997

White, Thomas

Candy	20	2012

Whitesnake

Is This Love	275	1987

White Town

Your Woman	17	1997

Whitewaits (See also Cause & Effect)

Island	59	2013

Whittaker, Roger

The Last Farewell	P	1975
New World In The Morning	P	1975

Who, Betty

A Night To Remember	13	2015
High Society	24	2015

Who, The (See also Roger Daltrey; Pete Townshend)

I Can See For Miles	P	1967
See Me, Feel Me/Listening To You	P	1970
Behind Blue Eyes	P	1971
Won't Get Fooled Again	P	1971
Baba O'Riley	P	1971
Love, Reign O'er Me	P	1973
Squeeze Box	96	1976
Who Are You	44	1978
Long Live Rock	97	1979
You Better You Bet	82	1981
Don't Let Go The Coat	84	1981
Eminence Front	132	1983

Wiedlin, Jane (See also Go-Go's)

Rush Hour	28	1988
Inside A Dream	31	1988
Lover's Night	57	1988
Song Of The Factory	73	1989

Wild Cherry

Play That Funky Music	13	1976

Wilde, Kim

Kids In America	107	1982

You Came	80	1988
Without Your Love	47	2016

Wilkinson, Kristin

Cowboy's Dream/All The Pretty Horses (Medley)	82	2001

will.i.am (See also Black Eyed Peas)

Beep (The Pussycat Dolls f/ will.i.am)	M	2006
What's Your Name	111	2008
OMG	4	2010
3 Words	8	2010
Photograph	20	2010
Scream & Shout	90	2013
Mind Your Business	133	2023

Williams, Andy

Butterfly	P	1957
House Of Bamboo	P	1959
Can't Get Used To Losing You/Days Of Wine And Roses	P	1963
It's The Most Wonderful Time Of The Year	X	1963
Kisses Sweeter Than Wine	P	1963
Born Free	P	1967
Music To Watch Girls Go By	P	1967
Love Theme From "Romeo And Juliet" (A Time For Us)	P	1969
(Where Do I Begin) Love Story	P	1971
Love Theme From "The Godfather" (Speak Softly Love)	P	1972

Williams, Deniece

Too Much, Too Little, Too Late (w/ Johnny Mathis)	M	1978

Williams, Hayley

Creepin'	71	2020

Williams, John

Main Title (Theme From "Jaws")	P	1975
Theme From "Close Encounters Of The Third Kind"	16	1978
Christmas At Hogwarts	X	2001

Williams, Joy

Before I Sleep	86	2015

Williams, Lucinda

Righteously	79	2003

Williams, Mason

Classical Gas	P	1968

Williams, Michelle

Unexpected Intro/Hello Heartbreak	7	2008

Williams, Pharrell (See also N*E*R*D)

Get Lucky	64	2013

W

Happy	139	2014
Feels	115	2017
Williams, Robbie (See also Take That)		
No Regrets	46	1999
Millennium	72	1999
Rock DJ	91	2000
Not Of This Earth	73	2001
My Culture	65	2003
Love Somebody	95	2003
Lovelight	85	2006
Bodies	42	2009
Last Days Of Disco	83	2009
Starstruck	38	2010
Difficult For Weirdos	57	2010
Williams, Roger		
Born Free	P	1966
Willis, Chris		
Love Is Gone	101	2008
Will Powers		
Adventures In Success	79	1983
Wilson, Al		
Show And Tell	P	1973
Wilson, Carl (See also The Beach Boys)		
Heaven	8	1981
Wilson, Lainey		
Never Say Never	83	2022
Wilson, Meri		
Telephone Man	71	1977
Wilson, Nancy		
What Are You Doing New Year's Eve	X	1963
Wings (See also Paul McCartney & Wings)		
Let 'Em In	60	1976
Silly Love Songs	90	1976
London Town	66	1978
With A Little Luck	111	1978
Goodnight Tonight	51	1979
Arrow Through Me	100	1979
Winston, George		
Thanksgiving / Joy	X	1982
Winter, Edgar, Group		
Frankenstein	P	1973
Winwood, Steve (See also Blind Faith; Traffic)		
While You See A Chance	44	1981
Arc Of A Diver	54	1981
Wire		
Four Long Years	87	2009

Wire Train		
Crashing Back To You	76	1992
Withers, Bill		
Ain't No Sunshine	P	1971
Lovely Day	38	1978
Wiz Khalifa		
Too Wild	69	2014
Wizkid		
Borrowed Love	40	2019
Wobble('s), Jah, Invaders Of The Heart		
Visions Of You	24	1992
Soledad	42	1992
Becoming More Like God	62	1994
Wolfgang Press, The		
Going South	35	1995
Womack & Womack		
Teardrops	30	1989
Wonder, Stevie		
I Was Made To Love Her	P	1967
My Cherie Amour	P	1969
Signed, Sealed, Delivered I'm Yours	P	1970
If You Really Love Me	P	1971
Superstition	P	1972
You Are The Sunshine Of My Life	P	1973
Living In The City	P	1973
Higher Ground	P	1973
Don't You Worry 'Bout A Thing	P	1974
Sir Duke	92	1977
Feeding Off The Love Of The Land	112	1991
Wong, David 黃大煒		
So Long	12	2000
秋天1944 (The Fall Of 1944)	20	2000
Wong, Faye 王菲 (Wong Fei)		
墮落 (Decadence / Duoluo)	M	1996
The Amusement Park (娛樂場) (w/ Cocteau Twins)	M	1997
新房客 (New Roommate / Xin Fang Ke)	M	2000
彼岸花 (Flower of Paradise / Bi'an Hua)	M	2000
Wonho 원호		
Lose	77	2022
Wood, Evan Rachel		
All Is Found	18	2020
Woods, Renn		
Aquarius	M	1979

W

Woods, Stevie		
Just Can't Win 'Em All	98	1982
World Order		
World Order (Welcome To Tokyo Remix)	75	2015
Wright, Betty		
Dance With Me	53	1978
Wright, Chely		
Say The Word	29	2019
Wright, Gary		
Love Is Alive	5	1976
Dream Weaver	15	1976
Really Wanna Know You	51	1981
Wroldsen, Ina		
Places	20	2017
Breathe	44	2018
Wynette, Tammy		
D-I-V-O-R-C-E	P	1968
Stand By Your Man	P	1968

X

X Ambassadors		
Chapter One: The Sleeping Giant/Beautiful Liar	34	2021
X-Perience		
I Feel Safe	32	2008
Personal Heaven	64	2008
Xscape		
Keep On, Keepin' On	65	1996
XTC		
Making Plans For Nigel	M	1979
Ten Feet Tall	43	1980
Generals And Majors	35	1981
Runaways	8	1982
Fly On The Wall	19	1982
Senses Working Overtime	49	1982
Great Fire	98	1983
This World Over	8	1985
Dear God	12	1987
Another Satellite	14	1987
Grass	90	1987
Chalkhills And Children	26	1989
War Dance	2	1992
Xu Shu Hao 許 書豪 (Haor Xu)		
不畏誰 (Amistad)	37	2017

Xymox (Clan Of Xymox)		
The Shore Down Under	17	1991
Believe Me Sometimes	99	1992

Y

YACHT		
Dystopia (The Earth Is On Fire)	67	2011
Yagnik, Alka		
Hindi Sad Diamonds	89	2001
Yandar & Yostin		
Sola Es Mejor	54	2022
Yang, Faith 楊乃文 (Yang Naiwen)		
我給的愛 (I Give You Love)	6	2000
Flow	8	2023
I'd Like To Give Up 亲爱的我不想努力了 (f/ Our Shame)	24	2024
Yanni		
Looking Glass	103	1987
The Keeper	35	2009
Yao Liu Yi (姚六一)		
In The Mist (雾里)	9	2024
Yardbirds, The (See also Eric Clapton)		
For Your Love	P	1965
Heart Full Of Soul	P	1965
Shapes Of Things	P	1966
Yatra, Sebastián		
Falta Amor	31	2020
Yazoo (Yaz) (See also Alison Moyet; Depeche Mode; Erasure)		
Nobody's Diary/State Farm	19	1983
Don't Go	42	1983
Only You	62	1983
Yeah Boy		
On My Mind	40	2017
Years & Years		
Desire	85	2015
Meteorite	68	2016
Palo Santo	43	2018
Hypnotised	10	2019
Play	39	2019
Dreamland	75	2020
A Second To Midnight	94	2021
Strange And Unusual	34	2022
Yeh, Sally 葉蒨文 (Sally Yip/Yip Sin-Man)		
潇洒走一回 (Walk Gracefully/Cool Walk)	20	1992

焚心以火 (Throw Heart To Fire)	65	1992

Yehonathan (Gatro)

On A Hot Summer Night/Just Another Summer (Hebrew Version)	93	2010

Yello

Desire	50	1985
Vicious Games	70	1985

Yellow Claw

Good Day	93	2017

Yellow Magic Orchestra (YMO) (See also Ryuichi Sakamoto)

Lotus Love	M	1983

Yes (See also Jon Anderson; Jon & Vangelis; Asia; Keats; The Buggles)

I've Seen All Good People (a. Your Move / b. All Good People)	P	1971
Roundabout	P	1972
Owner Of A Lonely Heart	32	1984
Leave It	94	1984

Yeter, Burak

Friday Night	40	2020
My Life Is Going On	57	2020

Yola

If I Had To Do It All Again	9	2021
Starlight	10	2021
Dancing Away In Tears	35	2021
Faraway Look	52	2021
Future Enemies	64	2024

Yorn, Pete

Undercover	91	2007

Yosefa

Place With No Name	9	1996
Coast Line	17	1996

Young, Adam (See Owl City)

Young, Neil (See also Crosby, Stills, Nash & Young)

Cinnamon Girl	P	1970
Southern Man	P	1970
Old Man	P	1972
The Needle And The Damage Done	P	1972
The Ways Of Love	129	1990
War Of Man	62	1992
Philadelphia	94	1994

Young, Paul

Come Back And Stay	38	1984
Love Of The Common People	51	1984
Wherever I Lay My Hat (That's My Home)	57	1984
Everytime You Go Away	104	1985
Losing Sleep (Still, My Heart)	61	1996

Youngbloods, The

Get Together	P	1969

Young-Holt Unlimited

Soulful Strut	P	1968

Young Love

Find A New Way	33	2007

Young Parisians

Jump The Next Train	29	2023

Young Rascals, The (The Rascals)

Groovin'	P	1967
How Can I Be Sure	P	1967

Yuna

Live Your Life	94	2012
Castaway	31	2019

Yung, Joey 容祖兒 / 容祖儿

Searching For Answers (答案之書)	36	2018

Z

Zager, Michael, Band

Let's All Chant	2	1978

Zager & Evans

In The Year 2525 (Exordium & Terminus)	P	1969

Zahn, Spencer

Quiet In A World Full Of Noise	111	2024

ZAYN (See also One Direction)

Dusk Till Dawn	125	2018

Zazie

Rose	20	1998
Ça Fait Mal Et Ça Fait Rien	4	1999
Tous Des Anges	13	1999
Made In Love	21	2000
Rue De La Paix	25	2002
On Éteint	39	2002
Rodéo	11	2005
La Pluie Et Le Beau Temps	18	2005
Doolididom	67	2005
Des Rails	17	2007
Je Suis Un Homme	44	2007
Yin Yang	83	2007
FM Air	75	2008
La Passion	83	2008
Let It Shine (radio edit)	63	2023
Là Où Je Vais	22	2024

Do you cherish the moment when a song
vibrates something in your home?

Epilogue

Music never dies with an artist; it plays forever.

My Sincere Thanks

Foremost, I must thank Mom and Dad. I think you raised a decent child, and I hope I made you proud.

And I have to thank all the music people in my life (current and past) for their support, for enduring my music over the years, for playing music-related games with me, for sharing long discussions about music, and mostly, for introducing great songs to me! I am forever grateful.

I have asked friends their favorite music artist of all time. Not everyone is able to answer this question so I often restate it in a different way: If you were on a deserted island and could only listen to music from one artist or band, who would it be?

From my friends and family who responded, in their honor I thank their favorite artists:

Art Garfunkel

Whitney Houston

Pet Shop Boys

Tears For Fears

John Mellencamp

Nilsson

Kelly Clarkson Akina Nakamori

George Michael Nine Inch Nails John Denver

Everything But Judy Collins Sheena Easton ABBA
Coldplay The Girl

Mariah Carey Patti Smith Depeche Mode

Def Leppard Ella Fitzgerald Boston Luke Combs

Daryl Hall & John Oates Elton John Sia David Bromberg

Janet Jackson Fleetwood Mac Madredeus Meat Loaf 311

Black Sabbath Calvin Harris Led Zeppelin Carpenters

Marvin Gaye Madonna Herb Alpert Keith Urban

Barbra Streisand George Harrison

Eurythmics Beyond Sérgio Mendes Beatles The 1975

Christina Aguilera Taylor Swift Tracy Chapman Tori Amos

*NSYNC Bee Gees Queen Rush Cleo Laine

Yoshiki Fukuyama The Driver Era

Lady Gaga

Joni Mitchell David Byrne David Bowie A - Mei

Tommy Bolin The Rolling Stones Supertramp

Mercedes Sosa Enigma Genesis Lucinda Williams

Dolly Parton Elle King Toto
Radiohead

Ollie Journey Mayday Prince

BB King Wong Fei

Spandau Ballet Bob Dylan

Utada Hikaru Michael Jackson

Talking Heads

George Benson

Olivia Newton-John

Perfume

BEGIN Westlife

John Coltrane

k.d. lang Sheila Majid

Phil Collins Song Dongye

Sohyang The Smiths

Phil Collins

Go-Go's Eagles india.arie Misa

Blondie Backstreet Boys **Heart** Earth, Wind & Fire

Jefferson Starship Michael Bublé **Soft Cell**

Jonathan Lee Ricky Hsiao Joy Division Guns N' Roses

Alison Krauss Air Supply Junior Vasquez

The Art Of Noise

English Beat Yumi Matsutoya Ed Sheeran Cher

Céline Dion The Cure The Cranberries Rage Against The Machine

Oingo Boingo/Danny Elfman

The Weeknd Amy Winehouse

Dan Fogelberg Jamiroquai

Green Day Etta James

XTC Joe Hisaishi **INXS** Traveling Wilburys

Marcell Siahaan Savage Garden Procol Harum **Adele**

Alison Moyet Diana Krall Eason Chan Tom Jones **KISS**

P!NK Bruce Springsteen Bon Jovi Namcha Jim Croce

Frank Sinatra Gogol Bordello Peter, Paul & Mary

Elvis Costello The Dramatics

Billy Joel Crosby, Stills, Nash & Young

Electric Light Orchestra Bonnie Raitt

Enya Sam Smith Jackson Browne

Annie Lennox

And I thank the radio station that exposed this teenager to music beyond the top hits: KTOE (1970s Mankato, Minnesota).

Final thanks to these record stores. I would never have found the music I love without you.

- The Lost Chord
- Electric Fetus
- Northern Lights
- Garage D'Or
- Oar Folkjokeopus
- Musicland
- Cheapos
- Virgin Megastore (Hong Kong)
- HMV (Hong Kong and Canada)

Please support your local music stores, venues, and artists! Always support the arts. Artists need us as much as we need them.

Final Thoughts about the Future

As I age and my remaining life gets shorter, my tastes have become more discerning and possibly more sophisticated, and I think this is reflected in my more recent year-end lists. I want to spend my remaining time with the best music—my old favorites, and new songs dissimilar to those I have heard before.

In the end, I am uncertain if this book will be loved or read by many . . . but still, I leave my small legacy in these lists. My songs are my epitaph (a very, very wordy epitaph) since I will have no gravestone that barely one generation beyond me would ever visit. Maybe a park bench somewhere lush and sylvan will forever bear my real name.

This book will exist somewhere, in a library, a coffee shop bookshelf, or in an attic of a music lover, collecting dust for decades, if humanity lasts that long. I can rest knowing I presented something important in my life; and in knowing I possess an ISBN.

Is my musical obsession of interest to others? I may not be an influencer; I am, after all, just me. But if I can "tune in & turn on" one person to a new song or artist, then I have fulfilled my mission of sharing music with the world. My desire is that this book is a gateway to new music for some, and a confirmation of shared musical tastes for others.

Some of these songs are waiting for a new audience. Many of my top songs have few hits when you examine the number of Shazam requests. I found one #1 song of mine where I was the only search.

It is my desire that my lists awaken musical memories of your own, generated by an obscure artist or a blast from your past. And I hope I gave you a few laughs along the way. (My personal editor found out I was once a janitor. She smiled.)

I dream one day to have a forum to discuss these songs and others' music. And to have a place to share my future year-end lists. Maybe a music-streaming channel, or a web page, though I am not a tech-savvy guy. Gee, I dread the idea of creating an ebook version. And I shy away from fame.

This is my musical love letter to the world and to the artists who made my life something special. I am grateful to every artist within. I hope my fervor and my enthusiasm for music shines! If this book becomes somewhat popular, my wish is to do some good in the world with the funds.

The world needs music more than ever. Without music, my life would not be as complete, as fulfilled, or as happy.

As I write this book, I notice disturbing trends, especially in one musical genre, against common decency toward all humanity. Truly sad when you have *coward[s] of the county* who fail to decry hate speech by caring more about money than being an example for a world where music stands for kindness, peace, and love. Get your acts together.

Speak out! I know some Chicks braver than y'all.

When you have a voice, use it. And not just to sing.

Of course, my book, my project, never really ends. The music, and my lists, will continue until I die. And like me, artists will come and go (so often too soon), and favorite musical styles will disappear like last year's fashion.

I dread the day the music dies.

In a fantastic, future dream world I can imagine my top 101 lists filled with songs recommended by you. How *Amazing* (#52, 2001; #14, 2017) does that sound?

Thank You . . . . (#70, 2015)

So Long . . . . (#71, 1978; #12, 2000)

Good Bye . . . . (#99, 2000)

Truly . . . . (#1, 2003)

Hard To Say Goodbye . . . . (#86, 2017)

Good Friends . . . . (#56, 1986)

Call Me . . . . (#82, 1980; legacy song, 1966, Chris Montez)

Here's Where The Story Ends . . . . (#14, 1990)

...*for now*.

The world spins as a turntable
to blend our overlapping rhythms
across time zones and oceans
till humanity merges in a song for peace.

Time for Music Games!

1. *What song titles come to mind for any of these words?*
   Or other words you choose.

Hand	**Open**	**Laugh**	**Hope**
Cat	**Red**	**Desert**	**Love**
Tree	**Lonely**	**You**	**World**
Smile	**Day**	**Run**	**Peace**

2. *Sing a mondegreen from your past to the person next to you.*

3. *Name your top three favorite songs, albums, or musical artists, composers, or groups.*

4. *A-Z songs: (Group activity) Sing a song title that starts with each letter of the alphabet. Take turns around the room or sing titles randomly.*

5. *View the original music videos for ten songs or artists you did not know before.*

Let's music!

Superior, Wisconsin, 1996

As I was preparing for a visit to my beloved gay bar—the Main Club—below my seventh-floor room in the Androy Hotel, an infomercial appeared on whatever murder or crime channel I was vaguely watching on the room's corner-ceiling TV. It wasn't more than seconds into the infomercial when I froze and stared at an ad for a CD compilation titled *Pure Moods*. It was like someone had read my musical mind when the TV voice-over intoned something along the lines of "But wait! You get Enigma, Deep Forest, Mike Oldfield, Sacred Spirit, Ennio Morricone, and Enya!"

As the song titles scrolled up the screen I was mesmerized! Then the ad played DJ Dado's version of *X-Files* and I knew I had to order this CD ("not available in stores!") despite owning 90 percent of the songs on the collection. I relive this memory when I hear any *Pure Moods* song, and I chuckle to myself each time about what a musical dork I am.

Over a decade later, in the same bar, a friend and I simultaneously began singing *Don't Call Me Baby* after another companion called one of us "baby." We immediately mused who sang it— sometimes it is more fun to try to remember something than to look it up instantly. Unsuccessful in our memories, I went outside for a smoke to think. I had barely lit my cig when I remembered the artist. I placed the cig on a ledge, still burning, and hurried inside as my friend was simultaneously running toward me. Upon sight of each other we screamed out the artist, "Madison Avenue!" And laughed at our musical madness.

This same friend and his partner used to manage the music talent for their cities' gay pride festival. In a past year, I happened to ask who it would be and he announced Uh Huh Her.

My response? "OMG, I love them!"

His reponse, "You are my only friend, outside of lesbians, who knows them. You wanna be their security at the concert?"

Um . . . "Hell to the yes!"

By the end of my security stint, there was only one lingering pest who I kindly guided away at the meet-and-greet after the awesome show. Bonus: They signed the CD I brought.

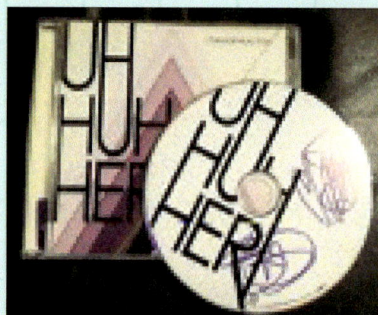

Klaus & Claus, 1982-1985

I struggled with this story and the songs I attach to two special people who share the same name, with a different spelling. One is a dear friend from my early twenties, a time when I really needed someone who understood me, the other my paternal grandfather. Let's call them Klaus and Claus. Where do I start?

Klaus appeared in my life near the end of college. Along with a mutual friend, we moved to the big city and became roommates. We were young, fun, and underfunded, with not a care in the world despite our meager incomes in the Reagan years. We had a blast during our time together in two roach-infested apartments. In one of them, the dining room was my bed, with a sheet providing "privacy." But the sheet did not protect me from the cockroaches.

Eventually we moved to separate addresses. I had a new roommate in an old brownstone, whereas Klaus and our mutual friend rented a carriage house on an alley near the art school they attended. I was selling shoes in the suburbs then, until my eventual career began a few years later. More on that when Grandpa appears in this tale.

We often went music shopping together (I was the only one who owned a car) and then we'd spend time in their carriage house, partying and sharing our latest musical finds. We always thought we owned artists before the rest of the world discovered them . . . Thomas Dolby, Baltimora, The Smiths, Yello, Thompson Twins, Yazoo—they all come to mind. Klaus was the friend who introduced me to Madonna when he bought her *Lucky Star/Everybody* 12-inch single. In turn, I shared the debut Tears For Fears album or Simple Minds's latest, unknown to us until the same day I purchased both based solely on their cover designs and song titles.

We shared so much music over the years, even when Klaus moved to New York City, so I find it difficult to settle on a definitive song that most reminds me of him. It could be *Pie Jesu* by Sarah Brightman, or *Music For Boys* by The Suburbs. I looked back at my year-end lists to find his name. You see, long ago, I used to write people's names next to the songs that reminded me of them. The first one I could find for Klaus was *The Day Before You Came* by ABBA. One of the final songs (as known to us at that time) from one of his favorite artists.

I wish I hadn't stopped listing names next to my songs some years ago, since it is now the only way I remember certain people from my past. But Klaus I can never forget. I can't imagine how my early adult life would have been without his friendship and encouragement.

Sadly, Klaus died after I knew him only a decade. He was my only close friend to die of AIDS, back when the disease was so misunderstood by the general public. His family, our mutual friend, and I were at his side in the hospital on his final day. I think of him often and wonder how my life would have been if he hadn't come into it; to remember the day before he came.

(continued)

When I look back at my life, I feel genuinely blessed to have had the opportunity to travel with all four of my grandparents. I was lucky. This music memory revolves around my grandpa Claus.

In 1985, he asked me if I would go to Norway with him so he could meet relatives and see the family farms. Our unique last name came from one of the farms we would visit (an old agrarian way to acquire a name, so it seems). Grandpa knew basic Norwegian. I knew only a few words.

He offered to pay for this journey since I did not have money for such a trip. While I planned it, purchased plane tickets, and booked hotel rooms, Grandpa got a passport and wrote letters to our Norwegian relatives about our arrival.

Mind you, this grandparent was special to me. I used to stay at his house as a boy and help him strip down old engines and other junk for scrap metal. We'd go to the town dump to find anything salvageable, then break it down in his garage and separate into piles of iron, steel, copper, zinc, and aluminum. I recall how I played with balls of mercury I took from old transistor tubes or other gizmos, and let the metallic drops roll around in my palms, sometimes covered in dirt. Did I know of the dangers back then? I am still alive.

I still have a metal protractor I found on a day we scavenged through garbage recently dumped by the local hospital. I am sure there were no HIPAA violations to be found.

After we had booked our trip, but before we left, I was offered my first well-paid job. This was great news until I realized vacation wouldn't be allowed during my initial six-month probation period. So I had a dilemma: take the job or go on the trip. I decided to speak with the division commissioner at my potential employer. He was quite understanding! He said I *had* to go on vacation with my grandpa but my probation period would be extended by the number of days I would be away.

So there we were, Grandpa Claus and I, enjoying an expensive beer at an outdoor bar in Oslo before we ventured into Gudbrandsdalen, where our American relatives originally came from. This bar was where I first heard Norway's current number-one single, *(I'll Never Be) Maria Magdalena* by Sandra. At that time, I didn't know of her soon-to-be famous husband, Michael Cretu, and his sounds of Sadeness. This was five years before Enigma became a sensation. A few years later I discovered a bootleg cassette of Sandra's greatest hits on the streets of Bangkok. That bootleg led me to purchase her CDs throughout the rest of my life.

We wandered the Norwegian countryside, meeting relatives on the family farms, playing cards and translating words with them, driving up and down fjords, exploring the high landscape of Blåhø (where I swear the tarns were impossibly angled as if about to spill their contents), and trying local foods in the various cities we visited. Grandpa was so happy, especially in Molde, the

(continued)

City of Roses, since he and my grandma had always grown roses in their garden at home. I recall a few hilarious moments, including when we laughed about graffiti written on a port-a-potty, "knulle rom." I told Grandpa what it meant. He grinned from the naughty interpretation. Or when Grandpa was giddily surprised by Ethiopian girls in front of us at an ice cream stand. He couldn't believe they spoke Norwegian! No matter where we went or what we did, throughout our trip, Sandra's song was playing.

When we returned to Oslo, prior to our flight home, I told Grandpa that I would go out when he went to bed. He certainly didn't know I was going to a gay bar.

At the bar a handsome guy my age named Anders approached me. After some time, we left the bar and ended up chatting (and kissing) on the king's lawn, in downtown Oslo, under a giant tree, caught in a heavy rain. There was no fence around the royal palace, at least not back then.

Eventually we went to his apartment nearby after the rain let up. He wanted to give me a gift. 1985 was the year USA For Africa's *We Are The World* was released. In his hand was an album, **Sammen For Livet**, by various Norwegian artists to raise money for the same cause. On that album was the other song that reminds me most of this wonderful adventure with Grandpa, *Healing Broken Hearts* by the Norwegian band Boys Voice. When I returned to my hotel around four o'clock in the morning, I discovered the door was locked with no attendant inside. Grandpa was a bit worried when he awoke after pounding on our room door. I found someone nearby at that early hour who knew how to access the hotel rooms at night.

I miss both Klaus and Claus very much. They died within years of each other—Klaus in his twenties, Claus in his nineties. Their legacies live on within me.

The Summer My City Died, 2020

2020. Everyone remembers that first horrendous year under the pall of COVID-19. Stores were shuttered, restaurants closed permanently; we canceled our travel plans, worked from home, and stopped visiting our elders. That year, the world essentially stopped. But I remember how the music stopped too.

It was February 2020 when I noticed the change musically. As you know, I keep a weekly top 10 chart of my favorite music, but by mid-February I was running out of likeable new songs to rank and track in my chart. One reason was all the libraries were closed so my accessible, new music supply ran dry. I could no longer attain convenient access to a wealth of songs to appreciate at home. So, I stopped creating a weekly chart. (Who would notice or care about my imaginative world?) I wasn't alone; Billboard magazine stopped the weekly "Dance Club Songs" chart since clubs were legally closed to protect us from ourselves.

In March, I realized new albums were being delayed including the much-anticipated **Chromatica** by Lady Gaga, which I was expecting in April. (Luckily, it was released in May.)

During the months of February through May, I decided to see more of my city and to spend most days outside birdwatching. It felt therapeutic to be alone in nature and to visit public art and murals in parts of my city previously unknown to me. I needed beauty during these months. COVID felt cold and dark.

By May, the world had seemingly learned how to navigate around the virus safely and life returned to some semblance of normalcy, though I still avoided most strangers and crowds. I began my weekly chart again with songs I had accumulated; and I learned to safely live in the viral world.

It was the day after Memorial Day. I was visiting mid-century modern churches around the Twin Cities. Most were still closed due to the virus, but a few invited me in to take pictures. I felt at peace with fond memories of my childhood congregation and church activities. Then I arrived home and saw what the rest of the world had watched that day. The video was from the night before—George Floyd's murder—and it was broadcast on international TV.

That evening, I felt so disgusted with people and the hatred in our world on so many levels, but I also felt the world would learn from this tragedy (and the scourge of COVID). We would become better people together.

Peaceful protests began against police brutality and racism, both here and around the world. Within a week, my city was on fire and infested by right-wing hooligans wreaking havoc and terrorizing our citizens. I saw them, firsthand, as they watched their fires burn, as they drove after midnight with their lights off, no license plates, and I read how they blended in with protesters to encourage destruction. I worried for my city and for America.

Fast-forward to August and the end of that summer. My city was mending; I trusted that the world was mending too. All that summer I continued visiting my city on my own adventures. On one of those days in late August, as I was about to turn off my car to take photos of an amazing mural in north Minneapolis, a few notes of a new song played on the radio. I froze. I kept the car running. Halfway through the song, I realized who the singer was. Miley Cyrus and her song *Midnight Sky*. It was an instant #1 song for me. And I played the video at home that night more than a few times.

Somehow this song became my memory song for Minneapolis's horrible, but soul-searching, summer of 2020. This song is linked to this watershed summer for my city and my life. In tragedy, music brings solace. And memories.

It was early in this first COVID winter of 2020 to 2021 that this book idea was born.